PROGRESSIVE
BLACK
MASCULINITIES

PROGRESSIVE BLACK MASCULINITIES

ATHENA D. MUTUA

EDITOR

Routledge
Taylor & Francis Group
New York London

Routledge is an imprint of the
Taylor & Francis Group, an informa business

Routledge
Taylor & Francis Group
270 Madison Avenue
New York, NY 10016

Routledge
Taylor & Francis Group
2 Park Square
Milton Park, Abingdon
Oxon OX14 4RN

© 2006 by Taylor & Francis Group, LLC
Routledge is an imprint of Taylor & Francis Group, an Informa business

Printed in the United States of America on acid-free paper
10 9 8 7 6 5 4 3 2 1

International Standard Book Number-10: 0-415-97687-1 (Softcover) 0-415-97686-3 (Hardcover)
International Standard Book Number-13: 978-0-415-97687-9 (Softcover) 978-0-415-97686-2 (Hardcover)

Visit the Taylor & Francis Web site at
http://www.taylorandfrancis.com

and the Routledge Web site at
http://www.routledge-ny.com

Dedication

To
Lumumba
Amani
Mwalimu
Each of whom continues to teach me more about life every day.
May you grow to be Progressive Black Men.

To
Kaybren, Lindani, Michael, and Gabriel
The young ones that inspire me.
May you too grow to be Progressive Black Men.

To
Loye and Erin
The ones who tickle my heart.
May you grow up surrounded by Progressive Black Masculinities.

Contents

Acknowledgments

Many people were instrumental in bringing about the writing, editing, and publication of this book. I would first like to thank the committee members who worked with me in conceptualizing and hosting the conferences on progressive black masculinities, held jointly at the State University of New York institutions, the University at Buffalo Law School, and the Buffalo State College. My sincere thanks go to Timothy Brown, Scott Johnson, Stephanie Phillips, and Ron Stewart. Their work was invaluable. I also received inspiration and direction from many other people. In particular I want to thank Devon Carbado and Angela Harris for their advice in the early formulation of the workshop and project, and Alex De Veaux for her continuing guidance, insight, and support throughout the project and the compilation of this book.

Each and every contributor to this book deserves my heartfelt thanks. These people not only attended the conferences but also put their immense talents toward exploring the project of progressive black masculinities. By name, these people are Tim Brown, Thema Bryant-Davis, Gay Byron, John Calmore, Patricia Hill Collins, Nathan Grant, Beverly Guy-Sheftall, Whitney Harris, Lisa Iglesias, Michael Kimmel, Bahati Kuumba, Teresa Miller, Mark Anthony Neal, and Stephanie Phillips. I owe a special thanks to Pat, Beverly, and Michael, who tirelessly encouraged me as I edited the book and shopped around for publishers, and to Teresa Miller who not only enthusiastically encouraged me throughout the book editing process but took time out of her busy schedule to help me proof many of the chapters.

I would also like to express my deep gratitude to the many faculty and staff at the Law School and the Baldy Center for Law and Social Policy at the University of Buffalo, who provided long-term support for this project. In particular I want to thank Nils Olsen, the dean of the Law School, who provided unwavering commitment to this project, to my scholarship in general, and to my career in teaching law. He has been an invaluable mentor. I also would like to thank Lynn Mather, director of the Baldy Center, and Laura Mangan, associate director of the Center, for their enthusiasm and steadfast sponsorship of the project from beginning to end. Further, every book project requires a dedicated research team. My sincere thanks go to my team in Buffalo, Annie Davey, Harvan Deshield, Jennifer Scarf, Joseph Schneider, and especially Jane Morris, all of whom performed this task with excellence.

The superb team at Routledge/Taylor & Francis provided much needed direction, encouragement and expertise in the process of bringing this work to the public. Many thanks to Matthew Byrnie, who walked me through the approval and publishing procedures, Rachael Panthier, who managed the production process, and Frederick Veith, who kept me on task.

My extended family has always been a cradle of love for me, providing me with their enduring support throughout my life. Margaret Johnson, my mom, has always been my greatest cheerleader and my finest model. Luther Johnson, my dad, has always been the giant on whose shoulders I have stood. The love and work ethic of these two pillars of my life have been essential to grounding my development, together with the love of my sister, Laurie Daniels; my brother, Darron Johnson; my cousin, Kim Horsely; and my aunt Carolyn Jones. Each of these individuals lead what I like to term *progressive black lives*. I also want to make special mention of Leonard Harrison, my maternal uncle, affectionately known as "Mzee," because of his thirty-year sojourn in Tanzania. In my life book, he is a tower of black nationalism and one of the unsung heroes of the American civil rights movement. He has always insisted that I be a critical thinker and has urged me to push the political boundaries in search of justice. My love and thanks to all of these people.

But it is because of my three sons that I produced this book. Even as I have raised them, I continue to learn a great deal from them. It is my fervent hope that Lumumba, Amani, and Mwalimu will be progressive forces in the spaces they occupy and will grow into progressive black men. I thank them for both inspiring and challenging me. And last but not least, I must thank Makau Mutua, the love of my life, my life partner, and friend. When I undertook this project he advised me to go out and find some black men to help me think through these issues. It was advice I heeded. However, this is my interpretation of much of that advice, and though the success of this text belongs to those named and many unnamed, I alone am to blame for any shortcomings it may have. I want to thank Makau for his patience, guidance, love, and support. Without it, you the reader and I the editor would unlikely be at this place right now.

Athena D. Mutua

Introduction: Mapping the Contours of Progressive Masculinities

ATHENA D. MUTUA

In 2001, scholars at the University at Buffalo Law School and Buffalo State College organized a workshop to explore the concept of progressive black masculinities and to examine the many supports and obstacles to their performance. The workshop was part of a larger project on progressive black masculinities that included a conference in 2002 and the presentation and development of the essays included in this book. This introduction briefly describes the tensions inherent in the concept of progressive black masculinities. It then discusses the development of this project, the themes and struggles that informed it, and presents a summary of the essays.

Progressive black masculinities are unique and innovative practices of the masculine self actively engaged in struggles to transform social structures of domination. These structures and relations of domination constrain, restrict, and suppress the full development of the human personality. Progressive masculinities are committed to liberating others and themselves from these constraints and therefore eschew relations of domination in their personal and public lives. This is no mean feat as masculinity itself is usually understood and practiced as a system of domination within the family, culture, economy, and political/legal structures of the United States.

Racism, too, is a system of domination. Thus it would appear that black men, particularly those who have been involved in the struggle against racism, would have an advantage in the project of asserting progressive masculinities. These black men have not only felt but also have seen, understood, and fought against the limiting deprivations imposed on the human personality and community by racism. This experience gives them an advantage; namely, they are accustomed to swimming against the tide and taking other folks along with them. This is true for some. But the wages of racism, and, sometimes, even the fight against racism, have operated in ways that impede the realization of progressive black masculinities. In addition, the ways in which racism is connected to and mutually supports other systems of domination—such as those related to matters of sex, gender, sexuality, and class—seem to stifle progressive black masculine practices. Yet progressive masculinities appear crucial to efforts seeking to transform the social structures and systems that reduce human potential, including the human potential of black people and black communities.

Inspiration

The workshop was inspired by two sets of discussions that reflected larger debates within black communities: one centering on the gendered nature of black men's oppression as exemplified by mass incarceration; the other centering on black men's complicity in systems of domination that oppress others but in the process also reinforce their own oppression. The first discussion emerged during a critical race theory course that my colleague Stephanie Phillips and I were teaching in spring 2000. The course featured a selection of class readings that juxtaposed discussions of certain features of slavery and current practices of mass incarceration, a complex of policies and practices that have had a devastating effect on black communities.[1] The similarities between the two systems were striking, including the limitations on personal mobility, the exploitation of black bodies largely for the benefit of other groups, and the ways in which both slavery and mass incarceration were used to consolidate white racial privilege.[2] This was an intriguing examination. In particular, as mass incarceration seemed to be something that happened more often to black men—as well as brown men—than to black women, we asked what was going on socially with regard to black men.

Commonsense explanations suggested that a complex array of social factors such as poverty, racism, the war on drugs, changed penal policies, and culturally specific behavior patterns gave rise to the mass incarceration of black men. Although various analyses weighted a host of factors, to the extent there was a focus on black and brown men, many studies suggested that racism played a part.[3] Black women, however, are also subject to some of these same conditions, including racism and poverty; but, though black women are experiencing rising levels of incarceration, their numbers do not begin to compare to those of black men. Michael Kimmel and others have suggested that violence and criminality, however defined, have a male face.[4] It is gendered.

And so we began to focus on this aspect of the problem. We wondered to what extent black men faced suspicion and the narrowing of their life opportunities because they were both black and men, and we suspected there was a host of these experiences. In other words, we posited that racism alone, even if it accounted for the disproportionate amount of poverty among black people, could not explain certain types of black male experiences. They seemed to have a gender component. That is, black men appeared to be targeted for certain kinds of treatment because they were both black and men.

Black nationalist discourses historically, though generally arguing that the societal mistreatment of black men was a function of racism, implied a gender component to black male oppression.[5] But they never quite took their own critique seriously. Black nationalists argued that black men were more threatening to the established order of white supremacy than black women; thus, the society, given its order, treated black men far worse than it treated black women or women in general. Further, others suggested that black men had developed culturally specific forms of behavior—some productive, others not—to resist this racist oppression, some of which produced problematic outcomes for black men.[6]

In addition, nationalist discourses at one time seemed to equate the black male condition with conditions of entire black communities[7] (see Kuumba, Ch. 13). Thus, the rest of the argument followed: To remedy the black communities' problems, the struggle against racism had to address primarily the conditions of black men, to center on their predicament. Remedying the conditions of black men meant providing them access to jobs and other opportunities that would allow them to be real men, defined by the established order as being in a position to lead, to provide for, and to control their environments and their families, including their women and children. With the absence of racism and black men firmly in the lead controlling all other members of the community, the problems in the community would disappear.[8]

In other words, providing black men access to patriarchal privilege was the answer to the oppressed conditions of black communities. Therefore, though these discourses posited that black men were oppressed because they were both black and men, there was little need to further develop a specific theory to explore the gender aspect of this phenomenon because, arguably, it was simply an aspect of the larger problem of racism. Apparently, the established order's social arrangements with regard to sex and gender were an accepted and agreed-upon fact.[9]

Black feminists, however, challenged this articulation of black communities' problems as well as its implied remedy on several fronts. First, black feminist writings suggested that the conditions of black male oppression did not entirely account for the nature of the oppression experienced by all community members. In particular, it did not account for the conditions of over half of the communities' population, that of black women. Black women's oppressed conditions, they argued, were not simply a product of white racism but were also a product of sexism, a system in which black men were also implicated.[10]

Second, this nationalist articulation did not necessarily account for the conditions of black children, both boys and girls. From this perspective, community problems that touched on women or children such as domestic violence, incest, child abuse, rape, and sexual harassment, while implicating racism and class structures that render black people disproportionately poor, were primarily attributable to sexist and patriarchal practices in which black men played a role. In addition, some argued, racism did not entirely account for the oppression of sexual minorities in the community, whether male or female.[11] However, though black feminists broadly explored the impact of the relationship between the dominant society's racism and its sex–gender system on black women, for the most part they initially did not apply their insights of this system to the experiences of black men[12] (see Phillips, Ch. 12).

Hence, both sets of discourses suggested that black people, including black men, contributed to problems in black communities and in the case of mass incarceration facilitated it through unproductive behavior. However, it seemed to us that neither black nationalist nor black feminist discourses adequately addressed the gendered and racial oppression of black men or gendered racism of black men.

Kimberlé Crenshaw's comments in the foreword of Devon Carbado's book *Black Men on Race, Gender, and Sexuality* (New York: New York University Press, 1999) were the second stimulus for the project. That book brought together a variety of black men to comment on the issues of race, gender, and sexuality.[13] The essays were both engaging and moving. However, Crenshaw commented that even though the book was a timely contribution to the topic, she nevertheless was dusting off her "Integrate Now" button. She suggested, in short, that few of the essays seemed to take seriously the idea of integrating gender and sexuality into black political consciousness. Rather, many of the essays still placed the male hetero subject in the center of black politics without engaging feminist and other critiques of the intersecting patterns of patriarchy and racism. She apparently awaited a more progressive engagement of race, gender, and sexuality by black men.[14]

We decided to take up the challenge of exploring what more progressive black masculinities might be. Given that black men's oppression appeared to be based on both race and gender, as well as class, sexuality, and a host of other oppressive social structures, we doubted that removing racism alone would free black men. Stated differently, we questioned whether racism could be eliminated without also attacking its gender, class, and sexual components. Further, we suspected that black male complicity in the subordination and oppression of others, including patriarchal practice, might also reinforce and contribute to their own subordination.

These two different angles—one about the gendered nature of black men's oppression and the other about the ways in which black men are complicit in domination, both their own and that of others—form the central theoretical explorations around which the conferences were organized.

In addition, the project had a broader political agenda. This entailed bringing a diverse community of academic scholars and activists together not only to map the current conceptions of progressive black masculinities but also to add these voices and our findings to the larger community debate about the roles and experiences of black men. This larger debate in the context of black communities was exemplified in the reaction to and discussion of the regressive book by Shahrazad Ali titled the *Blackman's Guide to Understanding the Blackwoman*.[15] It is also exemplified by the hundreds of books exploring the conditions of black men, mostly from a racial perspective,[16] and a smaller set of books and enterprises exploring the gendered aspect of black men's identity and experiences.[17] In the end, we hoped as a practical matter to build coalitions among the various proponents of different paradigms around the intersectional issue of race and gender. Further, we hoped to come out of the process not only with some ideas of what constituted progressive black masculinities but also with some activities through which people could both express and cultivate progressive black masculinities.

Constructing a Community

The planning committee approached the topic of progressive black masculinities primarily from a community perspective, though not exclusively so.[18] Conceptually, this meant we were inclined to invite primarily people from black communities that seemed to have a stake in progressive black masculine practice to participate in the project. Presumably, all black people—and perhaps other people as well—had such a stake, including black men, women, sexual minorities and black people from all classes and religions. They seemed to have a stake in this idea because what happened to black men affected what happened in these communities. Black men's issues and problems were community issues, even if the issues affecting them or the resolution of their issues did not constitute the sole set of concerns for these communities or begin to resolve all the concerns and problems facing a community.

At the same time, however, centering black men or focusing on black male issues—even ideas of progressive practice—seemed to reinforce older patterns of thought that insisted that men's issues were the most important issues in a community and therefore should be both the center of focus all of the time and should command most community resources. We simply rejected these ideas as a basis for our work and understood them largely as the discredited and flawed egotisms of male supremacist thinking. Further, as individuals and individuals within communities, we knew that though some of us would always work primarily on black male issues, others of us would explore other issues, conditions, and peoples. In addition, communities' various focuses would shift with their changing needs.

Concretely, a community approach to the project of exploring progressive black masculinities meant bringing together scholars and activists working in diverse fields and operating from different perspectives and paradigms on issues germane to black communities. Three factors influenced this vision and helped to determine the various groups of scholars that the project organizing committee initially invited.

The first was Carbado's book and others like it.[19] Carbado had brought together a variety of black men who worked in different disciplines and approached the subject matter of race, gender and sexuality from a variety of perspectives. Committee members planning the conference thought this was a successful approach and wanted to replicate it. However, they wanted to broaden its focus to include women and men as well as activists and scholars. Second, through its own discussions of the issues the committee had demonstrated that its diversity of views and expertise were useful in questioning and mapping different black male practices and various performances of masculinity. The committee consisted of five members. Two were legal scholars working from the perspective of critical race theory. The other three taught a number of courses on the topic of black men in their respective fields of criminology, sociology, and communications informed by Afrocentric thinking.

Third, the topic of progressive black masculinities, as it had developed in our own minds, evidenced contrary visions about the roles and experiences of black men by those writing from a black feminist perspective and those writing from more nationalist discourses. Thus, the committee wanted to try, at least, to bring leading scholars and activists from these two traditions together. The committee decided at this point to host two conferences. The first conference would be a roundtable dialogue and workshop to discuss and to define the notion of progressive masculinities as well as to chart the future for the larger conference. It would also however, among other things, center a discussion between black feminist scholars and Afrocentric thinkers, whose scholarship represented a strain of black nationalist thought.

The committee thought that black feminists had developed a sophisticated theory of the relationship between race and gender: intersectional theory.[20] Even though intersectional theory had been applied primarily to excavating the lives, experiences, and perspectives of black women, we believed it would nevertheless provide solid insights into the gendered racism of black men. However, intersectional theory had been interpreted in two ways that seemed to limit its power to explain the conditions of black men and for which, as Stephanie Phillips points out, black feminists had been criticized.

First, it was said to suggest that black men at the intersection of race and gender were subordinated by race and privileged by gender. As such, it seemed to imply that black men were not affected by racism that was gendered. Second, and related to the first idea, the theory seemed to suggest that because black women were subordinated by both gender and racism, they were doubly oppressed and thus more oppressed than black men. Though instances can be found where black women appear more subordinated than black men, as in the case of wage differentials, we challenged whether black men were privileged by gender and subordinated by race in all circumstances. We speculated that at times black men were oppressed by gender in addition to race. But we rejected the victim sweepstakes in which subgroups of an oppressed group such as blacks argued over who was more oppressed to claim the centrality of their cause within black communities. Instead, we suspected that black men, like black women, had unique experiences of gendered racism.

These ideas led the committee to the methodology it would use for the workshop. The committee would formulate questions relating to the gaps created by a particular theory's application to black men's conditions and the conditions more generally of black communites and its various members. Thus, the committee posed the following question to black feminists in the workshop: *Is the racialized gendered oppression that black men face exemplified in racial profiling, sexism? Or is it simply a product of racism? How does current black feminist thinking understand the gender analysis implicit in the older claim that white supremacy "castrates" black men?*[21]

The committee had different kinds of concerns with regard to Afrocentric thinkers. Afrocentricity is a strain of black nationalist thought. Though it is a contested term, Molefi Asante, one of its central articulators, suggests that Afrocentricity differs from black nationalism in that the latter is a political, economic, and cultural project whereas the former is a perspective.[22] Afrocentricity seeks both to develop and to draw on African and African diasporan knowledge, history, and experiences, including the experiences of blacks in America, to analyze the conditions and views of black people. Afrocentric work has been interpreted and criticized in a number of ways (see Mutua, Ch. 1). But the organizing committee's biggest concern was the critique of Afrocentricity as sexist and homophobic.[23] In earlier work, Asante argued that "homosexuality is a deviation from Afrocentric thought,"[24] whereas Haki Madhubuti, another Afrocentric thinker, was understood as bemoaning the decline of male dominance in the black community.[25] However, both seemed to have softened these positions in later work, and Afrocentric thinkers on the committee argued that the paradigm had grown beyond these limitations.

Some support for this position can be found in the literature.[26] In fact, Madhubuti's book *Tough Notes: A Healing Call for Creating Exceptional Black Men* issued a clarion call for men to participate in women's liberation. Yet a certain maleness to Afrocentric writings remains, which smacks of the patriarchy reminiscent of the black nationalist positions of the 1960s. For instance, Asante, in describing historical violence against African Americans in his 2003 book, used mostly examples of racist violence against black males even though the book is not about men.[27] Further, Na'im Akbar's book *Visions for a Black Man* supposedly provided a liberation program for black people but seemed to promote a male-centered vision.[28] In addition, Afrocentric thinkers have done a great deal of work on black men but have paid relatively little attention to the plight of black women or other members of black communities.[29] In fact, their most notable programs deal primarily with black males. These include their work to establish all- black male schools for black boys and their initiation or rites-of-passage programs for black male youths.

However, precisely because Afrocentric scholars have done considerable work on black men, we thought they could substantially add to a project on black masculinities. The question, though, became how they might define progressive and whether their definitions would be predicated on the domination of women and the exclusion of black sexual minorities. We thus posed the following question at the workshop to be directed to them: *Are there visions and practices of progressive black masculinities within Afrocentric imaginings that do not rely on*

heterosexuality and limited stereotyped roles of women? What does it mean to be
a black male and black female in the context of the United States?[30]

Also, the committee directed one other question to the workshop as a
whole. The committee's own analysis suggested that although many of the
prospective participants examined racism or sexism as social systems of
privilege and oppression, they shared a common outlook in their belief in
the agency of people. In other words, they believed that despite structural
oppression, people, both as individuals and groups, were capable of acting
both to define and to change their circumstances. With regard to black men,
they agreed that black men's agency was at a minimum shaped, hindered, and
constrained by racist oppression and potentially gendered racism, but this
agency—the ability to act on and to change their circumstances—remained.
At the same time, most of these participants seemed committed to the broader
issues of democracy, justice, and coalition building. With this in mind, the
committee drew on a statement by Cornel West in asking the following question:
How do black men practice and how might they be a part of building mature
black identities, coalitional strategies, and black cultural democracy, of the
sort that Cornel West suggests, in the oppressed space they occupy? What are
features of or how might progressive black masculinities be described?[31]

In addition to black feminists and Afrocentric theorists, the committee
also targeted a number of other groups for their participation in the workshop. These included critical race theorists, masculinities studies scholars, gay
activists, and queer theorists. Two of the committee members were critical
race theorists who argued that the theory's antisubordination stance should
infuse a definition of progressive black masculinities.

Critical race theory was developed in the legal academy. It holds that "race
and racism are endemic to the American social normative order and that law
is part of the social fabric of the country as well as its normative order."[32] Thus,
critical race theorists suggest that "law does not merely reflect and mediate
pre-existing racialized social conflicts and relations."[33] Rather, "it constitutes,
constructs and produces races and race relations in a way that supports" white
racial power and black subordination.[34] They support this claim by analyzing
cases, laws, and legal patterns to expose the ways in which law constitutes
and supports the status quo.[35] Their goal is not only to understand the bonds
between law and white racial power but also to change them.[36] Specifically,
they seek to work "toward the liberation of people of color as they embrace the
larger project of liberating all oppressed people."[37] The idea of working toward
the liberation of all people is captured in some critical race theory circles
and related scholarship as the stance and practice of antisubordination—an
active stance against all forms of domination or subordination.[38] Critical race
theory's antisubordination push or social justice orientation formed a central
proposal to the workshop in defining progressive and was later adopted as a
basis of the project.

The committee also thought it imperative to invite masculinities studies scholars to the workshop. These scholars draw on feminist insights but focus on men and men's lives and, thus, on masculinity as a gendered concept. They developed the concept of hegemonic masculinity, defined as a society's dominant masculine model, or what I call this society's ideal masculine model—a model to which society enforces compliance by privileging and rewarding those who come closest to it and penalizing those who stray or are distant from it. Masculinities scholars argue that hegemonic masculinity is the standard or ideal against which all men are measured and under which few measure up. Hegemonic masculinity is contrasted with subordinated masculinities, a term used to describe those groups of men subordinated by such things as class, race, and sexuality.

These scholars concede that the general study of such subjects as history, art, and science are studies about issues that men have constructed and thought were important but argue that these studies deal with man as an embodiment of a human ideal rather than with men as men.[39] Therefore, they argue, these studies fail to unpack how men feel, think, and experience themselves as men. Masculinities studies scholars suggest that although men are the dominant and privileged group, specifically vis-à-vis women, they often do not feel powerful as individuals. They thus react to feminist assertions of male power with incredulity, exclaiming, "What do you mean power? I have no power at all. My wife bosses me around, my kids boss me around, and my boss bosses me around. I'm completely powerless."[40] The theory thus arose from two different trajectories: one recognizing that men benefit from the social relations of patriarchal power and is profeminist and antisexist, and the other from men's movements that emphasized the pain and felt powerlessness of men, given the current needs and structure of society.[41] Both trajectories, however, embrace a male-affirmative approach to masculinity.

To the extent that masculinities studies is an antisexist movement, these scholars have argued that "[h]eterosexism is more fundamental to the dynamics of sexism than is, for example, racism or classism."[42] This is so in part because heterosexism seeks to compel and to privilege a certain kind of sexuality; namely, it promotes heterosexuality at the expense of gay, lesbian, and other sexual minorities' lives and ways of being. As such, this faction of masculinities studies scholars tends to support the movements of sexual minorities. Some critical race theorists also understand the gay struggle as a struggle for liberation from oppressive social systems. Basically these groups, like feminists, suggest that the United States has a sex–gender system that requires both social and sexual roles for women and men. These sexual roles compel heterosexuality, thereby excluding or denigrating same-sex practices. The gendered concept of hegemonic masculinity embraces this compulsion and, therefore, excludes gay being and practice from its definitions of masculinity.

Gay activism and theorizing, along with queer theory, it seemed to us, were crucial to any project with the goal of rethinking masculinity. Gay activism challenges the sex–gender system as being simply incompatible with reality. Gay, lesbian, bisexual, transgendered, and transsexual (GLBTT) people do exist, including in black communities. Further, their theorizing has helped to delineate and to elaborate the boundaries and limitations of the sex–gender system.[43] In addition, they have provided alternative ways of thinking about and of being masculine and have demonstrated other ways of being human. They have exposed the human cost of rigidly regulating and oppressing consensual adult sexual expression. Therefore, the committee targeted gay activists, scholars, and queer scholars, particularly black gay and other queer scholars, as indispensable to a workshop geared toward the community exploration of progressive black masculinities.

Successes, Absences, and the 2002 Conference

The workshop, as planned and executed, proved a stimulating event for all participants. However, one major absence plagued the project in its entirety: the failure of leading Afrocentric scholars to attend either the workshop or conference. The reasons for this are varied. Part of the fault lay in the committee's approach to invitations. The committee sought to invite people who were perceived as willing to engage in a day-long dialogue instead of the usual academic conference arrangement in which many speakers attend only for so long as it takes them to make their presentations. This desire on our part meant that several people, particularly some activists, were not able to make such a commitment. Further, the committee's decision to try to invite people who were known to be particularly capable of facilitating and participating in dialogue, despite their having clear positions on certain issues, also complicated the process. Though we used our own networks to attempt to learn more about various scholars and activists, our own limited knowledge meant that we did not invite enough scholars working within a particular field or paradigm to ensure that field or paradigm's representation.

However, it must be noted that a number of Afrocentric scholars expressed some hesitancy about participating in the project. Although this hesitancy may have resulted from a number of reasons, at least one scholar was clear about his discomfort. He found the inclusion of an antihomophobic position as part of the definition of progressive masculinities troubling. He suggested, as Asante had written, that homosexuality was contrary to the values of Afrocentricity. Thus, some of the particular perspectives and ideas we thought leading Afrocentric scholars might well be able to articulate are not among the essays written for this collection. This does not mean that the Afrocentric perspective is totally absent from this volume. In fact, a number of writers, including at least one of the organizing committee's members, write from an Afrocentric perspective, and still others draw on Afrocentric insights and writings about black men. Further, to the extent that Afrocentricity shares some ideas with black feminism, critical race theory, and certain masculinities studies scholars, these ideas are also captured in these essays. Nonetheless, this book offers one of only several efforts to engage a range of scholars around the idea and practice of progressive black masculinities. It is our hope that these ideas will continue to be developed by a host of different scholars in the future.

The success of the 2001 workshop augured well for the 2002 conference. The conference expanded the types of activists and scholars invited to present their expertise, views, and experiences of progressive black masculinities. In particular, the conference sought to include a wider range of topics and people. For instance, the committee sought and succeeded in bringing scholars to the conference who could talk knowledgeably about youth culture and about hip-hop in particular. Further, the committee sought to engage religious notions about gender. The workshop raised the question of whether ideas about progressive masculinities as antisubordination practice, both at the level of personal and political practice, were compatible with various religious doctrines. Women at the parallel conference for the United Nations Fourth World Conference on Women similarly questioned whether the common interpretations of the world's religions—defined as Judaism, Christianity, Islam, Hinduism, and Buddhism—were compatible with women's human rights. It was thought then as well as in the context of the progressive masculinities project that most religions are often interpreted as endorsing the complementary, hierarchal, and heterosexual-only roles for men and women and thus are potentially incompatible with women's human rights or progressive black masculinities. Though we were interested particularly in Christian and Muslim practice, as the majority of African Americans believe in one of these two faiths, only Christianity is explored in the essays included in this volume. Exploring progressive masculinities from a Muslim perspective as well as from other religious standpoints remain areas for future research. The tentative responses to whether current interpretations of Christianity might support progressive masculinities were a resounding "maybe." But given the historical prophetic Christian practices of African Americans,[44] support of such practices is possible (see Gay Byron, Ch. 6).

Finally, many speakers at the conference as well as writers in this book touch on the relationships among black men, notions of work, masculinity, and gendered racism. However, black men and work is a vastly under-explored topic from a progressive perspective, both in this text and in general. For example, no single article in this book attempts to tackle this web of issues, even at a theoretical level, perhaps because this topic is a book or series of books within itself. Yet, because the notion of work and the role of the provider have been fundamental to the ideology of hegemonic masculinity and in light of the high joblessness among black men, the transitioning of the American economy, globalization, and the entry in new ways with new impacts of other peoples and players in the world economy, this area is one that deserves additional, serious, and creative exploration and thought. We will explore and we hope others will explore these and other topics in the future.

The Essays

Many of the authors in this text embrace a social justice framework in their approach to examining black masculine practice and the conditions of black men's lives. Although the topics these authors explore emphasize different aspects of this framework, inherent in each essay is an understanding of progressive black masculinities as innovative performances of the masculine self that eschew dominance and are engaged in the struggle to transform social structures of domination. At the same time, as many of the authors point out, the structures of domination that limit and subordinate black men are not limited to racism alone but include other structures such as gendered racism, sexism, class, heterosexism, and so on. Consequently, in struggling to transform these structures, progressive black masculinities seek to liberate not only themselves but also others.

The book is divided into seven parts containing two or three chapters each. The first part is entitled "Theorizing Progressive Black Masculinities." My chapter of the same title opens this part. In it, I build on many of the ideas and schools of thought explored in this introduction for the purpose of clarifying the theoretical foundations of the book. I argue that the definition of progressive black masculinities is grounded in the twin projects of progressive blackness and progressive masculinities. I suggest that progressive blackness is an antiracist, and more generally an antidomination project committed to the existential wholeness and well being of black people and communities. However, I argue, as I have indicated here, that this project is undermined by commitments to ideal masculinity, which like racism is a system of domination. I spend some time explaining what ideal masculinity is and how it works. Progressive masculinities also is an antidomination political project but one that is committed in part to re-orienting masculine practice away from ideal masculinity, and by definition including a profeminist stance.

Beverly Guy-Sheftall, in Chapter 2 of this part, grounds many of the ideas about progressive black masculinities in the profeminist philosophies of some of our most heroic male leaders. Titled "Remembering Our Feminist Forefathers," Guy-Sheftall focuses on black history, drawing out the contributions a number of prominent black historical figures have made to feminist thinking. She notes that the history of feminism, particularly black feminism, is often told as if black men had no part in the development of the theory and practices. She corrects this omission by presenting the profeminist writings and what I would call progressive masculine writings of three legendary black men: Frederick Douglass, W. E. B. Du Bois, and Benjamin Mays.

The last chapter in this part is a thought piece. A thought piece is a short reflection essay meant to provoke thought and pose a question rather than explore an issue through sustained analysis. In this chapter, Elizabeth Iglesias ruminates on what it might mean to move into mature personhood, coalitional networks, and black cultural democracy in an anti-essentialist way. She suggests that maturity may mean evolving to a point where we see "the other" as ourselves. This kind of perspective, she suggests, might allow us to act as political agents beyond our own political struggles. She then goes on to question how ideas of black cultural democracy might handle dissent.

Part 2 entitled "Strength, Not Privilege or Domination," explains several dynamics inherent in American hegemonic or ideal masculinity. These include, 1) the notion of and the ways in which privilege works; 2) the ways in which black men may practice domination or assert privilege through hegemonic notions of masculinity; and 3) the ways in which black men are harmed by the American hegemonic system of masculinity. It suggests that progressive black masculinities are those that eschew domination and privilege as features of masculine practice. Michael Kimmel's chapter, "Toward a Pedagogy of the Oppressor," opens the part with a discussion of privilege. He sets out to explain what privilege is, what it means to have it, how it operates, and why those who have it must recognize it. He then examines what privilege for black men might mean and the ways it might manifest itself given racism. Patricia Hill Collins's essay, "A Telling Difference: Dominance, Strength, and Black Masculinities," follows, examining the harm that black men do to themselves when they internalize and occupy the limited images and spaces dictated to them by American hegemonic masculinity. She situates these harms in a racist gender ideology that relegates and defines black men as weak. Black men are considered weak, she explains, in part because hegemonic masculinity is a relational concept in which there are "real men" and then there are weak others against whom real men are defined. Real men are defined as not like women, not gay, not poor, not like boys, and not black. Instead, a "real man" under hegemonic masculinity requires that "men" dominate these identities and dominate in all circumstances, with this domination masquerading as strength. Collins encourages black men to reject domination as the central feature of masculinity and its black men-as-weak thesis, suggesting a number of ways in which this process might begin.

Part 3 titled "Christianity: Progressive Interpretations?" explores the compatibility of current Christian religious understandings with ideas of progressive masculinities. Gay Byron's chapter is first. It examines several biblical scriptures from Paul's letters that are often used to justify limited roles for women and to condemn gay life. She suggests these scriptures are interpreted literally and are used as authoritative guides for a Christian life in many black communities. This is so, even though black communities have rejected literal understandings of the injunctions supporting slavery, often found in the very same passages in which sexist injunctions are located. Using contemporary scholarship to interrogate these scriptures, she posits alternative interpretations of these passages and locates other Pauline scriptures that aid in the development of progressive masculinities. She then turns to extrabiblical texts to explore images and ideas that might inform progressive black masculine practice. Specifically she examines the life of Black Moses as a possible model. Whitney Harris' discussion of Christianity and progressive black masculinities is next and begins by him sharing his own personal experience as a black gay priest in the Catholic Church. He explains the ways in which he learned to engage in what he calls "loyal opposition," a practice meant to subvert the church's racist, sexist and homophobic orientation while remaining faithful to its message of salvation through Christ. He then turns to the message of Christ's life, suggesting that Christ refigured masculinity in his own time and explaining that progressive black men have to re-imagine God, reform their God talk, and refigure their own masculinity as Christ did.

Part 4, "From Unwanted Traffic to Prison," turns to an examination of the gendered racist oppression of black men. John Calmore's chapter "Reasonable and Unreasonable Suspects: The Cultural Construction of the Anonymous Black Man in Public Space (Here Be Dragons)" opens this part with his discussion of black men as unwanted traffic. He explains the ways in which the intersection of racial and gendered oppression is spatialized to produce black men as unwanted and as unwanted traffic. Employing cultural studies scholarship, he notes that all black men are subject to being constructed as unwanted traffic when they enter anonymous space — space in which they are personally unknown. However, he suggests that this construction has more dire consequences for black men who are working class or poor. Nevertheless, he argues that the community as a whole is injured by this situation and that black men must work in solidarity across the differences of class to remedy it. He then focuses on felony disenfranchisement as an example of this broad community injury and as an opportunity for men and black communities to act purposefully and in solidarity. Teresa Miller's chapter is a natural complement to Calmore's piece. One of the consequences of the construction of men as unwanted traffic is the heavy policing and imprisonment of black men. However, Miller in "Incarcerated Masculinities" focuses on the definitions and practices of masculinity in prisons. She argues that sexualized violence is what makes a man a "Man" in prison in the current moment and discusses the ways in which this practice is racialized. She then turns to the consequences of prison masculinities and of imprisonment itself on black men as well as to the consequences to the communities to which these men return after being released.

Turning next to the media's relation to this topic is Part 5 of the book, "Black Men in (Re)View." Nathan Grant opens this part. He comments on black men's limited access to the small screen (television) and the continuing importance of comedy given that it is in comedy that black men continue to have the greatest access as lead characters. He, therefore, focuses on two of the most commercially successful primetime shows with black male lead characters: *The Cosby Show* and *Martin*. In his essay "Mirror's Fade to Black: Masculinity, Misogyny, Class Ideation in *The Cosby Show* and *Martin*" he critiques both shows as failing to proffer progressive masculinities. *The Cosby Show*, he argues offered "fantasies" of upper-middle-class life while avoiding opportunities to discuss the real racial obstacles to elite class status for many black people. *Martin*, he suggests, presented distorted and silenced female images as the price required for black masculinity as domination. Tim Brown's chapter "Welcome to the Terrodome: Exploring the Contradictions of a Hip-Hop Black Masculinity" follows with a discussion of a highly publicized 2002 incident involving Allen Iverson. Brown demonstrates through an analysis of media coverage that the media reduced Iverson to the familiar stereotypes of black men as angry, violent, and sexually inappropriate. He suggests that the negative media attention in part was driven by ambivalence and hostility toward Iverson's hip-hop masculinity, a masculinity that has both progressive and regressive elements. He argues that despite racism and the society's tendency to denigrate blackness, that hip-hop is progressive in that it constructs an alternative identity that uncompromisingly uses and elevates blackness and black cultural practices, while also identifying with lower-class black life instead of white middle-class precepts. He suggest, however, that hip-hop is regressive because it imbibes and traffics in patriarchal and misogynist practices.

Part 6, "Black Feminist Engaged," discusses feminism in relationship to black masculinities. Phillips's chapter, the first in this part, is an excerpt from an earlier article she wrote in the 1990s.[45] I include it here because it examines the historical disagreement between black feminist and black male antiracist scholars over the competing claims that either black women are more oppressed than black men or that black men are more oppressed than black women. One claim asserts that women are doubly oppressed. The other, plays out in the trope "ain't nobody so free as a black woman and a white man." Phillips in "Beyond Competitive Victimhood: Abandoning Arguments that Black Women or Black Men Are Worse Off" focuses specifically on the feminist response, questioning it in relationship to ideas about gendered racism. Bahati Kuumba's chapter follows, explaining that the "promotion of progressive black masculinities is as necessary for achieving gender justice as is women's empowerment." Entitled, "Gender Justice: Linking Women's Human Rights and Progressive Black Masculinities," Kuumba suggests that black feminists have a stake in the development of progressive black masculinities. She then evaluates feminist approaches in engaging men in antisexist struggle in two specific institutional contexts, exposing the challenges in using feminist methods with men, as well as, interrogating the question of whether women's energies are best spent in this work.

The last part, "Walking the Talk," contemplates steps forward. Thema Bryant, in "Breaking the Silence: The Role of Progressive Black Men in the Fight against Sexual Assault" delineates the positions and steps progressive black men have and should take with regard to rape. Using her poetry to drive home the point, she explains the common misconceptions about rape, including the fact that large numbers of men have been raped. She leaves us hopeful with black folks "speaking, rapping, singing, [and] preaching" against this human tragedy. Mark Anthony Neal's chapter, "Bringing Up Daddy: A Progressive Black Masculine Fatherhood? ends the book on an inspiring note. At the center of his discussion are the loving stories about his daughter and his family's efforts to adopt a second child. Neal discusses such issues as father bias and nurturing in a patriarchal world and even the criminal allegations surrounding the musical icon R. Kelly, as he explores the various actions, issues, and concerns that might make one a profeminist, progressive black dad. His children, in addition to his work as a cultural analyst and scholar, provide him opportunities to engage the challenges of feminist ideas and progressive masculine practice in his life.

Notes

1. Eric Schlosser, "The Prison-Industrial Complex," *Atlantic Monthly* 282, no. 6 (December 1998); Loic Wacquent, "From Slavery to Mass Incarceration: Rethinking the Race Question in the U.S.," *New Left* 13 (January–February 2002).
2. Wacquent, "From Slavery."
3. See, for example, Marc Mauer, *Race to Incarcerate: Marc Mauer and the Sentencing Project* (New York: New Press, 1999).
4. Michael Kimmel, *The Gendered Society* (New York: Oxford University Press, 2003), noting that violence is a male activity.
5. Here I am thinking of the black nationalists of the late 1960s, particularly those who were a part of the black power phase. These include such activists as Eldridge Cleaver, Kwame Toure (formerly Stockley Carmichael), Amiri Baraka, Huey Newton, and H. Rap Brown. For a critique of some of this thinking see, e.g., bell hooks, *Ain't I a Woman: Black Women and Feminism* (Boston: South End Press, 1981), 95–96, discussing Baraka. General histories on 1960s black nationalism see Robert L. Allen, *A Guide to Black Power in America: An Historical Analysis* (London: Gollancz, 1970), 18–74, 108–239; Theodore Draper, *The Rediscovery of Black Nationalism* (New York: Viking Press, 1970); Herbert H. Haines, *Black Radicals and the Civil Rights Mainstream, 1954–1970* (Knoxville: University of Tennessee Press, 1988), 57–76; Alphonso Pinkney, *Red, Black, and Green: Black Nationalism in the United States* (New York: Cambridge University Press, 1976), 76–219; Robert Weisbrot, *Freedom Bound: A History of America's Civil Rights Movement* (New York: Norton, 1990), 222–61; and James Turner, "Black Nationalism: The Inevitable Response," *Black World*, January 1971, 4.
6. See, e.g., Richard Majors and others, "Cool Pose: A Symbolic Mechanism for Masculine Role Enactment and Coping by Black Males," in *American Black Male*, ed. Richard Majors and Jacob U. Gordon (Chicago: Nelson Hall, 1994), 246, 251–56, explaining that the cool pose adopted by many young black men produces problems when used in certain social, sexual, and educational context.
7. For works that critique black nationalism in this manner, see, e.g., Michelle Wallace, *Black Macho and the Myth of the Superwoman* (New York: Verso Classics, 1979); hooks, *Ain't I a Woman*, 87–117; Bahati Kuumba, *Gender and Social Movements* (Walnut Creek, CA: AltaMira Press, 2001); and Barbara Ransby, "Afrocentrism, Cultural Nationalism, and the Problem with Essentialist Definitions of Race, Gender, and Sexuality," in *Dispatches from the Ebony Tower: Intellectuals Confront the African American Experience*, ed. Manning Marable (New York: Columbia University Press, 2000), which critiques Afrocentricity.)
8. Ibid.
9. hooks, *Ain't I a Woman*, 87–117, which discusses the imperialism of patriarchy and Baraka's call for complementary and patriarchal roles for black women and men. The article also discusses the goals of the black power movement.

10. See, e.g., ibid.; Audre Lorde, "I Am Your Sister: Black Women Organizing across Sexualities," in *Feminist Theory Reader: Local and Global Perspectives,* ed. Carole R. McCann and Seung-Kyung Kim (New York: Routledge, 2003), 255–59; Lorde, *Sister Outsider: Essays and Speeches* (Trumansburg, NY: Crossing Press, 1984); Patricia Hill Collins, *Fighting Words: Black Women and the Search for Justice* (Minneapolis: University of Minnesota Press, 1998); Collins, *Black Feminist Thought: Knowledge, Consciousness, and the Politics of Empowerment* (Boston: Unwin and Hyman, 1990); Adrien Wing, ed., *Critical Race Feminism* (New York: New York University Press, 1997); Beverly Guy-Sheftall, *Words of Fire: An Anthology of African-American Feminist Thought* (New York: New Press, 1995); Toni Morrison, ed., *Race-ing Justice, En-gendering Power: Essays on Anita Hill, Clarence Thomas, and the Construction of Social Reality* (New York: Pantheon/Random House, 1992); Darlene Clark Hine, *Black Women in America: An Historical Encyclopedia,* 2 vols. (Brooklyn, NY: Carlson, 1993); Hazel V. Carby, *Reconstructing Womanhood: The Emergence of the Afro-American Woman Novelist* (New York: Oxford University Press, 1987); Paula Giddings, *When and Where I Enter: The Impact of Black Women on Race and Sex in America* (New York: William Morrow, 1984); hooks, *Feminist Theory: From Margin to Center* (Boston: South End Press, 1984); Alice Walker, *In Search of Our Mothers' Gardens: Womanist Prose* (San Diego: Harcourt Brace Jovanovich, 1983); and Angela Davis, *Women, Race, and Class* (New York: Random House, 1981).
11. See, e.g., Lorde, "I Am Your Sister."
12. Now many feminists have looked at masculinity. See Collins, *Black Sexual Politics* (New York: Routledge, 2004); hooks, *We Real Cool: Black Men and Masculinity* (New York: Routledge, 2003); Rudolph P. Byrd and Beverly Guy-Sheftall, eds., *Traps: African American Men on Gender and Sexuality* (Bloomington: Indiana University Press, 2001); and Darlene Clark Hine and Earnestine Jenkins, eds., *A Question of Manhood: A Reader in U.S. Black Men's History and Masculinity* (Bloomington: Indiana University Press, 2001). Also many black men recently have looked at masculinity as an aspect of male identity and the limitations it might pose. See, e.g., Devon Carbado, "The Construction of O.J. Simpson as a Racial Victim," in *Black Men on Race, Gender and Sexuality,* ed. Carbado (New York: New York University Press, 1999), 159–93; Michael Awkward, "You're Turning Me On": The Boxer, the Beauty Queen, and the Rituals of Gender," in ibid., 128–46; Phillip Brian Harper, *Are We Not Men? Masculine Anxiety and the Problem of African American Identity* (New York: Oxford University Press, 1996); Marcellus Blount and George Cunningham, eds., *Representing Black Men* (New York: Routledge, 1996); Ellis Cose, *A Man's World: How Real Is Male Privilege and How High Is Its Price?* (New York: Harper Collins, 1996); and Cose, *The Envy of the World: On Being a Black Man in America* (New York: Washington Square Press, 2002).
13. Kimberlé Crenshaw, "Foreword," in Devon Carbado, *Black Men on Race, Gender, and Sexuality,* ed. Carbado (New York: New York University Press, 1999).
14. Ibid.
15. Shahrazad Ali, *The Blackman's Guide to Understanding the Blackwoman* (Philadelphia: Civilized Publications, 1989).
16. See, e.g., Earl Ofari Hutchinson, *The Assassination of the Black Male Image* (New York: Simon and Schuster, 1997); and Jawanza Kunjufu, *Countering the Conspiracy to Destroy Black Boys,* vol. 4 (Chicago: African American Images, 1995).
17. See Carbado, *Black Men.*
18. Although the majority of these scholars identified as black, the conference participants overall were racially diverse with nonblack participants bringing particular issues of expertise, such as in masculinities studies, or with experience with comparative perspectives and coalition building, such as members of LatCrit, a group of legal scholars focusing on the Latino condition. For instance, Michael Kimmel was invited to the conference as one of the leading scholars in the field of masculinities studies. Further, several LatCrit scholars were invited to bring a focus on coalition building and possibly a comparative perspective about Latino men.
19. Devon Carbado, *Black Men on Race, Gender, and Sexuality,* ed. Carbado (New York: New York University Press, 1999); also see, e.g., *The American Black Male.* Though most of the essays in the book were written by black men, it included a few women contributors and scholars from a variety of fields. As such it seemed to be more of a community approach.
20. Though many black feminists have talked about the intersection of race and gender, Crenshaw was one of the first women to articulate it as a theory in Crenshaw,

"Demarginalizing the Intersection of Race and Sex: A Black Feminist Critique of Anti-discrimination Doctrine, Feminist Theory, and Antiracist Politics," *University of Chicago Legal Forum* (1989), 139–67.

21. Patricia Hill Collins was asked to present first on this question before the discussion was opened to the table.

22. Molefi K. Asante, *Erasing Racism* (Amherst, NY: Prometheus Books, 2003), 204.

23. See, e.g., Ransby, "Afrocentrism, Cultural Nationalism, and the Problem with Essentialist Definitions of Race, Gender, and Sexuality," in *Dispatches from the Ebony Tower: Intellectuals Confront the African American Experience*, ed. Manning Marable (New York: Columbia University Press, 2000), 216–223. However, Ransby's critique seems to be based on the earlier work of Haki Mudhubuti and Molefi Asante.

24. Asante, *Afrocentricity* (Trenton, NJ: Africa World Press, 1988), 56.

25. Madhubuti, *Black Men: Obsolete, Single, Dangerous? Afrikan American Families in Transition: Essays in Discovery, Solution, and Hope* (Chicago: Third World Press, 1990).

26. Asante, *The Painful Demise of Eurocentrism: An Afrocentric Response to Critics* (Trenton, NJ: Africa World Press, 1999), 99, says, "Afrocentricity is considered dangerous because it indicts Eurocentrism as racist, sexist, classist, and homophobic."

27. Asante, *Erasing Racism*.

28. Ransby, "Afrocentrism," 220.

29. Ibid.

30. Jerome Schiele was asked to initially address this question but was unable to attend the workshop.

31. Kendal Thomas provided the first response to this question. He is considered a critical race theorist and also has written a number of articles on the issue of gay black men.

32. Athena D. Mutua, "The Rise of Critical Race Theory in Law," in *Race and Ethnic Handbook* (Thousand Oaks, CA: Sage, forthcoming). An early version of this paper can be found at: http://72.14.203.104/search?q=cache:i6IIONnI54DcJ:222.law.buffalo.edu/baldycenter/pdfs/RacJusticeMutua05.pdf+Athena+Mutua&hl=en&gl=us&ct=clnk&cd=1

33. Ibid., citing Cheryl Harris.

34. Ibid.

35. Ibid.

36. Ibid., citing Harris and Crenshaw.

37. Ibid., citing Phillips.

38. Ibid., discussing LatCrit as a body of scholarship related to critical race theory and articulating the principle of antisubordination.

39. Harry Brod, ed., *The Making of Masculinities: The New Men's Studies* (Boston: Allen & Unwin, 1987).

40. Kimmel, "Foreword," in *Theorizing Masculinities*, ed. Harry Brod and Michael Kaufman (Thousand Oaks, CA: Sage, 1994), viii.

41. Kaufman, "Men, Feminism, and Men's Contradictory Experiences of Power," in Brod and Kaufman, *Theorizing Masculinites*, 156.

42. Brod and Kaufman, eds., "Introduction," *Theorizing Masculinities*, 5.

43. Darren Hutchinson, "Ignoring the Sexualization of Race: Heteronormativity, Critical Race Theory, and Anti-Racist Politics," *Buffalo Law Review* 47 (1999), 1–116; Francisco Valdes, "Queers, Sissies, Dykes and Tomboys: Deconstructing the Conflation of 'Sex,' 'Gender,' and 'Sexual Orientation,' in Euro-American Law and Society," *California Law Review* 83 (1995), 1–377; and Laurie Rose Kepros, "Queer Theory: Weed or Seed in the Garden of Legal Theory," *Law and Sex* 9 (1999–2000), 279–310.

44. See Cornel West, *Prophesy Deliverance* (Philadelphia: Westminster Press, 1982) for use of the term *prophetic Christianity*. The elements of prophetic Christianity include that every individual "should have an opportunity to fulfill his or her potentialities," given their equality before God, a belief in both the dignity as well as the depravity of people, and their imperfect ability to transform what is, as well as notions of freedom, democracy and hope. Ibid., 16–19; see also 101–8, which describes the prophetic Christian tradition in the African American experience calling it black theology.

45. Stephanie Phillips, "Claiming Our Foremothers: The Legend of Sally Hemings and the Tasks of Black Feminist Theory," in *Hastings Women's Law Journal* 8 (Fall 1997), 401–65.

Part 1
Theorizing Progressive Black Masculinities

1

Theorizing Progressive Black Masculinities*

ATHENA D. MUTUA

My children, three boys, jump up from the table and swing into various dance modes. One of their favorite songs is on the radio. They sing along, 'I ain't sayin' she's a gold digger, but she ain't messin' with no broke, broke…" This is the clean version of Kanye West's song, "Gold Digger." The original lyrics say, "She ain't messin with no broke Niggas."

Kanye West is one of the more interesting Hip-Hop artists, to my mind. In addition to his music, he is probably best known for his comments during a nationally aired live benefit concert, Hurricane Katrina Relief, in 2005. He critiqued the government's slow response in rescuing what appeared to be mostly black people stranded in New Orleans after the hurricane. Commenting first on the media's negative portrayal of black hurricane survivors and noting his own ambivalent response, West concludes: "George Bush doesn't care about black people." In that moment it seemed that West, in taking on George Bush, the president of the United States and the epitome of American ideal masculinity, had destroyed his music career. But West had merely stated what had undoubtedly crossed the minds of many in black communities across the country.

However, this was not the first time that West had spoken out in a controversial manner. A couple of months before the Katrina Hurricane, he had chastised the hip-hop community for its homophobia. He stated that hip-hop was supposed to be about "speaking your mind and about breaking down barriers, but that everyone in hip-hop discriminates against gay people." Explaining that his cousin was gay and that he loved him, he called on his hip-hop friends to just "stop it."

My kids were singing loudly now, the song, for them, had reached its crescendo: "We want freedom, we want freedom," they sang, "Eighteen years, eighteen years. And on the 18th birthday he found out (the kid) wasn't his." I join the kids in singing and dancing. "No, No, I exclaim, he didn't want freedom, if he had wanted freedom, he would have covered it up!" The kids laugh and keep dancing. They have heard me make this point before, or something similar.

* I would like to thank Hank Richardson, Rebecca French, Isabel Marcus, Teresa Miller, and Makau Mutua for reading earlier versions of this paper and providing insightful comments.

"Don't nobody force you to be a father". Or, "No! At the crucial moment (of engaging in intercourse) he was probably thinking that somebody else was supposed to be responsible for his sexuality. Ya got to be responsible for your own sexuality," I had laughingly counseled; using the song as a valuable "teaching moment." It would be some time before we bought the CD and learned that the lyrics in that section of the song were not "we want freedom," but rather we want prenupt (prenuptial agreements)! Oh well.

Called by *Rolling Stone* magazine West's "ode to women 'who ain't messin' with no broke niggas,'"(February 9, 2006), the song is about a seemingly problematic woman, who only dates men with money, has a handful of kids by different men, and who (she or some other woman in the song) uses her child support to buy a nice car, etc. But, West, the singer, loves this woman. This strikes me as an interesting twist, loving someone who is not perfect, given that few of us are. But the song nevertheless disturbs me because it is among a number of songs and articles that seem to suggest that most women, and apparently black women in particular, are gold-diggers. Now, I am sure the response to such a claim would be that gold-diggers are real, are part of our reality, on the one hand, and that the songs and comments are not referring to all women but simply to some. Nevertheless, the repetition of this idea unsettles me even as I know there are far more sexist and misogynist lyrics and comments out there.

My boys, young teenagers, have now burnt off some of their incredible energy and finished raiding the kitchen for a snack; it's time for homework!

Still reflecting on the song, I believe that black men, like Kanye West, courageously rail against racial domination, recognizing that racism is a system which primarily operates in the American society to support a white supremacist social order that privileges whites and subordinates black people. But many of the same black men embrace sexism, a system that operates to support American patriarchy or male supremacy, privileging men and certain understandings of masculinity and subordinating women and those marked as feminine. In other words, black men struggle against white racial domination but embrace masculinist gender and sexual domination. Though Kanye West seems to bring to the scene a more nuanced understanding of oppression, I wonder how many other black men get it... that is, do they understand that patriarchy and white supremacy are mutually reinforcing structures of domination that have complicated and negative consequences for black women but also for black men. And, I wonder if do they know that when black men embrace the patriarchy, they, among other things, undermine our struggle for racial justice.

In this chapter, I propose a definition of progressive black masculinities as the unique and innovative performances of the masculine self that on the one hand personally eschew and ethically and actively stand against social structures of domination.[1] On the other hand, they validate and empower black humanity, in all its variety, as part of the diverse and multicultural humanity of others in the global family. I argue that this definition is grounded in the twin concepts of *progressive blackness* and *progressive masculinities.* I suggest that both of these are political projects committed to eradicating relations of domination that constrain and reduce human potential. However, each project is directed toward different but overlapping groups of people—black people and men—and focuses on different systems of domination. The project of progressive blackness centers on the edification and empowerment of black people as part of a larger antiracist struggle and part of a still larger antidomination or antisubordination project. The project of progressive masculinities is similar but centers its efforts on reorienting men's concepts and practices away from ideal masculinity, which, by definition, requires the domination of men over women, children, and, yes, other subordinate, or "weaker" men as Patricia Hill Collins examines.

Black men are the focal point of this project. I suggest two basic points in discussing these projects. First that black men's embrace of ideal masculinity not only hurts black women, but also hurts black men and black communities as a whole. Second, I suggest that black men are not only oppressed by racism but that their oppression is gendered. In other words, they are oppressed by gendered racism.

The first part of this chapter lays out my tentative definition of progressive black masculinities. It then explores the ethical component of the project of progressive blackness. Specifically, through references to work by Cornel West on the Anita Hill/Clarence Thomas hearings and Michael Dyson on comments made by Bill Cosby, I argue that the project of progressive blackness is an ethical project. In other words, it is a principled commitment to the existential well-being, both materially and spiritually, of black people and black communities in their entirety, including their various constituent groups. To the extent that different parts of these communities, such as black women, poor blacks, or black sexual minorities, are constrained by different or multiple systems of domination, such as sexism, classism, or heterosexism, a commitment to the project of progressive blackness entails efforts to also transform these. As such, progressive blackness is a project to transform all systems of domination and to build coalitions with others who are ethically and actively committed not only to the struggle against racism but also to the struggle against domination and subordination in general.

I then note that the workings of American ideal, or hegemonic, masculinity are a hindrance to progressive masculine practice. The section on the American Masculine Ideal, therefore seeks to explain in some detail what the masculine ideal is, how it operates as part of the sex–gender system, the way in which men are socialized into it, and its relationship to the patriarchal order as a site of power. Here I argue that the central feature of masculinity is the domination and oppression of others; namely women, children, and other subordinated men. The section draws on insights from feminist theory, masculinities studies, and gay and queer theory as a way of defining the project of progressive masculinities.

The second part of the chapter analyzes a number of theories that seek to answer the question of where black men stand in relationship to hegemonic masculinity given their subjugation by racial oppression. Are they privileged by gender or oppressed by gender? Here the case is made that they both benefit and are disadvantaged by gender. The focus is the gendered racial oppression of black men. Specifically, the section looks at three theories. One theory examines the material conditions of black men in America and suggests that racism precludes black men from enjoying any of the unearned privileges associated with masculinity and in fact often precludes black men from enjoying the privileges of full personhood, personal competence, and humanity. But a careful analysis of this theory suggests that black men likely are oppressed because they are both black and men; that is, black men are oppressed by gendered racism whether or not they benefit as men in some form under the patriarchal order.

The second theory, intersectionality, applied to black men, is cognizant of black male conditions but also explores black men's status in relationship to black women to posit that black men are privileged by gender and oppressed by race. It too obscures the insight that black men may be constrained by gendered racism but adequately captures some of the situations of differential power between black men and black women. The third theory, multidimensionality, recognizes that black men are not homogeneous but rather are diverse by class, sexuality, religion, and other systems of subordination. It suggests that given the interconnectedness of patriarchy/sexism and racism, among other oppressive systems, black men, as a single multidimensional positionality, are in some contexts privileged by gender and sometimes oppressed by gendered racism. It also suggests that when the interconnectedness of multiple oppressive systems is ignored it undermines antiracist efforts.

The final parts of the chapter suggest reasons why black men should want to engage in a project of progressive black masculinities. It looks at the political and intellectual projects of various groups concerned with the welfare of black people including black nationalism; Afrocentricity; black feminist thought; black gay and lesbian, critical race theory; and black transformationist[6] ideas as well as relying on the experiential knowledge and history of black people. It suggests that to the extent black men are committed to the antiracist project of blackness, this project has always been concerned with the existential wholeness and well-being of black communities and black people. This well-being requires the promotion of black self determination, black self-love and appreciation and recognizes black agency, viewpoint—despite its diversity—and humanity in the context of a racist society inclined toward denigrating, humiliating, and limiting black humanity. This commitment is to the well-being of all of the constituent parts of black communities. These ideas bring the two sides of my definition of progressive black masculinities together. The last section of the chapter explores what it means concretely to be ethically and actively engaged in the progressive struggle of the sort contemplated by the project of progressive black masculinities.

Progressive Black Masculinities—Defined?

Simply stated, progressive black masculinities, on the one hand, personally eschew and actively stand against social structures of domination and, on the other, value, validate, and empower black humanity in all its variety as part of the diverse and multicultural humanity of others in the global family. More specifically, progressive black masculinities are, at a minimum, pro-black and antiracist as well as profeminist and antisexist. Further, they are male affirmative,[7] recognizing the humanity of men as men and rejecting early feminist formulations suggesting that men qua men are the enemy in the antisexist struggle. But progressive black masculinities are more than this. They are decidedly not dependent and are not predicated on the subordination of others. They instead promote human freedom for all, both in the context of their personal lives and in the outward manifestations of those personal lives in social, cultural, economic, and political contexts. As such, combining both *progressive blackness* and *progressive masculine* practice, progressive black masculinities are men who take an active and ethical stance against all social systems of domination and who act personally and in concert with others in activities against racism, sexism, homophobia and heterosexism, class and economic exploitation, imperialism, and other systems of oppression that limit the human potential of the black masculine self and others. This is challenging given normative—ideal and hegemonic—masculinity.

Progressive Blackness: An Ethical Project

Although many black people can be reactionary and there are any number of ways in which blackness and black culture can be employed in conservative, essentialist, and other counterproductive ways, I presume that most blacks abhor racism. That is, they stand against the racial domination and subordination of blacks that limit black agency and humanity. As Cornel West has so eloquently stated, "After centuries of racist degradation, exploitation, and oppression in America, being black means being minimally subject to white supremacist abuse and being a part of a rich culture and community that has struggled against such abuse. All people with black skin and African phenotype are subject to potential white supremacist abuse [and hence] have some interest in resisting racism—even if their interest is confined solely to themselves as individuals rather than to larger black communities."[8]

However, to be progressively black means something more than this. It recognizes that white supremacy is not just a belief system or an ideology but a structural system in which the ideology of white supremacy is deeply written into the conscious and unconscious patterns of people's behavior and into the very systems, institutions, and structures of American society.

Built on the extermination of large populations of Native Americans and the expropriation of their land; the enslavement, oppression, and exploitation of blacks; the subordination of Latinos and appropriation of portions of their land; and the initial exclusion of Asians as citizens all in an effort to create a white state,[9] the cultural value of white supremacy has been cultivated and institutionalized over several hundred years. This cultural value is so pervasive throughout society that whiteness is both the obvious and hidden norm against which most things are measured and is preferred in institutional settings that perpetuate themselves even in the absence of overt or conscious racist intent.[10] So for example, conversations about good schools often revolve around private or suburban schools, both of which code as white schools—not because black schools are inherently inferior but because a history of slavery, Jim Crow, segregation, government housing policies, and white flight have left "good" schools as "white" schools. To change this dynamic requires active intervention to disrupt the normal functioning of a society built on white supremacist foundations.

Progressive blackness therefore is this intervention. It is the ethical and active participation in antiracist struggles from the standpoint of black self identity and black communities' well-being. It intervenes to disrupt the normal economic, cultural, social, and political workings of white supremacy and consciousness. Latinaness, Native Americaness, Asian Americaness, and even European Americaness, among others, may also be projects meant to intervene and disrupt the normal psychological and instituionalized operations of white supremacy.

Ethical participation in antiracist struggles insists that the struggles not be dependent on or committed to the subordination of others. In addition it requires that participants be conscious of the relationships among "identities, class, culture, gender, sexual orientation, region, religion, age and the like."[11]

So for instance, within black communities, West critiqued as unethical what he calls racial reasoning, the practice of blacks ritually supporting particular black people simply because they are black without interrogating their commitments. He particularly criticized black leaders' initial response to the Clarence Thomas and Anita Hill hearings as unethical in part because although Thomas and Hill were black, black leaders failed to interrogate what they stood for in terms of the well-being of various black communities. Both of these people, according to West, supported "some of the most vicious policies to besiege black working and poor communities since Jim and Jane Crow segregation." He explained, "Both Thomas and Hill supported an unprecedented redistribution of wealth from working people to well-to-do people in the form of regressive taxation, deregulation policies, cutbacks and slowdowns in public service programs, take-backs at the negotiation table between worker and management, and military buildup at the Pentagon. Both ... supported the unleashing of unbridled capitalist market forces on a level never witnessed in the United State before that have devastated black working and poor communities."[12]

Further, racial reasoning in this instance was dependent on the subordination of black women. That is, it showed itself to be sexist and exclusionary, demonstrating a willingness to define the interest of the black community as corresponding to a narrow individual black male interest to the exclusion and suppression of those of black women. West thus criticized black leadership for failing to challenge Thomas's comment about his biological sister that reduced her to a stereotypical welfare cheat and their dismissal of Hill's sexual harassment claims. Hill's claims marked a departure from her otherwise "careerist addicted to job promotion [attitude which was] captive to the stereotypical self-image of the sacrificial black woman who suffers silently and alone."[13]

Thomas's comment about his sister as a welfare cheat also reveals the way cultural stereotypes often employ multiple systems of oppression to exact their sting. The welfare cheat is not simply a sexist comment but is also a racist one. Though it was meant to denigrate a black woman specifically, it nonetheless reinforced stereotypes about both women and blackness as lazy and as cheaters. Thus, Thomas unethically and for the purpose of his own individual aggrandizement sought bonding among men by trafficking in sexist discourse that also reinforced oppressive notions of blackness even while he misused the memory of black lynching.

Michael Dyson, too, commented on blackness as an ethical and political project. He recently challenged the ethics of Bill Cosby in using his celebrity and professional status to castigate the black community's most vulnerable members. Dyson charged that Cosby did so without articulating or even recognizing the structured oppressions that keep black people poor, such as policies promoting their imprisonment rather than their education or explaining the resistance to oppression implicit in a variety of their cultural practices.[14] As such, Cosby's comments were destructive and could be used by the racist right wing to justify further limiting poor black people's access to resources. Cosby castigated black youth for failing to stay in school, for failing to learn standard English and for engaging in activities that result in their incareration. He further castigated black parents for not adequately parenting their young. Finally, he commented that "lower economic and lower middle economic people [were] not holding up their end in this deal." Dyson suggested that Cosby's comments were particularly problematic and of questionable ethics, not because whites could misuse Cosby's comments, or because Cosby should not express his beliefs, but rather because, according to Dyson, Cosby had long refused to put that same status and professional success to use in the service of black communities well-being.[15]

Cosby's comments seem far less egregious than the racial reasoning employed in the context of Clarence Thomas and his Supreme Court nomination. Further, Dyson's criticism implicates the complicated issue of needed self-critique within black communities and the idea of cultural democracy (and thus dissent) that a project of progressive black masculinities embraces. Nonetheless, Dyson's criticism illustrates the link between ethics and community welfare.

In addition, here again two systems of domination were employed to make the cultural stereotype work. This time elitist comments reflecting class position—perhaps inadvertently—blame the poor for their own poverty and, though directed specifically against poor blacks, also suggest that black people in general are to blame for their own oppressed conditions. They thereby reinforce both classist and racist stereotypes.

Whether one agrees with Dyson's assessment of Cosby's career or not, the larger point becomes one of an ethical and active engagement in antiracist struggle that is not dependent on the subordination of others and is in pursuit of the expressive and material well-being of the entire community in all its variation. This variation includes black subgroups that are differentiated by class, sex, gender, sexuality, age, region, religion, and culture,[16] and particularly those differences on which structures of oppression have been erected. These structurally oppressed differences also serve as links, along with principled commitments, to other groups as potential coalitional partners.[17]

Exploring the subgroups that constitute black communities leads to three other insights that contribute to the definition of the project of progressive blackness: (1) The social construction of race, of which blackness is a part, is multidimensional; (2) the active stand against other forms of domination is the ethical extension of progressive black practice; and (3) coalition building against domination, not only with those within black communities but also with those outside of them, completes the ethical project of progressive black practice.

To the first insight, focusing on the subgroups within black communities, such as black women, black sexual minorities—some of which are women—or black Muslims, provides the insight that black identity is multidimensional. Black people are not just raced black but also are of different genders, sexes, classes, and religions, among others. Second, to the extent that members of black communities occupy identities that are structurally subordinated by other systems of domination such as class, gender, and sexuality, these systems also should be the focus of black antiracist struggle. This is so for two reasons. These other systems of domination should be a focus of black antiracist struggle because some black people's agency is constrained and affected by them. But second, given that these struggles, like the antiracist struggle, are based on claims that domination limits human potential, an ethical and principled position requires support of struggles also against these systems of domination.

Finally, as black subgroups find common ground with others with whom they share principled commitments and perhaps similar subordinated statuses, progressive blackness encourages coalition building around these issues. So for instance, black communities should stand against sexism because sexism limits the life chances of some members of the black community: black women. Thus, black women and other members of black communities should build coalitions with women generally who are committed to principles of antiracism and antisexism as limiting systems of subordination.

Seen from a different perspective, race itself also should be understood as multidimensional. That is, race, in which blackness is a project of black self-definition and in which whiteness has historically been a project of supremacy, can be understood as a system socially constructed on the basis of different types of human bodies.[18] This racial system assigns meanings to these different types of human bodies that justify and influence allocations of status and resources, both material and expressive, in a manner that privileges white people and whiteness and disadvantages black people and blackness, among others.[19] Racism operates and is bolstered through the economy, education system, religion, and other social systems and institutions and intersects with other systems of domination such as class, gender, and sex. To the extent that racism interacts with other systems of sexism, classism, and heterosexism, it is multidimensional. To eliminate racism, eliminating the other systems of oppression is likely necessary. At the same time, similar insights can be garnered from looking at racism as part of a larger system, which bell hooks refers to as the "White supremacist capitalist patriarchy"[20] and Francisco Valdes calls "the Euro-American Heteropatriarchy."[21]

Many of these ideas implicate the issue of black communities' very identities, including what it means to be black in the United States both as an individual matter and as communities, as well as, what the appropriate strategies (e.g., race consciousness, colorblindness) are for their affirmation. I return to this discussion later in this chapter, delving deeper into the discussion of progressive blackness as a political project. Suffice it to say for now that with regard to the appropriate strategies black people should pursue, though many of us who participated in the progressive black masculinities project viewed black identity as multiple, multilayered, and various[22] and the black community as multiple or imagined, most took a race-conscious approach.[23] This approach of race consciousness, or intentional blackness, seems particularly necessary as a social and political move because of the normativity of whiteness, where whiteness is assumed and in any event preferred as the standard. Such assumptions often negate or denigrate black experiences, black cultural traditions, black viewpoints—despite their variety—and black humanity, promoting instead their destruction or assimilation into whiteness as the price for admission into American citizenship and the privilege of humanness.

However, though one could assume that systematic racism might potentially spur progressive black practice, this seems less true for masculinity. Whereas blackness responds to and critiques racial domination, masculinity as a way of being and as currently practiced constitutes a social and political institution of domination. That is, it is defined, understood, believed, and practiced as domination over others. To the questions "What is a man? What is masculinity?"

the response is nothing if he is not in control of, in charge of, and dominates over everything else in his environment, including his own emotions, physical environments, women, children, and yes, other subordinate men.[24]

Whereas masculinity could of course be defined as caring and heroic, providing and sustaining, and ultimately humane, domination over others nonetheless is the central feature prevailing in notions and practices of normative masculinity in the United States. In fact, masculinity as domination is hegemonic.[25] That is, as a practiced understanding it is so pervasive that it rules over, suppresses, limits, and excludes other visions of masculinity through both coercion and complicity of all those involved. Further, like elite class domination and white racial power, masculinity as domination is structured and supported by the full range of social structures, including governmental, economic, religious, educational, media, and familial structures. These systems of domination—of race, class, and patriarchy—interact with one another and limit the human potential of groups over whom domination is exercised,[26] as each constitutes a site of power.

The American Masculine Ideal—Hegemonic Masculinity

The *masculine ideal* as feminists have shown, is informed by binary and dichotomous thinking that is endemic to Western thought. It is evidenced by common dualities such as white–black, good–evil, male–female, heterosexual–homosexual, and mind–matter.[27] These dualities are not equal but are hierarchical, with the first category representing the positive and preferred positionality and the second the undesirable and corrupted position.[28] Masculinity, the positive side of the male–female, man–woman dichotomy, is thus defined both as opposing and superior to the feminine. This duality is reflected in the traits supposedly confined to each category. Masculinity embodies socially valued traits. Men are to be strong, active, aggressive, reasoned, dominant, competitive, and in control. Femininity embodies the less socially valued traits. Women are to be weak, passive, receptive, emotional, nurturing, and subordinate.[29] These *cultural ideas*, as masculinities scholars insist, "don't describe women and men as they actually are,"[30] nor do they recognize that the ways "people feel and behave depends more on the social situation they're in than it does on some rigid set of underlying traits that define them in every circumstance."[31] These cultural ideas, instead, inform the ideal of masculinity in the American sex–gender system, which both feminists and masculinities scholars agree is backed by institutional and systemic power that rewards and penalizes those closest to the norm.

The Sex–Gender System

The sex–gender system basically says that men and women have both social and sexual roles. In these roles, which are related to the oppositional traits and are both hierarchal and complementary, men are to control their families and run the public world; women are to follow the masculine lead and to organize the private household.[32] Sexually, men are to be attracted to women, active in their pursuit of wealth and women, and active and penetrating in the world and in bed. Women, on the other hand, are to be attracted and attractive to men and passive and receptive both socially and sexually to men. A neat package, this system precludes and denigrates same-sex relations as deviant, devalued, and outside the preferred system. It is captured in the dichotomous thinking of the heterosexual–homosexual binary.[33] Further, intersexed people—those born with both female and male biological features—are to be changed surgically into male or female so that they can grow into men or women.[34]

Therefore, ideal masculinity is defined in opposition not only to women but also to homosexuality. A real man cannot be either feminine or gay. The ideal is also racialized and classed. Men are to be empowered, to be provided opportunities to fulfill their roles as leader and provider, and to be ensured dominance. This translates into policies that provide men the best and most key opportunities in the social world while circumscribing women's opportunities and human development to allow men the preferred positions. U.S. society has operated historically to provide this access to only certain men: those raced white and those who possess property. The boundaries surrounding race- and class-based privilege, though, have changed over time, as have the boundaries of manhood. For example, whiteness initially included primarily white Anglo-Saxon Protestant men. However, with immigration of a variety of ethnic groups from Europe, whiteness was expanded to also include men within these groups.[35] Further, initially only propertied men were provided certain privileges.[36] However, as Cheryl Harris argued, whiteness became a form of property, thereby expanding the group of white people.[37] In addition, the economic order expanded to make more men propertied, though this trend may be reversing. And finally, other changes have affected these boundaries. For instance, Clyde W. Franklin II, has argued that black men were considered boys until the 1960s, when they became nominal men.[38]

Nevertheless, the ideal man is currently an elite white heterosexual male. This is not a person but an ideal. And a man's masculinity is measured by how close he comes to the ideal. Though this ideal is dominant or hegemonic, it is not the only idea of masculinity. In fact, through the lived experiences of people and their interactions with their societies, multiple ideas and practices emerge to constitute masculinity differently over time and space.

Current ideal masculinity is the product of social processes prevailing in twenty-first-century America. It is different from the white rural estate-owning "genteel patriarch" of the late eighteenth and nineteenth century or the urban "heroic artisan" of the same period,[39] both of which have whiteness at their center. From this perspective, masculinity—both ideal masculinity and its multiple variations—is socially constructed, constantly changing, and dependent on time and place. It is not biologically determined; rather, as a gender concept, it is what we as a culturally specific community—both as a collective and as individuals—make of the biological difference between male and female. These concepts shift over time and also differ within cultures among various subgroups that construct distinct masculinities in response to the ways social processes act on them. As such, both individuals and groups have some agency in defining masculinity. However, neither groups nor individuals define and construct masculinities in a vacuum. Rather, they draw on other culturally prevalent notions and are constrained by various social structures. Further, much of what is defined as masculine within a group is both internalized and enacted as much as constructed and chosen.

Thus, although half of the children born are born male or remade into males, they are not born men.[40] Rather, they grow into men, learning the social expectations and cultural ideas of what a man is.

Socialization: Constructing Masculine Identity

My sons and I stop at a fast food restaurant along Route 15, somewhere in the middle of Pennsylvania. I am driving from our home in Buffalo to my parents' home in Baltimore. As they usually do, the boys are spending their spring break with their grandparents. As we enter the restaurant and the boys take off to the men's room, I notice a sign advertising a men's conference.

The conference is titled, "Training to Reign," and features a lion in the middle of the poster with a crown on the lion's head. There is much in this poster to critique. Instead however, I try to think of positive interpretations of it. As the poster attempts to appeal to everyday men, I change the word reign to lead. Lead sounds more democratic, to my mind, and one can certainly lead in everyday life. In fact, my sister-in-law chastises her twin sons by asking them whether they are leaders or followers when they are apparently following each other's lead in inappropriate action instead of each figuring out for himself more appropriate behavior.

My fourteen-year-old son emerges first from the bathroom, interrupting my thoughts. "Look," I say, "look at this sign." He quickly reads it, dismissively noting, "Hum, talking about male supremacist," as he moseys over to the ordering counter. Having in that instance made my concentrated efforts at positively interpreting the poster seem ridiculous, I reply, startled, "Male supremacist? I didn't know you knew such a phrase." "Oh Mom," he moans, "I'm not completely oblivious." I turn away as the smile spreads across my face. "That's my boy!" I think. "That's my child... that boy is the son of his parents...of his community? My heart warms, "perhaps his father and I have done at least one thing right? Perhaps young black men already know this stuff and there is hope for the world, after all."

Ian Harris, a masculinities scholar, explained that young boys are socialized to meet society's expectations of them and are "rewarded by their parents and teachers for conforming to gender-role standards ... [and] congratulated by their peers for performing like men. Mentors pat them on the back for their 'masculine' achievements."[41] In his study of 560 men, Harris distilled some two dozen types of dominate male gender norms or messages that boys or men hear about how men are supposed to behave. Many of these messages are conflicting and have dubious outcomes when enacted; many support idealized masculinity. These messages include men as adventurer, breadwinner, playboy, president, sportsman, tough guy, and warrior or instruct men to be the best they can, to be in control, to be self-reliant, to be stoic, or to make money—"a man is judged by how much money he makes or his status on the job." Harris argued that gender identity is the combination of biology on which dominant cultural norms, subcultural influences, and unique circumstances are imposed and constructed.[42] Children internalize dominant social norms but also internalize the norms of their specific subgroups. He explained, "Children who internalize social norms become cultural natives .... Boys from different subcultures—classes, kinship networks, ethnic groups, regional enclaves, religious communities—view the dominant ideology for masculinity with different lenses. From these perspectives, they construct complex gender identities full of idiosyncratic interpretations ... that contain common threads derived from dominant cultural norms and subculture influences."[43]

Franklin described the socialization process in a similar fashion but included peer groups as a significant socializing factor for youth entering the first phase of adult life. He suggested that the three most important socializing sources for children are the subculture group (the primary socializing factor), the peer group, and mainstream society. He posited that the contradictory messages in each make for the formation of complex identities. Thus, although men are greatly influenced by societal messages of what it means to be a man, their gender identity, as Harris notes, "can be conceived as [an individual] interpretation and acting out of how his social group interprets masculinity."[44] That is, men play a role in constructing their masculinity. Thus, from the time men are children, they are both shaped by and construct their identities as part of the socialization process and as part of various social groups.

Many of the messages men hear about what it means to be a man, particularly those associated with ideal masculinity, may be harmful to them and psychologically and socially problematic. For instance, the messages men hear often counsel them to suppress their emotions. This advice may result in alienating men from their own conscience and feelings, possibly leaving them conflicted, empty, and hard and leading to other antisocial consequences. Further, men may also be harmed by the narrow, limited, and restrictive roles they are told to play. Some suggest that women in some ways, despite restricted access to social opportunities and resources, currently may have an easier time constructing their identities because they are allowed a wider range of traits, roles, and ways of *being* that may better reflect them—who they are or who they want to be. In contrast, men, though often having greater access to more material resources and opportunities, arguably may be much more limited in their human expression of themselves because they have more narrow traits, roles, and messages about how to *be* from which to draw on in constructing their identities. This state of affairs may be more harmful to black men—and poor black men in particular—because they have less access to economic, social, and institutional resources and opportunities and are also subject to a range of disempowering and distorted stereotypes against which they must operate. Thus, to the extent that they internalize messages urging them to construct identities that conform to ideal masculinity, they may have even fewer resources to do so, and even fewer resources on which to construct healthy life-affirming and personally competent identities. This may lead to male identities based on more physical assertions and prowess involving physical toughness, violence, or sexuality, given the other social constraints. Some of these constrained expressions in turn often become the basis for both legitimate and illegitimate criticism and penalty.

Ideal Masculinity as Domination Masculinity, nevertheless, is a site of power. Power is a social phenomenon, the relations of which are institutionalized throughout the economic, political, and social area and to which compliance is enforced through penalties and rewards as well as legal and extralegal violence. Commenting on racial power, Harold Cruse noted that although America "idealizes the rights of the individual above everything else," the fact is that the "nation is dominated by the social power of groups, classes, in-groups and cliques—both ethnic and religious." He goes on to note, "The individual in America has few rights that are not backed up by the political, economic and social power of one group or another. Hence the individual Negro has, proportionately, very few rights indeed because his ethnic group (whether or not he actually identifies with it) has very little political, economic or social power (beyond moral grounds) to wield."[45]

Philosopher Hannah Arendt also commented on this idea, explaining that power is a collective phenomenon, something an individual can have only if society provides it. She explained, "Power corresponds to the human ability not just to act but also to act in concert. Power is never the property of an individual; it belongs to a group and remains in existence only so long as the group keeps together. When we say of somebody that he is 'in power' we actually refer to his being empowered by a certain number of people to act in their name. The moment the group, from which the power originated to begin with … disappears, 'his power' also vanishes."[46]

Gender, the structure of which masculinity is a part, is a description then not so much of the roles and traits of men and women but rather "of the actual social relations of power between men and women, institutionalized in society and internalized to varying degrees by its individuals." It is "socially structured and individually embodied."[47] Patriarchy describes the structure of men's social power that privileges and benefits men over women[48] but that does not privilege all men equally. Michael Kaufman noted that even though power can be understood as the human ability to develop human capacities, it is more often understood as the capacity to impose control over others and over material resources.[49] He explained that "in societies based on hierarchy and inequality ... people cannot use and develop their capacities to an equal extent ... .[Rather, one has power if one] can take advantage of differences between people ... .[50] The equation of masculinity with power is one that developed over centuries. It conformed to, and in turn justified, the real-life domination of men over women and the valuation of males over females. Individual men internalize all this into their developing personalities."[51]

Domination over others is one of the central understandings and practices of masculinity. Stated differently, normative masculinity is predicated on the domination of others. It relies on male group power to empower and to provide unearned privileges to those that come within its ambit, namely males, but provides greater privileges to those who come closest to the established or ideal norm. It thereby seduces men into compliance with its promise of greater privilege vis-à-vis the other, whether women, gay men, or countless others differentiated by race, class, ethnicity, age, or nationality. Further, it not only requires domination over others but also is defined in relationship to and in opposition to others.

This domination is exercised through the entire range of social institutions and systems and employs specifically the tools of the economy, cultural representation, and violence, both legal and nonlegal,[52] to exclude, to exploit, to marginalize, and to disempower women as well as certain other men.[53] Further, men's use of these tools is justified in relationship to the traits often assigned to masculinity such as physical strength, public action, economic control, sexual domination, and aggressiveness. Men's justified dominion over these tools and the prescription of domination in general imbue masculinity with an association with violence and contribute to a culture of male-enacted violence. For an example, the high incidence of domestic violence by men against women may indicate that men are using violence to try to control and dominate over their partners. Minimizing sanctions for this violence, in law for example, may indicate the society's tolerance for this type of behavior.

For an economic example, a department store was recently sued for allegedly steering women into lower paying positions. Such steering ensures that men occupy the vast majority of decision-making and higher paying positions within the store, and to the extent that steering, and a variety of other practices which frustrate women's advancement, are replicated throughout the society, it may well result in men exercising financial control in their individual families. It is clear that men constitute the vast majority of the politicians, judges, captains of industry and highest paid workers. These institutional practices are encouraged by the sex/gender ideologies that suggest that women should stay at home, are not responsible for their families, or are never interested in good-paying jobs or career advancement.

These ideas inform the contours and the struggles implicit in the project of progressive masculinities. This project is about reorienting male practices and performances of masculinity to eschew domination as a central feature. Further, it requires the active support and edification by men of those against whom masculine domination has been exercised, including women, sexual minorities, and other men subordinated by race, class, and other systems of subordination. In short, it requires action to transform the institution of masculinity as a system of domination.

Given this understanding of hegemonic masculinity and the project of progressive masculinities, where do black men fit? What can be said of black masculinities, which are constrained, at a minimum, by racism and certainly markets and are therefore something less than dominant? And further, though some black men are clearly progressive by the definition already provided, what would it mean for more black men to practice progressive black masculinities, and why, given the privileges of masculinity, would they want to?

Theoretical Positionings of Black Men in Ideal Masculinity

Where do black men fit in all of this? Some scholars suggest that racism precludes black men from exercising and in any way benefiting from the privileges of masculinity; from being "real men" (apparently as defined by ideal masculinity). They do so by looking at the lived conditions of black men. But this analysis nonetheless implies that black men are oppressed because they are both black and men; that is oppressed by gendered racism. The idea of gendered racism accounts for representations, or stereotypes, and practices directed toward black men because they are both black and men.

Others argue that black men, at the intersection of race and gender, are oppressed by race but are privileged by gender, by which they understand black men to be privileged over women and particularly over black women. They compare not only the conditions of black men to black women but also the relationships between black men and black women. Although the theory in some ways obscures the impact of gendered racism against black men, I suggest that intersectional theory can be interpreted in a more nuanced fashion that recognizes that black men in some contexts benefit from unearned privileges in this patriarchal society but are nonetheless sometimes oppressed by gender and race in the form of gendered racism. Ultimately, I argue for a multidimensional understanding of black men as a single social position—*blackmen, one word*—and under which black men are both sometimes privileged by gender and oppressed by gendered racism, often in different contexts.

Black Male Conditions in the U.S.: Gender Privilege?

Some scholars, including Afrocentric scholars, can be read to suggest that because black men are oppressed by race, they are in no position to benefit from the privileges afforded men under a patriarchal sex–gender system that oppresses women and others in part to benefit men. They point to the fact that black men are economically subordinated in segmented and separated job markets that leave them in much lower-paying jobs than whites and often leave them unemployed outright. Though black women are also segmented into lower-paying jobs, it is argued they may be able to find jobs and may do so increasingly given the changing nature of the economy. The economy is adding more lower wage service jobs and is losing the manufacturing jobs that historically employed mostly men and paid them higher wages. They also point to the fact that black men are disproportionately and increasingly incarcerated, leaving them warehoused in the nation's prisons and thereafter deprived of opportunities to provide for themselves and their families. Further, they argue that black men have been culturally stigmatized in a way that justifies their increased surveillance, subjects them to the microaggressions of clutched purses and profiling that psychologically injure and constrain them, and dismisses and lowers expectations of their humanity. These same conditions are experienced by black boys, resulting in higher suspension rates from schools and disproportionate placement in special education programs, which among other things render them increasingly less educated and less likely to grow into productive men. These arguments are borne out by the following facts:

- Black men have the lowest life expectancy rate of any group within the United States.[54]
- Black male suicide rates doubled between 1980 and 1995, constituting the third leading cause of death among black men.[55]
- Black men have the highest rate of diabetes among all men. Cardio-vascular ailments prematurely kill four of every ten black men.[56]
- Homicide is even more problematic than disease; in 1998 black men represented seven of ten murder victims.[57]
- Using 1998 figures, black men earned on average seventy-one cents for every dollar earned by white men. College graduates do better, earning seventy-two cents for every dollar earned by comparable white graduates. (Black women earned about seventy-six cents for every dollar black men earned. Even of college graduates, black women's median income was 87 percent of black men's earnings.)[58]
- As of 2003, black male teens experienced the lowest employment ratios (i.e., employment relative to population) in fifty years, at less than 20 percent.[59] It has not been this low since the historic decision in *Brown v. Board of Education.*

- The period between 2000 and 2002 saw the year-round idleness, where blacks did not work at all during the year, at 21 percent for black males of almost all ages, 20–64, compared to 12 percent for Asian men and 10 percent for white men. 44 percent of black men without high school diplomas or a GED were idle for the entire year.[60]
- Employment rates for young, less-educated black males are much lower than for whites and lower in cities than in suburbs, the gap widening over the last decade.[61] These mark the spatial inequalities wrought by the city/suburban split of segregated living and the increasing isolation of black populations.[62]
- Nationwide, black men were incarcerated 9.6 times the rate of white men. Other studies suggest that 12 percent of black men between twenty and thirty-four years of age are in jail or prison compared to only 1.6 percent of white men of similar age. And 28 percent of black men can expect to be imprisoned during their lifetimes.[63]

These statistics confirm conditions of deprivation for many black men and represent not only blocked opportunities for black men in terms of realizing ideal masculinity and its proscriptions to be providers but also their lack of opportunities to become productive and contributing members of society. These conditions also hinder men in developing the self-esteem that is often associated with work. Work may not only provide an opportunity for people to make a living but may provide also a sense of competence and self-fulfillment.

However, whereas Afrocentrics and others analyze these problems as resulting primarily from the racist structure of the society, their focus on black men belies their emphasis. That is, their focus illustrates that black men are not only oppressed by racism but also may be harmed by the gender oppression implicit in the notion of gendered racism. Further, these conditions do not mean that black men are not in many ways privileged by the patriarchal sex–gender system through the operation of sexism and gender oppression nor does it mean there are no representations of black men as masculine. Rather, as Franklin suggested, multiple forms of black masculinities exist. These have adapted in, varying degrees, to the realization that black men's opportunities to attain ideal masculinity have been blocked. He described them as follows:

"Conformist Black masculinity," which "continue[s] to accept mainstream society's prescriptions and proscriptions for heterosexual males";[64]
"Ritualistic Black masculinity,"[65] which recognizes blocked opportunities but continues to "play the game" without believing or really questioning it;
"Innovative Black masculinity," which "exaggerates one aspect of traditional masculinity which *can* be achieved in order to receive desired responses."[66] He referred to some of the rap music that denigrates women and is sexually explicit but achieves the desired goal of material

success as nonthreatening examples of this type of masculinity. Violent, drug-dealing masculinities are examples of more lethal ones.

"Retreatist Black masculinity," which has "grown weary of participating in a system that denies the means for achieving common goals"[67] and as such, has opted out through such things as drugs, homelessness, welfare dependency;

"Rebellious masculinity," which rejects the dominating precepts of American ideal masculinity.[68]

The last group is where progressive masculinities are located. These may well draw on innovative strategies but are focused on realizing the well-being of black men and others. The other types of masculinities that Franklin described have all been seduced into understanding and practicing masculinity in some form as a system of domination over others.

Intersectional Theory: Privileged by Gender, Oppressed by Race?

A second theory that contributes to the study of black masculinities in the context of hegemonic masculinities is intersectional theory. Intersectional theory was developed by black feminists for the purpose of examining black women's lives. The theory was first articulated by Kim Crenshaw, a black feminist working within the law from the perspective of critical race theory.[69] Intersectional theory challenges a single-axis framework for understanding black women's oppression. The single-axis framework suggested that black women were either oppressed by race or were oppressed because of gender and did not account for black women's oppression structured by both sexism and racism. Crenshaw used the traffic intersection to describe structural intersections of systems of domination. The intersection had cars coming from various directions: one direction for race, another for sex, and a third for some other socially structured force. She suggested that in an accident it is often too difficult to tell which axis caused the accident, and oftentimes more than one axis was at fault. Applied to black women, the theory seemed to imply that they were doubly burdened and worse off than black men, a topic undertaken by Stephanie Phillips in this volume.

When this theory was applied to black men, it was often interpreted to suggest that black men were subordinated by race but privileged by gender.[70] In other words, as black people, black men were oppressed by race, but as men, black men were privileged by gender. This understanding seemed to capture a host of practices and realities. For instance, it seemed to capture the fact that although the median income for working black men is less than that of working white men, it is, nonetheless, higher than the median income for black women. Further, it seemed to capture the fact that it is all too often black men who comprise the leadership roles in the black community, roles they often appropriate to themselves vis-à-vis women because they are men. For example, black clergy, who feature significantly among black leadership, also often agree and promote the position that women should not become religious ministers or pastors and thereby limit women's opportunities to leadership positions via this avenue.

However, this understanding failed to address practices such as racial profiling that seemed to happen to black men because they were both black and men. In other words, black men under these circumstance did not seem to be privileged by gender and oppressed by race but rather oppressed by both race and gender. The idea that black men were privileged by gender and subordinated by race undermined the potential of intersectional theory to further delineate differences among men. Black men are not just some undifferentiated group; they are not just raced and gendered but also are distinguished by class, age, and region. Potentially the intersections were many and varied.

But intersectionality theory can be interpreted in other ways that render it a more nuanced theory. First, it might suggest that black men are dominant and unjustly privileged in the private realm of the black community, which constitutes a family of sorts; but that black men are subordinated publicly, meaning their masculinity is subordinated within the larger society outside of the black community. Here black communities are seen as inhabiting private space within the public–private dichotomy of male and female spheres of influence. This is a sexist, and racist framework, in part, because it relegates black men to a space *made* marginal and to which women are supposed to be limited while in many ways supporting men's control over this space often at women's expense. Nevertheless, it may better capture the dynamics within the black community that often yield black men in leadership positions. It may also capture the dynamic within black communities of privileging black men's victimization over black women's victimization as in the Thomas–Hill context,[71] or even where black women are victimized by black men as through rape as Thema Bryant makes clear in Chapter 14. But it fails to account for the way in which, as John Calmore explains in Chapter 8, young black men may be over-policed and constructed as unwanted traffic even within their own communities.

Another way to interpret the intersectional theory as applied to black men is to understand it as pointing out that many social structures contribute to the construction of individual and group identity and that to determine what a particular intersectional identity means requires scholars to look to the context. In other words, when applying intersectional theory to the black male experience, one must look to the context of a particular situation to determine whether black men are being privileged or oppressed by gender or any other structure that intersects with it.[72]

Multidimensionality Theory: Privileged by Gender
and Oppressed by Gendered Racism

A third theory that contributes to understanding the ways black masculinities are positioned in relation to hegemonic masculinity is multidimensionality theory, an emerging theory that grew out of intersectionality. Many black feminists and critical race theorists have contributed to its development. However, a number of gay/queer theorists producing scholarship in the areas of critical race theory[73] and LatCrit[74] have made substantial contributions to its development.[75] Multidimensionality theory directs focus to the various and multiple social structures that oppress and constrain the agency of individuals and groups in uniquely distinctive ways.

Multidimensionality has three insights. First, it recognizes that an individual has many dimensions, some that are embodied by human traits, such as skin color, sex, earlobe length, and eye color, and others that are expressive, such as being Methodist or Catholic or a cat owner or dog owner. In addition, each individual possesses a unique set of traits and ways of being. As such, communities encompass a diversity of unique and uniquely positioned individuals. Recognizing this uniqueness suggests that no group or community effort can represent every single person in his or her individuality.

Second, however, some of these dimensions are "materially relevant" in that society structures systems of privilege and disadvantage on the basis of them.[76] That is, society over time develops meanings and systems around either particular traits such as color or, say, religious differences that justify and influence the allocation of both status and material resources, privileging some group traits or dimensions over others. So for instance, although the color of a person's skin has been developed as materially relevant, being a dog owner has not. And though earlobe length might in another society bring with it certain meanings and privileges, it is not materially relevant in the United States. Here the focus is on systems of domination, including class, race, and sexuality.

Third, the various systems of disadvantage and privilege or systems of domination interact with one another and are mutually reinforcing. So for instance, elite white heterosexual men occupy each of the privileged sides of the race, sex–gender, and class systems within the United States and as such constitute the most privileged and advantaged people within the system who represent the idealized norm.

Multidimensionality provokes several related ideas. It suggests that as all groups are made of unique individuals who predictably are positioned differently with regard to the various systems of domination, all groups are coalitions of different people and different groups of people.[77] Further, the intersection of two or more systems of disadvantage may produce unique categories and experiences. For example, although intersectional theory might suggest that black men are privileged by gender and oppressed by race, multidimensionality might capture the experience and phenomenon of racial profiling by suggesting that black men are sometimes oppressed because they are blackmen—one socially and multidimensionally constructed positionality. Thus, to the extent the various systems of disadvantage are mutually reinforcing, the elimination of only one system, such as race, while weakening the overall structure of domination, is unlikely to change the oppressed conditions of black people.

Multidimensionality also provides insight into certain social tendencies. One tendency is for cultural stereotypes to be multifaceted. In other words, cultural stereotypes, in which specific groups are targeted, may employ more than a single system of oppression to stigmatize the disadvantaged group.[78] So for instance, the historical stereotype of black men as violent, sexually aggressive, and lazy employs not only racialized images—even though race is not mentioned; rather, black men are being referenced—but also images that are classed, sexualized, and gendered.[79]

Another tendency is that within multidimensional groups, like black communities, the most privileged people within the group often cling to the socially privileged aspects of their identities. So for instance, it is not surprising that while calling on sisterhood, white women feminists often used their whiteness to assert their domination over black women and the growing feminist field, or that those black men who understand themselves as oppressed by race often assert their masculinity as justification for their representational race status in which they assert dominion for speaking for black people.[80] In doing so the actors are complicit with and conform to the understandings of domination implicit in the privileged sites within these systems. They often assert them to bond with other similarly privileged people or to exert dominion over or to exclude more disadvantaged people within the community.

This is problematic because it reinforces the very system against which these groups are fighting by undermining solidarity, as in solidarity among women. In addition, it strengthens their secondary statuses within the privileged system. So for instance, black men's appeals to the masculine ideal strengthen ideal hegemonic masculinity. But ideal masculinity is raced white and understands black masculinity as secondary. The assertion therefore reconfirms black men's secondary status and reinforces black subordination.[81] And finally, these moves increase the possible success of opponents that seek to divide groups along these cleavages of difference in a divide-and-rule ploy.

Because of these tendencies, groups that engage in political projects must do so not simply on the basis of shared disadvantage or victimhood; they must come together on the basis of shared commitments and accountability to one another.[82] In this way multidimensionality also highlights the potential for coalition building.

Relating the Project of Progressive Blackness to Progressive Masculinities

What is the relationship between blackness as a political project to hegemonic masculinity, and ultimately to progressive masculinities? I suggest here that the political project of blackness has always been primarily concerned with the elimination of domination. The ideas in black communities about what domination entails—simply race, gender, class, or something else—and which strategies should be employed to counter domination have differed over time and among different individuals and groups of black people. However, underneath these different visions is a striving for black people's well-being, which has been variously interpreted to encompass black self-determination and self-appreciation as well as the recognition of black agency, viewpoint, and humanity.

I now turn to several political or intellectual black movements to illustrate the program of antidomination and black edification. I survey black nationalism, Afrocentricity, black feminist thought, and briefly black gay and lesbian thought, as well as tranformationist ideas for three reasons. First, having focused on the disagreements between Afrocentrists and black feminists in the introduction, I want to demonstrate that both their scholarship as well as the scholarship of black gay and lesbian and transformationists share some basic concerns and approaches to the well-being of black people. Second, I seek to make apparent the justification for black people's commitment to the eradication of domination, as well as its depth and breadth. I do so to suggest that this commitment is incompatible with a simultaneous commitment to the domination inherent in ideal masculinity in part because it recognizes the harm domination does to human potential. Stated differently, the legitimacy of a claim to self-determination is wholly undermined by a commitment to limiting the self-determination and agency of others. Third, this exploration brings together the two sides of the definition proffered: Progressive black masculinities are both about a stance against domination and a commitment to the valuation and empowerment of black humanity.

I begin with a brief analysis of black nationalism because I believe it articulates the elements that are crucial to the material and spiritual welfare of black communities. These elements both best capture the harms caused to black people by white supremacy as exercised through racism and remain in many ways the articulated basis of the project of blackness.

Black Nationalism

Black nationalism is a political, economic, and cultural project that emphasizes black self-determination, self-definition, and self-love.[83] Captured in part in the theories of people such as Martin Delaney, Alexander Crummell, Douglass, Booker T. Washington, Du Bois, Garvey, Elijah Muhammad, and Malcolm X,[84] its primary goals are to pursue black people's control over their own destinies, self-determination, and to affirm black humanity.[85] The goal of pursuing black people's control over their own destinies was primarily a political–economic project, illustrated most dramatically in Garvey's organizational efforts, including his Back to Africa movement and the economic self-sufficiency and self-help ideology and practices of Elijah Mohammed through the Nation of Islam. This project is also captured, for example, in the critiques by Malcolm X and others of the integrationist approach to black education in the 1960s.[86] They rejected what they saw as the implication within the integrationist movement that black schools were inherently inferior. They argued that the problem of black education was a problem of resources and control—that is, black control over the school, teacher staffing, and curricular content.[87] Malcolm X explained, "A school system in an all-white neighborhood is not [considered] a segregated school system. The only time it's segregated is when it is in a community other than white, but at the same time controlled by whites. So my understanding of a segregated school system ... is a school that's controlled by people other than those who go there. . . . [However] if we can get an all-black school, one that we can control, staff it ourselves with the type of teacher who has our good at heart, with the type of book that has many of the missing ingredients that have produced this inferiority complex in our people, then we don't feel that an all-black school is necessarily a segregated school."[88]

The project of affirming black humanity is meant in part to counter the potential inferiority complex engendered by racism but also to reflect the agency of the black personality manifest both before and after the colonial encounter. The project of affirming black humanity, though political in many respects, is primarily a cultural endeavor. It stresses black self-love, which by definition rejects white supremacist ideology that denigrates black people as inferior and without a history or agency. It focuses on the way African Americans have survived and have claimed human dignity despite the dehumanizing processes of American slavery, segregation, and institutionalized racism. This survival turned on African Americans' cultural responses to these oppressive conditions. These responses are seen as distinctive, encompassing a mixture of various cultural strands (i.e., African, Amerindian, and European),[89] but are most notably tied to and influenced by Africans and the cultural practices the African slaves first brought with them. These are captured in various black art forms, including music and aesthetic presentations, ways of communicating, family structure, certain values, and philosophical orientations, which represent the more mobile forms of African cultural expression.[90] Black nationalism remains a strain of thought prevalent in black communities and is shared by most black intellectuals who work on issues of concern to or who claim to write from the perspectives of black communities.[91] In fact, integrationists of the Sixties would probably agree with many of these ideas.

However, black nationalism goes further: It sees African Americans as a nation, viewed by some as an internally colonized nation and others as an ethnic group.[92] It suggests that black communities should not have to give up their culture, admittedly constructed in the furnace of white supremacy and linked to a distinctive African cultural fingerprint.[93] This they argue, drawing on Du Bois,[94] would amount to what Gary Peller has called a "painless genocide,"[95] in which black communities and people would be assimilated, absorbed, and dissolved into whiteness and the white culture's limited vision of America. Further, they argue that African Americans should be linked to Africa and diasporan Africans through the politics of Pan-Africanism.

These themes remain a part of black thinking and conceptualization. For instance, the idea of self-determination remains in some quarters as a political, economic project with separatist orientations,[96] whereas in others it has come to more closely relate to the idea of agency, or the ability to act or to act in concert with others.[97] In this sense, it is both an individual and community asset, recognizing not only that individuals act and know themselves through communities but also that the individual's well-being is linked to the well-being of communities. Stated differently, to the extent that a society subordinates a particular group, even its most liberated members will suffer the ill effects of their group's subordination. In any case, systems of subordination limit and constrain self-determination and agency. These ideas of self-determination and black self-appreciation remain a part of black philosophy and a basis for the project of blackness, as is evidenced by Afrocentric, black feminist, gay and lesbian, and tranformationist thought.

Afrocentricity

Afrocentricity, though a contested term, embodies many of the broad themes found in black nationalism. As an intellectual tradition first fully articulated by Molefi Asante, Afrocentricity is situated in many black studies programs in American universities. Afrocentricity took up the *cultural* project seemingly apparent in black nationalism and inherent in its goals of promoting black self-respect. It does so by seeking to delineate and to articulate black perspectives and a black worldview on the full range of issues involving African and African Diaspora peoples.[98] In doing so, Afrocentricity seeks to develop the scholarship and knowledge base about African and diasporan African cultures and the links among them.

Its central goal, however, is to center blackness and reclaim black agency.[99] The idea here is that black people are subject to cultural domination. They argue that blacks have been seen and see themselves through Eurocentric lenses—that is, through a lens centered on a European worldview, complete with white supremacy, which declares whites as the primary agents and actors in history and in all areas of life and which relegates black people to the role of spectators and objects of history and current life. To the extent that black people often see themselves through Eurocentric eyes, they are "misoriented because [they are] culturally disoriented,"[100] as Eurocentricity generally assigns and is institutionally organized to convey the message that all that is black is evil, pathological, and degenerate and makes no contribution to the rest of humanity. This disorientation, together with white internalized and institutionalized racism, stifles the realization of the black nationalist goals of black self-love, self-definition, and self-determination in the political and economic arenas. Afrocentricity seeks to use the knowledge gathered about a unique "African cultural system"[101] or an African cultural fingerprint that African Americans share, to analyze and critique black behavior from a black perspective, thereby centering and revealing black agency. They also seek to reorient this agency in a congruent and productive way by stressing values such as community, harmony, spirituality, responsibility to family and community, and emotional and intuitive—in addition to rational—ways of knowing. These, they argue, are central to an African cultural system.[102]

As such, Afrocentricity involves an ideological project of fighting white cultural domination by grounding black cultural appreciation within both the minds of people and the sociopolitical order, through, for example, entrenching multiculturalism.

However, Afrocentrics have been criticized for romanticizing African and African American history and for being reactive in a number of their ideas.[103] Further, they have also been criticized for promoting a sweepstakes of black authenticity (i.e., who is authentically black) that essentializes black identity, does not recognize the multiplicity of black identity, and fails to question the ethics of a particular position, authentic or not.[104] Latent in both of these critiques seems a concern that Afrocentricity objectifies black culture and understands or promotes it as static and unchanging as opposed to dynamic and adapting. Whatever African American culture is, it is different from what it was in the past and will and should be different in the future. This does not mean that it should not exist or that it might not in some ways carry forward a cultural fingerprint. It simply means that it will change and will adapt itself within the social environment of its times.

Afrocentricity has also been criticized for being sexist and homophobic.[105] Although the theory's stance on these issues seem to be in a state of flux, there remains a certain maleness to Afrocentric writings that smack of patriarchy,[106] which is in part reflected in some of their most notable programs. These deal primarily with black males and include their work to establish all-black male schools for black boys and their initiation of rites-of-passage programs for black male youths. Yet it is in this work where Afrocentricity makes contributions to theorizing about the positioning of black men in relation to hegemonic masculinity. Though they might analyze the conditions of black men through the lens of racism and argue that their problems are the consequences of racist cultural domination rather than a combination of racist cultural domination and gender hegemony, their conclusions belie their argument.[107] Nevertheless, Afrocentricity is committed to the project of black edification through revealing black agency and directing that agency toward black edification. Further, Afrocentricity highlights the problems of cultural domination and as such can be said to stand against certain forms of domination.

To the extent that domination is a concern and that the edification of the black community is its goal, a limited concern—as opposed to a practical focus—on only the domination of black men within black communities, as critics have charged, undermines the goals of the Afrocentric project. That is, it undermines community empowerment because it is only concerned with part of the community. But it also undermines others' participation in their movement because of its own apparent disregard for the harm of others. Stated differently, why should black women, for instance, share or care about Afrocentric concerns, particularly where their proposed program requires women's subordination? And finally, it belies the question of whether black male empowerment can be accomplished without taking into account the ways black men are differently positioned by class, sexuality, or other structures of domination, which may also harm black men.

Black Feminist Thought

Black feminists have also engaged in a project of promoting black self-appreciation and self-determination through revealing black women's agency and humanity. That is, they agree that black people have agency and as such are "subjects and conscious actors in the creation of history and culture rather than the passive recipients of someone else's actions."[108] This idea is reflected in Toni Morrison's comments on the place of Afro-American literature:[109] "[I]t is no longer acceptable merely to imagine us and imagine for us. We have always been imagining ourselves. We are not Isak Dinesen's 'aspects of nature,' nor … Conrad's 'unspeaking.' We are the subject of our own narrative, witnesses to and participants in our own experience, and, in no way coincidentally, in the experience of those with whom we have come in contact. We are not, in fact, 'other.' We are choices."[110]

Black people have not only actively imagined themselves; they have also been actively involved in creating themselves and their culture despite tremendous social constraints.[111] Black feminism, a diverse and complex body of scholarship, focuses on the experiences, writings, activities, and insights of both scholarly and ordinary black women's lives as a way of demonstrating their agency and humanity. Further, they have argued that black women's ideas and activities contribute to critical social theory, including the feminist theory on which they draw and in which they participate.[112] So for instance, Patricia Hill Collins suggested that Sojourner Truth's question of "Ain't I a Woman?" exposed the culturally constructedness of womanhood.[113] Further, she argued that the limitations of black women to domestic and agricultural work for much of American history has provided them unique insights into positions of subordination—both their own and others.[114]

Nevertheless, black feminists have consistently and emphatically insisted that the lives of black women are oppressed not just by race but also by sex, class, and more recently by sexuality, drawing on work of people such as Sojourner Truth, Martha W. Stewart, Francis E. W. Harper, Anna Julia Cooper, Ida B. Wells, Mary Church Terrell, and Zora Neale Hurston. They have suggested that the structures of domination impacting their lives are interlinked, connected, and mutually reinforcing.

Black feminists have concentrated on race and sex, in particular, as intersecting social structures of oppression that have limited and constrained black women's lives and agency. They have argued that black women's lives have been affected not just by race but also significantly by sexism and the gendered structure of oppression. They contend that black women's experiences, activities, and insights have been suppressed and oppressed due to the functioning of racism among white men and women—including white feminist women—and sexism by white and black men—including black nationalists. They challenge the articulation of the goals of black struggle as the establishment of a patriarchal order. This, according to them, is inconsistent with its stated concern for the community, as these communities include black women and patriarchy limits black women's agency in some of the same ways that race is thought to limit black men's agency. They also have begun to challenge the idea that black men's life-chances are simply affected by race. Rather, as Collins argues in this volume, stereotypes about black men have always been not only raced as inferior but also sexualized and gendered as deviant. In other words, black men are depicted as sexually out of control, as violent brutes, drawing on both images of race and gender.

Further, in her critique of a definition of feminism as being primarily about women's social equality, hooks noted that all men are not equal[115] and thus defines feminism as something more than social equality with men. Rather, she explains that "feminism is a struggle to end sexist oppression. Therefore, it is necessarily a struggle to eradicate the ideology of domination that permeates Western culture on various levels as well as a commitment to reorganizing society so that the self-development of people can take precedence over imperialism, economic expansion, and material desires."[116] Feminism defined in this way addresses the social structures of oppression that, according to hooks, direct attention to the differing ways women are subordinated, including those who are also subject to racial and class-based domination. It also suggests that although the focus is on transforming sexism as a system that primarily disadvantages women, to be effective, it must also address the ways women are differently positioned by way of class, race, and sexuality. In so directing attention, it begins to capture other structures of domination and their effects on other people including men.

Under this formulation and to the extent that black feminists agree with it, they are committed to active engagement in dismantling domination and the promotion of human flourishing for people in general, for black people and women in particular, and for black women specifically. From this perspective, the project of progressive blackness entails the edification of black people and the elimination of all forms of domination that limit this edification for all those raced as black. But in addition, it must address and must build coalitions with people committed to the elimination of all forms of subordination, including racism, sexism, heterosexism, and classism.

Although black feminist women dominate this field, black male feminist and profeminist black men have joined their efforts in standing against sexism and gendered oppression as part of and in addition to antiracist struggle. These include men such as Michael Awkward, Luke Harris, Devon Carbado, and Mark Anthony Neal. They grapple with exactly what the terms *black male feminist* or *profeminist black men* mean, but they understand sexism to be a system of domination that privileges men. Further, they recognize the ills of domination in its various forms and the need to edify subordinated identity, including blackness, others who are racially oppressed, such as Native Americans, women, sexual minorities, and poor and working-class people. Though still developing, their goals seem to be on the one hand to develop the "women" within themselves and to support their mothers, sister, and daughters. But on the other hand they seek to articulate and make visible—from the standpoint of men—their privileges as men.[117] That is, their project is to fill out the picture of the other side of the relation of power, their own privilege. So for instance, they seek to acknowledge and to explain the ways black men head most of the black institutional spaces at the expense of and often to the exclusion of black women.

Black Gay and Lesbian Thought

Black gay, lesbian, bisexual, transgendered, transsexual, (GLBTT) and other sexual minorities have also keenly felt the need to articulate, to expose, and to promote the human agency and self-determination of black people. James Baldwin has been a leading figure in discourses about black agency. From him, as Kendall Thomas suggests, black gay men not only learned to live in this world as black men but as gay men. But the community efforts of GLBTT people often have been undermined and dismissed. For instance, Bayard Rustin's participation in the civil rights movement was restricted in part because he was gay.

Audre Lorde spoke to these issues within black communities in her essay "I Am Your Sister: Black Women Organizing across Sexualities." She discussed dealing with differences between black people and urged black women to "recognize that unity does not require that we be identical to each other. Black women are not one great vat of homogenized chocolate milk. We have many different faces, and we do not have to become each other in order to work together.[118]... When I say I am a Black feminist, I mean I recognize that my power as well as my primary oppressions come as a result of my Blackness as well as my womanness, and therefore my struggles on both these fronts are inseparable. When I say I am a Black Lesbian, I mean I am a woman whose primary focus of loving, physical as well as emotional, is directed to women."[119]

She then challenged people who insist that "Black Lesbians are not political ... and are not involved in the struggles of Black people,"[120] highlighting many of her own efforts in the struggle while all the time a black lesbian. She then went on to list other black gay and lesbian people who were also voices in the black struggle, including Langston Hughes, Alice Dunbar-Nelson, Angelina Weld

Grimke, Bessie Smith, Ma Rainey, and Lorraine Hansberry.[121] She commented that the "terror of Black Lesbians is buried in that deep inner place where we have been taught to fear all difference—to kill it or ignore it."[122] Lorde then restated and reminded her sisters that "I am a Black Lesbian, and I *am* your sister."[123]

Lorde defined *heterosexism* as "a belief in the inherent superiority of one form of loving over all others and thereby the right to dominance" and *homophobia* as "a terror surrounding feelings of love for a member of the same sex and thereby a hatred of those feeling in others."[124] She is one of many who have advocated and analyzed the patriarchal sex–gender system that not only privileges men but also promotes domination on basis of heterosexuality.

Though GLBTT people differ on the best way to analyze the role of sexuality in life, GLBTT scholarship, drawing on feminist scholarship, has largely been about unpacking the sex–gender system and the sexuality hierarchy, for the two are related. First, the sex–gender system assigns not just social roles to biological males and females but also sexual roles. These sexual roles mandate that men be only sexually attracted to and be intimate with women and vice versa. Women occupy the inferior and subordinate positions in this complementary system. Married relations between men and women are held to be the basis of the family unit, with the nuclear family understood and promoted as the idealized family. In this sense, not only is same-sex desire and intimacy devalued but to the extent heterosexuality is rejected as the basis for a family, such rejection is seen as undermining the family unit, potentially corrupting children, and opening up a sexual can of worms that have little to do with consensual adult sexual love and expression.

Although the oppression GLBTT people face is fundamentally linked to maintaining the current sex–gender system, human sexuality and desire have also been subjugated by fear and taboo as well as by systems of oppression. The breadth and diversity of human sexuality and desire constitutes a separate field of inquiry, as do the systems of heterosexism and homophobia, which are meant to constrain it. These help to keep the sex–gender system afloat and to suppress human sexual diversity. The expansion of studies to explore this diversity continues to expand, and GLBTT and queer people are at the heart of this exploration and expansion.

Transformationist

Manning Marable described yet another "ideological tendency within Black public discourse and inside the struggles to define the African American community."[125] He referred to this tradition as "transformationist," or the radical perspective, and characterized it as "the collective efforts of black people neither to integrate nor self-segregate but to transform the existing power relationships and the racist institutions of the state, the economy and society.... .

[This] necessitates the building of a powerful protest movement, based largely among the most oppressed classes and social groups, to demand the fundamental restructuring of the basic institutions and patterns of ownership within society. Toward this larger goal, the building of black institutions is an essential process, in providing the resources for African American people to survive and resist."[126] Again, this group is committed to black self-determination, black agency, and black humanity. But they are committed to a larger goal, namely, restructuring the system so that all people will be in a position to live well, to define themselves outside social stereotypes, to appreciate themselves, and to act ethically in accountable ways toward themselves and others.

This, too, is the antisubordination project. But this group would emphasize that a project refusing to address the economic relations of domination and exploitation that both underpin and shape the racial and sex-based systems of oppression cannot transform the latter. For instance, when Hurricane Katrina struck New Orleans, many people questioned whether the inadequate evacuation plans and the slow rescue of those who remained there during the hurricane were the result of racism. However, when the question is seen from the perspective of the people themselves, it seems obvious that those who remained in New Orleans in the wake of Hurricane Katrina did not do so because they were black but because they lacked the resources to leave the city. This was compounded by political and economic choices that assumed adequate wealth while ignoring growing poverty levels in the United States and thus assumed an order to evacuate the city was sufficient to save lives. For a different example, the declining availability of work that pays life-sustaining wages affects not only blacks but also increasingly broad groups of Americans as well as millions in underdeveloped countries. In the United States, those unable to find jobs, including young black men, are vulnerable to being pressed into service as cannon fodder in imperialist wars, often against other people of color. These wars are meant to reinforce and to sustain the white supremacist capitalist system that such people otherwise might be inclined to resist.

The struggle must be fought on all fronts with human liberation and the material well-being of all as the goal. Confronting and transforming an economic system that prizes self-interest, consumption, and commodification of everything for the benefit of a few to one that places people and their human development at its center will be an essential component of this struggle.

Summary

Even though these subgroups within the black community have had different focuses, each has been committed in some ways to the political project of blackness in the context of white supremacist America and American practice. The project of progressive blackness encompasses all of these groups and their various struggles to the extent they are committed to the elimination and transformation of domination in all its forms. As such, it is a project about the existential wholeness of black communities, the material and spiritual well-being of those communities and its peoples in all their diversities, and the linking of black people with others similarly committed.

Ethical and Active Participation

Black feminists have sometimes been accused of raising issues that distract from the struggle. Some feminists have accused them of distracting and undermining the feminist struggle by inserting issues of race. Some black scholars have similarly agued that black women raising the issue of sexism are distracting and diverting resources from the struggle against racism. These concerns will inevitably be raised as objections against a project that advocates for the active and ethical engagement in multiple struggles to transform the structure of domination and subordination on which the current American order is based. Implicit in these concerns is a concern about time and energy, focus and conflicts.

Each of us is a finite being with only so much time and energy to commit, in addition to daily living, to the active involvement of multiple struggles. Focused energy is probably better than scattered energy.[127] Thus, as a practical matter most people will be actively and heavily committed to one struggle. This is fine. In addition, it is hoped that each person brings his or her own unique innovative practices, performances, and gifts to those endeavors in which he or she finds passion. However, there is a difference between concentrating energy in one direction, as a practical matter, and assuming that this one effort is the whole. Most of our efforts will be within one aspect of a much bigger picture. Keeping the bigger picture in mind and the way struggles are linked perhaps hinders us from taking positions that subordinate and minimize efforts that are companions to our own, as well as taking positions that might reinforce the structures of domination against which we are fighting. In addition, keeping the bigger picture in mind might also aid us in spying and in taking advantage of coalitional possibilities, which presumably will increase our chances of success.

Further, though actively engaging in the antisubordination struggle may mean that much of our energies are engaged in a single aspect of the struggle, in our everyday lives we are undoubtedly presented with multiple micro-activities to strengthen multiple movements. These activities may involve reorienting our family lives. It may mean refusing to be silent when people with whom we are in the company make disparaging remarks about black men, women, gay men, transgender people, or the disabled. These moments become opportunities to strengthen antisubordination sensibilities.

At the same time, celebrating, playing, signifying, and calling out our difference may well be the fun of life. Here homogeneity is not the goal. Rather, the goal is to be in the process of changing and creating a society where we can appreciate our differences and can see in it our strengths.

And finally, our involvement in of struggles may well bring us into conflicts with other progressive people about priorities and goals. These are inevitable. Joan Williams suggested a code of ethics that may help to guide our efforts and our conflicts. She proposed four rules, parts of which I quote.

"Allow for differing priorities."[128] We cannot continuously address all facets of an issue. "Progressive people have different priorities. We need to respect that."

"Recognize there will be zero sum moments."[129] There will be moments when we will disagree and when our projects will be diametrically opposed. For example, as between a queer activist who believes pornography provides a link for gay teens in contrast to a MacKinnnon-like feminist who believes all pornography is linked with the exploitation of women. Try to control the bitterness of the disagreement and leave windows open for other coalitional efforts.

"Do no harm .... Zero sum moments are the exception ... where progressive agendas diverge,"[130] simply do no harm. For example, in trying to aid women, feminists should not demonize black women; in trying to aid men, black men should not demonize gay men.

"Be as inclusive as possible."[131] The more the merrier.

Conclusion

I have argued that progressive black masculinities are unique and innovative performances of the masculine self that, on the one hand, personally eschew and actively, ethically stand against social structures of domination and, on the other, that value, validate, and empower black humanity—in all its variety—as part of the diverse and multicultural humanity of others in the global family. As such, progressive black masculinities embrace a fully liberatory agenda. Progressive black masculinities sit at the intersection of a progressive black political project and a progressive masculinities political project. The first insist on the existential wholeness of black communities and black people and their connections to others in the human family and the transformation of systems of domination that confine and limit them. The latter are committed to transforming the systems of domination of men over women, sexual minorities, and other men specifically, as well as other systems that differently limit others.

Further, I suggest that although black men are oppressed by race, they are sometimes privileged by gender and other times are the specific targets of gender racism. That is, even though patriarchal gender oppression as a system is geared toward the subordination of women, men and black men in particular are harmed by the patriarchal order in two ways. One, hegemonic masculinity and the sex–gender system commit them to dominating over others and to constraining their human expression to limited, often socially problematic traits. Further, black men as subordinate masculinities are subject to stereotypes and are the target of efforts that understand them not simply as black but as the gendered multidimensional category blackmen — for starters. And finally, I suggest that to the extent black men engage in hegemonic masculine practice, they may well be reinforcing the system of racist oppression that they often seek to eliminate.

Notes

1. By performances I mean ways of being, ways of living. Here I am drawing on Butler's and Kimmel's work. See, e.g., Judith Butler, "Imitation and Gender Insubordination," in *Inside Out: Lesbian Theories, Gay Theories*, ed. Diana Fuss (New York: Routledge, 1991), 13–32; and Michael S. Kimmel, *The Gendered Society* (New York: Oxford University Press, 2000) on "doing gender" and noting that in our interactions with others we rely mostly on secondary sex characteristics that we can see and the ways in which they are dressed up. Thus, he discusses gender as a performance, 100–106.

2. A diagram of this order might look like this:

   (assignment)race →→→(system)racism →→→ (order)white supremacy

3. "Mission Statement of Black Men for the Eradication of Sexism, Morehouse College 1994," in *Traps: African American Men on Gender and Sexuality*, ed. Rudolph P. Byrd and Beverly Guy-Sheftall (Bloomington: Indiana University Press, 2001).

4. Sumi Cho was one of the first people that I heard use this sort of term in discussing racialized sexual harassment. Sumi K. Cho, "Converging Stereotypes in Racialized Sexual Harassment: Where the Model Minority Meets Suzie Wong," in *Critical Race Theory: The Cutting Edge*, 2d ed., ed. R. Delgado and J. Stefancic (Philadelphia: Temple University Press, 2000), 532–542.

5. Masculinity is part of the patriarchal order. The patriarchal order is supported through the conscious, unconscious, and institutional habits of people and institutions. Where people fit in this order is determined by biological sex and the cultural assignment of traits associated with that biology. Further, the sex–gender system, because it believes in the hierarchal and complementary roles of the sexes, also compels a heterosexual order which is supported through homophobia and heterosexism among other things. This system can be diagramed in a way that is similar to the diagram of racism in a white supremacist order. However, though the systems are similar in their operation there are significant differences. Diagramed, the system of patriarchal gender oppression and sexism might look like, this:

   (assignment) sex/gender → (system) sexism/gender oppression→ (order) patriarchy or male supremacy
   ↓
   sexuality (biological/social assignment)
   ↓
   (system)homophobia and heterosexism
   ↓
   compulsory heterosexuality order

6. Manning Marable, ed., *Dispatches from the Ebony Tower: Intellectuals Confront the African American Experience* (New York: Columbia University Press, 2000).

7. Ibid.

8. Cornel West, *Race Matters* (Boston: Beacon Press, 1993), 25. See also Patricia Hill Collins, *Black Feminist Thought: Knowledge, Consciousness, and the Politics of Empowerment* (Boston: Unwin and Hyman, 1990), 28, which makes a similar point. She discusses the interdependence of thought and action and notes that standpoints of the oppressed "can stimulate resistance."

9. See, generally, Ronald T. Takaki, *A Different Mirror: A History of Multicultural America* (Boston: Little Brown and Co., 1993) which discusses some of the "founding fathers" of the U.S. and notes that some of them believed that America should be a white country. He then discusses and interprets a variety of efforts as constituting parts of the project of constructing a white country.

10. Kimberlé Crenshaw, "Race, Reform and Retrenchment: Transformation and Legitimation in Anti-discrimination Law," *Harvard Law Review* 101, no. 7 (1988), 1331–87; Michael Omi and Howard Winant, *Racial Formation in the United States from the 1960s to the 1990s* (New York: Routledge, 1994); Athena Mutua, "The Rise of Critical Race Theory in Law," in *Handbook Series of Race and Ethnic Studies*, ed. Collins and John Solomos (Thousand Oaks, CA: Sage Publications, 2006).
11. Michael Eric Dyson, *Is Bill Cosby Right? Or Has the Black Middle Class Lost Its Mind?* (New York: Basic Civitas Books, 2005), 40.
12. West, *Race Matters,* 29.
13. Ibid., 30.
14. Dyson argues that throughout his career, Bill Cosby took a colorblind approach to race, presenting his race as incidental to his humanity. He adamantly adhered to this approach, refusing to be drawn into the civil rights movement or to speak or act as a leader of blacks, but he also refused to engage his professional comedy to unpack or expose stereotypical thinking. Dyson also suggests that Cosby's comments further stigmatize the poor and can be used by conservatives to justify further shrinking aid to the poor in part because his comments are blind to the institutional structures and policies that foster poverty in general and black poverty specifically. Further, he notes that practices such as poor blacks choosing unique names for their children or stylizing their bodies are in part cultural responses to racism. When seen in a historical context they contain resistance to the racist and oppressive social structures that limit black potentiality. Whether Dyson is wholly correct in his analysis of Cosby's career is arguable. As Dyson notes, Cosby's Ph.D. dissertation adequately deals with the educational problems of race. Further, Cosby has been a big supporter of historically black colleges and educational efforts. Thus, the claim that he has not used his status to promote black well-being is debatable. Dyson, *Bill Cosby.*
15. Dyson, *Bill Cosby,* 15–57.
16. Ibid.
17. A. Mutua, "Rise of Critical Race Theory," citing Stephanie Phillips.
18. Omi and Winant, *Racial Formation.*
19. Ibid.
20. bell hooks, *Killing Rage: Ending Racism* (New York: H. Holt & Co., 1995), 78.
21. Francisco Valdes, "Identity Maneuvers in Law and Society," *University of Missouri Kansas City Law Review* 71, no. 2 (2002), 387, which notes that the U.S. structure combines a particular strain of "patriarchy, heterosexism, and capitalism."
22. Ibid.; see also Dyson, *Bill Cosby.*
23. A. Mutua, "Rise of Critical Race Theory"; Collins, *Black Feminist Thought*; Dyson, *Bill Cosby.* However, West suggested that blackness would not have any meaning except in the context of a race-conscious society. West, *Race Matters,* 25. Thus, in the absence of such a society, race consciousness would be unnecessary. Afrocentric thinkers might reply that it does not mean that some sort of African or ethnic consciousness would cease to exist.
24. See, generally, Michael S. Kimmel, *The Gendered Society* (New York: Oxford University Press, 2000); Collins, *Black Feminist Thought.*
25. Kimmel, *Gendered Society.*
26. Ibid.
27. Crenshaw, "Race, Reform."
28. Jacques Derrida, *Dissemination*, trans. Barbara Johnson (Chicago: University Press, 1981).
29. Allan G. Johnson, *The Gender Knot: Unraveling Our Patriarchal Legacy* (Philadelphia: Temple University Press, 1997), 61.
30. Ibid., 61.
31. Ibid., 61–62.
32. Karen Engle, "After the Collapse of the Public/Private Distinction: Strategizing Women's Rights," in *Women and the Market: Collapsing Distinctions in International Law* (Toronto: Toronto University Press, 1994).
33. See, generally, Darren Hutchinson, "Ignoring the Sexualization of Race: Heteronormativity, Critical Race Theory, and Anti-racist Politics," *Buffalo Law Review* 47 (1999), 1–116; Hutchinson, "Identity Crisis: 'Intersectionality,' 'Multidimensionality,' and the Development of an Adequate Theory of Subordination," *Michigan Journal of Race and Law* 6, no. 3 (2001), 285–317; Hutchinson, "'Unexplainable on Grounds Other than Race':

38 • Athena D. Mutua

The Inversion of Privilege and Subordination in Equal Protection Jurisprudence," *University of Illinois Law Review* 2003 (2003), 615–700; Hutchinson, "Critical Race Histories: In and Out," *American University Law Review* 53, no. 6 (2004), 1184–1215; Francisco Valdes, "Queers, Sissies, Dykes and Tomboys: Deconstructing the Conflation of 'Sex,' 'Gender,' and 'Sexual Orientation' in Euro-American Law and Society," *California Law Review* 83 (1995), 1–377; Laurie Rose Kepros, "Queer Theory: Weed or Seed in the Garden of Legal Theory," *Law and Sex* 9 (1999–2000), 279–310; Max H. Kirsch, *Queer Theory and Social Change* (2000); Eric Savoy, "'That Ain't All She Ain't': Doris Day and Queer Performativity," *Out Takes: Essays on Queer Theory and Film*, ed. Ellis Hanson (Durham, NC: Duke University Press, 1999), 151–82; John D'Emilio, "A New Beginning: The Birth of Gay Liberation," in *Sexual Politics, Sexual Communities*, ed. D'Emilio (Chicago: University of Chicago Press, 1998), 223–39; "Queers Read This" (distributed at New York City Gay Pride Parade, 1990), reprinted in William B. Rubenstein, ed., *Cases and Materials on Sexual Orientation and the Law*, 2d ed. (St. Paul, MN: West Publishing, 1997); Judith Butler, "Imitation and Gender Insubordination," in *Inside Out: Lesbian Theories, Gay Theories*, ed. Diana Fuss (New York: Routledge, 1991), 13–32; and Sandi Farrell, "Reconsidering the Gender–Equality Perspective for Understanding LGBT Rights," *Law and Sexuality* 13 (2004), 605–703.

34. Stephanie Riger, "Rethinking the Distinction between Sex and Gender," in *Power, Privilege and the Law: A Civil Rights Reader*, ed. Leslie Bender and Daan Braverman (St. Paul, MN: West Publishing, 1995), 232–39.
35. See Takaki, *Different Mirror*, 139–65, 277–310, which explores how the Irish and the Jews, respectively, became white.
36. For example, the Constitution initially allowed only those with a certain amount of property to vote.
37. Cheryl Harris, "Whiteness as Property," *Harvard Law Review* 106, no. 8 (1993), 1707–91.
38. Clyde W. Franklin II, "'Ain't I a Man?' The Efficacy of Black Masculinities for Men's Studies in the 1990s," in *The American Black Male*, ed. Richard Majors and Jacob U. Gordon (Chicago: Nelson-Hall Publishers, 1994), 271–283.
39. Kimmel, "Masculinity as Homophobia: Fear, Shame and Silence in the Construction of Gender Identity," in *Theorizing Masculinities*, ed. Harry Brod and Michael Kaufman (Thousand Oaks, CA: Sage Publications, 1994), 121–24.
40. Ibid.
41. Ian Harris, *Messages Men Hear: Constructing Masculinities* (Bristol, PA: Taylor & Francis, 1995), 10.
42. Ibid.
43. Ibid.
44. Ibid.
45. Harold Cruse, *The Crisis of the Negro Intellectual* (New York: William Morrow & Co., Inc., 1967), 7–8.
46. Kimmel, "Masculinity," 137, citing Hannah Arendt, *On Revolution* (New York: Viking, 1970), 44.
47. Kaufman, "Men, Feminism, and Men's Contradictory Experiences of Power," in Brod and Kaufman, *Theorizing Masculinities*, 159.
48. See Harris, *Messages Men Hear*, 18, standing for the proposition that patriarchy is a social system that benefits men. Harris quotes Rich's book *Of Women Born: Motherhood as Experience and Institution* (Bantam Double Dell, 1976) to note, "Patriarchy is the power of fathers: a familial–social, ideological, political system in which men—by force, direct pressure, or through ritual, tradition, law and language, customs, etiquette, education and the division of labor—determine what part women shall or shall not play, and in which the female is everywhere subsumed by the male. It does not necessarily imply that no woman has power, or that all women in a given culture may not have certain powers."
49. Kaufman, "Men, Feminism," 145, citing C. B. McPherson.
50. Ibid.
51. Ibid., 146.
52. Here I am drawing on Pharr's ideas of economic, violence, and homophobia as tools to sustain the system of patriarchy and heterosexist oppressions. See Suzanne Pharr, "Homophobia: A Weapon of Sexism," in *Power, Privilege, and Law: A Civil Rights Reader*, ed. Leslie Bender and Daan Braverman (St. Paul, MN: West Publishing, 1995), 252–63.

53. Iris Marion Young, "Five Faces of Oppression," in *Power, Privilege, and Law: A Civil Rights Reader*, ed. Leslie Bender and Daan Braverman (St. Paul, MN: West Publishing, 1995), 66–80.
54. "Black men remain the group with the lowest life expectancy. Those born in 1999 are expected to live to the age of 67.8, which is about 7 years less than for comparable White men (74.6). Among women born in 1999, blacks are expected to live to the age of 74.7, and whites to age 79.9." Cassandra Cantave, Dietra Lee, and Roderick Harrison, "African-Americans and Health," Joint Center Data Bank, http://www.jointcenter.org/DB/factsheet/lifexpec.htm. See also "Premature Mortality in the United States: Public Health Issues in the Use of Years of Potential Life Lost," *Morbidity and Mortality Weekly Report* 35, no. 2S (December 19, 1986): 1–11, http://www.cdc.gov/mmwr/preview/mmwrhtml/00001773.htm.
55. "Suicide among Blacks," Healthyplace.com, Depression Community, http://www.healthyplace.com/Communities/Depression/minorities_5.asp.
56. "What about Men? Exploring Inequities in Minority Men's Health," W.K. Kellogg Foundation, June 12, 2002, http://www.wkkf.org/Pubs/Health/CommunityVoices/31zt4iqkqymlsxrx2zobfgq4_20020730082714.pdf.
57. Ibid.
58. Harrison and Cantave, "Earnings of African Americans," Joint Center Data Bank, http://www.jointcenter.org/DB/factsheet/earnings.htm.
59. Andrew Sum and others, *Trends in Black Male Joblessness and Year-Round Idleness: An Employment Crisis Ignored* (Chicago: Alternative Schools Network, June 2004).
60. Council of Economic Advisers for the President's Initiative on Race, "Labor Markets," in *Changing America: Indicators of Social and Economic Well-Being by Race and Hispanic Origin* (Washington, DC: U.S. Government Printing Office [GPO]), 23, http://www.gpo.gov/ eop/ca/.
61. Paul Offner and Harry Holzer, "Left Behind in the Labor Market: Recent Employment Trends among Young Black Men," Center on Urban & Metropolitan Policy, Georgetown Public Policy Institute http://www.ssc.wisc.edu/irpweb/publications/dps/pdfs/dp124702.pdf.
62. Ibid.
63. David A. Harris, "The Stories, the Statistics, and the Law: Why 'Driving while Black' Matters," *Minnesota Law Review* 84, no. 2 (1999) 301.
64. Clyde Franklin II, "'Ain't I a Man?' The Efficacy of Black Masculinities for Men's Studies in the 1990s," in Majors and Gordon, *American Black Male*, 280.
65. Ibid.
66. Ibid., 281.
67. Ibid.
68. Ibid., 280–82.
69. A. Mutua, "Rise of Critical Race Theory."
70. "Mission Statement," 201.
71. Devon Carbado, "The Construction of O.J. Simpson as a Racial Victim," in *Black Men on Race, Gender, and Sexuality: A Critical Reader* (New York: New York University Press, 1999), 159–93; and Toni Morrison, *Race-ing Justice, En-gendering Power: Essays on Anita Hill, Clarence Thomas, and the Construction of Social Reality* (New York: Pantheon Books, 1992).
72. I owe this insight to Stephanie Phillips. She understood the intersections to mean that such designations as race, gender, and class applied to all situations but that what the situation actually meant culturally required scholars to look to the specific context. She also suggests that there may be no meaningful difference between intersectional and multidimensial theory.
73. Critical race theory is a theory and body of scholarship developed in law for the purpose of analyzing and exposing the connections between law and white racial power. It also seeks to change this relationship and to contribute to the liberation of oppressed people. See my introduction to this volume; see also A. Mutua, "Rise of Critical Race Theory," which cites the following resources for information about critical race theory. K. Crenshaw and others, eds., *Critical Race Theory* (New York: New Press, 1995); R. Delgado and J. Stefancic, eds., *Critical Race Theory: The Cutting Edge*, 2d ed. (Philadelphia: Temple University Press, 2000); J. Perea and others, eds., *Race and Races: Cases and Resources*

for a Diverse America (St. Paul, MN: West Group, 2000), 551–61; Delgado and Stefancic, *Critical Race Theory: An Introduction* (New York: New York University Press, 2001); C. Harris, "Critical Race Studies," *UCLA Law Review* 49 (2002), 1215–40; F. Valdes, J. Culp, and A. Harris, eds., *Crossroads, Directions, and a New Critical Race Theory* (Philadelphia: Temple University Press, 2002); Delgado and Stefancic, eds., *The Latino/a Condition: A Critical Reader* (New York: New York University Press, 1998); F. Wu. *Yellow* (New York: Basic Books, 2002); K. Aoki. "The Scholarship of Reconstruction and the Politics of Backlash," *Iowa Law Review* 81 (1998): 1467–88; T. Saito, "Alien and Non-Alien Alike: Citizenship, 'Foreignness,' and Racial Hierarchy in American Law," *Oregon Law Review* 76 (1997), 261–345; and R. Chang, "Toward an Asian American Legal Scholarship: Critical Race Theory, Post-Structuralism, and Narrative Space," *California Law Review* 81 (1993), 1241–1323.

74. LatCrit, which stands for Latina and Latino critical theory, is a body of scholarship related to critical race theory but focusing on the conditions of Latino/a communities and identities. A. Mutua, "Rise of Critical Race Theory." See also LATCRIT: Latina and Latino Critical Theory at http://www.latcrit.org, which lists the many publications of LatCrit symposia and colloquia.

75. These two scholars are Darren Hutchinson, particularly in Hutchinson, "Ignoring the Sexualization"; and Valdes, "Identity Maneuvers"; and Valdes, "Beyond Sexual Orientation in Queer Legal Theory: Majoritarianism, Multidimensionality and Responsibility in Social Justice Scholarship or Legal Scholars as Cultural Warriors," *Denver University Law Review* 75, no. 4 (1998).

76. Valdes, "Under Construction: Latcrit Consciousness, Community, and Theory," *California Law Review* 85, no. 5 (1997), 1087–1142.

77. Crenshaw, "Demarginalizing the Intersection of Race and Sex: A Black Feminist Critique of Antidiscrimination Doctrine, Feminist Theory, and Antiracist Politics" (University of Chicago Legal Forum, 1989); and Crenshaw, "Mapping the Margins: Intersectionality, Identity Politics, and Violence against Women of Color," *Stanford Law Review* 43 (1991), 1299.

78. See, generally, Nancy Ehrenreich, "Subordination and Symbiosis: Mechanisms of Mutual Support between Subordinating Systems," *University of Missouri Kansas City Law Review* 71, no. 2 (2002), 251–324.

79. See also ibid.

80. Ibid.

81. Ibid.

82. See hooks, *Killing Rage.*

83. Molefi K. Asante, *Erasing Racism* (Amherst, NY: Prometheus Books, 2003), 104, 240; West, *Race Matters*, 95–105, which discusses Malcolm X's nationalist viewpoint.

84. Cruse, *Crises of the Negro*, 5.

85. West, *Race Matters*, 98.

86. Gary Peller, "Race-Consciousness," in *Critical Race Theory: The Key Writings that Formed the Movement*, ed. Crenshaw and others (New York: New Press, 1997), 127–159.

87. Ibid.

88. Ibid., 128.

89. West, *Race Matters*, 101, which notes the culturally hybrid character of black music and religion that makes it distinctive.

90. Cornel West, *Prophesy Deliverance* (Philadelphia: Westminster Press, 1982), 31, 86.

91. See, generally, Marable, *Ebony Tower*; A. Mutua, "Rise of Critical Race Theory"; West, *Race Matters*; and Asante, *Erasing Racism.*

92. See Peller, "Race-Consciousness"; and Nikhil Pal Singh, "Toward an Effective Antiracism," in Marable, *Dispatches from the Ebony Tower*, 31–52.

93. A. Mutua, "Rise of Critical Race Theory."

94. W. E. B. Du Bois, *The Souls of Black Folks* (New York: W. W. Norton & Company, 1999), 11; see also Dyson, *Bill Cosby*, 47, note 63.

95. Peller, "Race Consciousness."

96. Afrocentricity may be read this way.

97. This is how I interpret hooks, to use the term in hooks, *Killing Rage.*

98. Asante, a central conceptualizer of Afrocentric theory, suggest that Afrocentricity is not a matter of color but a perspective. Asante, *The Painful Demise of Eurocentrism: An*

Afrocentric Response to Critics (Trenton, NJ: Africa World Press, 1999), 112. It is primarily an orientation and approach to data. Ibid. "Afrocentricity [is] an intellectual theory for analyzing African behavior." Ibid., 109, grounded "in the autonomy of the African agency." Ibid., 108.

99. Ibid.; see also Marable, *Ebony Tower*, 16–17.

100. Asante, *Painful Demise*, 80, which refers to African scholar Kwame Anthony Appiah; see also Merlin R. Langley, "The Cool Pose: An Africentric Analysis," in Majors and Gordon, *American Black Male*, 231–44, which describes a psychological theory put forth by scholars such as Azibo and Baldwin.

101. This is a term used by Asante, Asante, *Afrocentricity* (Trenton, NJ: Africa World Press, 1988).

102. Jerome Schiele, "The Contour and Meaning of Afrocentric Social Work," *Journal of Black Studies* 27, no. 6 (July 1997), 805–8; Makau Mutua, "The Banjul Charter and the African Cultural Fingerprint: An Evaluation of the Language of Duties," *Virginia Journal of International Law* 35, no. 2 (1995), 339–81; see also Maulana Karenge, *Kwanzaa: A Celebration of Family Community and Culture* (Los Angeles: University of Sankore Press, 1999); and, generally, Asante, *Afrocentricity* (Trenton, NJ: Africa World Press, 1988), which notes that Afrocentricity has five distinguishing characteristics: (1) an intense interest in psychological location as determined by symbols, motifs, rituals, and signs; (2) a commitment to finding the subject-place of Africans in any societal, political, economic, or religious phenomenon with implications for questions of sex, gender, and class; (3) a defense of African cultural elements as historically valid in the context of art, music, and literature and a defense of a pan-African cultural connection based on broad responses to conditions, environments, and situations over time; (4) a celebration of "centeredness" and agency and a commitment to lexical refinement that eliminates pejoratives, including sexual and gender pejoratives about Africans or other people; and (5) a powerful imperative from historical sources to revise the collective text of African people as one in constant and consistent search for liberation and Maat [justice].

103. Leith Mullings, "Reclaiming Culture," in Marable, *Dispatches from the Ebony Tower*, 212, which describes Afrocentricity's "attempt to highlight the importance of culture, to reclaim history, and to correct the distortions of Euro centrism" being a mirror in its negation of Eurocentrism. It also asserts that Afrocentricity is a child of Eurocentrism.

104. West, *Race Matters*, 25–29, which discusses racial reasoning.

105. For example, in earlier work Asante argued, "Homosexuality is a deviation from Afrocentric thought." Asante, *Afrocentricity*, 102. However, Haki Madhubuti has been seen as bemoaning the decline of male dominance in the black community. Madhubuti, *Black Men: Obsolete, Single, Dangerous? Afrikan American Families in Transition: Essays in Discovery, Solution, and Hope* (Chicago: Third World Press, 1990). For example, Asante, *Erasing Racism*, 96, says, "Afrocentricity is considered dangerous because it indicts Eurocentrism as racist, sexist, classist, and homophobic." This seems to suggest that Afrocentrism is not any of these. And Madhubuti's book titled *Tough Notes: A Healing Call for Creating Exceptional Black Men* (Chicago: Third World Press, 2002) issued a clarion call for men to participate in women's liberation.

106. See the introduction to this volume, in which I argue, for instance, that in describing historical violence against African Americans in Asante's book *Erasing Racism*, he uses mostly examples of violence against men, even though the book is not about men. Further, Na'im Akbar's book, *Visions for Black Men* (Nashville, TN: Winston-Derek Publishers, 1991), supposedly provides a liberation program for black people but seems to promote a male-centered vision. See Barbara Ransby, "Afrocentrism, Cultural Nationalism, and the Problem with Essentialist Definitions of Race, Gender, and Sexuality," in Marable, *Dispatches from the Ebony Tower*, 220. Further, Afrocentrics have done a great deal of work on black men but have paid relatively little attention to the plight of black women or other members of black communities. However, many believe that sexism and heterosexism as part of Afrocentricity is changing as the theory develops—at least for some Afrocentric scholars.

107. For instance, their and others' work on education highlights the way most school curriculums are Eurocentric, highlighting European achievement, reinforcing African absence, and promoting America as white, even though America has always been multilingual and multicultural and in some ways distinctly African. This, along with a complex of other factors, are said to affect the learning prospects of African American children.

Although such biases must necessarily affect African American girls, Afrocentric activist such as Kunjufu, in noting the higher suspension rates of black boys and their higher numbers in special education, has drawn attention to the fact that, among other factors, most of the teachers in American schools are white middle-class women. These women, he suggests, are likely bringing white middle-class gendered values to the classroom and thus are insensitive to various black cultural practices as displayed distinctly by black boys. Further, he argues that these teachers often in fact have lower expectations for black boys. This examination seems to suggest that the complex dynamics that play out in the educational system are raced, gendered, and classed.

108. This language is akin to Ransby, "Afrocentrism," 217, in her discussion of Afrocentrics.
109. Morrison, "Unspeakable Things Unspoken: The Afro-American Presence in American Literature," in *The Black Feminist Reader*, ed. Joy James and T. Denean Sharpley-Whiting (Oxford: Blackwell Publishers Ltd., 2000), 31.
110. Ibid., 31–32.
111. Collins, "The Social Construction of Black Feminist Thought," in James and Sharpley-Whiting, *Black Feminist Reader*, 184, which notes that black women "have been neither passive victims of nor willing accomplices to their own domination." And suggesting that their resistance challenges thinking that subordinate groups either identify with the powerful and have no independent interpretation of their oppression or that their understandings are inferior.
112. Collins, *Black Feminist Thought*.
113. Collins, "The Politics of Black Feminist Thought," in *The Feminist Theory Reader: Local and Global Perspectives*, ed. Carole R. McCann and Seung-Kyung Kim (New York: Routledge, 2003), 330.
114. Ibid., 327.
115. hooks, *From Margin to Center* (Boston: South End Press, 1984), 18.
116. Ibid., 24.
117. Carbado, "Construction."
118. Audre Lorde, "I Am Your Sister: Black Women Organizing across Sexualities," in McCann and Kim, *Feminist Theory Reader*, 255.
119. Ibid., 256.
120. Ibid.
121. Ibid.
122. Ibid.
123. Ibid., 259.
124. Ibid., 255.
125. Marable, *Dispatching the Ebony Tower*, 19.
126. Ibid.
127. Joan Williams, "Fretting in the Force Fields: Why the Distribution of Social Power Has Proved So Hard to Change," *University of Missouri Kansas City Law Review* 71, no. 2 (2002), 500.
128. Ibid.
129. Ibid.
130. Ibid., 501.
131. Ibid.

2

Remembering Our Feminist Forefathers

BEVERLY GUY-SHEFTALL

I wonder what it would take to fully integrate gender and sexuality into Black political consciousness. What would it take for our public intellectuals, the self-appointed spokespersons, the opinion leaders and the like, to go beyond lip service given to "unity" and "common interest" to articulate a political sensibility that embraces substantive equality as a value within our community?

Kimberlé Williams Crenshaw, in *Black Men on Race, Gender, and Sexuality*, Devon Carbado, 1999

Not only have Black women made contributions to feminist history, Black men have made contributions as well.

Aaronette M. White, *Womanist*, 2001–2002

African American men's contributions to progressive gender or profeminist activism have been largely ignored in black political history. This is so even though there is a growing body of scholarly work about black men and black masculinities.[1]

These silences surrounding a significant aspect of black men's commitments to social justice compelled the publication of *Traps: African American Men on Gender and Sexuality*.[2] This anthology, which I coedited with Rudolph P. Byrd, is the first of its kind that historicizes writings by black men who have examined the meanings of the overlapping categories of race, gender, and sexuality and who have theorized these categories in the most expansive and progressive terms. The first imperative of *Traps* was to contest and to dispel the widely accepted notion that black men have been hostile to feminism and played no part in its development. This erasure has occurred within the scholarship concerning the evolution of feminism in the United States and discussions of black politics as well. It is important to recall that Frederick Douglass was among the first men in the United States to publicly endorse and support the elective franchise for women. He was the only black person and one of only thirty-two men to attend the historic Women's Rights Convention in Seneca Falls, New York, in 1848. In one sense, *Traps* calls all American

43

men, but particularly African American men, to reclaim a radical tradition of commitment to feminist struggle and to remember our gender-progressive forefathers.

Despite the commitment of some African American men to eradicate sexism and heterosexism, black liberation has been conceptualized, generally speaking, in narrow terms that focus heavily on recuperating black manhood, on constructing patriarchal families, and on ending racism. Hegemonic black nationalist discourse, characterized by both masculinist and heterosexist frameworks, has been particularly influential within activist and intellectual communities and has stifled the development of more egalitarian models of black empowerment free from the ideological traps of sexism and homophobia. Put another way, the tendency to conflate black freedom with black manhood, our uncritical acceptance of traditional conceptions of gender, the celebration of normative and rigid constructions of black masculinity, and persistent denials about homosexuality have prevented African Americans from establishing the truly revolutionary communities that Toni Cade Bambara challenged us to imagine over thirty years ago in her groundbreaking anthology, *The Black Woman.*[3]

Her compelling essay, "On the Issue of Roles," was the first to interrogate the pitfalls of the African American community's uncritical embrace of dominant cultural definitions of masculinity and femininity: "Generally speaking, in a capitalist society, a man is expected to be an aggressive, uncompromising, factual, lusty, intelligent provider of goods, and the woman, a retiring, gracious, emotional, intuitive, attractive consumer of goods.... [W]e have not been immune to the conditioning; we are just as jammed in the rigid confines of those basically oppressive socially contrived roles."[4] Anticipating a fundamental premise of the emerging field of women's studies, she understands from her study of postcolonial Africa, Asia, the South Seas, and the Americas that gender—conceptions of what it means to be male and female—is a cultural construction. She noted, "Cultures have conceived of man/woman in a variety of ways [and] 'human nature' is a pretty malleable quality."[5] Recalling the more egalitarian nature of some societies before contact with Europeans and Christianity, she explained, "There is nothing to indicate that the Sioux, Seminole, Iroquois, or other 'Indian' nations felt oppressed or threatened by their women, who had mobility, privileges and a voice in the governing of the commune."[6] With respect to our African ancestors, she asserted, "the woman was neither subordinate nor dominant, but a sharer in policymaking and privileges."[7] Painfully aware of the "antagonism between the sexes,"[8] Cade insists that we fashion "revolutionary selves, revolutionary lives, revolutionary relationships"[9] by abandoning dysfunctional definitions of manhood and womanhood, which stifle the development of healthy black communities. It is fair to assert that Cade is in some ways a spiritual daughter of Du Bois and like-minded black foremothers who envisioned a gender-progressive world very different from the one in which they were socialized.

Although it is clear that Cade's admonitions were largely ignored during the male-dominant and revolutionary Sixties, and later, many of us would like to believe that a gender revolution within our communities is still possible. Literary critic Michael Awkward, echoing Cade in his admonitions concerning the necessity of an active disloyalty to patriarchy, wrote a pioneering essay in which he reminded us that "androcentric practices are learned, are transmitted by means of specific sociocultural practices in such effective ways that they come to appear natural." However, "through an informed investigation of androcentric and feminist ideologies, individual men can work to resist the lure of the normatively masculine."[10] In his call for theorizing a black male feminism, Awkward went on to assert that "while gendered difference might be said to complicate the prospect of a non-phallocentric black male feminism, it does not render such a project impossible."[11] What is needed, he argued, is an acknowledgment that "feminism represents ... an incomparably productive, influential, and resilient ideology and institution" and that "certain instances of afrocentric feminism provide Afro-American men with an invaluable means of rewriting—of *re-vis(ion)ing*—ourselves."[12] After a description of his childhood, in which he articulated his difficulty achieving a "gendered self-definition" because he was only able to define himself with regard to his gender in oppositional ways—that is, what he did not want to become—he asserted the value of black feminism, and Afro-American women's literature, which he embraced as a sophomore student at Brandeis University in 1977. "[It] helped me move toward a comprehension of the world, of aspects of my mother's life, and what a man against patriarchy could be and do."[13]

The radicalizing and transformative potential of an embrace of black feminist discourse among young black men would become even more apparent over the next two decades. Listen to the transgressive discourse of a small group of Morehouse College students who founded an organization called "Black Men for the Eradication of Sexism" in 1994. Their mission statement asserts the following:

We believe that although we are oppressed because of our color, we are privileged because of our sex and must therefore take responsibility for ending that privilege;

We believe that our relationships with women must be based on the principle of equality;

We recognize that present Eurocentric notions of manhood and masculinity are damaging to the psyche of Black men and must be replaced with a holistic interpretation of manhood that acknowledges the oneness of women and men;

We believe that sexism is a global form of oppression of no less importance
    than any other form of oppression;
We believe that sexist oppression against women pervades every aspect of
    our communities and must be eradicated.[14]

Their final statement is a testament to their solidarity with black women and
offers the possibility of reconciliation: "As we fight alongside our sisters we
struggle to become whole; to deprogram ourselves. We have organized into
one body because we know in our hearts and minds that as we hold our sisters
back so will we hold ourselves back."[15]

Feminist Forefathers: Mays, Douglass, and Du Bois

Benjamin Elijah Mays

Though the young Morehouse men may have been unaware of their connections
to a small group of feminist forefathers, their departed elders, it is instructive
to remember the legacy of black men whose progressive writings about gender and the oppression of black women are a significant, if invisible, aspect of
black political discourse. I daresay that these Morehouse students may have
also been surprised to learn that they were connected as well to one of the most
revered figures in the history of the college. In his autobiography, *Born to Rebel*
(New York: Scribner, 1971), former president of Morehouse College Benjamin
Elijah Mays reveals the origins of his feminist sensibility with respect to the
treatment of black women as he recalls his own patriarchal, abusive household
and the impact it had on his own adult behavior.

> I cannot say that my home life was pleasant. Quarreling, wrangling,
> and sometimes fighting went on in our house. I got the impression early
> on that Father was mean to our mother. He fussed at her; and when he
> drank too much he wanted to fight and sometimes did. All too many
> times we children had to hold him to keep him from hurting Mother. He
> would take out his knife and threaten to cut her. Often at night, we were
> kept awake by Father's loud and abusive raging. I think if Mother had
> said nothing, there would have been fewer arguments. But Mother had to
> talk back. Our sympathy was with her … . Largely under the influence of
> my mother, I made a vow at twelve years of age that I would never drink
> liquor … . My decision was not based on religious or moral grounds but
> on what I saw drinking do to my father and our family. (p. 9–10)

Though Mays, perceived primarily as a race man, was not privy as an undergraduate at Bates College to the kinds of classes Awkward and Morehouse
students would take long after he left the presidency, his autobiography
does reveal an understanding of the evils of male dominance, at least in the
domestic arena.

Frederick Douglass

An examination of the still-neglected topic of African American men and feminism usually begins with the writings and activism of Frederick Douglass and William E. B. Du Bois.[16] Without question, Douglass was one of the most outspoken advocates during the nineteenth century for the full emancipation of women in all areas of their public lives. A fellow suffragist, Fannie Barrier Williams, acknowledged shortly after Douglass's death in 1895 the debt owed to him by lovers of liberty everywhere, especially women:

> He so lived not only that men might be free and equal and exalted, but that women, too, by the same emancipating forces, might come equally into the estate of freedom …. His eloquence on behalf of women's rights to the equalities of citizenship is a lasting justification of woman's claims and contentions for perfect liberty. By right of his manly confidence in woman… Mr. Douglass was easily the strongest and best friend American women ever had among the great men of the republic. The history of progressive women in this country cannot be written without grateful acknowledgment to the helpful and inspiring influence of the incomparable friend of all humanity, Frederick Douglass.[17]

Though Douglass is known primarily as an anti-slavery crusader, he was deeply committed to an independent, organized movement to achieve equal rights for women. On July 14, 1848, his newspaper, the *North Star,* carried the historic announcement of the Seneca Falls Convention, the first women's rights gathering in the United States. In addition, a constant reminder to his readers of his commitment to the rights of women was the slogan, which appeared on every issue of the *North Star*—"Right Is of No Sex." At the 1848 convention, when Elizabeth Cady Stanton's resolution that "it was the duty of the women of this country to secure for themselves their sacred right to the elective franchise" seemed headed for defeat, Douglass, at a critical juncture, asked for the floor and delivered an eloquent plea on behalf of woman's right to the vote.[18] The resolution was then put to a vote and was carried by a small margin. In 1888, a few years before his death, Douglass recalled his role at the Seneca Falls Convention and told the International Council of Women:

> There are few facts in my humble history to which I look back with more satisfaction than to the fact … that I was sufficiently enlightened at that early day, when only a few years from slavery, to support your resolution for woman suffrage. I have done very little in this world in which to glory except this one act—and I certainly glory in that. When I ran away from slavery, it was for myself; when I advocated emancipation, it was for my people; but when I stood up for the rights of woman, self was out of the question, and I found a little nobility in the act.[19]

Similarly, in his autobiography he explained why he became a woman's rights man: He believed that all persons are created equal and should therefore have the right to participate fully in the affairs of government.

> Recognizing not sex nor physical strength, but moral intelligence and the ability to discern right from wrong, good from evil, and the power to choose between them, as the true basis of republican government … I was not long in reaching the conclusion that there was no foundation in reason or justice for woman's exclusion from the right of choice in the selection of the persons who should frame the laws, and thus shape the destiny of all the people, irrespective of sex.[20]

W. E. B. Du Bois

In her compelling essay, "The Souls of Black Women Folk in the Writings of W. E. B. Du Bois," literary critic Nellie Y. McKay called our attention to what makes Du Bois a unique figure in African American life: "The extent to which he includes the influences of women's experiences, and especially those of black women, on his thinking; his recognition of gender oppression; and his acceptance of the worth of his emotional and spiritual feelings makes his works distinctive."[21] Here McKay is referring to his emphasis on the soul—the sensitive, feeling component of the self—as opposed to the intellectual, rational component stereotypically considered to represent masculinity. She also asserted that Du Bois's three autobiographies "demonstrate that Black women have been central to the development of his intellectual thought."[22] McKay reminded us of his indication in *The Autobiography of W. E. B. Du Bois: A Soliloquy on Viewing My Life from the Last Decade of Its First Century* that "he always had more friends among Black women than among Black men; that he was less attracted to relationships with the men of the race because many of them 'imitated an American culture which [he] did not share.'"[23] McKay also went on to assert, "We also know that he was aware that the folk were not all men. If anything can be said about his views on the souls of Black women folk, it is that he felt that they had struggled through to an even higher plane than Black men had."[24] Furthermore, his "perceptions of the 'souls of Black folk'—that spiritual essence that made survival and transcendence possible for an entire race in spite of indescribable oppression, was most obvious in his discourse on Black women."[25]

Though largely ignored, Du Bois's essay "Of the Meaning of Progress," which appears in *The Souls of Black Folk*, reveals his progressive gender politics, which he seemed to have developed at a fairly early age.[26] While he was an undergraduate student at Fisk University in 1886, he went for two consecutive summers to teach at a school for poor rural blacks in Tennessee. The essay includes the heroic, long-suffering black female figure Josie—the young school girl who had impacted him most—and one of the most poignant portraits of a black community struggling to survive and trying to maintain a sense of dignity in the most desperate circumstances. The plight of females in this tiny community is perhaps the most memorable aspect of his recollections. Ten years after graduating from Fisk, Du Bois returned to the hills of Tennessee and learned of Josie's death and the troubles her family and others had endured; her life, like the lives of many poor black women, had been tough and consumed with unrelenting labor and very little happiness. Following the tragedy of her brother Jim having to leave town because of a racial incident, "Josie grew thin and silent, yet worked the more."[27] Unfulfilled as an adult, "Josie shivered and worked on, with the vision of schooldays all fled, with a face wan and tired,—worked until, on a summer's day, some one married another; then Josie crept to her mother like a hurt child, and slept—and sleeps."[28] Here Du Bois reminded us of her unfulfilled dreams and her loneliness. Listening to the life struggles of another family, Du Bois learned from Uncle Bird that a neighbor, "Thenie[,] came wandering back to her home over yonder, to escape the blows of her husband. And the next morning she died in the home that the little bow-legged brother, working and saving, had bought for their widowed mother."[29] This brief allusion to domestic violence illustrates Du Bois's sensitivity to the particular plight of women; in this case, black families suffer the indignities of racial oppression, including lynching and poverty. Black women also suffer at the hands of their menfolk.

In his riveting essay, "The Damnation of Women," which McKay referred to as "one of his most moving discourses on the plight of Black women,"[30] Du Bois, as committed to women's rights as is Douglass, spoke autobiographically and politically about the women of his youth: "my mother, cousin Inez, Emma, and Ide Fuller. They represented the problem of the widow, the wife, the maiden, and the outcast … . They existed not for themselves, but for men; they were named after the men to whom they were related and not after the fashion of their own souls."[31] In his feminist critique of patriarchy, which renders women unable to forge their own identities, Du Bois anticipated the contemporary women's movement, which would articulate the plight of disempowered women in male-dominant societies. He was also critical of the institution of marriage, which in the case of his cousin, Inez, resulted in a life of misery. "What was marriage? We did not know, neither did she, poor thing! It came to mean for her a litter of children, poverty, a drunken, cruel companion, sickness, and death."[32] Du Bois' use of the term "litter" to describe Inez's family situation suggests an oppositional viewpoint with respect to the joys of motherhood. His refusal to idealize matrimony and mothering is underscored in his subsequent analysis of the urgency of forging a new world for women. He imagined a world of free women, set loose from the traps of patriarchy: ignorance, economic dependence, obligatory motherhood, and domestic confinement. "The future woman must have a life work and economic independence. She must have knowledge. She must have the right of motherhood at her own discretion. The present mincing horror at free womanhood must pass if we are ever to be rid of the bestiality of free manhood; not by guarding the weak in weakness do we gain strength, but by making weakness free and strong."[33]

Throughout the essay, he spoke eloquently about both the plight and contributions of black women. In the 1920s, this was his assessment of the race with respect to gender matters: "As I look about me today in this veiled world of mine, despite the noisier and more spectacular advance of my brothers, I instinctively feel and know that it is the five million women of my race who really count."[34] Furthermore, the accumulated assets of the black community were "wrung [largely] from the hearts of servant girls and washer women" who "toil hard" and have their value "trod under the feet of men."[35] He also defended the beauty of black women against the "defective eyesight" of the white world and sang the praises of such heroic figures as Sojourner Truth and Harriet Tubman. And then there is his most moving tribute to black women, which captures his sensitivity to the peculiar history of African American women:

> For their hard past, I honor the women of my race. Their beauty—their dark and mysterious beauty of midnight eyes, crumpled hair, and soft, full-featured faces … . No other women on earth could have emerged from the hell of force and temptation which once engulfed and still surrounds Black women in America with half the modesty and womanliness they retain. I have always felt like bowing myself before them in all abasement, searching to bring some tribute to these long-suffering victims, these burdened sisters of mine, whom the world, the wise, white world, loves to affront and ridicule and wantonly to insult.[36]

And finally, he offered this particularly scathing attack on white America: "I shall forgive the white South much in its final judgment day; I shall forgive its slavery, for slavery is a world-old habit; I shall forgive its fighting for a well-lost cause … but one thing I shall never forgive, neither in this world nor the world to come: its wanton and continued and persistent insulting of the Black womanhood which it sought and seeks to prostitute to its lust."[37]

Conclusion

Mays, Douglass, and Du Bois are our feminist forefathers. Given in particular Douglass's and Du Bois's passionate commitment to the eradication of gender oppression and Du Bois's unusual sensitivity to the plight of black women historically, I articulate here how we might make use of this legacy's embrace of feminist ideologies in a contemporary context.[38] Du Bois is certainly an important male figure with respect to his contributions to our understanding of the need for struggle around the emancipation of women, especially African American women, but I believe his writings represent new visions of manhood that are liberating and healing. At the beginning of this new century, black women and men—indeed, all men and women—must struggle for "revolutionary selves, revolutionary lives, revolutionary relationships,"[39] which Toni Cade Bambara asserted three decades ago. Rejecting the traps of patriarchy and sexism, which Du Bois compelled us to do sixty years ago, black folk, in particular, might continue our journey toward freedom in racist America in even more compelling ways and will offer new visions and possibilities for this nation, the world, and generations yet unborn. Du Bois boldly asserted in 1920 that "the uplift of women is, next to the problem of the color line and the peace movement, our greatest modern cause," though what is mainly remembered is what he said about the color line.[40] These three urgent issues remain: the eradication of the oppression of women and people of color and building and sustaining a world of peace with justice. Embracing Du Bois's prophetic vision would have pointed the way toward the creation of a world in which racism, sexism, and violence might be relics of the past. Du Bois's rejection of a patriarchal political culture, which stifles women and robs the world of their potential contributions, is one example of gender-progressive thinking on the part of an African American male who remains one of our most revered intellectuals. It is important to remember and honor the legacy of the feminist forefathers who understood that eradicating the twin evils of racism and sexism was urgent. We can now imagine the viability of the idea of progressive black masculinity in all its complexity because of them.

Notes

1. Useful texts in this regard include Richard G. Majors and Jacob U. Gordon, eds., *The American Black Male: His Present Status and His Future* (Chicago: Nelson-Hall Publishers, 1994); Majors and Janet Mancini Bilson, *Cool Pose: The Dilemmas of Black Manhood in America* (New York: Lexington Books, 1992); Darlene Clark Hine and Earnestine Jenkins, eds., *A Question of Manhood: A Reader in U.S. Black Men's History and Masculinity*, vols. 1 and 2 (Bloomington: Indiana University Press, 1999); Devon W. Carbado, *Black Men on Race, Gender, and Sexuality* (New York: New York University Press, 1999); Donald Belton, ed., *Speak My Name: Black Men on Masculinity and the American Dream* (Boston: Beacon Press, 1995); Christopher B. Booker, *"I Will Wear No Chain!": A Social History of African American Males* (Westport, CT: Praeger, 2000); Daniel Black, *Dismantling Black Manhood: An Historical and Literary Analysis of the Legacy of Slavery* (New York: Washington Square Press, 2002); and W. Lawrence Hogue, *The African American Male, Writing, and Difference: A Polycentric Approach to African American Literature, Criticism, and History* (Albany: State University of New York Press, 2003).
2. See Rudolph P. Byrd and Beverly Guy-Sheftall, eds., *Traps: African American Men on Gender and Sexuality* (Bloomington: Indiana University Press, 2001).
3. Cade, *The Black Woman: An Anthology* (New York: Mentor, 1970), 102. See Farah Jasmine Griffin, "Conflict and Chorus: Reconsidering Toni Cade's *The Black Woman: An Anthology*," in *Is It Nation Time?: Contemporary Essays on Black Power and Black Nationalism*, ed. Eddie S. Glaude, Jr. (Chicago: University of Chicago Press, 2002), for a discussion of gender issues.
4. Cade, *Black Woman*, 102.
5. Ibid., 103.
6. Ibid., 104.
7. Ibid., 103.
8. Ibid., 101.
9. Ibid., 110.
10. Michael Awkward, "A Black Man's Place in Black Feminist Criticism," in Byrd and Guy-Sheftall, *Traps*, 178.

11. Ibid., 179.
12. Ibid., 181–82.
13. Ibid., 187.
14. Reprinted in Byrd and Guy-Sheftall, *Traps*, 201.
15. Ibid.
16. See the pioneering work of Gary L. Lemons, who has written extensively about black men's feminist forefathers. Lemons, "To Be Black, Male, and Feminist: Making Womanist Space for Black Men on the Eve of a New Millennium," in *Feminism and Men: Reconstructing Gender Relations*, ed. Steven P. Schacht and Doris W. Ewing (New York: New York University Press, 1998), 43; and Lemons, "'When and Where [We] Enter': In Search of a Feminist Forefather-Reclaiming the Womanist Legacy of W. E. B. Du Bois," in Byrd and Guy-Sheftall, *Traps*, 71. His unpublished manuscript, *Memoir of a Black Boy Outsider: From the Margin of Masculinity to Pro Feminist Professor*, is also useful in this regard. Also see Philip Foner, ed., *Frederick Douglass on Women's Rights* (Westport, CT: Greenwood Press, 1976); Kalamu ya Salaam, *Our Women Keep Our Skies from Falling* (New Orleans: Nkombo, 1994); Nellie Y. McKay, "The Souls of Black Women Folk in the Writing of W. E. B. Du Bois," in *Reading Black, Reading Feminist: A Critical Anthology*, ed. Henry Louis Gates, Jr. (New York: Meridian, 1990); Aaronette M. White, "Ain't I a Feminist?: Black Men as Advocates of Feminism," *Womanist Theory and Research* 3, no. 2 (2001–2002); Luke Charles Harris, "The Challenge and Possibility for Black Males to Embrace Feminism," in *Black Men on Race, Gender, and Sexuality: A Critical Reader*, ed. Devon Carbado (New York: New York University Press, 1999); and Joy James, *Shadowboxing: Representations of Black Feminist Politics* particularly the essay "Fostering Alliances: Black Female Profeminisms" (New York: St. Martin's, 1999).
17. Fannie Barrier Williams, *Woman's Era* 2 (April 1895).
18. Foner, *Frederick Douglass*, 13–14.
19. Ibid., 113.
20. Frederick Douglass, *Life and Times of Frederick Douglass* (New York: Macmillan, 1962), 472–73.
21. Nellie Y. McKay, "The Souls of Black Women Folk in the Writing of W. E. B. Du Bois," in Henry Louis Gates, Jr., ed., *Reading Black, Reading Feminist: A Critical Anthology* (New York: Meridian, 1990), 229.
22. Ibid.
23. Ibid. See W. E. B. Du Bois, *Autobiography of W.E.B. Dubois: A Soliloquy on Viewing My Life from the Last Decade of Its First Century* ed. Herbert Aptheker, (New York: International Publishers, 1968).
24. Ibid.
25. Ibid., 230.
26. Du Bois, *The Souls of Black Folk* (New York: Penguin, 1996), originally published in 1903.
27. Ibid., 58.
28. Ibid., 58–59.
29. Ibid., 61–62.
30. McKay, "Souls," 236–37.
31. Du Bois, *Darkwater: Voices from within the Veil* (New York: Harcourt, Brace, 1921), 163.
32. Ibid.
33. Ibid, 164–65.
34. Ibid., 179.
35. Ibid., 179, 182.
36. Ibid., 185–86.
37. Ibid., 172.
38. In this chapter, I am concerned with Du Bois's critiques of patriarchal gender conventions—that is, his progressive writings about gender matters. Here I am not examining his own behavior or what we know about his personal life and his treatment of women, as these have been revealed in several biographies, including Gerald Horne, *Race Woman: The Lives of Shirley Graham Du Bois* (New York: New York University Press, 2000), a biography of Du Bois's second wife, or *David Levering Lewis, W.E.B. Du Bois: Biography of a Race, 1868–1919* (New York: Henry Holt, 1993) 2 vols. a comprehensive biography of Du Bois. The discrepancy between Du Bois's gender ideologies and his

actual practice is the subject of another work. The work of Lemons is important in this regard, however. See also Round Table Discussion of W.E.B. Du Bois's "The Damnation of Women," coordinated by Shirley L. Poole, *Crisis* XX (November–December 2000):1–16, which includes a multilogue among a group of women, myself included, that discusses the essay from their contemporary vantage points.
39. Cade, *Black Woman*, 110.
40. Du Bois, *Darkwater*, 181.

3

Toward Progressive Conceptions of Black Manhood LatCrit and Critical Race Feminist Reflections: Thought Piece, May 2001

ELIZABETH M. IGLESIAS

Questions:

How do black men practice and how might they be part of building mature black identities, coalitional strategies, and black cultural democracy, of the sort that Cornel West suggests, in the oppressed space they occupy? What are the features of progressive black masculinities, or how might they be described?

These questions intrigue me because they evoke three notions I have long considered central to the development of any liberation strategy: (1) the nature and meaning of *maturity* in the development of one's personal identity, and the relationship among the substance of one's personal identity, the formation of political identities, and the relationships one has with others, both intimate and social; (2) the role of race in the way one conceptualizes the ethical norms, political objectives, and practical strategies of coalitional solidarity—understood specifically as a commitment to inter- and intragroup justice; and (3) the meaning of *democracy*, not limited to the contestation for control of the state apparatus but understood more comprehensively as the realization of egalitarian participatory norms and practices in all fields of social life including the microhierarchies that structure interpersonal relationships within the family, the workplace, and the organization of religious spaces.

In this brief thought piece, my purpose is not to suggest that any one answer exists to any of these questions but that each question invites further questions, depending on the subject position from which the questions are asked and answered. Thus, I approach these questions self-consciously, as a woman of color, positioned professionally in the legal academy of the United States at a time when the emergence of a critical race feminist theory began to explore the subordination of women of color within the United States generally and the civil rights movement in particular. Further, my approach to these questions is critically informed by the insights and experiences I am gaining through my efforts to birth and nurture the development of LatCrit theory—a project I have always conceptualized as a struggle to produce a liberation strategy that addresses and resolves the intragroup differences that too often have rendered Latina/o identity a political battleground for so many different liberation projects at the intersection of race, nationality, gender, sexual orientation, language proficiencies, and class.

In addressing the three notions triggered by the questions posed above, my purpose is to share some of the insights I have developed over the last ten years doing liberation struggle in the belly of the legal academy. These insights draw on my early efforts to articulate a critical race feminist position on the relationship between the feminist struggle for women's sexual autonomy and the meaning and substance of mature masculinity and femininity.[1] I also draw on my more recent efforts to articulate a LatCritical theory of political identity, intergroup justice, and human connection that is relentlessly anti-essentialist in its commitment to achieving liberation through antisubordination practices.[2]

At the same time, I want to raise more general questions about the relationship between the project of producing Afrocentric imaginings and what I consider a common project of critical race feminist and LatCrit theory. In my view, critical race feminism and LatCrit theory share a common project of producing anti-essentialist, antisubordination, coalitional theory. "Essentialism" and "anti-essentialism" are key concepts in LatCrit and Critical Race Feminist theory. Generally, "essentialism" is a label applied to claims that a particular experience or perspective reflects the common interests of a broader group, as when working class men purport to define the class interests of "workers," or when white women purport to define the interests of all "women" without acknowledging intragroup differences and the relations of subordination and domination that are organized around differences such as race, sexual orientation, language proficiencies, national origin, and age. For a more extensive exploration see Elizabeth M. lglesias, "Latcrit Theory" Some Preliminary Notes Towards a Transatlantic Dialogue, 9" *U. Miami Int & Comparative L. Rev. 1, 3* (2000–01). Critical race feminism seeks to give meaning and content to coalitional solidarity among women of color.[3] Similarly, in the production of LatCrit theory I have sought to theorize, to perform, and ultimately to institutionalize the practice of coalitional solidarity among the marginalized and oppressed of any color. I raise these more general questions as a general source of unease, because at this particular moment—before the workshop discussions have unfolded—I am earnestly wondering whether the two liberation projects at the heart of both critical race feminism and LatCrit theory are in fundamental conflict with the project of producing Afrocentric imaginings. And if they are not in fact in conflict, then I am wondering what kinds of Afrocentric imaginings will effectively reveal the points of convergence and potential solidarity between Afrocentrism and the anti-essentialist commitments underpinning critical race feminism and the LatCrit project. I am also excited because, in my view, this workshop presents the potential for a genuinely substantive and mutually respectful opportunity to explore whether anti-essentialism and Afrocentricity can find common ground.

On Mature Men

Six years ago, as I struggled to recover from, and to reflect on, the end of my first (and only) marriage, I wondered whether there was any way to articulate a vision of masculinity that would enable, rather than suppress, the possibility of deeply intimate sexual relationships between women and men. The conceptual results of that struggle are reflected in my article "Rape, Race, and Representation,"[4] where I drew on resources of Jungian psychology to articulate the sorts of personal power which men and women need to access in order to negotiate, in meaningful and mutually affirming ways, the impact of sexual desire as an interpersonal experience while recognizing sexuality as a commodified, constitutive, cultural practice. Part of the challenge was to cut through the essentialized visions of masculinity and femininity, as articulated both in mainstream culture and in the discourses of white feminist theory. Both discourses posit essentialized imaginings of masculinity as a dominant and suppressive factor in the subordination of women, with mainstream culture glorifying that domination and white feminist theory condemning it. Cutting through these representations was in part dependent on seeing men and women as human beings and on recognizing sexuality as an expression of the embodiment of a spiritual self. The other part of the challenge was to articulate the practices through which individual men and women could perform new forms of masculine and feminine identity, as well as to challenge the belief that liberation was a prerequisite to, rather than the end product of, the performance of new forms of masculinity and femininity. To cast liberation as an end product rather than as a prerequisite is to say that if you or I want to become mature human persons, you and I need to begin to act like mature humans, regardless of costs. In my view, the construction of a new reality follows the performance of a new identity rather than the performance of a new way of being and doing, following a new reality created by some revolution "out there."

Since then, I have had occasion to reflect further on the meaning of mature personhood in the context of struggling to articulate the ways in which LatCrit theory should approach the meaning of *difference*. Though the question of difference raises many issues, here my point is that the encounter with difference is also a call and a challenge to each and all persons to reach a level of maturity that enables us to see the Other as ourselves.

As I have written elsewhere, "Otherness and difference are gifts, avenues of insight beyond our own particularities, windows on the world we might behold if ever we could see beyond our own contingency and beyond our finitude—a glimpse of God."[5] Evolving as political agents presupposes our evolution as human beings. Thus, the question, "How do black men practice and how might they be part of building mature black identities?" is from this perspective the same profound question we are each and all called to answer from our different subject positions: How do we make ourselves into existentially grounded, compassionate, and effective instances of human agency?

On Coalitional Solidarity

The theory and practice of coalitional solidarity has been a major concern of my work beginning with earlier attempts to center *women of color* as a distinct identity category in the articulation of critical legal theory and has continued and expanded in and through my efforts to develop LatCrit theory. This particular intellectual history colors my response to and reflections on the question, "How do black men practice and how might they be part of building … coalitional strategies?" From one perspective, my initial answer would be, "Well, the same way any of us do": by finding a way of viewing the elimination of one's own subordination as a part—but not the whole—of the project and by seeing how the elimination of one's subordination depends on the liberation of others as well. Ultimately, one's liberation cannot be real or genuine if it depends on the subordination of others.[6]

However, I also am intrigued by the question when I think of it like this: It is not enough to say that each of us—those who share a commitment to the realization of justice and liberation—is fundamentally called to the same political and spiritual challenge. It is not enough because each of us is called to this challenge from the very different positions we occupy as subjects. Thus, the way I attempt to develop and to perform coalitional strategies depends as much on my ability to imagine what the project entails as it does on the particular subject position from which I am called to do it. For example, as a person privileged by class and professional status, I do it by investing in and identifying with the struggle for economic justice of the materially dispossessed; as a person privileged by U.S. citizenship, I do it by investing in and identifying with the struggles for liberation from this country's brutality in the field of foreign affairs and national security; and as a Cuban American, I do it by asserting my Cuban identity even as I dissent from the regressive and reactionary positions so oftentimes attributed—rightly—to Cuban American political identity. Thus, the question by analogy becomes, "How does a black man perform antisubordination coalitional solidarity with those whose subordination is different from his own?" Even the statement of this identity begs further specification; that is, how does a queer black man, a rich black man, a U.S. citizen black man perform coalitional solidarity with men and women who do not share his particular privileges or his particular subordinations? It seems he would have to do so from where he stands and, then, in relationship to and in support of other marginalized persons.

On Cultural Democracy

As I imagine the concept of *cultural democracy*, it is an effort to reflect on the implications of democratic principles for the organization of social relationships beyond a narrow focus on the state apparatus. In my view, the concept of cultural democracy evokes a demand for equality and participation in every aspect of cultural life. Against this backdrop, I am interested in how notions of equality and the right to participatory involvement in the process of self-determination cohere with political and theoretical projects that ground liberation in Afrocentric imaginings. Indeed, I have two questions for my Afrocentric brothers and sisters. First, how does an Afrocentric vision of liberation address internal dissent—that is, the dissent of individuals or peoples of African descent who define their liberation in relationship to their experiences as women, as mixed race, as third world, or as queer people? Dealing with internal dissent is the central problem confronting any project that purports to invoke democracy, whether cultural or other, in its liberation agenda. Second, democracy, by its very nature, implies the decentralization of power and always creates the possibility that one will not have sufficient power to combat positions and projects one views as regressive. Thus, my second question is whether the concept of a cultural democracy can account for power asymmetries, and if so, how.

These brief notes express some of my preworkshop reflections on the project of building progressive black masculinities.

Notes

1. See Elizabeth M. Iglesias, "Rape, Race, and Representation: The Power of Discourse, Discourses of Power, and the Reconstruction of Heterosexuality," *Vanderbilt Law Review* 49, no. 4 (1996), 869.
2. See Iglesias, "Identity, Democracy, Communicative Power, International Labor Rights and the Evolution of LatCrit Theory and Community," *University of Miami Law Review* 53, no. 4 (1999), esp. 617–29, on "rotating centers" as epistemological and political imperative in the evolution of coalitional theory and praxis. See also Iglesias and Francisco Valdes, "Religion, Gender, Sexuality, Race, and Class in Coalitional Theory: A Critical and Self-Critical Analysis of LatCrit Social Justice Agendas," *Chicano-Latino Law Review* 19 (1998), 503.
3. See, e.g., Elizabeth M. Iglesias, "Structures of Subordination: Women of Color at the Intersection of Title VII and the N.L.R.A. Not!," Harvard Civil Rights-Civil Liberties Law Review 28 (1993): 395–503.
4. Iglesias, "Rape, Race."
5. Iglesias, "Identity, Democracy," 653.
6. Iglesias, "Structures of Subordination," 473–78 (elaborating reasons why individual liberation depends on the equality and actualization of "others").

Part 2
Strength, Not Privilege or Dominance

Toward a Pedagogy of the Oppressor[1]

MICHAEL KIMMEL

This Breeze at My Back

To run or walk into a strong headwind is to understand the power of nature. You set your jaw in a squared grimace, your eyes are slits against the wind, and you breathe with a fierce determination. And still you make so little progress.

To walk or run with that same wind at your back is to float, to sail effortlessly, expending virtually no energy. You do not feel the wind; it feels you. You do not feel how it pushes you along; you feel only the effortlessness of your movements. You feel like you could go on forever. It is only when you turn around and face that wind do you realize its strength.

Being white, or male, or heterosexual in this culture is like running with the wind at your back. It feels like just plain running, and we rarely, if ever, get a chance to see how we are sustained, supported, and even propelled by that wind.

In recent years, the study of discrimination based on gender, race, class, and sexuality has mushroomed, creating a large literature and increasing courses addressing these issues. Of course, the overwhelming majority of the research has explored the experiences of the victims of racism, sexism, homophobia, and class inequality. These are the "victims," the "others" who have begun to make these issues visible to contemporary scholars and laypeople alike. This is, of course, politically as it should be: The marginalized always understand first the mechanisms of their marginalization; it remains for them to convince the center that the processes of marginalization are in fact both real and remediable.

When presented with evidence of systematic discrimination, majority students are often indifferent and sometimes even defensive and resistant. "What does this have to do with me?" they ask. The more defensive of them immediately mention several facts that, they believe, will absolve them of inclusion into the superordinate category. "My family never owned slaves," "I have a gay friend," and "I never raped anyone" are fairly typical responses. Virtually none seems able to discuss white people as a group. Some will assert that whites are dramatically different from one another and that ethnicity and religion are more important than race; others maintain that white people, as a group, are not at all privileged. And virtually all agree that racism is a problem of individual attitudes—prejudiced people—and not a social problem.

Such statements are as revealing as they are irrelevant. They tell us far more about the way we tend to individualize and personalize processes that are social and structural. And they also tell us that majority students resist discussions of inequality because it will require that they feel guilty for crimes someone else committed.

Even students willing to engage with these questions also tend to personalize and to individualize them. They may grudgingly grant the systematic nature of inequality, but to them, racism, sexism, and heterosexism are bad attitudes held by bad people. They are eager to help those bad people see the error of their ways and to change their attitudes to good attitudes. This usually will come about through better education, they say.

We, who are white, heterosexual, male and/or middle class need to go further; we need to see how we are stakeholders in the understanding of structural inequality, how the dynamics that create inequality for some also benefit others. Privilege needs to be made visible.

Exciting new research in a variety of disciplines, including sociology, literature, and cultural studies is examining what previously passed as invisible, neutral, and universal. We now can see how the experience of privilege also shapes the lives of men, white people and heterosexuals. Such an inquiry, long overdue, will enable us to more fully understand the social dynamics of race, class, gender, and sexuality and how they operate in all our lives.

Making Privilege Visible

To be white, or straight, or male, or middle class is to be simultaneously ubiquitous and invisible. You are everywhere you look; you are the standard against which everyone else is measured. You are like water, like air. People tell you they went to see a woman doctor, or they say they went to see the doctor. People tell you they have a gay colleague, or they tell you about a colleague. A white person is happy to tell you about a black friend, but when that same person simply mentions a friend, everyone assumes the person is white. Any college course that does not have the word *woman* or *gay* or *minority* in the title is, de facto, a course about men, heterosexuals, and white people. But we call those courses literature, history, or political science.

This invisibility is political. This was first made visible to me in the early 1980s, when I participated in a small discussion group on feminism. In one meeting, in a discussion between two women, I first confronted this invisibility. A white woman and a black woman were discussing whether all women were, by definition, *sisters,* because they all had essentially the same experiences and because all women faced a common oppression by men. The white woman asserted that what bonded them was that they were both women, in spite of racial differences. The black woman disagreed.

"When you wake up in the morning and look in the mirror, what do you see?" she asked.

"I see a woman," replied the white woman.

"That's precisely the problem," responded the black woman. "I see a *black* woman. To me, race is visible every day, because race is how I am *not* privileged in our culture. Race is invisible to you, because it's how you are privileged. It's why there will always be differences in our experience."

As I witnessed this exchange, I was startled, and I groaned—more audibly, perhaps, than I had intended. Being the only man in the room, someone asked what my response had meant.

"Well," I said, "when I look in the mirror, I see a human being. I'm universally generalizable. As a middle-class white man, I have no class, no race, and no gender. I'm the generic person!"

Sometimes, I like to think that it was on that day that I became a middle-class white man. Sure, I had been all those before, but they had not meant much to me. Since that time, I have tried to understand how race, class, and gender did not refer only to other people marginalized by race, class, or gender privilege. Those terms also described me. I enjoyed the privilege of invisibility. The very processes that confer privilege to one group and not to another are often invisible to those on whom that privilege is conferred. What makes us marginal or powerless are the processes we see, partly because others keep reminding us of them. Invisibility is a privilege in a double sense—hiding the power relations that are kept in place by the very dynamics of invisibility, and in the sense of privilege as luxury. It is a luxury that only white people have in our society not to think about race every minute of their lives. It is a luxury that only men have in our society to pretend that gender does not matter.

Even though this story took place over twenty years ago, I was reminded of it recently when I went to give a guest lecture for a female colleague at my university. (We teach the same course on alternate semesters, so she always gives a guest lecture for me, and I do one for her.) As I walked into the auditorium, one student looked up at me and said, "Oh, finally, an objective opinion!"

All that semester, whenever my female colleague opened her mouth, what this student saw was a woman, biased. But when I walked in, I was, in this student's eyes, unbiased, an objective opinion. Disembodied Western rationality—standing right in front of the class. This notion that middle-class white men are objective and that everyone else is biased is the way inequalities are reproduced.

Let me give you another example of how power is so often invisible to those who have it. Most of you have e-mail addresses, and you write e-mail messages to people all over the world. You have probably noticed that there is one big difference between e-mail addresses in the United States and e-mail addresses of people in other countries: Their addresses have country codes at the end of the address. So, for example, if you are writing to someone in South Africa, you put "za" at the end, or "jp" for Japan, or "uk" for the United Kingdom, or "de" for Germany (Deutschland). Even if you write to someone at a university in another country, you have to use a country code, so, for example, it would be "ac.uk" for an academic institution in Britain, or "edu.au" for an educational institution in Australia. But when you write to people in the United States, the e-mail address ends with "edu" for an educational institution, "org" for an organization, "gov" for a federal government office, or "com" or "net" for commercial internet providers. Why is it that the United States does not have a country code?

It is because when you are the dominant power in the world, everyone else needs to be named. When you are in power, you need not draw attention to yourself as a specific entity, but, rather, you can pretend to be the generic, the universal, and the generalizable. From the point of view of the United States, all other countries are "other" and thus need to be named, marked, noted. Once again, privilege is invisible. In the world of the Internet, as Michael Jackson sang, "we are the world."

There are consequences to this invisibility: Privilege, as well as gender, remains invisible. And it is hard to generate a politics of inclusion from invisibility. The invisibility of privilege means that many men, like many white people, become defensive and angry when confronted with the statistical realities or the human consequences of racism or sexism. Since our privilege is invisible, we may become defensive. Hey, we may even feel like victims ourselves.

I was reminded of this reaction from the privileged recently when I appeared on a television talk show opposite three angry white males—three men who felt that they had been the victims of workplace discrimination. The show's title, no doubt to entice a large potential audience, was "A Black Woman Took My Job." In my comments to these angry men, I invited them to consider what the word *my* meant in that title: that they felt the jobs were originally theirs, that they were entitled to them, and that when some other people got the job, those black women were really taking their jobs. But by what right is that his job? By convention, by a historical legacy of such profound levels of discrimination we have needed decades of affirmative action to even begin to make slightly more level a playing field that has been so decidedly in one direction.

Our task is to begin making privilege visible.

The Invisible Knapsack

One way to understand how privilege works—and how it is kept invisible—is to look at the way we think about inequality. We always think about inequality from the perspective of the one who is hurt by the inequality, not the one who is helped. Take, for example, wage inequality based on gender. We are used to hearing that women make about seventy-one cents for every dollar made by a man. In that statistic women's wages are calculated as a function of men's wages; men's wages are the standard (the $1) against which women's wages are calculated. In this way, the discrimination against women is visible—doing the same job, they earn less, just because they are women.

But what if we changed the statistics? What if we expressed men's wages as a function of women's wages? What if we said that for every dollar earned by a woman, men make $1.34? Then it would not be the discrimination that was visible—it would be the privilege. Just for being a male, a male worker received an additional thirty-four cents. This is what sociologist R. W. Connell calls the *masculinity dividend*—the unearned benefits that accrue to men just for being men.

One could easily apply this model to race, class, and sexuality. And several of the authors in this volume probe their own experiences as a way to enable others to see what had earlier been invisible. Perhaps no one has done that more successfully than Peggy McIntosh, in her celebrated essay on what she calls the *invisible knapsack*. The invisible knapsack contains all the little benefits that come to us simply because we are white, or straight, or middle class, or male. We have to open up that knapsack, dump its contents out, and take a look at all the very different ways that these ascribed characteristics—those we were born with—have become so obscured that we have come to believe that the events of our lives are the results of achieved characteristics.

Making gender, race, class, and sexuality visible—both as the foundations of individual identity and as the social dynamics of inequality—also means that we pay some attention to the differences among them as well. Often students argue that gender is different from race, because, as one of my students put it, "you have to live every day with a person of the opposite sex, but you don't have to live so intimately with people of another race." Leaving aside the potential racism or heterosexism of such a statement—one might, after all, live intimately with someone of a different race, or one might not live with someone of the opposite sex—this student does point to an important issue: Just as all forms of inequality are not the same, all forms of privilege are not the same.

For example, race and gender appear, at least on the surface, to be based on characteristics present at birth: one's sex or race. That means that they are always visible to an observer—well, at least nearly always; there are, of course, people who change their biological sex, or who dress differently from established norms, or those who try to pass as members of another race, or even those, like Michael Jackson, who seem to be using draconian surgical techniques to be taken for another race entirely. Thus, the privileges based on gender or race may feel even more invisible because those privileged by race and gender did nothing to earn their privilege.

On the other hand, sexuality and class are not immediately visible to the public. One can more easily pass as a member of a privileged group. But sexual minorities also may feel that their identity is not a social construction but is the fulfillment of an inner essence; that is, it is more like race and gender than it is like class. Whereas race and biological sex may be evidently inborn, biologically based or "God-given" sexuality also feels like that to both heterosexuals and homosexuals.

Class, however, does not feel like this. In fact, class seems to feel exactly the opposite: as a status that one was not born with but that one has earned. Class is less visible than the other dimensions because though our objective position in an economic order depends on empirically measurable criteria (e.g., income, occupation, education), class as an everyday experience rests on other people's evaluation of our presentation of self. It is far easier to pass as something we are not—both for people of modest means to affect the lifestyle of the rich and famous and for very wealthy people to affect the styles of the poor. Although most of us would like to have everyone think we are wealthier than we actually are, it is often the case that the truly wealthy want everyone to think they are less wealthy than they are. We may dress up while they dress down.

Often we associate ourselves with the trappings of the class to which we aspire as opposed to the class from which we actually come. Take, for example, fashion. I am reasonably certain that most of the readers of this chapter have, at some point in their lives, gone bowling. And I am equally certain that very few readers, if any, have ever played polo. And yet I would bet that many of you would be very happy to shell out a lot of money for a garment that identified you as a polo player (e.g., a Ralph Lauren Polo shirt with a little polo player on it) rather than for an equally well-made garment with a little bowler on it. In fact, you would be eager to pay a premium on that Polo shirt precisely because the brand has become associated with a class position to which you can only aspire.

Class can be concealed, and class feels like something we have earned all by ourselves. Therefore, class privilege may be the one set of privileges we are least interested in examining because it feels like it is ours by right, not by birth. All the more reason we should take a look at class.

The Souls of White (and Straight and Middle-Class and Male) Folk

This is a difficult thing to do, and there is no question but that it will make us feel uncomfortable. It is unpleasant to acknowledge that all the good things that have happened to you are not simply the result of your hard work and talent and motivation but are the result of something over which you had no power. Sometimes it makes us feel guilty, other times defensive. Sometimes we just feel powerless. "What can I possibly do to change this massive system of inequality?"

In a culture such as ours, all problems are thought to be individual problems, based on bad attitudes, wrong choices, or our own frailties and addictions.

When confronted with structural or social problems, we think the solutions are either aggregated individual solutions—everyone needs to change his or her attitude—or that the solutions do not exist. A single, lone individual has no chance, we think, to change the system. You cannot fight City Hall.

We feel powerless, impotent. We can become mired in guilt. Some people argue that guilt is a negative emotion and that we should not have to feel guilty for the things that happened generations—even centuries—ago. Occasionally, someone is moved by that guilt to attempt to renounce his or her privilege. Books counsel us to become race traitors or to refuse to be a man.

And sometimes such a posture feels moral and self-righteous. Guilt is not always a bad emotion after all. How would you feel about a German student saying, "I really don't want to feel guilty about what happened here; after all, I never personally sent a Jew to the gas chambers"? Or about white South Africans who proclaimed that they never actually benefited from apartheid, since they got their jobs and their wealth by virtue of their hard work and determination?

Guilt may be appropriate, even a necessary feeling—for a while. It does not freeze us in abjection but can motivate us to transform the circumstances that made us feel guilty in the first place, to make connections between our experiences and others', and to become and remain accountable to the struggles for equality and justice around the world. Guilt can politicize us. Perhaps that is one reason why we often resist it?

Though noble in their intention, however, this posture of guilty self-negation cannot be privileged people's final destination as we come to understand how we are privileged by race, class, gender, and sexuality. Refusing to be men, white, or straight does neither the privileged nor the unprivileged much good. One can no more renounce privilege than one can stop breathing. It is in the air we breathe.

And it is embedded in the architecture that surrounds us. Renouncing privilege ultimately substitutes an individual solution for a structural and social problem. Inequality is structural and systematic, as well as individual and attitudinal. Eliminating inequalities involves more than changing everyone's attitude.

Trying to rid oneself of bad attitudes and renouncing one's unearned privilege also, finally, brings us no further than the feelings of impotent despair we often feel in the face of such overwhelming systemic problems. We feel lonely. We feel isolated from our friends, our families, or our classmates. It is the loneliness of the long-distance runner against the wind.

The struggles against inequality are, however, collective struggles: enormous social movements that unite people across geography, race, religion, class, sexuality, and gender. Participating in these struggles to end inequality brings one into a long history of those who have stood alongside of the victims of oppression, those who have added their voices to the voices of those who had been earlier silenced. Examining our privilege may be uncomfortable at first, but it can also be energizing, motivating, and engaging.

A Method of Analysis

In examining privilege, we should consider using an intersectional approach to explore the ways in which race, class, gender, and sexuality intersect and interact. This method was first developed by women of color, who argued that the variables of race, class, gender, and sexuality could not be separated in understanding their experiences. This was a response to the traditional studies of race, which focused on race alone and usually ended up focused narrowly on men of color, and to women's studies, which often focused only on the experiences of white women. But some of these theorists asked different questions: Where does the black person stop and the woman begin? How can one analyze the totality of one's experience without examining the ways in which all these categories coincide, collide, contradict?

An intersectional analysis in this instance would explore the ways in which race, gender, class, and sexuality interact in the lives of those who are privileged by one or more of these identities. Examining the ways in which we are privileged as well as those ways in which we are not privileged will enable us to understand our society more fully and to engage us in the long historical process of change.

Intersectionality and Black Masculinities:
Regressive and Progressive Masculinities

An intersectional approach opens enormously fruitful avenues in the construction, celebration, and nurturing of progressive black masculinities. For example, one can see the claiming of unexamined male or heterosexual privilege by black men as a strategy in the struggle against racism. Black feminists have long pointed to the ways they have felt pressured by black men to give priority to the struggle against racism, to withhold their critiques of black male sexism, so as not to disturb some ideal of racial unity. In this way, claiming masculinity becomes a compensatory strategy: If racism is experienced as emasculating, as it is, then expressing a virulent masculinity becomes a method of reclaiming human dignity.

Indeed, it is often the case that those whose masculinity is undermined by racism, heterosexism, or classism seek the vigorous reassertion of traditionally patriarchal ideals of masculinity as a compensation, a restoration. Thus, for example, does one often see hypermasculine posturing among black, gay, and working-class men?

However, though these actions may seem to compensate for racism as an emasculating structure, they simultaneously reproduce the disempowerment of black women. What intersectionality implies is that this method also reproduces the very inequalities it is meant to challenge. What sort of masculinity can gay men claim as honorable if it results in the further disempowerment of lesbians in particular and of all women in general? What sort of masculinity can black men claim as honorable if it results in the further denial of black women's humanity?

It is in this context that the facile defensiveness of many black men about obviously sexist and homophobic music, poetry, literature, and other cultural forms must be seen. It may be that some of the more virulently sexist and homophobic gansta rap, for example, is an accurate portrayal of life in the inner city and therefore is perceived as a vigorous defense of a group whose masculinity is denied by a racist society at every turn. But at what cost? The casual misogyny and homophobic rage divides the black community from its natural allies—black women (straight or gay) and gay black men—who all know a thing or two about oppression. That is simply too great a cost.

What is more, the casual sexism and homophobia also reproduce the oppression of straight black men, providing a justification for the denial of manhood to black men within a racialized society. "You see," one can almost hear the establishment saying, "those black men are like animals. Look at how they treat their women! They don't deserve to be treated with respect, like men." The very mechanism that black men thought would restore manhood ends up being the pretext on which it is denied.

There is yet another cost to this casual taken-for-granted misogyny and homophobia: the reproduction of those oppressions and the claiming of privilege by an unprivileged group. Were the sorts of things said in some rap songs about women or about gays said about, say, Jews or about black men by white people, it would be seen as intolerable and would never get on the radio, in books, or in poetry slams. The racist or anti-Semitic content would be obvious immediately. Why is it that the sexism and homophobia in so much of mainstream popular culture—and here I decidedly do not single out gangsta rap or poetry slams—do not merit the same sort of cultural scrutiny and generate the same sort of outrage?

But racism tends to problematize the masculinity of the "other" by declaring him—black, gay, ethnic minority—to be simultaneously too masculine and not masculine enough. It is a problem I often call the *Goldilocks paradox*, after the old fairy tale in which everything was either too hot or to cold, too big or too small, but rarely "just right." Racism, heterosexism, and class oppression are justified because the masculinity of the "other" is not just right. There is a problem with it, and therefore the inequality we observe is the natural outcome of that problematic masculinity.

Racism images black men as both hypermasculine and hypomasculine. Black men are violent rapacious beasts, out-of-control animals, and weak, irresponsible, welfare-dependent deadbeat dads. One can see how gangsta rap therefore justifies racist images, even as white suburban boys buy it like crazy. Gay men are both weak, effeminate sissies and so voraciously carnal that straight men can only watch their sexual adventures with awe and wonder—and thus their oppression and HIV is a consequence of their behavior. See how it works?

But also included here is something else, something important. Just as black men have sought to use the trappings of patriarchy, of male privilege, to restore and to revive a damaged sense of masculinity—hypermasculine overcompensation—it is equally true that some black men have used their problematized masculinity to redefine it, to forge a strategy of resistance to such images. It never fails to amaze my students—at least the white students who typically embrace the notion of black masculinity as hypermasculine overcompensation—to learn that married black men do more housework than white men or even that working-class white men do more housework than middle-class white men, although middle-class white men do have more progressive ideologies about sharing housework.

Here is a strategy of resistance, an effort to turn racist stereotypes on their heads, to forge alliances with black women, and to embrace a new vision of masculinity that only the marginalized can begin to articulate. There are many such seams in the edifice of a culture built on dramatic inequalities based on race, class, gender, and sexuality, because that culture is also sustained by stereotypic images of the marginalized that justify their continued marginalization as somehow derived naturally from their obvious shortcomings as men. Exploring and exploiting these seams require alliances across class, race, ethnicity, gender, and sexuality, since attempting to claim the privileges of one means the further marginalization of all.

Here, I believe, the best allies that black men have for the development and sustenance of progressive black masculinities are, and will continue to be, black feminist women. For just as a black woman, those many years ago, first explained to me the ways in which privilege was invisible, so too have black feminist women consistently demanded support from black men, and have believed that only through that alliance can the struggles against sexism and racism be joined.[2]

Notes

1. This essay is a revised version of the introduction to Michael Kimmel and Abby Ferber, *Privilege* (Boulder, co: Westview, 2003). I am grateful to the conference organizers, and especially to Athena Mutua, for their critical comments and to Abby Ferber for her comments on the original draft.
2. Although it is not evident from my usage here, I mean the word *joined* in both its meanings: the joining together of the two struggles and the initiation of the struggle in the first place.

5

A Telling Difference: Dominance, Strength, and Black Masculinities

PATRICIA HILL COLLINS

Black mothers love their sons and raise their daughters.

African American adage

Introduction

African Americans typically think that gender relations are a private, domestic concern, mainly reflecting the love relationships between heterosexual men and women. Even those who see the harmful effects of gender oppression on African Americans still wish to define issues of gender and sexuality solely within the context of black civil society, as an internal black community concern. Place the public issue of race first, they counsel, and leave the more private issues of gender and sexuality for us to work out among ourselves. Relying on ideas about family to construct ideas about race, this approach sees African Americans as participating in a large, imagined racial family that must always put on a good face for a critical white public. The adage "Don't air dirty laundry in public" speaks to this black community norm of keeping these and other family problems hidden.

What these approaches fail to grasp is that commonsense notions about gender have long been used to construct ideas about racial difference that are central to racism in the United States. In other words, ideas about white racial normality and black racial deviancy draw heavily on ideas about gender and sexuality. Specifically, sex roles among whites—which embrace ideas of strong men and weak women—allegedly constitute normal and ideal gender practices. African Americans have been evaluated against this sex role ideology, which by its very nature disadvantages black people and stigmatizes them as deviant.[1] Because the racial normality attributed to whites has been defined in gender-specific terms, African American progress, or lack thereof, in achieving white gender norms has long been used as a marker of racial progress and has often been used to explain and to justify racial inequality itself.

Two commonsense understandings have framed gendered assumptions of black deviancy. One is the idea that African Americans are thought to have women who are too strong and men who are too weak. Because Western sex-role ideology is premised on ideas of strong men and weak women, the seeming reversal of strong women and weak men stigmatizes African Americans as inferior. African American men have been harmed by this conflict, presumably because it obscures the fact that black men have never been allowed to achieve the ideal of the real man of white middle-class masculinity yet have been evaluated using these criteria.[2] The strong black women–weak black men thesis has taken an especially pernicious form in the post–civil rights era. Increasingly, the thesis has been used less to describe outcomes of racial oppression and more often has been identified as its cause. Thus, gender relationships between African American men and women are more often depicted as one of perpetrator and victim where African American men are too weak because African American women are too strong.

Within the strong women–weak men thesis, two specific sites of African American social organization allegedly are responsible for producing weak men. One site is the putatively flawed relationship between mothers and sons, where strong black mothers baby their sons yet raise their daughters in their own, too-strong image. As a result of flawed gender socialization, black men fail to learn how to control themselves and succumb to weaknesses of unrestrained violent acts or sexual irresponsibility. The other site is composed of the troubled love relationships between black men and women, one that also reflects the allegedly flawed gender socialization within African American families. Apparently the combination of strong women with weak men is inherently explosive. In essence, this framework creates images of African American men as victims, not of racism and class exploitation but at the hands of their mothers, sexual partners, and other black women in their lives. To the extent that black men internalize this myth, black women within their own communities become the enemy, and black men are encouraged to adopt strategies that seek dominion over black women instead of attacking the race and class structures that subordinate them. Not only do they potentially lose black women as allies, but also their own contributions to the survival of a people as evidence of strength is minimized.

In conjunction with the thesis of strong women–weak men, a second commonsense understanding also constructs ideas about alleged gender deviancy among African Americans generally and within black masculinity in particular. This is the thesis of strong men, weak men. The meanings attached to masculinity are not limited to domination and control over women but extend to domination over other men and to exclusive control over the economic, political, and social order. To the extent that only white men have been allowed to exercise this type of overarching dominion, hegemonic masculinity is defined in terms of white masculinity. Consequently, this thesis, by definition, constructs black masculinity as subordinate. Using white masculinity as a yardstick for a normal masculinity grounded in ideas about strength as dominance, African American men become defined as subordinates, deviant, and allegedly weak, and black men's purported weakness as men is compared to the seeming strength of white men. Despite a complicated reality that structurally subordinates both black men and black women to white men, black men's subordination nevertheless becomes ideologically defined as a weakness in relation to both black women and white men.

Definitions of black masculinity in the United States reflect a narrow cluster of controlling images situated within a broader framework that grants varying value to racially distinctive forms of masculinity. Arrayed along a continuum, virtually all of the representations of black masculinity pivot on questions of weakness, whether it is a weakness associated with an inability to control violent impulses, sexual urges, or their black female heterosexual partners or a weakness attributed to men whose lack of education, employment patterns, and criminal records relegate them to inferior social spaces. One end of the continuum contains images of black men as beasts who pose varying degrees of threat to white society. These are the threatening, sexualized, and occasionally violent representations that have long populated American science, social science, and popular culture. Representations of black men as beasts that were created in defense of African colonialism evolved into those of black men as bucks who required slavery's domestication, and both were followed by post-emancipation images of African American men as rapists and thugs who could not handle their newfound freedoms. These images equate black male strength with wildness and suggest that an allegedly natural black male strength must be tamed by family, civilization, and, if all else fails, the military or the National Basketball Association. The other end of the continuum holds representations of safely tamed Negroes who pose little threat to white society. As domesticated Negroes, representations such as Sambo, Uncle Tom, and Uncle Ben signify castrated, emasculated, and feminized versions of black masculinity whose feminization associates them with weakness. Once the connection is made, men can no longer be considered real men.

Black men are harmed and constrained by these images and the underlying vision of masculinity as dominance. To the extent that they internalize this thesis, their own strategies to combat their oppression will be misguided. Thus, the fallacy of both the strong black women–weak black men thesis attributed to gender relations of black men and women and the strong white men–weak black men thesis of hegemonic masculinity is that both counsel black men to embrace unrealistic strategies for dealing with relations of dominance. Progressive black masculinities require rejecting not only the images currently associated with black masculinity but also the structural power relations that cause them. In particular, uncoupling ideas about strength from ideas about dominance might enable more black men to tell the difference between the two.

Clearing Space for Black Masculinities: Challenges to Dominant Gender Ideology

Historically, Western antiracist scholarship and social policy failed to challenge these gendered assumptions about African Americans, arguing instead that, if given the chance, black men and women would be just like white Americans. In this context, African American and mainstream scholars alike embraced a traditional gender ideology that proscribed distinctive and complementary gender roles for black men and black women. They also uncritically accepted societal perceptions of masculinity that upheld both the strong black women–weak black men thesis and the strong white men–weak black men thesis. Collectively, African Americans also failed to challenge these gendered assumptions. Using race- and class-based paradigms, the majority of African Americans continued to see racism and class exploitation as structural processes that limited their life chances. Yet few considered how sexism and its concomitant gender ideology structured schools, jobs, housing, health care, and other social institutions in ways that also profoundly shaped their lives. Because African Americans implicitly accepted the interpretive framework of complementary gender roles, they challenged neither the strong women–weak men thesis associated with American racial ideology nor the strong men–weak men thesis concerning American masculinity. Instead, many African Americans argued that black poverty and political powerlessness could best be addressed by approximating more closely the gender roles of dominant society. Within this logic, gender normality became a sign of racial progress, and racial progress became measured in gender-specific forms.

Since the early 1970s, three developments have disputed this taken-for-granted gender ideology. Collectively, they catalyzed new analyses of black masculinity. First, African American women advanced a black feminism that challenged both African Americans' seemingly uncritical acceptance of dominant gender ideology as well as white feminism's critique of patriarchy. Second, breaking from mainstream interpretations of masculinity as rooted in male biology, men's studies scholarship analyzed masculinity as a gendered, socially constructed structure of power. Third, gay, lesbian, and bisexual studies and the development of queer theory revealed how sexuality was not only socially constructed but remained integral to ideas about masculinity. Together, these three areas created space for new discussions of black masculinity.

Black Feminist Theory

Western feminists criticized the two-parent, nuclear family as one site of women's oppression and as central to perpetuating dominant gender ideology. But because much Western feminism focused on the experiences of middle-class white American or Western European women and men, it inadvertently privileged the family forms of this population. By analyzing the realities of black women's lives, Toni Cade Bambara, Pauli Murray, Audre Lorde, Angela Davis, and other early modern black feminists pointed out that race was equally if not more important in black women's lives. These women argued that race constituted an important axis in constructing gender ideology overall and that African American women had a distinctive place at the intersections of race, class, gender, and sexuality.[3] By critiquing the assumed sisterhood thought to exist among all women, black feminist thinkers suggested that gender ideology operated in racially specific ways. In particular, the representations of normative femininity were revealed as being middle class, white, and unattainable by the majority of African American women. Moreover, not only did black women confront race and class oppression, but both the image and the reality of strong black women also made the image and the reality of normative white femininity possible. Black feminists did not simply want to be judged by the standards of normative white femininity. Rather, they questioned the desirability of normative conceptions of femininity and advanced a black feminist analysis of the race and class dynamics of Western constructions of femininity itself.[4] This black feminist critique was quite effective in opening up new political venues within Western feminism, especially for collaboration among women across differences of race, ethnicity, and class. But how effective would such a critique be in confronting a deeply entrenched black gender ideology and in catalyzing analyses of black masculinity in particular? Could black feminist analyses make a dent in the strong black women–weak black men thesis?

New analyses of black masculinity that were informed by the major tenets of black feminism were sorely needed.[5] Moreover, black men needed to be at the forefront of developing such analyses if they were to be effective in changing black men's lives. These new analyses of black masculinity might also facilitate revisiting black feminist analyses of black femininity, much of which was developed in heated dialogues with white women and within the context of a focus on women. Would African American men engage in serious political critique of masculinity as a form of race and gender power and also engage in honest dialogues with black women?

The reaction of African American men to black feminist analyses of masculinity in the 1970s and 1980s gave an early answer: a resounding no. Black male responses and resistance to the ideas of African American women thinkers suggested that any black intellectual production or leadership that decentered black men and the assumptions of black male victimization under racism would be rejected.[6] When African American women pointed out the black male privileges gained under sexism, black men accused them of colluding with the white supremacist emasculation of black males. Charged with black male bashing, Alice Walker, Ntozake Shange, and Michelle Wallace, among others, found themselves treading carefully through a minefield of gender and race controversy. Sadly, black male antifeminists targeted the works of these and other black women writers precisely because many men believed that black women writers who wrote about black women somehow were bashing black males.

Not all black men took this stance. Sociologist Clyde Franklin's work on black masculinity drew on gender as a category of analysis well before his contemporary counterparts. Political scientist Manning Marable's classic 1983 essay "Groundings with My Sisters: Patriarchy and the Exploitation of Black Women" remains a groundbreaking piece in the context of the backlash against black feminism in the 1980s.[7] As black feminism has become more institutionalized, many more African American men have become receptive to its ideas. For example, Michael Awkward has engaged the ideas of black feminist criticism by noting how black men have multiple places within it. The corpus of work by historian Robin D. G. Kelley reflects a sustained familiarity with the ideas of black feminism. This growing receptivity to the ideas of black feminism, in turn, enabled black male intellectuals to apply the gendered analyses advanced within black feminism to the question of black masculinity.[8]

Men's Studies

Scholarship that analyzed masculinities as part of a gendered structure of power constituted a second development that spurred new thinking about black masculinity. Men's studies emerged in conjunction with a men's movement and was influenced both by the theoretical turn toward social constructionism within Western social science and, more importantly, by Western feminism—although this debt is not typically acknowledged. In contrast to the apolitical and ahistorical framework of traditional sex role theory, men's studies typically approached masculinity as part of a system of gender power. As sociologist R. W. Connell contends, studying men was just as important as studying women for analyzing gender relations: "To understand a system of inequality, we must examine its dominant group—the study of men is as vital for gender analysis as the study of ruling classes and elites is for class analysis."[9] Rejecting the term *patriarchy* as overly simplistic, men's studies scholars introduced the phrase *hegemonic masculinity* to refer to the dominant form of masculinity in any given society, as well as marginalized and subordinated masculinities that characterize the experiences of men whose race, class, religion, ethnicity, age, sexuality, or citizenship category placed them within subordinated groups. This move in turn created the space to view representations of white masculinity and black masculinity not as descriptions of nature inherited from nineteenth-century biological science but as social constructions rooted in American race relations.

Some key features characterize hegemonic masculinity in the United States. First, hegemonic masculinity is defined in relation to the subordination of women and to other subordinated and marginalized masculinities.[10]

Second, hegemonic masculinity does not refer to a personality type or an actual male character. Rather, it describes sets of prescriptive American social norms, symbolically represented, that operate as a crucial part of daily, routine activities.[11] Third, the constellation of ideas and social practices that constitute hegemonic masculinity are accepted, rejected, and performed by men from diverse social class groupings, racial or ethnic groups, ages, and religions. Whereas men are not equal in their ability to control the very definitions of masculinity itself, the vast majority of men in the United States know the rules that govern masculinity and, in some fashion, are complicit in upholding them.[12] Finally, the power relations in the United States that construct these relational masculinities enable the erasure of whiteness, class privilege, and assumptions of heterosexuality—in short, the workings and structures of hegemonic masculinity itself. As a result, hegemonic discourses of American masculinity operate as unquestioned truths. Ironically, despite the ubiquity of gender, race, class, and sexuality in constructing American masculinity, masculinity can be discussed without referencing these systems at all.

Over time, this literature on masculinities devoted increasing attention to the socially constructed nature of hegemonic masculinities in relation to a variety of other constructed masculinities across differences of class, race, ethnicity, and sexuality. Masculinity was seen as highly heterogeneous and relational, with the relationships of different masculinities to one another emerging as an important area of study.[13] Thus, from the perspectives of subordinated groups, it became clear that all masculinities possessed hegemonic ideas—a situation resulting in, for example, white men encountering a hegemonic white masculinity that dictates what a white man should be and do, and, likewise, black men encountering equally hegemonic ideas about what a black man should be and do. In a sense, there are levels of hegemonic masculinity, all designed to maintain a pecking order among American men.

Queer Theory

The growth of queer theory within American universities in the 1990s sparked fresh perspectives on black masculinity. Influenced both by social movements by lesbian, gay, bisexual, transgendered and transsexual (LGBTT) people and the constructionist turn in the American academy, queer theory challenged earlier frameworks that viewed heterosexuality and homosexuality within the binary of normal and deviant. However, social constructionist analyses suggested that sexual identities of all sorts, including homosexuality, were formed gradually through a series of stages as well as being a subculture or set of cultures maintained by socialization and boundary negotiation.[14]

The proliferation of language describing various sexualities, such as lesbian, gay, bisexual, transgendered and transsexual (LGBTT), illustrates this development. Queer theory now has multiple meanings, from a useful shorthand way to speak of LGBTT experiences to a theoretical sensibility that stresses transgression and permanent rebellion.[15] Initially accepting traditional assumptions that homosexuality did not exist among African Americans, much queer theory reflected the thesis that all homosexuals are white. However, LGBTT people of color have challenged this white bias.

The new sexualities research enabled LGBTT black people to advance analyses that have unsettled long-standing notions concerning homosexuality and African Americans. For one, many LGBTT black people have criticized the extent and contours of homophobia within African American communities.[16] The interpersonal and political relationships between white and black LGBTT people constitute another theme that has received considerable attention.[17] Still other work has aimed to unseat the assumed whiteness of homosexuality by investigating how homosexuality existed in precolonial Africa and in other black societies in the African Diaspora.[18] In contesting the assumptions that black gays and lesbians have not existed within African American communities, historical and ethnographic work on black urban communities has helped to dispel these myths. Finally, 2000 marked the publication of the first national social science survey that investigated the attitude of LBGTT African Americans about marriage, employment, family, hate crimes, and other issues of concern.[19]

The increasing visibility of scholarship on blacks and homosexuality as well as that of black gay, lesbian, bisexual, transgendered, and transsexual people themselves has also had important implications for rethinking black gender ideology. By destigmatizing alternative sexualities and by challenging the normative assumptions of heterosexuality, queer theories created space for black gays and lesbians to criticize the core ideas of black gender ideology. For example, as Harlon Dalton contended, "My suspicion is that openly gay men and lesbians evoke hostility in part because they have come to symbolize the strong female and the weak male that slavery and Jim Crow produced ... . [L]esbians are seen as standing for the proposition that 'black men aren't worth shit.' More than even the 'no account' men who figure prominently in the repertoire of female blues singers, gay men symbolize the abandonment of black women. Thus, in the black community homosexuality carries more baggage than in the larger society."[20] Not only does Dalton's thesis unsettle notions of the assumed whiteness of homosexuality; his argument also links patterns of homophobia within African American communities to the broader gender ideology that affects all African Americans.

Collectively, the growth of black feminist theory, the emergence of new paradigms of masculinity within men's studies, and queer theory's contributions to new sexualities research changed the context for analyzing black masculinities. Within this context, several African American male and female scholars have begun serious investigations in search of new progressive black masculinities. Works by Kobena Mercer, Rudolph Byrd,

Beverly Guy-Sheftall, Devon Carbado, Michael Awkward, Kendall Thomas, and Marlon Riggs, among others, draw on this new interpretive context to challenge many of the assumptions that have guided former studies of black masculinity.[21] These new approaches search for fresh analyses of progressive black masculinities that are not predicated on anyone else's subordination. In other words, these new approaches aim to unpack the association of hegemonic masculinity, dominance, and strength, with an eye toward creating new definitions of black masculinity that can tell the difference between dominance and strength.

Hegemonic Masculinity, Dominance, and African American Men

Hegemonic Masculinity Defining Masculinities

In the United States, hegemonic masculinity is installed at the top of a hierarchical array of masculinities. All American men are evaluated by how closely they approximate the distinguishing features of a hegemonic masculinity situated at the top. Masculinity becomes organized as a three-tiered structure: those closest to hegemonic masculinity, predominantly wealthy white men—but not exclusively so—retain the most power on the top; those men who are situated just below have greater access to white male power yet remain marginalized; and those males who are subordinated by both of these groups occupy the bottom. Hegemonic masculinity requires these marginalized and subordinated masculinities. All masculinities, including those assigned to or defined by African American men, are evaluated by how closely they approximate dominant social norms.

Men from varying races, classes, and sexualities jockey for position within this hierarchy of masculinities. For example, like African American men, the vast majority of Latino and Asian American men are excluded from the category of hegemonic masculinity. Instead, they are assigned social scripts of marginalized masculinities, the former because of dedication to family and the latter due to representations of hard work and being a model minority. Latino and Asian American men who falter can be demoted to the subordinated masculinity reserved for African American men. Those who manage to approximate the norms of hegemonic masculinity may enter the inner circle, often as honorary white men. Not surprisingly, this hierarchy of successful and failed manhood matches up to the white normality–black deviancy framework that accompanies racism, to the heterosexual–homosexual binary that supports heterosexism, to structures of age that grant seniority to older males over younger ones, and to a class system that grants propertied individuals more power and status than those who lack it.

Hegemonic white masculinity is fundamentally a relational construct with boundaries defined through a series of oppositional relationships whereby normal masculinity becomes defined in opposition to women, gay men, poor and working-class men, boys, and black men.[22] In other words, hegemonic masculinity is a concept shaped by ideologies of gender, age, class, sexuality, and race. Ideas about groups formed within these ideologies, for example, women or LGBTT people, constitute an important benchmark for defining a hegemonic masculinity that must constantly construct itself. Without these groups as ideological markers, hegemonic masculinity becomes meaningless. Each of these groups serves as an important social group for constructing the ideas of hegemonic white masculinity as well as actual social practices of dominance that maintain power relations that privilege elite white men. As social groups, women, gay men, poor and working-class men, boys, and black men are socially stigmatized with a particular form of weakness that is juxtaposed to the seeming strengths of hegemonic white masculinity. Hegemonic masculinity reflects a cognitive framework of binary thinking that defines masculinity in terms of its difference from and dominance over multiple others. This dominance is the strength of hegemonic white masculinity.

Real Men Are Not Like Women   Under conditions of hegemonic white masculinity, because real men are primarily defined as not being like women, they are essential to constructions of masculinity based on strength, dominance, and control. Lacking allegedly female characteristics of passivity, emotionality, dependency, and submissiveness, real (i.e., white) men are forceful, analytical, responsible for women, and willing to exert authority over them, if not violence against them, when necessary. The oppositional use of women in the construction of masculinity is so widespread that it has become transparent. For example, boys on American sports teams are routinely ridiculed for playing like girls. A major insult hurled at men is that they are soft like women. Within this ideological framework, it is not enough simply to not be like women: Men must engage in certain types of relationships with women to know that they are real men. Women, however, can define their femininity without men, for example, as mothers and as caregivers in their families. Ironically, female dependency is typically seen as a desirable attribute for women, yet women's feminine identity does not depend on males staying in their place. Men, in contrast, require control and dominance over women—which takes many forms—to know that they are real men. Men placed in situations where they become too closely aligned with women or, worse yet, seem to be dominated by women suffer a loss of manhood. Such men are viewed as being emasculated or pussy whipped. The weak-men thesis of black-gender ideology clearly reflects the perception that African American men's seeming failure to control their women is a sign of weakness. Uncritical acceptance of dominant-gender ideology places African American men and women in an adversarial relationship where women who do not let men be men become blamed for black male behavior. Abusive men routinely blame their partners for their own violent behavior—if she had been more of a woman (i.e., submissive), she would have let him be more of a man (i.e., strength as domination).

Real Men Are Not Gay   Another important benchmark of constructing hegemonic white masculinity concerns the treatment of heterosexuality: Real men are also not gay or homosexual. Under hegemonic white masculinity, gay men mark the contradictions that plague male heterosexuality itself: Heterosexual men should only be sexually attracted to women. Avowedly heterosexual men belittle gay men because they see gay men as being like women. In particular, gay men submit to the sexual advances of other men and are penetrated like women, sexual practices that lead heterosexual men to stereotype gay men as sissies, faggots, or effeminate men. Connell provided some insight as to why this is the case: "In the dynamics of hegemony in contemporary Western masculinity, the relation between heterosexual and homosexual men is central, carrying a heavy symbolic freight. To many people, homosexuality is a negation of masculinity, and homosexual men must be (therefore) effeminate."[23] Black gay men are routinely stereotyped as effeminate and weak, even though the majority of black gay men do not fit this profile. Despite this fact, African American perceptions of homosexuality often see it as a sign of weakness within individual black men. Ron Simmons summarized some the arguments given by many African American intellectuals and community leaders for the presence of homosexuality. One explanation is that the emasculation of black men by white oppression allegedly causes homosexuality. Gay black men are those who were conquered by real white men. Another argument points to the breakdown of the black family structure and loss of male role models as fostering weak men, some of whom turn to homosexuality. Another explanation suggests that homosexuality in the black community is a sinister plot by white racists as a form of population genocide—gay black men do not reproduce under this scenario.[24] In this context, heterosexual African American men may hesitate to align themselves too closely with gay black men for fear of being stigmatized as homosexuals.

Real Men Are Not Poor   Maintaining middle- and upper-class status constitutes yet another benchmark for constructing hegemonic white masculinity. In this scenario, real men are not dependent on others but rather are financially independent to the point where they can support others. They take responsibility for their families by getting married, going to work, and providing a home for their wives and children. In addition, this dimension of hegemonic white masculinity demonstrates how white male dominance in the public sphere of the political economy articulates with male dominance in the private sphere of family. Under the tenets of hegemonic white masculinity, middle- and upper-class white men should be in charge and in control both in the context of their families and in work. They not only direct and provide for their families as a signal of independence rather than dependence but also direct their families and others in the workplace. In contrast to the depiction of elite white men, unemployed and underemployed poor men, regardless of race, are often depicted as lazy even where jobs and job training are unavailable. Further, such men are also portrayed as sexual renegades who run from one woman to another. African American men bear the brunt of this stereotyping of poor men who lack financial means. Within mass media, black men are frequently depicted as pimps and hustlers who live off women or other family members. Black men without money are routinely depicted as irresponsible, with the number of children they father with their unmarried partners often used as evidence for their sexual irresponsibility and refusal to grow up.[25]

Real Men Are Not Boys Boys constitute yet another benchmark used to construct hegemonic white masculinity. Real men do not resemble or behave like boys, namely, immature and irresponsible males who have not yet been properly socialized. Possessing an adult male body constitutes one important factor that distinguishes boys from men. Adult males have facial and body hair and are physically muscular. In contrast, boys lack body hair and are physically weaker—they are quasi-women. When it comes to sexuality, boys are virgins. The fact that they have not yet penetrated a woman signals that they remain unfamiliar with this form of potential dominance over women. In fact, the absence of heterosexual sexual activity means that boys lack a sexual identity, a prerequisite for hegemonic white masculinity. They are rendered premasculine. Economically, boys are normally unemployed and are not expected to support themselves or others. Moreover, just as subordinated men must submit to hegemonic white masculinity, boys are expected to submit to adult male authority—most notably, their fathers. Ironically, holding fast to boyhood may be one way that some African American men gain protection from the harsh penalties that affect adult black men. Because young black men learn early on that the standards applied to them differ from those applied to everyone else, becoming adults may place them in danger. Marita Golden described her fear for her son Michael growing up in Washington, D.C.: "[M]y son careened into adolescence. I heard the deepening of Michael's voice, witnessed the growth spurts that propelled him to a height that echoed his father's, saw the sudden appearance of muscles … . I was flushed with trepidation. Soon Michael would inhabit that narrow, corrupt crawl space in the minds of whites and some black people too, a space reserved for criminals, outcasts, misfits, and black men. Soon he would become a permanent suspect."[26] Golden knew that her son had to leave boyhood behind, but she saw all too clearly the costs of doing so.

Real Men Are Not Black Finally, race is an important benchmark in constructing hegemonic white masculinity in the United States. Within American society, black men as a group, by definition, are denied the full entitlements of hegemonic white masculinity because they are black. The fact of blackness excludes black men from participating in hegemonic masculinity because, if they do so, they decenter the assumed whiteness of those installed in the center of the definition itself. The best that black men can do is to achieve an honorary place bestowed on them by white men. If the very definition of masculinity is predicated on the subordination of the vast majority of black men, then it becomes extremely difficult to become an adult black man without grappling with the profound contradictions of this system of American masculinity. In essence, African American men's threat to elite white male power arises not simply from a perceived racial difference but also from the potential for gender equality among men. In other words, differences among men must be maintained or hierarchies of race, class, and sexuality all fail.

Summary   Within this context, varying combinations of remaining unpartnered with a woman, of rejecting heterosexuality, of being unemployed or living in poverty, of being a nonadult male, or being socially classified as black become the criteria for attributing marginalized and subordinated masculinities to racial, ethnic, working-class, and gay men. Depending on where males are placed along the continuum, they encounter variations of marginalized and subordinated masculinities. Dominant-gender ideology reflects a combination of these benchmarks that have been repackaged as representations or controlling images routinely applied to different groups of men. Here distinctions among men of color make them less manly in very distinctive ways. Relegated to the very bottom of hierarchies of masculinity, perceptions of black masculinity in America signal deviancy and thus provide important examples of what not to be. African American men find themselves between a rock and a hard place of being unable to achieve masculinity within the standards reserved for white men and of resisting the forms of black masculinity offered to them by those same white men. Overall, ideas about white masculine strength remain normative to the point where black men must struggle to claim legitimate space as men. Moreover, alternative ideas about black masculinity advanced within black male groups and within African American communities may further complicate this nexus of meanings of black masculinity. Competing definitions of black masculinity—some defined by white men, others by black men, and still others in terms of African American community norms—all coalesce in a value system that may create conflict for individual African American men.[27]

Dominance and Its Consequences for African American Men

Developing progressive black masculinities thus requires rejecting not simply the narrow representational spaces reserved for black men within American culture but the entire structure of masculinity predicated on dominance. Clearly, the current system has negative consequences for large numbers of African American men. Moving toward new definitions requires rethinking the connections between strength and dominance.

Not only is black masculinity typically represented as the opposite of hegemonic white masculinity; American characterizations of manhood also define masculinity in terms of physical, sexual, and economic dominance. Dominance constitutes a defining feature of American society overall, yet when it comes to definitions of masculinity, strength and dominance are closely intertwined. Regardless of race, class, sexuality, or citizenship status, ideas about physical, sexual, and economic dominance pervade both the social institutions that regulate male behavior as well as representations of masculinity created by those very same institutions. Within this overarching framework, African American men encounter a narrow set of representations of black masculinity that also encourage them to define black masculinity in terms of black male dominance. Across differences of social class, sexuality, age, and ethnicity African American men confront, contest, and capitulate to a constellation of masculinities grounded in concepts of dominance.

Physical Dominance   Physical dominance, aggressiveness, and the use of violence to maintain male power constitute a central feature in definitions of hegemonic white masculinity that African American men must confront in crafting progressive black masculinities. The value placed on physical dominance has significant implications for African American men who find themselves boxed in by ideas of subordinated black masculinities. In a climate that defines aggressiveness and the use of violence as important markers of masculinity, women, gay men, and boys are seen as lacking aggression or the willingness or ability to use violence effectively. These traits have been interpreted as inherent to their seemingly effeminate or soft natures. Stated differently, black male violence against women, against gay men of all races, and among themselves constitutes a triad of aggressive behavior that takes on added importance for African American men whose power within the broader political economy remains compromised. At the same time, black men's adoption of violence as evidence of strength harms them and others. All men are expected to be in control, to the point of using violence, yet men's access to the apparatuses of violence differs depending on their race and social-class classifications.[28] For example, elite white men run the army and the police forces—they have the authority to manage the legitimate use of force while not appearing to be violent at all. White males also control forms of structured violence, as in sports, which is as an arena for symbolic violence within American society. In contrast, working-class and poor black men have access to street weapons, and many use their own bodies as weapons.

The media is culpable in constructing different texts of physical dominance that alternately celebrate or demonize the physicality attributed to black men. In some cases, the physical strength and aggressiveness thought to reside in black men's bodies generate admiration, whereas in others these qualities garner fear. On the one hand, the bodies of athletes and models are admired, are viewed as entertaining, and are used to sell a variety of products. For example, Keith Harrison, an African American male model for the Polo clothing line, never speaks but symbolizes a black male body that should be admired. Similarly, the hip-hop magazine *Vibe* relies heavily on black male models and athletes to sell gym shoes, clothes, CDs, and other trappings of hip-hop culture. African American professional athletes reveal varying degrees of acceptance and rejection within a mass media that constructs black men by their physicality and then markets images of boxers, basketball players, and football linemen—less so, quarterbacks—to a seemingly insatiable public.

On the other hand, the image of the feared black male body also reappears across entertainment, advertisement, and news. Mass-media marketing of thug life to African American youth diverts attention away from social policies that deny black youth education and jobs. It also seems designed to scare whites and African Americans alike into thinking that racial integration of seemingly poor and working-class black boys—the allegedly authentic blacks—is dangerous. Black men who have seen purse-clutching white women cross the street on catching sight of them know that their physical presence can be enough to invoke fear, regardless of their actions and intentions. This reaction to black men's bodies emboldens police to stop motorists in search of drugs and to command black youth to "assume the position" for random street searches. Racial profiling is based on this very premise—the potential threat of physical dominance and violence caused by African American men's bodies. Across the spectrum of admiration and fear, the bodies of black men are what matters.

Black men who understand black masculinity through the lens of physical dominance often demand respect from those they see as being weak. For example, in his important work *Code of the Street,* sociologist Elijah Anderson was "concerned with why it is that so many inner-city young people are inclined to commit aggression and violence toward one another."[29] Anderson found that in some of the most economically depressed urban neighborhoods, rules of civil law had been replaced among young black men with a set of informal rules of behavior organized around a desperate search for respect. Respect—and the credible threat of vengeance—became highly valued for shielding ordinary young African American men from the interpersonal violence of the street. As Anderson pointed out, "The code of the street emerges where the influence of the police ends and personal responsibility for one's safety is felt to begin, resulting in a kind of 'people's law,' based on 'street justice' … . In service to this ethic, repeated displays of 'nerve' and 'heart' build or reinforce a credible reputation for vengeance that works to deter aggression and disrespect, which are sources of great anxiety on the inner-city street."[30]

Ironically, this commitment to physical dominance, to being tough, and to adhering to the code of the street can disconnect black men from family networks, all in the name of saving black male pride. Despite the fact that families headed by black women are not inherently inferior, the absence of men in the lives of their children constitutes a real loss for African American families. Male children may express this loss more forcefully, at least in the media, but its effects are profound for girls as well. The meaning of an absent father for black boys in particular circulates throughout black popular culture. From the television show *Good Times*, through works as disparate as the choreography of Bill T. Jones, to the music of Tupac Shakur, African American men comment on the pain that many feel at their inability to be fathers to their own children—beyond biological coupling—and of not having had fathers of their own when they were young. Those who cannot challenge dominant ideas about masculinity remain trapped in a derogated space of irresponsible deadbeat dads. Only by rejecting prevailing social norms can black men start the process of healing from the damage done to them.[31]

Sexual Dominance Sexual dominance constitutes another important component of hegemonic white masculinity that black men must rethink in crafting progressive black masculinities. In constructing a hierarchy of sexual dominance and subordination, the sexual practices attributed to women, gay men, working-class men, and boys become interrelated benchmarks for defining masculinity. "Heterosexual masculinity did not predate homophobia but instead was historically produced along with it."[32] In this context of male dominance, women are derogated because they are soft, weak, and can be penetrated or fucked. The dual meaning of the term *fuck* speaks to the fusion of sexuality and violence in constructing normative white masculinity. By internalizing notions of dominant masculinity, black men can harm themselves and others. In a context that denies African American men access to wealth and power, the physical dominance of having strong and athletic bodies as well as sexual dominance associated with the phallus become especially important. James Baldwin was one of the first authors to grapple with the significance of the penis to black masculinity and within a society that uncritically accepts the tenets of hegemonic white masculinity. Baldwin noted the ways in which an image of black men as walking phalluses minimizes their humanity while also serving as a justification for limiting their potential: "I think that I know something about the American masculinity which most men of my generation do not know because they have not been menaced by it in the way that I have been. It is still true, alas, that to be an American Negro male is also to be a kind of walking phallic symbol: which means that one pays, in one's own personality, for the sexual insecurity of others."[33]

This theme of reducing black men to the penis reappears in contemporary popular culture, high and low. For example, Kobena Mercer claimed that the photographs of renowned photographer Robert Mapplethorpe invoke this deep taproot of black sexual prowess created within Western imaginations.[34] Mapplethorpe's exhibitions often raised controversy primarily due to the depiction of gay sadomasochistic rituals and of nude black male bodies. Mercer noted that the photographs of gay male sadomasochistic rituals invoke a subcultural sexuality that consists of doing something. In contrast, black men are "confined and defined by their very *being* as sexual and nothing but sexual, hence hypersexual."[35] Mapplethorpe's *Man in Polyester Suit* is especially exemplary in that the photograph eliminates all identifying features of masculinity except hands (objects to service whites) and an exposed black penis (sexuality).[36] The image, which is a commodity, reduces a black male body to a fragmented body resembling the commodification of black women's bodies under chattel slavery.[37]

Gail Dines analyzed the treatment of black men in *Hustler* magazine, a popular pornographic periodical whose primary readership consists of working-class white men. Dines argued that movies and magazines featuring black men focus on two categories of the black male body: the size of the black penis and the alleged insatiable sexual appetite black men have for white women. Searching for a similar pattern in *Hustler*, Dines found that black men were most often depicted in cartoons as caricatures and that the humor centered on the size and deployment of the black male penis. Using the depiction of King Kong as a frame of reference, Dines observed, "While the original Kong was lacking a penis, the Hustler version has as his main characteristic, a huge black penis that is often wrapped around the "man's" neck or is sticking out of his trouser leg. The penis, whether erect or limp, visually dominates the cartoon and is the focus of humor. This huge penis is depicted as a source of great pride and as a feature which distinguishes black men from white men."[38] In this sense, the penis becomes the defining feature of black men that contributes yet another piece to the commodification of black male bodies.[39] Though black men's humanity is minimized by this image, their embrace of it also has significant cost for them and the community.

The association of masculinity and sexual dominance also is constructed through black men's perceptions of gay sexuality. The growth of prison culture in the 1980s seemingly has had an important influence on African American social organization, especially black youth culture. In particular, the arrest and imprisonment of black street gangs in the 1970s and 1980s led to organized gang structures within prisons. Prison gangs inevitably became connected to their street gang counterparts; in fact, many join gangs while in prison, primarily for protection. As the line between street gangs and prison gangs blurred, so did the distinctions among prison culture, street culture, and youth culture. With record-high numbers of African American men incarcerated, consensual and forced sexual contact among men in prison has become more common.[40] Many of these men are eventually released from prison.

Within this context, the presence of sexual relations between males does not automatically construct both men as homosexuals. Rather, dominance matters. Men who are treated as if they were women—that is, by submitting to the sexual advances of other men and being orally or anally penetrated—are feminized and become less manly men, their masculinity severed, equated with castration. They are transformed into girls (i.e., lacking a penis), sissies, or faggots by engaging in sexual acts reserved for women—being penetrated—or having an immature or small penis like that of a prepubescent boy. In contrast, men who penetrate and who are on top retain their heterosexuality. In fact, their masculinity may be enhanced by a hyperheterosexuality proven through sexually dominating men. Within popular culture, basketball star Dennis Rodman exercises this kind of hyperheterosexual dominance by wearing a wedding dress, by dying his hair blonde, and by appearing in women's clothes without anyone accusing him of being like a girl or a sissy. There are several outcomes of this association. For one, it minimizes, excludes, and limits the lives of gay men and their possible contributions to the community as a whole. Further, it limits possibilities of brotherhood across sexuality. In addition, this vision seems to reinforce notions of sexuality as violence, dominance through penetration. This hurts women and men. And finally, with each of these areas, black male acceptance, internalization, and complicity reinforce the larger system that subordinates them.

Political and Economic Domination   Dominance in the political economy constitutes another feature of masculinity in the United States that affects the prospects for developing progressive black masculinities. During the post-civil rights era, poor and working-class African American men experienced growing rates of permanent unemployment and underemployment that made it even more difficult to bring home a family wage. Many African American men work in the informal labor market, primarily the global drug industry, as an alternative to employment in the formal labor market. Many have prison records as convicted felons, a stigma that disqualifies black men from the franchise and thus precludes many men from invoking their voting rights as citizens to change labor laws and criminal justice procedures.[41] The convergence of these factors renders African American men less able to contribute financial support to their families. As a result, black men can be viewed as irresponsible boys who do not fulfill their obligations as men whereas white men are real men because they do. When combined, the strong black women–weak black men thesis and the strong white men–weak black men thesis counsel black men to embrace unrealistic strategies for dealing with the economic exploitation and political disempowerment of dominance. Confronted with a barrage of images that depict black men as lazy, irresponsible boys who are unwilling to or unsuitable for work and that counsel men to look for work, it becomes hard to see how difficult it is actually to find good jobs.[42] In the context of globalization characterized by job flight, mechanization, and downsizing, and punitive domestic social welfare policies that leave black boys and men in poor schools and with bad housing, poor opportunities and prison records, economic dominance as modeled by elite white men seems a distant dream.

African American men, women, and children as well as broader American society currently pay a tremendous price when African American men resist being relegated to a space of weakness through shows of physical, sexual, or economic dominance. Black men who uncritically accept definitions of masculinity grounded in dominance can cause harm to others as well as to themselves. Domestic violence, incest, child abuse, broken homes, rape, and hate crimes against LGBTT black people all stem in some fashion from ideas about masculinity and assumptions of male dominance.

African American men pay a high price for confusing dominance with strength because they are always on display, with any sign of letting down one's guard misinterpreted as a sign of weakness. Novelist John Edgar Wideman described the price he paid in coping with the pressures of constant surveillance:

Coming home from the university, from people and situations that continually set me against them and against myself, I was a dangerous person. If I wanted to stay in one piece and stay in school, I was forced to pull my punches. To maintain any semblance of dignity and confidence I had to learn to construct a shell around myself. Be cool. Work on appearing dignified, confident. Fool people with appearances, surfaces, live my real life underground in a region where no one could touch me. The trouble with this survival mechanism was the time and energy expended on upkeep of the shell. The brighter, harder, more convincing and impenetrable the shell became, the more I lost touch with the inner sanctuary where I was supposed to be hiding. It was no more accessible to me than it was to the people I intended to keep out. Inside was a breeding ground for rage, hate, and dreams of vengeance.[43]

Wideman's struggles point to the destructive costs to men themselves, and to those who love them, of not being able to uncouple strength from dominance in defining black masculinity.

Telling the Difference: Dominance, Strength, and Progressive Black Masculinities

Black men do immense damage to themselves, to women, and to children, all under the banner of protecting their manhood. The need to tell the difference between strength and dominance in defining progressive black masculinities raises several interrelated questions: How might African American men craft progressive black masculinities that are not predicated on the dominance and exploitation of others? How might progressive black masculinities not grounded in dominance help African American men develop affirming social relations with their sexual partners, with their parents, siblings, and children, and with one another? What specific strategies might help African American men redefine notions of strength within progressive black masculinities?

Moving forward by redefining strength to develop progressive black masculinities requires meeting two fundamental challenges. First, black men must learn to recognize and to relinquish privileges, both real and imagined, gained through domination—in particular, the benefits and costs attached to sexism and heterosexism. Relinquishing benefits of dominance is difficult because it inevitably fosters marginalization and alienation from those very groups that long served as places of belonging. As one black male feminist pointed out, "Like black women feminists advocating against racism, black men supporting women against sexism find ourselves on the margins of both black liberation and women's movements."[44] Similarly, because masculinity is so heavily reliant on heterosexism for meaning, black men may also be hard pressed to relinquish the benefits they gain under heterosexism as a system of power. As Carbado pointed out:

> Heterosexual privilege is one of the few privileges that straight Black men *know* they have—not being a "sissy, punk, faggot." This is not to say, of course, that Black male heterosexuality has the normative standing of White male heterosexuality. It does not; straight Black men continue to be perceived as heterosexually deviant (potential rapists of White women) and heterosexually irresponsible (jobless fathers of children born out of wedlock). Still, Black heterosexuality is closer to White male heterosexual normalcy and normativity than is Black gay sexuality. And many straight (or closeted) Black men will want to avoid even the suspicion of homosexuality ... . Challenging heterosexual privilege creates (homo)sexual identity suspicion.[45]

Rejecting the seductive privileges offered by prevailing ideas about masculinity constitutes a complex project for African American men. Yet giving up the seeming benefits of sexism and heterosexism would establish much-needed space to do something else. Relinquishing privilege may initially seem like a loss, but by refusing to subordinate others black men would potentially gain new allies and new relationships. For example, black men who struggle to relinquish the seeming benefits they gain under sexism might come to see black women as equals and partners. Why try to dominate someone whom you accept as your equal? A strong black woman would no longer be a threat to a black man who need not worry whether he can measure up. Similarly, black men secure in their sexual identities as heterosexuals would have little need to worry about everyone else's sexual orientation.

A second challenge in developing progressive black masculinities concerns incorporating an ethic of personal accountability in relation to women, children, parents, siblings, and one another. Black men must rejoin black families and communities and reject the dual theses of strong women–weak men and strong men–weak men that currently box them in. Despite the deeply embedded nature of social scripts about black masculinity within American culture, African American men need not accept them. Although it is important to remember that historical patterns of black sexual politics provide the overarching context for black men's behavior, each individual African American man is responsible for his actions and the choices he makes in everyday life.

Personal accountability to self and others means rejecting the negative outcomes of the weakness thesis and redefining black male strength in terms of relationships with others. For example, black men's inability to find well-paying work that would allow them to support their families encourages far too many to leave. Yet economic contributions to a family's well-being can take many forms that go beyond bringing home a big paycheck. Black men may be saving their pride by avoiding the seeming stigma of weakness attributed to men who cannot support their families, but the children and female partners they leave behind sorely miss them. Definitions of masculinity that would enable black men to see their worth in more than a steady paycheck would create space for new ideas for black male strength. Weak black men may actually be those who desert their families, as opposed to the strong ones who stay, even if they cannot earn a living wage.

New definitions of black masculinity grounded in the strength of commitment to families, communities, or social justice principles might create space for black men to redefine black male strength in affirming ways. Rejecting views of black masculinity grounded in dominance would enable black men to question troublesome behavior by themselves and others that hurts black women, black children, and each other. Patterns of troublesome behavior can range from the seemingly benign to the dangerous. For example, many black men have great difficulty even seeing issues that are important to black women, let alone showing support for black women or taking action in regard to these issues. As Carbado pointed out, "Men are systematically conditioned not even to notice what women want."[46] Not seeing the women in their lives as equals fosters a range of behaviors, from ignoring women to hitting them.

Overall, new definitions of progressive black masculinities can only be as effective as each individual black man allows them to be in his everyday life. African American men can reject dominance masquerading as strength by engaging in loving, committed, honest relationships with their partners, children, parents, neighbors, and friends. Many men already do so, yet their behaviors are not routinely celebrated or even recognized. Take, for example, asha bandele's rendering, in her memoir *The Prisoner's Wife*, of her husband, Rashid's, perceptions of new definitions of black manhood:

> I think you deserve a man who isn't afraid of you, and who isn't afraid of
> everything that brought you pain, and who will face that pain with you,
> no matter how ugly it is. You deserve a man who knows how to make you

laugh, asha. You deserve a man who will tell you when you're wrong, and who will listen when you tell him he's wrong, and a man who is going to be just as open as you are, and just as free with his thoughts as you are, and just as willing to struggle with himself as you are. And a man who wants to make the world a better place as much as you want to make it a better place. You deserve a man who loves your poems, and who wants to hear you read them again and again and again. You deserve a man who's not afraid of being passionate, and who loves to kiss all of you, not just your mouth, but all down your back, on the bottom of your feet. You deserve a man who wants to cook for you, and raise babies with you, and be old and tired with you. And I think that these things are the least of what you deserve. What you deserve is a man who will always protect you. Protect you with his life if he has to.[47]

Rashid's words may not seem like the radical change envisioned by the call to develop progressive black masculinities, but his words provide an important starting point. Rashid has no privilege to reject and decides to be personally accountable for himself in the context of his partnership with his loved one. In the space of prison where domination is so clear, he strives for a new source of black masculine strength.

Notes

1. Sex role theory has generated considerable critique. Michael Messner summarized five common problems with sex role theory: (1) it focuses on individualistic, voluntary levels of analysis and minimizes institutional power relations; (2) it implies a false symmetry between men and women that masks gender oppression; (3) it normalizes the male sex role and measures deviance from a falsely universalized—that is, middle-class, white, and heterosexual—norm; (4) it relies on binary ideas about gender that reify biological notions of male and female sex categories; and (5) it fails to explain changes in gender ideology, especially resistance. Messner, "The Limits of 'The Male Sex Role': An Analysis of the Men's Liberation and Men's Rights Movements' Discourse," *Gender & Society* 12, no. 3 (1998), 258. Messner pointed out that sociologists do not use the terms race roles or class roles when describing other social inequalities: "We may speak of race or class *identities*, but we do so within the context of an understanding of the historical dynamics of race and class *relations*." Ibid., italics in original. R. W. Connell offered a comparable critique: "The conceptualization of gender through role theory ... reifies expectations and self-descriptions, exaggerates consensus, marginalized questions of power, and cannot analyze historical change." Connell, "A Very Straight Gay: Masculinity, Homosexual Experience, and the Dynamics of Gender," *American Sociological Review* 57, no. 6 (1992), 735. By the 1980s, a more historicized and politicized language of gender relations virtually supplanted the language of sex role theory within sociology, although not within psychology, education, social work, and other disciplines.
2. A series of research projects implicitly took up this theme of black male disadvantage within the domestic sphere as a fundamental problem. For example, William Julius Wilson's incisive ethnographic work on African American inner-city neighborhoods stressed male disadvantage in urban labor markets as the source of problems within black American communities. Wilson, *When Work Disappears: The World of the New Urban Poor* (New York: Knopf, 1996). Wilson is certainly right, but at the same time little mention is made of female disadvantage. For other work in this tradition, see Noel Cazenave, "Race, Socioeconomic Status, and Age: The Social Context of American Masculinity," *Sex Roles* 11 (1984), 639–56; Clyde W. Franklin II, "Surviving the Institutional Decimation of

Black Males: Causes, Consequences, and Intervention," in *The Making of Masculinities: The New Men's Studies*, ed. Harry Brod (Boston: Allen & Unwin, 1987), 155–69; Andrea G. Hunter and James E. Davis, "An Exploration of Afro-American Men's Conceptualization of Manhood," *Gender & Society* 6 (1992), 464–79; and Hunter and Davis, "Hidden Voices of Black Men: The Meaning, Structure, and Complexity of Manhood," *Journal of Black Studies* 25 (1994), 204–40.

3. For classic works, see Audre Lorde, *Sister Outsider: Essays and Speeches* (Freedom, CA: Crossing Press, 1984); Combahee River Collection, "A Black Feminist Statement," in *But Some of Us Are Brave*, ed. Gloria T. Hull, Patricia Bell Scott, and Barbara Smith (Old Westbury, NY: Feminist Press, 1982); Pauli Murray, "The Liberation of Black Women," *Voices of the New Feminism* 10, no. 2 (1970); and Toni Cade, ed., *The Black Woman: An Anthology* (New York: Mentor, 1970).

4. Patricia Hill Collins, *Black Feminist Thought: Knowledge, Consciousness, and the Politics of Empowerment* (New York: Routledge, 2000), 3–26.

5. For a comprehensive treatment of the core themes of black feminism, see ibid., 45–226.

6. For a good example of African American men's reactions, see Robert Staples, "The Myth of Black Macho: A Response to Angry Black Feminists," *Black Scholar* 10, no. 6 (1979).

7. *How Capitalism Underdeveloped Black America* (Boston: South End Press), 69–104.

8. Franklin's early work clearly broke from his black male counterparts. See Franklin, "Black Male-Black Female Conflict. Individually Caused and Culturally Nurtured," *Journal of Black Studies* 15, no. 2 (1984), 139–154. For representative work on black men, see Franklin, "Surviving the Institutional Decimation of Black Males: Causes, Consequences, and Intervention," *The Making of Masculinities* (Boston: Allen & Urwin, 1987). For representative works, see Manning Marable, *How Capitalism Underdeveloped Black America: Problems in Race, Political Economy, and Society* (Boston: South End Press, 1983), ch. 3, 69–104; Michael Awkward, "A Black Man's Place(s) in Black Feminist Criticism," in *Representing Black Men*, ed. Marcellus Blount and George P. Cunningham (New York: Routledge, 1996); and Robin D. G. Kelley, *Freedom Dreams: The Black Radical Imagination* (Boston: Beacon, 2002), 135–56.

9. Connell, "Very Straight Gay," 736.

10. Messner, "When Bodies Are Weapons: Masculinity and Violence in Sport," *International Review for the Sociology of Sport* 25 (1990), 205.

11. Margaret Wetherell and Nigel Edley, "Negotiating Hegemonic Masculinity: Imaginary Positions and Psycho-Discursive Practices," *Feminism & Psychology* 9, no. 3 (1999), 335–56, esp. 336.

12. Connell, *Masculinities* (Cambridge: Polity Press, 1995).

13. Connell, "Very Straight Gay"; Connell, *Masculinities*.

14. Connell, "Very Straight Gay"; Steven Seidman, "Introduction," *Queer Theory/Sociology*, ed. Seidman (Cambridge, MA: Blackwell, 1996), 1–30; Connell, *Masculinities*; Seidman, *Beyond the Closet: The Transformation of Gay and Lesbian Life* (New York: Routledge, 2002).

15. Seidman, "Introduction," 11.

16. Delroy Constantine-Simms, ed., *The Greatest Taboo: Homosexuality in Black Communities* (New York: Alyson Books, 2000); Cathy J. Cohen and Tamara Jones, "Fighting Homophobia versus Challenging Heterosexism: 'The Failure to Transform' Revisited," in *Dangerous Liaisons: Blacks, Gays, and the Struggle for Equality*, ed. Eric Brandt (New York: New Press, 1999), 80–101.

17. Brandt, *Dangerous Liaisons*, esp. Barbara Smith, "Blacks and Gays: Healing the Great Divide," 15–24; Cohen and Jones, "Fighting Homophobia."

18. Gloria Wekker, "*Mati*-ism and Black Lesbianism: Two Ideal Typical Expressions of Female Homosexuality in Black Communities of Diaspora," in Constantine-Simms, *Greatest Taboo*, 149–62; and Cary Alan Johnson, "Hearing Voices: Unearthing Evidence of Homosexuality in Precolonial Africa," in Constantine-Simms, *Greatest Taboo*, 132–48.

19. Juan Battle and others, *Say It Loud, I'm Black and I'm Proud: Black Pride Survey 2000* (New York: Policy Institute of the National Gay and Lesbian Task Force, 2002).

20. Harlon L. Dalton, "AIDS in Blackface," in *Black Men on Race, Gender, and Sexuality*, ed. Devon W. Carbado (New York: New York University Press, 1999), 333.

21. Awkward, "A Black Man's Place(s)"; Carbado, *Black Men,* esp. Awkward, "'You're Turning Me On': The Boxer, the Beauty Queen, and the Rituals of Gender," 128–46; and Marlon T. Riggs, "Black Macho Revisited: Reflections of a SNAP! Queen," 306–11; Kobena Mercer, *Welcome to the Jungle: New Positions in Black Cultural Studies* (New York: Routledge, 1994); Kendall Thomas, "'Ain't Nothin' Like the Real Thing': Black Masculinity, Gay Sexuality, and the Jargon of Authenticity," in *Representing Black Men,* ed. Marcellus Blount and George P. Cunningham (New York: Routledge, 1996), 55–72; Rudolph P. Byrd and Beverly Guy-Sheftall, eds., *Traps: African American Men on Gender and Sexuality* (Bloomington: Indiana University Press, 2001); and Johnetta B. Cole and Guy-Sheftall, *Gender Talk: The Struggle for Women's Equality in African American Communities* (New York: Ballantine, 2003).
22. Michael S. Kimmel, "Masculinity as Homophobia: Fear Shame, and Silence in the Construction of Gender Identity," in *Men and Masculinity: A Text Reader,* ed. Theodore F. Cohen (Belmont, CA: Wadsworth Thomson Learning, 2001), 29–41.
23. Connell, "Very Straight Gay."
24. Ron Simmons, "Some Thoughts on the Challenges Facing Black Gay Intellectuals," in *Brother to Brother: New Writings by Black Gay Men,* ed. Essex Hemphill (Boston: Alyson Publications, 1991), 211–28.
25. The treatment of poor and working-class men on television talk shows illustrates how this ideology is constructed within mass media. For a comprehensive analysis, see Collins, *Black Sexual Politics: African Americans, Gender, and the New Racism* (New York: Routledge, 2004).
26. Marita Golden, *Saving Our Sons: Raising Black Children in a Turbulent World* (New York: Doubleday, 1995), 68.
27. Jay C. Wade, "African American Men's Gender Role Conflict: The Significance of Racial Identity," *Sex Roles: A Journal of Research* 34, nos. 1–2 (1996), 17.
28. As Messner pointed out, "[T]o suggest that violence is an essential feature of maleness [is inaccurate] … . Most males are not comfortable committing acts of violence. … Violent behavior is learned behavior, and some men learn it better than others." Messner, "When Bodies Are Weapons," 205.
29. Elijah Anderson, *Code of the Street: Decency, Violence, and the Moral Life of the Inner City* (New York: W. W. Norton, 1999), 9.
30. Ibid., 10.
31. Mark Anthony Neal, *Soul Babies: Black Popular Culture and the Post-Soul Aesthetic* (New York: Routledge, 2002), 68.
32. Connell, "Very Straight Gay," 736.
33. James Baldwin, *Nobody Knows My Name* (New York: Vintage, 1993), 217.
34. Mercer, *Welcome to the Jungle,* 171–220.
35. Ibid., 174.
36. Ibid., 186.
37. Barbara Omolade, *The Rising Song of African American Women* (New York: Routledge, 1994), 7.
38. Gail Dines, "King Kong and the White Woman: Hustler Magazine and the Demonization of Black Masculinity," *Violence against Women* 4, no. 3 (June 1998), 294.
39. Sexual prowess is only one characteristic way of measuring a black male sexual dominance that is so important to constructions of black masculinity. Black men's ability to father children—but not to support them—constitutes another characteristic of social constructions of black male sexual prowess.
40. Joanne Mariner, *No Escape: Male Rape in U.S. Prisons* (New York: Human Rights Watch, 2001); Teresa A. Miller, "Sex and Surveillance: Gender, Privacy and the Sexualization of Prison," *George Mason University Civil Rights Law Journal* 10, no. 2 (2000), 291–356; and William F. Pinar, *The Gender of Racial Politics and Violence in America: Lynching, Prison Rape, and the Crisis of Masculinity* (New York: P. Lang, 2001).
41. John O. Calmore, "Race-Conscious Voting Rights and the New Demography in a Multi-racing America," *North Carolina Law Review* 79, no. 5 (2001).
42. For discussions of how the global economy has affected the status of black men as workers, see Wilson, *When Work Disappears*; and Wilson, *The Truly Disadvantaged: The Inner City, the Underclass, and Public Policy* (Chicago: University of Chicago Press, 1987).

43. John Edgar Wideman, *Brothers and Keepers* (New York: Penguin, 1984), 32.

44. Gary L. Lemons, "To Be Black, Male and 'Feminist'—Making Womanist Space for Black Men," *International Journal of Sociology and Social Policy* 1, no. 2 (1997), 45.

45. Carbado, "Epilogue: Straight Out of the Closet: Men, Feminism, and Male Heterosexual Privilege," in Carbado, *Black Men*, 431.

46. Wilson, *When Work Disappears*; Wilson, *Truly Disadvantaged*; and Carbado, "Epilogue," 420.

47. asha bandele, *The Prisoner's Wife: A Memoir* (New York: Scribner, 1999), 112.

Part 3
Christianity: Progressive Interpretations?

PART 3
Cultural and Linguistic Diversity: Perspectives

6

Images of Masculinity in the Pauline Epistles: Resources for Constructing Progressive Black Masculinities, or Not?

GAY L. BYRON

Introduction

I find myself resisting popular notions of black masculinity ... . We're faced with redefining what masculinity is. We're faced with constructing a masculinity for all of us, one that will be useful as opposed to disempowering ... . We need a masculinity that brings us more into contact with one another. A masculinity that is intimate and humane.

Essex Hemphill[1]

There is no longer Jew or Greek, there is no longer slave or free, there is no longer male and female; for all of you are one in Christ Jesus.

The Apostle Paul[2]

Poet Essex Hemphill and Paul the apostle on the surface have little in common. Seldom, if ever, would these two men appear together in discussions about masculinity. Yet Paul and Hemphill both point to the goals and challenges involved in understanding the complex roles and symbolic representations of masculinity in early Christian writings. More specifically, Paul and Hemphill read together call attention to the nexus among black identity, masculinity, and the Bible.

The purpose of this chapter is to provide a brief survey of the New Testament Pauline epistles as a springboard for raising questions about the ways these letters might function in the task of constructing progressive black masculinities.[3] I choose to explore representations of masculinity through an analysis of the Pauline Epistles in part because these writings have had a pervasive influence over Protestant and Catholic church leaders as they define and emulate models of masculinity and continue to wield unlimited authority over many interpreters of the Bible. More importantly, however, I focus on the Pauline Epistles because these letters are used as definitive authority to support current ideologies on the correct gender and sexual roles for men and women in African American Christian communities. In other words, they are used as evidence of authoritative texts for the development of norms, doctrine, and teachings about how men and women in these communities are supposed to act, both socially and sexually. Tragically, several key passages in these writings have been used to perpetuate sexist and homophobic values in these communities, often eclipsing more liberatory passages by Paul on which human interaction might be based and, consequently, limiting discussions that might lead to more nuanced and multivalent images of masculinity in African American communities.[4]

What follows then is an attempt to identify some of the images of masculinity in the Pauline writings that have traditionally served to reinscribe sexist and homophobic values in African American communities. After a brief review of the literature on the New Testament and masculinity, I argue that many of the Pauline discussions about women's roles and same-sex relations in early Christian communities invariably create images of masculinity that are oppressive and counterproductive to the task of constructing progressive black masculinities. However, a more critical understanding of the context in which these letters were written may provide a basis for reinterpreting and rearticulating these scriptures in a way that is consistent with Paul's eschatological challenge in Galatians. I suggest that rearticulating and even rejecting scriptures used to justify oppression have been central to the practice of African American biblical interpretation and may be useful in dealing with some of the more problematic interpretations of Pauline texts.

I also identify several Pauline texts that offer alternative—more liberative—models of masculinity. These models include cultivating practices of humility, resistant struggle, and bold acknowledgment of weaknesses. Finally, I suggest that other sacred sources, such as ancient monastic writings, and theoretical paradigms might facilitate discussions about progressive black masculinities. Specifically I look at the example of the desert father known as Ethiopian Moses.

Literature on the New Testament and Masculinity

The conference that gave rise to this volume has provided a rare and unique opportunity for me to survey the Pauline writings and to suggest some possible ways this material might function in the task of constructing progressive black masculinities.[5] Since the mid-1990s biblical scholars have begun to examine representations of masculinity in the New Testament.[6] A few scholars have provided provocative discussions about male images in the Bible, and others have explored the intersection among masculinity, sexuality, and religion.[7] In addition, numerous studies deal with the topics of homosexuality, homoeroticism, and same-sex relations in the ancient world and throughout the Bible.[8] But there is generally no attention to the subject of masculinity as it relates to understanding either early Christianity and blacks in antiquity or the implications of such material for contemporary discussions about the experiences of African American men.[9] This absence also includes explorations of the Pauline texts as they might relate to black masculinity.[10]

Although not explicitly addressing the issue of black masculinity, New Testament scholar Clarice J. Martin provided a cogent analysis of some of the Pauline texts that have had an adverse affect on the lives of African Americans, especially with regard to teachings about slavery and the roles of women. In an essay titled "The *Haustafeln* (Household Codes) in African American Biblical Interpretation," C. Martin reviewed the divergent African American hermeneutical approaches to the regulations about slaves and women in the *Haustafeln,* codes that sometimes in a single chapter exhort wives to obey their husbands, children to obey their parents, and slaves to obey their masters.[11] In particular, she isolated a vexing question with respect to the interpretation of these authoritative biblical texts: "Why is the African American interpretive tradition marked by a forceful critique and rejection of a literalist interpretation of the slave regulations in the *Haustafeln*, but not marked by an equally passionate critique and rejection of a literalist interpretation regarding the subordination of women to men in the *Haustafeln*?"[12] She carefully responded to this question by demonstrating the blind spots some African American religious leaders and biblical interpreters—presumably male interpreters—have with respect to interpreting sections of the New Testament that are paradigmatic of the complex, interlocking systems of oppression that affect African American communities today.[13] She ultimately concluded that a womanist reflection on the hermeneutical paradoxes and tensions evident in African American biblical interpretations should "take seriously the need to create and implement responsible ethical guidelines for the dismantling of the gender hierarchy of African American men and women,"[14] a process in my view that would aid in redefining masculinity and men's roles. To this end, she suggested strategies for promoting more equitable and liberative faith communities.[15]

Specifically, C. Martin's analysis of the household codes indicates how African Americans learned to reinterpret and even dismiss the authority of literalist, proslavery regulations in the Pauline texts in a variety of creative and subversive ways. They did so by affirming the ways "the Bible witnessed to an all-powerful, liberating God who in Jesus Christ was concerned for the ultimate and holistic liberation of all of humanity."[16] This prohumanity hermeneutic is supported by passages such as "God made from one every nation of humanity [*anthrōpoi*] to live on all the face of the earth, having determined allotted periods and the boundaries of their habitation" and "For by one Spirit we were all baptized into one body—Jews or Greeks, slaves or free—and all were made to drink of one Spirit."[17] This emphasis on the universal parenthood of God is a fundamental proposition of the black Christian tradition.[18]

Moreover, African Americans dismissed the authority of proslavery interpretations of biblical texts. For example, as Howard Thurman recounted, his grandmother, a former slave, would not permit him to read the sections from the Pauline letters that dealt with slavery, evidencing one of many ways African Americans have always appealed to a canon within the canon when it came to developing prescriptive guidelines for their faith.[19] Thus, I suggest that in the same way that African Americans have learned to either reinterpret or dismiss the authority of proslavery biblical texts, they can also learn to rearticulate and even to dismiss the literalist authority of texts that support other forms of oppression.

The Pauline writings have not only been used to justify slavery in the past, they continue to be used to justify sexism and to silence those who identify with or embody expressions of sexuality that deviate from prescribed—hetero-sexual—norms in African American Christian communities. This oppression, marginalization, and, indeed, silence undergird the sexism and homophobia that are systematically hurting and dividing African American communities and churches. Similar to the ways in which racism supports practices, ideas, and institutional structures that limit blacks to only occupying certain places in society, sexism declares and supports structures that limit women to assume their so-called rightful place in the home or the domestic sphere. Likewise, homophobia ensures that gays and lesbians have a place in the closet—if any at all. Each of these oppressive ideologies limits the human potential of the individuals who make up the groups.

Furthermore, it is evident that both sexism and homophobia impede visions of masculinity. Instead of men having the freedom to define them-selves in the image of God, sexist and homophobic ideologies often lead men to define images of themselves in society, community, and religious norms and structures that privilege certain heteropatriarchal views of masculinity and that penalize other life-affirming views of masculinity that recognize the full and unique humanity embedded in each man or woman.

Fortunately, now many African American theologians, cultural critics, historians, and others are trying to break the silence and to carve out new spaces for dialogue, critique, and transformation. For example, womanist theologian Kelly Brown Douglas, in her book *Sexuality and the Black Church*, argued that leaders of the church, as well as scholars of religion, should develop a "sexual discourse of resistance."[20] By this she challenged her colleagues to break the cycle of silence and to create a safe space for sustained analysis of the complex factors that have led to the pervasive misogyny and homophobia in existence in African American religious communities. Her goal is to "move all Black women and men closer to enjoying the fullness and uniqueness of their humanity."[21] Sociologist and religious historian Elias Farajaje-Jones also identified strategies for breaking the silence related to homophobia in African American communities.[22] In 1993, he called attention to several biblical texts that have been misinterpreted with respect to the condemnation of lesbian, gay, bisexual, and transgendered (LGBT) people.[23] He prophetically challenged black theologians to join in the struggle against heteropatriarchy, the source of multiple forms of oppression.[24] Similarly, cultural critic Michael Eric Dyson suggested that the black church must develop a theology of homoeroticism, or "queerness," that would build bridges between gay and lesbian and straight black church members.[25] Ethicist G. Kasimu Baker-Fletcher proposed a radical reconstruction of African American maleness through the systematic debunking of the ways black males have bought into patriarchal ideals of masculinity.[26] Baker-Fletcher contended that the voices of lesbian and gay Christians must be taken seriously if new models of masculinity are to emerge in the black church.[27] All of these interpretations offer important steps toward developing a more expansive definition of masculinity and eradicating the ideological traps associated with sexist and homophobic teachings in the black church.[28] But a reinterpretation of key biblical passages, which invariably provide authority for these traps, is still needed for a more authentic level of discourse about black masculinities.

Images of Masculinity in the Pauline Epistles: Sources for Sexist and Homophobic Ideologies

The thirteen Pauline writings in the New Testament were not all written by the apostle Paul. Most New Testament scholars agree that Paul wrote seven of the letters—Romans, First and Second Corinthians, Galatians, Philippians, Philemon, and First Thessalonians—during the middle of the first century C.E. About a generation later, another group of letters known as the deutero-Pauline epistles—Colossians, Ephesians, and Second Thessalonians—were written by authors who pseudonymously wrote in Paul's name. Approximately another generation after this, around the end of the first century or the beginning of the second, another group of Pauline writings known as the Pastoral Epistles—First and Second Timothy and Titus—were also pseudonymously written in Paul's name.[29] Thus, three generations of Pauline writings reflect the different interests of the authors and the various influences in their communities during the time the epistles were generated. This tripartite distinction becomes significant when trying to assess Paul's teachings about masculinity because many of the texts considered sexist or homophobic are usually attributed to Paul, when in fact they were more likely written years later by pseudonymous authors. This is particularly so in regard to some of the scriptures on women and their roles and status in the early Christian communities.

Paul worked with both women and men as he traveled throughout the Mediterranean sharing his understanding of the Christian faith. Romans 16 provides a long list of the persons who assisted Paul in various capacities, including many women such as the benefactor and deacon Phoebe,[30] the risk-taker and trusted colleague Prisca,[31] and the apostle Junia.[32] Paul also worked with Euodia and Syntyche[33] and Tryphaena and Tryphosa[34] and responded to the concerns of Chloe's people.[35] Although Paul did not seem to have problems with women praying and prophesying during worship,[36] he did render a complex hierarchical teaching about women's clothing and hair that is sometimes misappropriated in many contemporary Christian communities. Also, readers should bear in mind that many of Paul's teachings and admonitions about women, marriage, and sexual vices were addressing specific concerns and circumstances that were challenging the early Christians at various stages in their historical development.[37] These teachings were not necessarily intended to become universal authoritative statements about women's leadership roles or sexual practices.

In this section, I examine several Pauline texts, three commenting on women's roles, each taken from a different generation of Pauline letters: one from Paul's undisputed letters, First Corinthians 14:33b–35; one from the deutero-Pauline tradition, Colossians 3:18–4:1; and one from the trito-Pauline tradition, Second Timothy 3:1–7. I then discuss two of Paul's undisputed letters commenting on same-sex relations: Romans 1:26–27 and First Corinthians 6:9–10. In all of these examples, the images of masculinity invariably lead to sexist and homophobic appropriations in African American Christian communities, even if this was not the intent of the original authors.[38] In each, a greater understanding of the historical context in which they were written may provide a basis for reinterpreting them consistent with the exhortation of Galatians: "There is no longer male and female; for all of you are one in Christ Jesus."

First Corinthians contains an exemplary text that has been used to support and to justify the exclusion of women from ordained ministry and to relegate women to silence and submission: "As in all the churches of the saints, women should be silent in the churches. For they are not permitted to speak, but should be subordinate, as the law also says. If there is anything they desire to know, let them ask their husbands at home. For it is shameful for a woman to speak in church."[39] Many New Testament scholars have discussed how this passage is likely a later editorial insertion that reflects aptly the teachings of a later generation of the church's development. Indeed, First Corinthians 14:33b–35 is remarkably similar to teachings contained in one of the Pastoral Epistles written during the late first or early second century: "Let a woman learn in silence with full submission. I permit no woman to teach or to have authority over a man; she is to keep silent."[40]

From the examples about women cited earlier in this section, it is clear that Paul knew of prophetic women in the early Christian communities and relied on women throughout the course of his missionary activities. Thus, the teachings about women assuming more subordinate and silent roles in the church must have been generated during a period after Paul's ministry by those apparently threatened by the activities of women in the community. Unfortunately, such texts about women are used to fuel the sexist attitudes that exist in contemporary African American communities, drawing them into the ideological trap of sexism.

In one of the deutero-Pauline writings, there are further teachings about the roles of husbands and wives:

> Wives, be subject to your husbands, as is fitting in the Lord. Husbands, love your wives and never treat them harshly. Children, obey your parents in everything, for this is your acceptable duty in the Lord. Fathers, do not provoke your children, or they may lose heart. Slaves, obey your earthly masters in everything, not only while being watched and in order to please them, but wholeheartedly, fearing the Lord. Whatever your task, put yourselves into it, as done for the Lord and not for your masters, since you know that from the Lord you will receive the inheritance as your reward; you serve the Lord Christ. For the wrongdoer will be paid back for whatever wrong has been done, and there is no partiality. Masters, treat your slaves justly and fairly, for you know that you also have a Master in heaven.[41]

This text is an example of ancient household codes. As noted earlier, C. Martin provided a cogent reinterpretation of the household codes that brings into perspective how well-meaning African American male interpreters take offense to the slave regulations but fail to reject the equally oppressive injunctions about women in this text.[42] In the household codes, masculinity is understood through the male-ruled family unit, or *paterfamilias*, wherein the head of the household exercises control over other persons: a wife, his offspring, or male and female slaves. It is based on a hierarchical understanding of relationships that disregards mutuality and respect for all those represented in the household. As C. Martin indicated in her examination of the household codes, African American interpreters must continue to find ways to break free of the literalist authority this text continues to wield with respect to how men and women define themselves in relation to one another and to God. This is where the eschatological challenge of Galatians 3:28–29 can become the new nonhierarchical paradigm for relationships that transcend gender. There is much potential in this material for constructing progressive black masculinities.

One final example about attitudes toward women in early Christianity is from the second pastoral letter addressed to Timothy:

> You must understand this, that in the last days distressing times will come. For people will be lovers of themselves, lovers of money, boasters,

arrogant, abusive, disobedient to their parents, ungrateful, unholy, inhuman, implacable, slanderers, profligates, brutes, haters of good, treacherous, reckless, swollen with conceit, lovers of pleasure rather than lovers of God, holding to the outward form of godliness but denying its power. Avoid them! For among them are those who make their way into households and captivate silly women, overwhelmed by their sins and swayed by all kinds of desires, who are always being instructed and can never arrive at a knowledge of truth.[43]

Feminist scholars have already called attention to the ways this text is a response to powerful, influential women in the community.[44] But New Testament scholars are now raising questions about the ways the teachings in the Pastoral Epistles might be drawing attention to models of masculinity in early Christianity. For example, Jennifer A. Glancy argued that the pastoral letters reflect the efforts of an author trying to promote a more favorable form of masculinity: one favored among elite educated men in the first and second centuries and that preserved conservative imperial gender norms.[45] Such a model of masculinity includes the following: "someone who is blameless, married only once, whose children are believers, not accused of debauchery and not rebellious ... . [H]e must not be arrogant or quick-tempered or addicted to wine or violent or greedy for gain; but he must be hospitable, a lover of goodness, prudent, upright, devout, and self-controlled."[46] In effect, the author of this material was trying to counterbalance other modes of masculinity that may have captured the imagination of early Christians and may have disrupted the social order and control of their households,[47] that is, alternative postures of masculinity represented by persons such as John the Baptist, Jesus, and Paul—all of whom renounced prescribed matrimonial and paternal roles.[48]

This same phenomenon of competing modes of masculinity exists in contemporary discussions about African American manhood. Discussions in mainstream media and throughout many books and essays about black men are focused on black middle-class, presumably heterosexual, married men.[49] This narrow normative heterosexist paradigm for understanding black manhood prohibits communities from tuning in to the voices and experiences of black men who may embody alternative modes of masculinity. An exploration of progressive black masculinities must include the full spectrum of African American manhood, including those who renounce mainstream values and choose to love other men.

In this vein, Paul's letter to the Romans probably contains the most scathing commentary about same-sex relations in the New Testament: "For this reason God gave them up to degrading passions. Their women exchanged natural intercourse for unnatural, and in the same way also the men, giving up natural intercourse with women, were consumed with passion for one another. Men committed shameless acts with men and received in their own persons the due penalty for their error."[50] As I suggest later in this section, a literal interpretation of the text is problematic because it is not clear what practices Paul is actually criticizing, and his teachings may simply reflect his social, cultural, and historical location as a Jewish man in the first century. Further, the commentary is tangential to Paul's main point, which is that all humanity is sinful. As such, these comments were not meant to convey a universal authoritative statement about homosexuality.

Paul wrote his letter to the Romans in approximately 58 C.E. when he was at the point of formulating a more sustained explanation of his teachings about the Christian faith. After the customary salutation (Rom. 1:1–7), thanksgiving (Rom. 1:8–15), and the engaging description of the power of the gospel (Rom. 1:16–17), Paul launched into a carefully designed argument about the sinfulness or fallen state of humanity (Rom. 1:18–3:20) and used Romans 1:26–27 as an extreme example of the consequences of sin.

This text has been used historically to chastise and to condemn gays and lesbians. Most Christian communities are not able to move beyond the literal reading of the text and to explore the ancient context in which Paul's use of this sexually loaded illustration took place. Some have argued that Paul is condemning homosexual acts carried out by heterosexual persons; others suggest that Paul is condemning a particular type of homosexuality that was widespread in Greco-Roman antiquity—pederasty.[51] The scholarship suggests that drawing direct parallels between the ancient and modern contexts is wrought with pitfalls.[52] But for most interpreters of this material, especially in African American communities, such literal and uncritical readings of this text support the marginalization of LGBT persons.

Clearly, Paul was communicating to his audience the consequences of falling away from God:

So they are without excuse; for though they knew God, they did not honor him as God or give thanks to him, but they became futile in their thinking, and their senseless minds were darkened. Claiming to be wise, they became fools; and they exchanged the glory of the immortal God for images resembling a mortal human being or birds or four-footed animals or reptiles. Therefore God gave them up in the lusts of their hearts to impurity, to the degrading of their bodies among themselves, because they exchanged the truth about God for a lie and worshiped and served the creature rather than the Creator, who is blessed forever! Amen.[53]

Paul's use of this example is reflective of his religious, cultural, and social location. As a Jew, Paul had to be well aware of the holiness code in Leviticus that denounced same-sex relations (Lev. 18:22; 20:13). As an urban Greco-Roman male, he also had to be aware of the many expressions of same-sex practices in the ancient world.[54] Although the example in Romans 1:26–27 is tangential to the larger point Paul was attempting to make—all of humanity is sinful—its placement in the text is enough to draw attention to a particular segment of humanity and thus to provide ammunition for later interpreters who might want to condemn those who adhere to homosexual lifestyles and practices. The thorny debate about this text is unresolved. But for purposes of constructing progressive black masculinities, I suggest that this text is not a useful source, for it invariably draws interpreters into the ideological trap of homophobia.

In another example from First Corinthians, Paul provided an extensive list of vices that prevents a person from inheriting the kingdom of God. Paul's letter to the Corinthians, written to help curtail the dissensions that existed in the newly formed Christian community at Corinth, is filled with ethical exhortations and discussions about sexuality. In First Corinthians 6:9–10, Paul once again denounced those in Corinth who engage in sexual vices: "Do you not know that wrongdoers will not inherit the kingdom of God? Do not be deceived! Fornicators (*pornoi*), idolaters, adulterers, male prostitutes (*malakoi*), sodomites (*arsenokoites*), thieves, the greedy, drunkards, revilers, robbers—none of these will inherit the kingdom of God."

New Testament scholar Dale B. Martin provided an extensive analysis of the Greek terms *malakoi* and *arsenokoites* in this text.[55] These terms have been taken to refer to people who engage in male homosexual activity.[56] D. Martin discussed how contemporary interpretations of *arsenokoites* and *malakos* as condemning modern homosexuality have been driven, in part, by ideological interests in marginalizing gay and lesbian people.[57] Moreover, he concluded that naive attempts by conservative Christians to derive ethics from a simple reading of the Bible leads to imputing destructive ideologies to the text.[58] Similar to Romans 1:26–27, Paul's teachings about fornicators, idolaters, and male homosexuals in First Corinthians 6:9–10 are not a useful source for constructing progressive black masculinities.

The Pauline writings are clearly problematic. Although Paul may not have been trying to oppress women or to denounce those who engaged in so-called unnatural relations, the way this material is situated in the New Testament and is used to signify sinful behavior is enough to cause many to reject altogether Paul and his teachings. Unfortunately, however, in African American Christian communities these biblical passages are loaded with authority and provide the raw material for reinscribing sexist and homophobic attitudes that effectively marginalize and silence a very significant segment of God's humanity. Peter J. Gomes, a minister and professor of Christian morals, described incisively what is at stake: "The 'authority' of Scripture to which preachers almost universally appeal, in the traditions of the black church, is an authority derived from the cultural consensus of the people in their understanding not so much of the text but of their own fears and hopes, anxieties and ambitions."[59] Until black church leaders and other interpreters of this material are able to grapple with their own fears and hopes, anxieties and ambitions, these texts will continue to do ideological and spiritual damage throughout African American communities. Furthermore, these texts distort the possibilities that exist in the Pauline writings for constructing progressive black masculinities.

Images of Masculinity in the Pauline Epistles: Sources for Liberative Models of Masculinity

Thus far I have discussed Pauline texts generally used in African American communities to reinforce sexist and homophobic values. Because of the pejorative interpretations of texts dealing with women and homosexuality, it is often difficult to find anything redeemable about Paul and his teachings. I suggest, however, that the Pauline writings offer a number of alternative—more liberative—images of masculinity that might prove useful for constructing progressive black masculinities.

One particularly important aspect of masculinity that has been largely ignored in African American communities is humility. Paul, in his letter to the Philippians, emphasized how important it is to take on this spiritual discipline: "Do nothing from selfish ambition or conceit, but in humility regard others as better than yourselves. Let each of you look not to your own interests, but to the interests of others. Let the same mind be in you that was in Christ Jesus … ."[60] With these words used to introduce the Christ hymn in Philippians 2, verses 6–11, Paul was directing his audience to cultivate the ascetic virtue of humility by imitating Christ. Paul, throughout the letter, was advocating a type of political asceticism that encouraged the Philippians to withdraw from allegiance to earthly political structures and to engage in a program of redefining an alternative reality that is able to transform historical and social circumstances.[61] This realignment of political allegiances does not discourage activism but calls for a more focused and grounded commitment to activism rooted in values that will lead to building a stronger sense of community and citizenship—in Christ.[62]

The Pauline writings also point to a model of masculinity that emphasizes spiritual formation. In the deutero-Pauline letter to the Ephesians, the author exhorted the community to respond to dangers and threats by putting on the full armor of God: "Finally, be strong in the Lord and in the strength of his power. Put on the whole armor of God, so that you may be able to stand against the wiles of the devil. For our struggle is not against enemies of blood and flesh, but against the rulers, against the authorities, against the cosmic powers of this present darkness, against the spiritual forces of evil in the heavenly places. Therefore take up the whole armor of God, so that you may be able to withstand on that evil day, and having done everything, to stand firm."[63] This type of spiritual formation is exemplified in the life and teachings of mystic, theologian, and pastor Howard Thurman. For Thurman, true manhood resided in transcending gender and in cultivating a genuine and all-encompassing spiritual life.[64] Thurman envisioned the worshiping moment as the opportunity to pierce through the spiritual forces of evil that separate God's humanity based upon gender, ethnicity, class, sexual preferences, or any other distinction.[65] This emphasis on spiritual formation will enable African American men to recognize their own humanity and the humanity of others. As Hemphill suggested, it would lead to building much more intimate and humane relationships while building coalitions to fight against various forms of oppression.

Another model of masculinity exemplified by Paul is his resistant struggle through bold acknowledgment of his weaknesses. Paul's weaknesses can be understood in two ways: (1) those that result from his own limitations and frailties; and (2) those that result from living in oppressive conditions.

In Romans, chapter 7, Paul explicitly acknowledged his personal weaknesses:

> I do not understand my own actions. For I do not do what I want, but I do the very thing I hate. Now if I do what I do not want, I agree that the law is good. But in fact it is no longer I that do it, but sin that dwells within me, that is, in my flesh. I can will what is right, but I cannot do it. For I do not do the good I want, but the evil I do not want is what I do. Now if I do what I do not want, it is no longer I that do it, but sin that dwells within me … . Wretched man that I am! Who will rescue me from this body of death? Thanks be to God through Jesus Christ our Lord![66]

Seldom, if ever, are African American males given the space to acknowledge the ways they have fallen short of their own expectations, of the expectations of others, or of the expectations of God. In a society where only the strong survive, it is virtually impossible to find the courage or the words for acknowledging weaknesses and limitations. But Paul boldly acknowledged his weaknesses—and sins—and admitted that his salvation and deliverance came from God.

Paul also acknowledged that his weaknesses were not just personal; they stemmed from many different sources embedded in his religious, social, and cultural worlds. In Second Corinthians 4:7–12, he effectively summarized his apostolic hardships and challenges, which reflect a condition of weakness rooted in larger societal structures and systems:

> But we have this treasure in clay jars, so that it may be made clear that this extraordinary power belongs to God and does not come from us. We are afflicted in every way, but not crushed; perplexed, but not driven to despair; persecuted, but not forsaken; struck down, but not destroyed; always carrying in the body the death of Jesus, so that the life of Jesus may also be made visible in our bodies. For while we live, we are always

being given up to death for Jesus' sake, so that the life of Jesus may be made visible in our mortal flesh. So death is at work in us, but life in you.[67]

In U.S. society, African American males generally are not encouraged to acknowledge or to reflect on their failures, or weaknesses, on a communal or societal level. Filmmaker Isaac Julien made a powerful observation in this regard: "We have to be willing to engage in a process of thinking through our failure as black men in this society. Black masculinity has always been a 'failed masculinity' in relationship to white male colonialism. Black macho discourses of empowerment will never truly reach us where we live. There is something interesting we can learn from our so-called failure, because our failure also contains our resistance."[68] For Julien, "failure to live 'up' to oppressive masculinity is a part of what it means to be queer."[69] His observations were in response to questions about the merits of the Million Man March and the Nation of Islam, but he raised a poignant challenge to those seeking to develop a more expansive definition of black masculinity. What might happen if African American men were able to understand their failures as a critique of white supremacy and affirm the words of Paul: "God's grace is sufficient, God's power is made perfect in my weakness"?[70] This type of hermeneutic of resistance has the potential to radically alter the ways boys are nurtured and conditioned for manhood. It also provides opportunities to imagine and to practice alternative forms of masculinity.[71] So the failed masculinity Julien described resonates with the teachings of Paul, who said, "I will boast all the more gladly of my weaknesses, so that the power of Christ may dwell in me. Therefore I am content with weaknesses, insults, hardships, persecutions, and calamities for the sake of Christ; for whenever I am weak, then I am strong."[72]

What we find in the Pauline writings are competing modes of manhood and multiple representations of masculinity. Generally, masculinity is understood through the heteropatriarchal ethos that privileges the man who is married, with children, head of the household, and natural-sex oriented. But many other images would serve as useful sources for constructing progressive black masculinities. The images of humility, spiritual formation, and resistant struggle through the bold acknowledgment of weaknesses and failures offer powerful tools for engaging in a deeper level of discourse not only about models of masculinity but also about the implications for understanding larger sociopolitical and theological questions that affect African American men.

Many might argue that the Bible, especially the Pauline Epistles, is not the most fertile resource for constructing progressive black masculinities. But given the fact that many still resort to this material for guidance and instruction for living the Christian life and for shaping the moral values of African American children, it is imperative that scholars of the New Testament provide critical readings of this material to offer some alternative paradigms for understanding the meaning of these teachings in light of the diverse experiences of African American males and females in the twenty-first century. Critical readings of the misogynist and homophobic texts that have been used to reinforce dominating images of masculinity in African American communities call for an interdisciplinary hermeneutic of resistance that subverts the heteropatriarchal authority embedded in biblical narratives. Yet it is naive to assume that the answers to the deep webs of hegemonic oppression embedded in the ideological traps of misogyny and homophobia can be handled through the critical reinterpretation of the Bible alone. The next section demonstrates the merit of also appealing to extrabiblical sources.

Other Useful Sources for Constructing Progressive Black Masculinities

The examples cited already in this chapter indicate that the Pauline letters have the potential to serve as either lethal or liberative sources for constructing progressive black masculinities. Yet it is obvious that the Pauline writings are not the only available sources for constructing progressive black masculinities. Many other biblical and extrabiblical sources could also yield important insights for understanding masculinity in general and the ways black masculinities are represented in particular. The task of exploring other biblical sources is beyond the scope of this chapter, but a review here of at least one extrabiblical source demonstrates the value of utilizing other sacred writings as sources for constructing progressive black masculinities.

One such example is the story contained in monastic writings about the fifth-century desert father known as Ethiopian Moses.[73] He has been venerated as one of the great desert fathers for his extreme self-control and ascetic virtue of humility, although his early life was far from virtuous. Moses was a slave who had been driven out of his master's house because of his bad moral character.[74] He later became the leader of a group of robbers and committed many evil deeds and murders. After his encounter with the teachings of monasticism, Moses subsequently converted from his troubled past and eventually pursued the monastic life. Despite the fact that Moses was curiously praised for overcoming his blackness during a period of testing before his ordination,[75] through him we can begin to see an alternative mode of masculinity in the ancient world. In fact, Moses provides an alternative model of masculinity that might be useful for contemporary discussions about progressive black masculinities. Moses exemplified a type of self-control that allowed him to persist in the face of all obstacles until he defeated the demons trying to distract him.[76] In many respects, he is quite similar to the progressive Paul (introduced in the previous section), who invoked masculine images of humility, spiritual formation, and resistant struggle.

What is most important in the story about Ethiopian Moses is the way he is represented as a black man. In fact, his ethnicity appears to be a source of confusion and consternation as one anonymous desert father describes:

"The Fathers wished to put Moses to the test. They treated him with contempt, saying "Why does *this Ethiopian* come into our midst?"[77] Moses responded to such questioning with humility and silence, two virtues that are characteristic of resistant struggle.[78] Moses is considered exemplary not because he was married to a submissive wife or was the head of a household, but rather because he was able to exhibit self-control in the face of ridicule and insults, to renounce his destructive deeds and habits of the past, and to acknowledge his weaknesses by relying on a power much greater than his own. Moses forged a new identity by an inward transformation that ultimately called for an outward reappropriation of his worldly realities. Moreover, the ethnic and color-symbolic language about Moses calls attention to the complex web of social, cultural, and political challenges that existed in late antiquity.[79]

Moses is also a paradigmatic figure for those attempting to understand progressive black masculinities today. He embodies a complex set of spiritual virtues, social and political realities, community values, and liberative practices that are useful for reorienting dialogues about African American men and the meanings of masculinity. Many contemporary discussions about masculinity or black males are framed by those who are trying to shape a certain heteropatriarchal understanding of African American men and their sociopolitical realities. This extracanonical text about Ethiopian Moses challenges those interested in constructing progressive black masculinities (1) to examine alternative models of masculinity and (2) to critique the ways stories and descriptions of black men are represented in media and popular culture—some of the things this volume attempts to do.[80]

Summary and Theoretical Considerations: An Interdisciplinary Quest for Progressive Black Masculinities

The images of masculinity in the Pauline writings are both illustrative and limiting when it comes to understanding progressive black masculinities. I propose that it is important to acknowledge the problematic nature of these texts that allude to sexism and homophobia and then to search for alternative models of masculinity embedded in the Pauline writings. It is not enough, however, to stop with the Pauline material. There are many images of masculinity throughout biblical and extrabiblical writings. Beyond these ancient sources, there is now a burgeoning number of books and essays written by and about the experiences of African American males.[81] Many of these writings document the urgent impetus for alternative models of masculinity by intentionally undermining conventional macho idealizations of black men. Unfortunately, critical engagement with the various sources—especially the Bible—that have led to the macho idealizations is lacking.

To understand the potential in the Pauline writings, it is necessary to adopt an interdisciplinary theoretical paradigm that brings together the expertise of many different scholars to engage and to dismantle the ideological traps of sexism and homophobia. A recent volume edited by Vincent L. Wimbush titled *African Americans and the Bible* provides an impressive example of the type of interdisciplinary scholarship that might bring nonbiblical scholars into a more critical conversation with biblical texts. In this volume, Wimbush assembled scholars from various disciplines and gave them the charge of examining the various ways African Americans have engaged the Bible, have rejected the Bible, have reread the Bible, or have dismissed the Bible altogether. In fact, he raised the question, "What would happen if African Americans became the very center of biblical interpretation?"[82]

I refer to this volume for two reasons. First, it may provide a theoretical model for how scholars can begin to apply an interdisciplinary approach to the exploration of the topic of progressive black masculinities. Although there are several anthologies about black men and masculinities, none of them embraces a common theoretical theme beyond the naming and classification of black male experiences in the United States.[83] These anthologies tend to provide a smorgasbord of intellectual musings about masculinity but fail to provide a theoretical linchpin for dissecting the multiple sources of oppression that have shaped the ways discourses—especially religious discourses—about masculinity have developed.

Second, *African Americans and the Bible* demonstrates how African Americans have historically applied radical and subversive readings of biblical texts and in many ways have reinvented the Bible to facilitate their own survival in a strange and oppressive land. Wimbush argued in the opening essay that it is possible to shift the focus from a narrow interrogation of the biblical texts to a broader spectrum of including the ways interpreting communities have appropriated the texts and, in some respects, have become texts themselves. Thus, it is possible to go beyond the Bible and to appeal to sources from the African American experience for constructing progressive black masculinities. Slave narratives, rap music, poetry, art, and communities of interpreters can be used as source material in addition to, or possibly in lieu of, prescribed biblical writings.

In this chapter, I provide a suggestive framework for understanding the range of possibilities that exist for examining images of masculinity in the Pauline writings. Despite the many possibilities, there are still limitations. Through the use of contemporary studies about black male masculinities, I am able to move beyond the limitations and to discover liberative interpretations of the Pauline material that might serve as resources for constructing progressive black masculinities. I am hoping that this exploration will generate a starting point for interdisciplinary dialogue and theoretical reflection that will spark new images and models of black masculinity, which according to Paul transcend gender ("There is no longer male and female") and are, in the words of Hemphill, more "intimate" and "humane."

Notes

1. Don Belton, "Where We Live: A Conversation with Essex Hemphill and Isaac Julien," in *Speak My Name: Black Men on Masculinity and the American Dream*, ed. Belton (Boston: Beacon Press, 1995), 210–11.
2. Gal. 3:28. All biblical translations, unless otherwise noted, are from the New Revised Standard Version (NRSV) of the Bible.
3. For purposes of this chapter, the Pauline Epistles are divided into three categories: Paul's seven undisputed letters (Romans, First and Second Corinthians, Galatians, Philippians, First Thessalonians, and Philemon); a second generation of Pauline writings known as deutero-Pauline Epistles (Colossians, Ephesians, and Second Thessalonians); and a third generation of Pauline writings known as Pastoral Epistles (First and Second Timothy and Titus).
4. Although this conference was devoted to exploring progressive black masculinities and the implications for African American communities, European, Latin, and Asian American communities are also afflicted with sexism and homophobia.
5. A conference titled "Exploring, Constructing, and Sustaining Progressive Black Masculinities" was held at the Baldy Center for Law & Social Policy, State University of New York at Buffalo, April 12–14, 2002. The religion session was titled "Black Masculinities and Religion: Rearticulating Doctrine and Understanding Possibilities." The discussants were asked to "address the question whether adherence to the Abrahamic religions (Judaism, Christianity, and Islam) can be consistent with construction of Black masculinities that are neither sexist nor homophobic. An affirmative response to the question requires, among other things, that many passages of scripture be reinterpreted or rejected. Our discussion will start with a demonstration that, from a liberal theological perspective, such scriptural exegesis is both necessary and possible." I am grateful to the conference organizers, especially Stephanie Phillips, for inviting me to participate in this session and Athena Mutua for reading this chapter with much care and for offering many helpful editorial suggestions.
6. See Stephen D. Moore and Janice Capel Anderson, eds., "New Testament Masculinities," in *Semeia Studies* (Atlanta: Society of Biblical Literature, 2003), 45. This volume contains an excellent bibliography of masculinity studies (pp. 23–46); see pp. 36–9 for books and articles related to the New Testament and early Christianity.
7. See, for example, Moore, *God's Beauty Parlor: And Other Queer Spaces in and around the Bible* (Stanford, CA: Stanford University Press, 2001); Moore, *God's Gym: Divine Male Bodies of the Bible* (New York: Routledge, 1996); Stephen B. Boyd, W. Merle Longwood, and Mark W. Muesse, eds., *Redeeming Men: Religion and Masculinities* (Louisville, KY: Westminster John Knox Press, 1996); and Gerard Loughlin, "Refiguring of Masculinity in Christ," in *Religion and Sexuality*, ed. Michael A. Hayes, Wendy Porter, and David Tombs (Sheffield, England: Sheffield Academic Press, 1998).
8. See, for example, Robin Scroggs, *The New Testament and Homosexuality: Contextual Background for Contemporary Debate* (Philadelphia: Fortress Press, 1983); Bernadette J. Brooten, *Love between Women: Early Christian Responses to Female Homoeroticism* (Chicago: University of Chicago Press, 1996); Martti Nissinen, *Homoeroticism in the Biblical World: A Historical Perspective* (Minneapolis: Fortress Press, 1998); and Robert E. Goss and Mona West, eds., *Take Back the Word: A Queer Reading of the Bible* (Cleveland: Pilgrim Press, 2000).
9. One notable exception is David Brakke, "Ethiopian Demons: Male Sexuality, the Black-Skinned Other, and the Monastic Self," *Journal of the History of Sexuality* 10, nos. 3–4 (2001), 501–35; Brakke did not address contemporary questions related to black masculinities in this article.
10. See, for example, Brigitte Kahl, "No Longer Male: Masculinity Struggles behind Galatians 3:28?" *Journal for the Study of the New Testament* 79 (2000), 37–49.
11. Clarice J. Martin, "The *Haustafeln* (Household Codes) in African American Biblical Interpretation: 'Free Slaves' and 'Subordinate Women,'" in *Stony the Road We Trod: African American Biblical Interpretation*, ed. Cain Hope Felder (Minneapolis: Fortress, 1991), 206. For scripture references, see Col. 3:18–4:1; Eph. 5:21–6:9; and 1 Pet. 2:18–3:7.
12. Ibid., 225.
13. Ibid., 226–27. Although C. Martin is alluding to male interpreters in her essay, many African American women also have these blind spots when reading the household codes.

14. Ibid., 228. For a definition of *womanist hermeneutics*, see C. Martin, "Womanist Biblical Interpretation," in *Dictionary of Biblical Interpretation*, ed. John H. Hayes (Nashville: Abingdon, 1999), 655–58. See also Ann Holmes Redding, "Not Again: Another Look at the Household Codes," in *Eve & Adam: Jewish, Christian, and Muslim Readings on Genesis and Gender*, ed. Kristen E. Kvam, Linda S. Schearing, and Valarie H. Ziegler (Bloomington: Indiana University Press, 1999), 456–63.
15. C. Martin, "Household Codes," 228–31.
16. Ibid., 216.
17. Acts 17:26—the NRSV translates *anthrōpoi* as *men* instead of the more inclusive term *humanity*—and 1 Cor. 12:13.
18. C. Martin, "Household Codes," 216–17; see also Peter J. Paris, "The Bible and the Black Churches," in *The Bible and Social Reform*, ed. Ernest R. Sandeen (Philadelphia: Fortress Press, 1982), 134–35.
19. For a detailed discussion about Thurman's account and the ways African Americans have created their own canons—or authoritative texts—see Renita J. Weems, "Reading Her Way through the Struggle: African American Women and the Bible," in Felder, *Stony the Road We Trod*, 60–72. See also Howard Thurman, *Jesus and the Disinherited* (Boston: Beacon Press, 1996), 30–31.
20. Kelly Brown Douglas, *Sexuality and the Black Church: A Womanist Perspective* (Mary knoll, NY: Orbis Books, 1999), 68–83.
21. Ibid., 8.
22. Elias Farajaje-Jones, "Breaking Silence: Toward an In-the-Life Theology," in *Black Theology: A Documentary History—Volume II: 1980–1992*, ed. James H. Cone and Gayraud S. Wilmore (Maryknoll, NY: Orbis Books, 1993), 139–59.
23. Lev. 20:10–16; Ezek. 16:49–50; Luke 10:10–13; Rom. 1:26–27. See Farajaje-Jones, "Breaking Silence," 151–52.
24. Farajaje-Jones, "Breaking the Silence," 158. See also Renee L. Hill, "Who Are We for Each Other?: Sexism, Sexuality and Womanist Theology," in Cone and Wilmore, *Black Theology*, 345.
25. Michael Eric Dyson, "When you Divide Body and Soul, Problems Multiply: The Black Church and Sex," in *Traps: African American Men on Gender and Sexuality*, ed. Rudolph P. Byrd and Beverly Guy-Sheftall (Bloomington: Indiana University Press, 2001), 325.
26. Garth Kasimu Baker-Fletcher, *Xodus: An African American Male Journey* (Minneapolis: Fortress Press, 1996).
27. Ibid., 35–36.
28. For a provocative discussion about the ideological traps of sexism and homophobia, see Byrd and Guy-Sheftall, *Traps*. According to Byrd and Guy-Sheftall, "Monolithic constructions of gender and sexuality whose potency is derived, respectively, from a strong identification with the practices of sexism and historically sanctioned homophobia are the traps into which we all have fallen. The deconstruction and dismantlement of these ideological traps, which are both internally and externally imposed, are a matter of considerable urgency to us all." Ibid., xiii.
29. For more background on this topic, see Calvin J. Roetzel, *The Letters of Paul: Conversations in Context*, 4th ed. (Louisville, KY: Westminster John Knox Press, 1998).
30. Rom. 16:1–2.
31. Rom. 16:3–4; Prisca was also called Priscilla in Acts 18:2.
32. Rom. 16:7.
33. Phil. 4:2–4.
34. Rom. 16:12.
35. 1 Cor. 1:11, 11:18.
36. 1 Cor. 11:2–16.
37. See, e.g., 1 Cor. 5:1–13, 7:1–40, 11:2–16.
38. It is worth reiterating at this point that sexist and homophobic interpretations of Paul's writings are not limited to African American communities. They exist among people of various ethnic backgrounds (e.g., European, Asian, Hispanic) in both Protestant and Catholic communities.
39. 1 Cor. 14:33b–35.
40. 1 Tim. 2:11–12.

41. Col. 3:18–4:1; cf. Eph. 5:21–6:9.
42. C. Martin, "Household Codes," 227–31.
43. 2 Tim. 3:1–7.
44. See discussion in Carol A. Newsom and Sharon H. Ringe, eds., *The Women's Bible Commentary*, expanded ed. (Louisville, KY: Westminster John Knox Press, 1998).
45. Jennifer A. Glancy, "Protocols of Masculinity in the Pastoral Epistles," in *New Testament Masculinities*, ed. Moore and Anderson (Atlanta: Society of Biblical Literature, 2003), esp. 238–49, in which Glancy cited examples of elite models of masculinity. Such models emphasize control of the behavior of the various members of the household—wives, children, and slaves—and self-control, especially with respect to passions and pleasures, anger, greed, and drinking. Cf. 1 Tim. 3:1–13 and Titus 1:5–11. I am grateful that my colleague Jennifer Glancy shared with me a copy of her essay before its publication, and that she offered a close, critical reading of an earlier draft of this chapter.
46. Titus 1:6–8.
47. Titus 1:10–11.
48. Glancy, "Protocols," 250.
49. See, for example, Bob Herbent, "Who Will Help the Black Man?" *New York Times Magazine,* December 4, 1994, 74; and Robert Staples, *Black Masculinity: The Black Male's Role in American Society* (San Francisco: Black Scholars Press, 1982).
50. Rom. 1:26–27.
51. Pederasty is sexual activity between adult men and boys. For a detailed analysis of this institution in the ancient world, see Scroggs, *New Testament.*
52. See Nissinen, *Homoeroticism*; Scroggs, *New Testament*; Brooten, *Love between Women*; and H. Darrell Lance, "The Bible and Homosexuality," *American Baptist Quarterly* 8 (1989):140–51.
53. Rom. 1:20c–25.
54. For a detailed treatment on this topic, see Craig A. Williams, *Roman Homosexuality: Ideologies of Masculinity in Classical Antiquity* (New York: Oxford University Press, 1999).
55. Dale B. Martin, "Arsenokoites and Malakos: Meanings and Consequences," in *Biblical Ethics and Homosexuality*, ed. Robert L. Brawley (Louisville, KY: Westminster John Knox Press, 1996), 117.
56. For other meanings of the terms, see ibid., 118–28.
57. Ibid., 117.
58. Ibid., 118.
59. Peter J. Gomes, "Black Christians and Homosexuality: The Pathology of a Permitted Prejudice," *African American Pulpit* 4 (Summer 2001), 33.
60. Phil. 2:3–5.
61. Scroggs, "Paul the Prisoner: Political Asceticism in the Letter to the Philippians," in *Asceticism and the New Testament,* ed. Leif Vaage and Vincent L. Wimbush (New York: Routledge, 1999), 187.
62. Phil. 4:20.
63. Eph. 6:10–14.
64. Alton B. Pollard III, "Magnificent Manhood: The Transcendent Witness of Howard Thurman," in Boyd and others, *Redeeming Men*, 222.
65. Ibid., 230.
66. Rom. 7:15–20, 24–25a.
67. 2 Cor. 4:7–12.
68. Belton, "Where We Live," 215.
69. Ibid.
70. 2 Cor. 12:9a.
71. Patricia Hill Collins, for example, encouraged black men to reject the ideology of masculinity as domination, and to understand their weakness—in terms of not being able to sufficiently dominate others—as their strength. See her chapter in this volume.
72. 2 Cor. 12:9b–10.
73. Kathleen O'Brien Wicker, "Ethiopian Moses (Collected Sources)," in *Ascetic Behavior in Greco-Roman Antiquity: A Source Book,* ed. Wimbush (Minneapolis: Fortress Press, 1990), 329.
74. Ibid., 331.

75. For a full analysis of this text and several other early Christian writings that discuss Ethiopians and blacks, see Gay L. Byron, *Symbolic Blackness and Ethnic Difference in Early Christian Literature* (New York: Routledge, 2002).

76. For another provocative interpretation of this text, see Brakke, "Ethiopian Demons," 527–33. Utilizing postcolonial theory, Brakke argued that Ethiopian Moses is employing "resistant mockery."

77. Anonymous, *Apoph. Patrum*, 3; Byron, *Symbolic Blackness*, 117.

78. Phil. 2:3–11.

79. Byron, *Symbolic Blackness*, 118–20.

80. See also ibid., 122–29.

81. See, for example, Belton, *Speak My Name*; Phillip Brian Harper, *Are We Not Men?: Masculine Anxiety and the Problem of African-American Identity* (New York: Oxford University Press, 1996); Joseph L. White and James H. Cones III, *Black Men Emerging* (New York: W.H. Freeman, 1999); Byrd and Guy-Sheftall, *Traps*; Ellis Cose, *The Envy of the World: On Being a Black Man in America* (New York: Washington Square Press, 2002); Na'im Akbar, *Visions for Black Men* (Nashville: Winston-Derek Publishers, Inc., 1991); Haki Madhubuti, *Black Men: Obsolete, Single, Dangerous?* (Chicago: Third World Press, 1990); and Staples, *Black Masculinity*.

82. Wimbush, "Introduction: Reading Darkness, Reading Scriptures," *African Americans and the Bible* (New York: Continuum, 2000), 1–43.

83. See, for example, Belton, *Speak My Name*; Byrd and Guy-Sheftall, *Traps*; Devon Carbado, ed., *Black Men on Race, Gender, and Sexuality: A Critical Reader* (New York: New York University Press, 1999); and Herb Boyd and Robert L. Allen, eds., *Brotherman: The Odyssey of Black Men in America* (New York: Ballantine Books, 1995).

7

Progressive Black Masculinities and a Christian Experience: An Autobiographical Perspective

WHITNEY G. HARRIS

Is adherence to Christianity consistent with the construction of progressive black masculinities that are neither sexist nor homophobic? I was asked to respond to this question as a panelist at a conference on progressive black masculinities. Although I am an ordained minister with a degree in theology,[1] I am not a professional theologian. In fact, I am what is referred to in the black South as a "jack-leg" preacher, i.e., one who is recognized as a reverend but who is neither a pastor nor considered a major religious leader of the community. Although I have been ordained for over twenty years, I have spent very little time as a full-time minister. It is clear then, that I could not respond to the question from either the professional theologian's perspective or from that of a pastor. Instead, I chose to respond from an autobiographical perspective informed by black liberation theology.[2]

Within this framework, three tasks are embraced. First, I sketch the role that my experience as an African American gay priest in a racist and homophobic Roman Catholic Church plays in my development as a black male committed to progressive masculinities. Second, I discuss various images of God and the challenge of creating new images that support and are consistent with progressive black masculinities. Third, I argue, based on examples of Christ's life, that the images of Christ must be rescued from the forces of oppression and refigured into images supportive of progressive black masculinities. I further suggest that Christ initiated a refiguring of masculinity during his own time that provides a model for similar efforts today.

My Soul Looks Back and I Wonder: "How I Got Over"[3]

"Father, you preach like a Baptist." I can think of no better way to begin a brief sketch of my spiritual journey than with this often-heard comment. Over the past twenty-two years, whenever I have had the privilege of delivering a sermon or some other occasional speech, invariably at least one person, and usually a number of people, have said to me, "Father, you preach like a Baptist."

Many of the members of Sacred Heart Catholic Church, where I served as an adjunct priest for thirteen years, assumed that because of my preaching style, I was a convert to Catholicism. Or as one sister stated it, "Father, you got Catholicism in your heart but you got deep-down black folks' Protestant religion in your soul."

When I look back and wonder how I got over—how I survived life's challenges with dignity—the answer is clear. It is my religious faith. The faith I received at St. Martin DePorres Roman Catholic Chapel and the religion that I "got" at Morning Star, Evergreen, and Mount Zion Baptist Churches formed my "Old Ship of Zion."[4] My faith is steeped in the Roman Catholic tradition into which I was baptized a few weeks after my birth. When I think *religion,* I think *Catholic.* My assent to that reality, which is beyond me, flows from my Catholic faith. My fundamental opinions regarding the issues of life and death are shaped by my Catholic faith. For example, my opposition to the death penalty is as much the fruit of my Catholic faith as it is the fruit of my social consciousness as an African American. But the practice of my faith has been informed also by my experiences at black Baptist churches.

St. Martin DePorres Chapel was a small black Catholic community that served the few African American Catholics who could not be active members of the white Our Lady of LaSalette Catholic Church. Though they could attend liturgy on Sunday at the white church, African Americans had to sit in the back pews and could only go to communion after all of the white attendees had done so.[5] Somehow, despite the biting racism of the Catholic Church, the faith expressed by the African American elders of DePorres community became my faith. However, at a very early age I became aware of the contradiction between the teachings proclaimed by the Catholic Church and its lived experience. In fact, because of the radical stance I witnessed from both my parents and from other elders, I became the catechism student who asked the priests and other catechism teachers uncomfortable questions such as, "Why do we have to sit in the back when we go to LaSalette?" Or, "Father if we are all made in the image and likeness of God, why are colored people required to sit in the back at the white church?" These were simply some of the first skirmishes I had with the Catholic Church as a white racist institution. Perhaps one of the most poignant examples of my later struggles with the church came during my first assignment after my ordination. I was assigned to the campus ministry chapel at a large university in Louisiana. On the first Sunday that I led the celebration of the Eucharist, known as Mass, a white female refused to receive Holy Communion from me. She whispered, "Father I don't have anything against you, but I'm not ready to receive communion from black hands yet." Still, though I cursed and struggled against the racism of the church, I kept the faith I had received from the teachings of the African American men and women at DePorres.

Loyal Opposition

Perhaps the person who did the most to keep me in and loyal to the Catholic Church was my maternal grandmother. Of course my mother, also a very staunch Catholic, played a very important role in this struggle. Over the years, she has served her faith community in many capacities. However, it was in witnessing my grandmother's faithfulness to God and to her church that helped me to look beyond what she called "the grievous faults of racism and homophobia of the Catholic Church." She was a divorced mother of two who considered herself often down but never out. Her strength and her commitment to the church despite adversity and the church's hypocrisy set an example of loyalty that I would emulate years later.

Not only did my grandmother serve as my connection to the Catholic Church, but she also called me out as a gay male. Though she was dedicated to Catholicism, a religion that denounces homosexual behavior as a sin, she announced that I was gay without criticism and malice. More importantly, nothing in our relationship changed; she continued to treat me in a warm and loving manner. In addition, she often protected me from the wrath of other family members and acquaintances who did not know quite what to do with a punk in the family.[6] No one dared called me Winetta in her presence.

While my grandmother provided me with a model for loyalty to the church despite its faults, my maternal uncle, also very committed to the Catholic faith, provided me with a model of action for expressing opposition to the church's oppressive practices. My uncle was a serious Catholic who maintained his dignity as a black man in the face of the church's racism. For example, he had the only car in my mother's family. He was responsible for providing rides to worship services, family visits, and medical appointments as well as visits to other family members. Uncle Tee, as we called him, was very generous and almost always provided the needed ride. However, he refused to provide a ride to anyone going to the "white church." He argued, "Mass can't be any good if they don't let colored people sit where they want to sit." He added, "God don't know anything about color." If someone missed Mass at DePorres, my uncle would often provide a ride to the next closet African American Catholic church, some thirty miles away. Also, I remember that when a cousin was ordained a priest, my uncle, along with the rest of the family, made sure that every white Catholic in our small town knew that we had a family member who was a priest.[7] My uncle proudly announced that not one white boy from Our Lady of LaSalette had ever been ordained a priest. For him this was the ultimate victory.

Without a doubt, my uncle consciously saw himself protesting the racism in the church while maintaining his dignity as a Catholic black man. In doing so, he modeled for me an approach for coping with the contradictions within the Catholic Church. It was a model of subversive action against racism in the institution while remaining faithful to the church's message of salvation and hope. This model provided me with a paradigm of oppositional action that shaped my own struggles against racism, homophobia, and later sexism within the church. Further, though today my uncle might be considered one step from an "Uncle Tom" because he did not leave the racist white institution, for me he nonetheless represented an African American masculinity that was progressive. Within the framework of his understanding of Catholicism, he not only critiqued "Holy Mother Church"—not an easy task for a barely literate African American layperson—but also engaged in positive subversive action against its racist practices.

This subversive element of my religious experience was certainly fueled by my religious experiences at the local Baptist churches. More often than not, the leaders of these churches were at the forefront of the various civil and human rights activities in which I was involved as a child. A. H. Northfolk, a deacon and treasurer at the local baptist church, served as the unofficial advisor to the first organized movement in which I became involved—Black Brothers for Community Advancement.[8] At the same time, these churches provided me with another vision and image of God that sprung from the black experience of slavery: the image not of God of the masters but rather of God of the oppressed. These experiences provided further content to the model of oppositional and subversive action against oppressive practices.

On a personal level, like Uncle Tee I have used this model as a strategy for overcoming many challenges while retaining my dignity as an African American male. For example, when a local bishop decided to close the Office of Black Catholics, I used the only occasion I have ever had to preach at a cathedral to publicly denounce, in his presence, his decision to close the office. The general consensus of those present was that this was the first time a bishop had been publicly chastised in his own cathedral. Few priests had dared to publicly criticize the bishop in any forum, much less from the cathedral pulpit.

Though I doubt that Uncle Tee would have endorsed my actions, his subversive behavior provided the paradigm for my reflection and subsequent behavior. His private war against the racism he encountered in the Roman Catholic Church provided me with the getting-over strategy—the poise of dignity that arises from survival—that empowered me to out the bishop in his own cathedral. This model has helped me to discover and to shape my masculine self.

From Resisting Racism to Resisting Heteropatriarchy: New Versions of Black Masculinity

It is this same paradigm of loyal opposition that I have embraced to live as an openly same-gender-loving Catholic priest. Initially, however, I teetered at closet doors. During the early years, I was not so much out of the closet as I refused to deny that I was a homosexual. I never denied my sexual orientation. In fact, during my early years as a priest I devoted a great deal of time to the establishment of a local chapter of Dignity, a national organization for gays and lesbians and their allies. I attended my first Dignity meeting while a seminarian at St. Augustine Seminary in Toronto, Ontario, Canada. In the early 1980s, most people assumed that every priest working with Dignity was a homosexual.

So, even though during the early years of my priesthood my openness was not nearly as bold or honest as it became in later years, once again my ability to be among the loyal opposition provided me with the strategy to get over—to survive with dignity. Over the years, many African Americans have told me that those few of us who dared to live openly gay lives served not only as a model for them but also as a source of strength as they discovered or embraced their sexual orientation. To quote one young man, "Father Harris, when I was a teenager, though we weren't close and I didn't participate in your youth group, just seeing you as an out gay black man helped me out. It was good seeing a high-profile black gay man." Another man said to me, years later, "Father Harris, when you were at St. Anthony Church, I came out to my family and used you to argue that I could be a homosexual, a black man, and a Catholic Christian. Because you were a priest and they liked you, they didn't get as mad at me as they could have because then they would have had to get mad at you. Being 'born' Catholic, they couldn't criticize a priest."

Male African American ministers who live openly gay lives are not only the product often of successful strategies combating racism and homophobia but also contributors to notions of progressive black masculinities.[9] One of the most prominent openly gay African American ministers is Peter Gomes. An American Baptist minister, Gomes is a member of Harvard University's Faculty of Arts and Sciences and of the Faculty of Divinity. In addition, he is the minister of Harvard's Memorial Church.[10] In his book *The Good Book: Reading the Bible with Mind and Heart*, he not only acknowledged his own homosexuality but also warned others about the abuse of scripture to support homophobia.[11] Gomes also challenged Christian communities to accept the Bible's mandate to allow the full inclusion of women in all facets of the church's affairs and ministries.[12]

We are developing new styles of progressive black masculinities, in that our lives challenge the model that says that one has to be tough in order to be considered a real African American man. Though I am not suggesting that all gay African American ministers fit the gay male stereotype of being effeminate, simply being an openly gay male minister challenges the community's perception of what it means to be an African American male. Out African American gay ministers also challenge the stereotypical view that gay is a white thing. This is especially true among African Americans who accord a high level of respect to ministers. In my experience, gay male ministers provide a model of progressive black masculinity that challenges the myth that real black men are not gay.

Ministers who live openly gay lives also help to make a place at the table for new approaches to doing masculinity within the context of African American religious communities. Our very presence challenges the prevailing model of the black preacher. The controlling feature of that model is a man's man who, at least according to the prevailing stereotype, hustles women with the same vigor that he regales the congregation on Sunday mornings with sermons straight from the mouth of God. Michael Dyson told an interesting story about a visiting revivalist who rails against fornication and marital infidelity with a thrilling sermon. Once the ministers have reclined to the pastor's study, the revivalist says to the host pastor, "Who is that woman with those big breasts?" And the revivalist goes on to say, "Well, Doc, do you think you could fix me up with her?" The pastor promised to see if he could arrange the "hook-up."[13]

Gay black ministers offer another version of masculinity. Those of us who allow our homosexuality free rein within the context of our work as ordained ministers are examples of doing masculinities that are Christian, black, and homosexual. For me, life as an openly black gay minister was a very important part of my Christian witness, or testimony. It was a key moment of telling my story of how I got over. My hope is that my lifestyle provided a vision, ever so blurry, of how some elements of progressive black masculinities might look. I believe this is true for all African American gay male Christian ministers who seek to live both authentically black and authentically homosexual lives. Hopefully, we are models of black men who, while faithful to our Christian calling, are seriously engaged in the work of constructing progressive black masculinities. Gay ministers also are, by their approach to doing masculinity, inviting African American Christians to rethink their images of God.

New Images of God: What Does the Face of God Look Like?

Creating new images of God is a challenge that must be embraced if African American men are to remain faithful to the Christian community and to create new ways of doing progressive black masculinities. The images of God, who stands behind both the Bible and the Christian traditions, form the primary model of masculinity for Christian men.[14] African American men in particular and black Christians in general must change the image of God from great white patriarch to one more aligned and consistent with black progressive masculinities. Of course, a prerequisite for reimagining God is recognizing that all of our descriptions of God are but approximations. All of our descriptions of God are reductive because they reduce God to the human experience, as an image or essence or intellect.

As such, imagining God is a language-bounded exercise. Therefore, part of birthing new images of God involves critiquing our God talk.[15] The language one uses to talk about God not only shapes what one says about God but also provides the vehicle by which the individual imagines God. For example, our image of God sitting on a throne somewhere up yonder is only accessible through a language that flows from a hierarchical worldview. The use of this language system supports the image of a Great White Patriarch God. Most African American male Christians' image of God has been influenced by the representation and language of the white patriarchy. This certainly was my initial image of God. It was also the language I used to talk about the divine.

Fortunately, early on I drew from Morning Star, Evergreen, and Mount Zion Baptist Churches other ways not only of doing God talk but also of envisioning God. On Sunday mornings when Sister Mae Phillips sang, "He made me. He saved me. God brought me and I can feel him walking by my side," I sensed a real dissonance between the white God of St. Martin DePorres and Sister Phillips's God. I knew that the white DePorres's God would not be "walking by my side" as I walked, after church services, up the railroad tracks back to the New Addition.[16] The "precious Lord" that Sister Julia Parsons sang about over at Mount Zion could not possibly be the son of a white God. No white man I knew would "take my hand and lead me through a storm." My image of God slowly evolved away from the white patriarch. To be sure, it was years before I let go of the patriarchal image. However, by my early teen years, the white God of my childhood was dead. Of course, growing up during the mid-twentieth-century civil rights era provided a healthy context for my emerging black awareness and influenced my religious experience.

Thus, not only my image of God but also my God talk was more closely aligned with the God of the oppressed than with the God of the Catholic Church.[17] African American men involved in the Christian religion must change the image of God from great white patriarch to one more aligned with images consistent with black progressive masculinities. Following the example of our African American ancestors who changed the image of God of the master's image given to them by their slave masters to the image of God of the captain of the ship of Zion, African American men must discover new images of God. The God of the masters must become the God of the oppressed.[18] Here, the oppressed are not limited to people of color but extend to all oppressed peoples, including homosexuals and women.

This image of God not only allows but also demands that its male adherents embrace masculinities that are neither sexist nor homophobic. The God of the oppressed becomes the God who stands firmly with all who have labored under the burden of patriarchy—even white males who experience their own form of patriarchal oppression. As African American males identify with the God of the oppressed, they unite with him in the struggle against the powers and principalities that support and sustain oppression and discrimination. Masculinities born and nurtured in the bow of the ship of Zion captained by the God of the oppressed embody this God's liberating spirit and are committed to the struggle against oppression.

What does this mean concretely? First, a liberating masculinity is a progressive masculinity because it rejects not only sexism but also all forms of oppression. Personally, my appreciation of the second-class status of women in many religious communities increased as my representation of God moved away from the exclusively dominant male to an image that was inclusive of all of humankind. For example, my image of God does not allow room for the exclusion of women from ordination because they are females. Therefore, I am among a growing number of Roman Catholic priests who are publicly challenging the exclusion of women from the ordained ministry. My opposition is not tied to the decline in the number of priests; rather, it reflects my belief in the equality of all of humankind. To do less is to bask in male privilege rather than to side with the God of the oppressed. And as Sister Phillips reminded us, "God is the father to the fatherless, the mother to the motherless." Clearly, God is beyond the limits that gender classifications define.

Second, a significant moment in my evolving masculinity is acknowledging the male privilege I enjoy within the various contexts of Christian communities. Access to the pulpit is just one of the many gender-determined benefits I enjoy as a member of my faith community. Another more subtle privilege is what I refer to as the extra voice at the table of decisions. Despite being fewer in number than females, males have a greater voice in the governance and decision-making process in most faith communities. Certainly, women do the mule work of most faith communities, but they are usually not the major decision makers.[19] A part of my evolving masculinity is challenging this injustice that flies in the face of my concept of Christianity. In fact, more than any other sin of the church, with the possible exception of racism, sexism most threatens my continued membership in the Christian religion. As my sense of what it means to be a male becomes more in tune with God and with the evolution of humanity, it becomes increasingly difficult for me to be involved with groups that engage in exclusionary behavior.[20] Black male oppression of black women certainly is informed by racism, but at the heart of this oppression within religious communities is the disease of patriarchy. Arguably, all forms of oppression within faith communities are based on the masculine hegemonic image of God that pervades Christian theologies and practices. If black Christian men are to create progressive masculinities, I can think of nothing more urgent than the fight against patriarchy in the black church community.

Refiguring the Masculinity of Christ—Christ as a Model for Refiguring Masculinity

Who is Jesus? This is the central question for every adherent to any of the many Christian traditions. James Cone, the father of black liberation theology correctly stated, "Christian theology begins and ends with Jesus Christ."[21] Although the concept of God is a key question in all of the religions of the book as well as many others, Christianity is shaped both communally and individually by how individuals and faith communities construct their Christology. Christology is the study of the life of the earthly Jesus and the experience of the risen Jesus known as the Christ. It seeks answers to the perennial question, "Who is Jesus?"

Over the years, Christian African Americans have provided numerous answers to this question. Clearly, one answer has been the so-called white man's Jesus. This Jesus is depicted on the covers of numerous Sunday school pamphlets and other religious paraphernalia used in black churches. He is proclaimed in the thousands of other-world sermons preached by an army of African American ministers at eleven o'clock on Sunday mornings in thousands of churches across the country. Dietrich Bonhoeffer referred to this image as the "cheap grace" Jesus.[22] For him, most Christians' Jesus is an anemic deity who supports the status quo and who offers no critique of the racist and sexist institutional church or of society. He is a safe Jesus because his concern is up yonder and not down here. Because he is an other-world Jesus, Christians need not bother challenging the current oppressive patriarchal social structure both within and without the churches. The oppressed should simply see their suffering as what one does to merit heaven. Thus, there is cost neither to the individual nor to the faith communities for being a Christian. This image of Jesus is woefully inadequate for men seeking to embrace new forms of masculinity that are inclusive and liberating rather than exclusive and oppressive.

For black men to remain faithful to the Christian tradition while living lives rooted in progressive masculinities, there must be a refiguring of the image of Christ.[23] As with God, black men's image of Jesus must not be limited by the traditional culture-bound portrayals of him. African American men must liberate Jesus from the clutches of the white Christians who have used him as an instrument of oppression.[24]

For me, this process started sometime in the late Sixties when my mother gave me a copy of a picture of Jesus with an Afro hairstyle. She suggested that I replace the white Jesus on my wall with the real Jesus. Of course, as Catholics, at least during the Fifties and Sixties, the picture of Mary, the Mother of Jesus, held almost as important a place as Jesus. So my brother and I, with the blessings of my mother, simply blackened our picture of Mary. She thereby became a credible mother for Jesus. This simple act was a revolutionary moment in my spirituality. Through it my brother and I rescued Jesus from the clutches of white racists and made him one of us.

African American men who wish to remain faithful to Christianity while embracing new ways of doing masculinity must also rescue Jesus from his white captives. The Jesus of the New Testament is not the Jesus of the status quo in either the white or black churches. According to Cone, "Jesus' sole reason for existence [was] to bind the wounds of the afflicted and to liberate those who are in prison."[25] In the American context, Jesus cannot be the model for black men unless he is refigured. Black men cannot allow "the white condition to determine the meaning of Jesus for us."[26] Black men engaged in doing progressive masculinity must save the savior from those who would destroy his image by enshrining him in whiteness, a whiteness defined in part by its commitment to the status quo of domination. At the same time, people of color must resist the temptation to limit Jesus by barricading him in this time—bound by cultural experiences including those defining what a man is.

The point of departure for refiguring Jesus is examining the life of the historical Jesus—the one born in a stable to humble parents.[27] His birth identifies Jesus with the downtrodden and the oppressed. "Jesus' messiahship means that He is one of the humiliated and the abused, even in his birth."[28] My understanding of Jesus' birth has had a profound impact on my perception of my role as a black man in America. For example, I reject the interpretation of Jesus' lowly birth as a means of blessing and spiritualizing the value of living in poverty and of being victimized by various sociopolitical institutions. Rather, I see his birth as a critique of the victimization of oppressed people by the rich and powerful. For me, Jesus' birth is an invitation to join in the struggle against the captives of the poor and oppressed. As I see it, through his birth Jesus identified with the oppressed not simply as oppressed people but also by becoming one of the humiliated and the abused. He identified with them in their struggle against the powers and principalities that held them captive.[29]

Over time, my definition of the disempowered grew from people of color to include women, gays, persons with disabilities, the homeless, and all others trapped in the dehumanizing stables of the world. Therefore, inherent in my understanding of my African American maleness is my commitment to the liberation of all oppressed peoples. For example, there is no room in my understanding of myself as a black man for the oppression and subordination of women. Consequently, my participation in the feminist and womanist movements, albeit with a sense of humility and otherness, is a manifestation of my understanding of the Jesus experience and its claim on my life. It makes clear that one can adhere to Christianity and at the same time can forge ahead with the construction of progressive black masculinities that are neither sexist nor homophobic.

On a personal level, my interaction with females is certainly informed by my immersion in the spirit of Jesus. It is not possible for me to be in communion with Jesus and not to recognize that women share equally in the humanness that is being set free by Jesus' liberating spirit. Jesus, though rooted in his culture through his humanness, was not totally trapped in the hegemonic masculinity of his time. For example, his adventure with the Samaritan woman not only challenged important political and religious tenets but also defied the prevailing definition of Jewish masculinity.[30] Specifically, his mere act of acknowledging the presence of a woman, and in particular a non-Jewish woman, was a radical departure from the manner in which men treated women. First, Jewish men did not even acknowledge women from their own group in public, so Jesus' conversation with the Samaritan woman provides a powerful insight into his appreciation for and treatment of women. Second, "[n]ot only was it unheard of for a rabbi to speak familiarly with a woman in public but also for a Jew to request water of a Samaritan."[31]

Jesus, then, did not accommodate his performance of masculinity to the prevailing code of manliness; rather, he initiated a refiguring of masculinity. Thus, the devaluing of women, in whatever form, is anathema to the life and message of Jesus. Clearly, my understanding of Jesus' relationship with women informs my own performance of masculinity vis-à-vis women. The Samaritan woman scenario serves as a paradigm for African American men attempting to adhere to one of the Christian faith traditions and to embrace new forms of progressive black masculinities. The Jesus story provides a model for refiguring masculinity.

At the risk of sounding stereotypical, let me say that my so-called feminine qualities—for example, to nurture—are fostered by my relationship with Jesus. For example, his insistence on being available to the children, uncommon behavior for a man in his culture, provides a paradigm for my nurturing self.[32] On one level, the story is about Jesus breaking into a form of domesticity prescribed for the women of his day. By responding to the concerns of the children, he was doing the work of women. On another level, the children symbolize the little ones, the dispossessed.[33] Both messages present a caring Jesus who serves as a model for those doing the work of birthing new progressive black masculinities. Both provide an opportunity to refigure Jesus into an image that serves as a powerful paradigm for progressive African American men.

Conclusion

Is adherence to Christianity consistent with the construction of progressive black masculinities that are neither sexist nor homophobic? Yes. It is possible for African American Christian males to construct progressive black masculinities. In fact, some of that work is already being done. For example, several years ago, a group of black men, including myself, at Sacred Heart Catholic Church formed a group called Men against Violence. Granted, the name of our group is problematic, as our work is almost always done in cooperation with women, but the goals are twofold. The adult males gather each week to ponder the issues concerning our performance of masculinity vis-à-vis our understanding of and commitment to the Jesus experience and his rejection of violence. A part of this process is refiguring Jesus in light of our growing understanding of him as the incarnation of the God of the oppressed.

Cone warns that "[t]he gospel bears witness to the God who is against oppression in any form, whether inflicted on an oppressed group from the outside or arising from within an oppressed community."[34] Black males who profess faith in Jesus Christ must join with God in the struggle against all forms of oppression. Even though this is clearly just one aspect of what I hope are the emerging forms of black progressive masculinities—given the racism, sexism, and homophobia in American society—it is a cornerstone on which black men of the Christian faith must build new ways of being progressive black men who are neither sexist or homophobic.

Notes

1. Baccalaureate in theology (St. Paul University, Ottawa, Ontario, Canada, 1979).
2. Special thanks to Stephanie Phillips, State University at Buffalo School of Law, for suggesting that I use an autobiographical approach to express my views on this topic.
3. This is an African American religious song that was popularized by gospel singers such as Clara Ward and Mahalia Jackson.
4. This is a spiritual song made famous by Mahalia Jackson. The words and music are by Alfred McCrary, Nanni Byl, and Daniel Kosmalski. It is not to be confused with the concept of *getting over*, which suggests that one's success is the product of negative behavior such as abusing and oppressing others.
5. Both churches had the same pastor who lived in the rectory at Our Lady of LaSalette.
6. *Punk* was used most often to refer to homosexual or suspected homosexual males.
7. Father Dominic Carmon (now Bishop Carmon) is my uncle's second cousin. In south Louisiana a second cousin is considered a close relative.
8. Approximately ten African American male adolescents formed this group to work for improvement in Mossville, Louisiana, the all–African American community in which I lived during high school. I do not recall anything we did, but I remember the pride we had in creating the organization.
9. Clearly the same could be said for black lesbian ministers; however, because this work is autobiographical, the issues relating to lesbians must await another day.
10. Peter Gomes, *The Good Book: Reading the Bible with Mind and Heart* (San Francisco: Harper, 2002), 164.
11. Ibid, 165.
12. Ibid, 120–125.
13. Michael Dyson, "When You Divide Body and Soul, Problems Multiply: The Black Church and Sex," in *Traps: African American Men on Gender and Sexuality*, ed. Rudolph P. Byrd and Beverly Guy-Sheftall (Bloomington: Indiana University Press, 2001), 309.
14. Howard Eilberg-Schwartz, "A Masculine Critique of a Father God." *Tikkun* 10, no. 5 (1995), 58–62.
15. David C. James, *What Are They Saying about Masculine Spirituality?* (New York: Paulist Press, 1996).
16. The New Addition was one of the segregated African American neighborhoods in the town where I spent my childhood.
17. James H. Cone, *God of the Oppressed* (New York: Seabury Press, 1997).
18. Ibid.
19. The term *mule* is borrowed from Patricia Hill-Collins, *Fighting Words: Black Women and the Search for Justice* (Minneapolis: University of Minnesota Press, 1998); and Zora Neale Hurston, *Mules and Men* (New York: Negro Universities Press, 1969).
20. James H. Cone, *Risks of Faith: The Emergence of a Black Theology of Liberation, 1968–1998* (Boston: Beacon Press, 1999).
21. James H. Cone, *A Black Theology of Liberation* (Maryknoll, New York: 1989).
22. Dietrich Bonhoeffer, *The Cost of Discipleship* (New York: Macmillan, 1959).
23. Gerard Loughlin, "Refiguring of Masculinity in Christ," in *Religion and Sexuality*, ed. M. Hayes, W. Porter, and D. Tomb (Sheffield, UK: Sheffield Academic Press, 1998).

24. Cone, 1989.
25. Ibid.
26. Ibid.
27. Luke 2:7 New American Bible (Camden, NJ: Thomas Nelson, 1971).
28. Ibid.
29. Ibid.
30. John 4:1–44 New American Bible (Camden, NJ: Thomas Nelson, 1971).
31. Bruce Vawter, "The Gospel According to John," in *The Jerome Biblical Commentary*, vol. 2, ed. Raymond E. Brown, Joseph A. Fitzmyer, and Roland E. Murphy (Englewood Cliffs, NJ: Prentice-Hall, 1968), 431.
32. Matthew 19 New American Bible (Camden, NJ: Thomas Nelson, 1971).
33. John McKenzie, "The Gospel According to Matthew," in Brown and others, *Jerome Biblical Commentary*, 96.
34. Cone, *Risks of Faith*.

Part 4
From Unwanted Traffic to Prison

8

Reasonable and Unreasonable Suspects: The Cultural Construction of the Anonymous Black Man in Public Space (Here Be Dragons)*

JOHN O. CALMORE

Men are not born, growing from infants through boyhood to manhood, to follow a predetermined biological imperative encoded in their physical organization. To be a man is to participate in social life as a man, as a gendered being. Men are not born; they are made. And men make themselves, actively constructing their masculinities within a social and historical context.

Michael S. Kimmel and Michael A. Messner[1]

What is a Black man in an institutionally racist society, in the social system of modern capitalist America? The essential tragedy of being Black and male is our inability, as men and as people of African descent, to define ourselves without the stereotypes the larger society imposes upon us, and through various institutional means perpetuates and permeates within our entire culture.

Manning Marable[2]

Introduction

I take the generalized cultural construction of African Americans as *unwanted traffic* from the Supreme Court's 1981 decision in *City of Memphis v. Greene*,

---

* This parenthetic reference is taken from James Baldwin, "Here Be Dragons," in *Traps: African American Men on Gender and Sexuality*, ed. Rudolph P. Byrd and Beverly Guy-Sheftall (Bloomington: Indiana University Press, 2001), 207, 209. I invoke this description of black masculinity to call attention to its state of confusion and complexity, its misunderstood and fear-inducing presence within and without the race of black people. This chapter is adapted from a work in progress, a book titled *Random Notes of an Integration Warrior* (forthcoming, 2007).

in which the court endorsed and legitimated a street closing that blocked traffic from a black neighborhood through a white one.[3] Although the majority of the court characterized the closing as a mere inconvenience, Justice Thurgood Marshall in dissent saw it as "a monument to racial hostility."[4] From the court's legitimation, society more generally has viewed blacks, particularly males, as unwanted traffic. In fact, some argue that the decision may have legitimated the development, during the 1980s and 1990s, of many communities that built iron gates and neighborhood barricades.[5]

The particular cultural construction of the anonymous black man in public space prompts an ambivalent societal gaze toward him, a gaze that may reflect both reasonable and unreasonable suspicion. As a result, people tend to despise, to fear, and to avoid him. As arrest, inmate, and probationer records indicate, moreover, the black man as unwanted traffic often translates more precisely into the criminal element that must be apprehended, prosecuted, and sent away.[6] This complex imagery is well captured in the observation of one black journalist who stated, "To almost all cops and most of society, I am a criminal who happens not to have committed his first crime."[7]

The black man is the paradigmatic representation of unwanted traffic.[8] As the term *unwanted traffic* suggests, the negative representation flows with black males through time and across space, from youth to elder years and from predominantly black settings to predominantly white or mixed settings. Because of the high degree of residential segregation, most black men are perceived as unwanted traffic within the very neighborhoods that should represent supportive homeplaces. Thus, as Elijah Anderson described in his neighborhood study, a struggle emerges for common ground and shared moral community. He observed that an overwhelming number of young black males in the neighborhood he studied "are committed to civility and law-abiding behavior."[9] These males, however, find it difficult to negotiate public space because many others do not see them in this way. It appears that the stigma of skin color, age, gender, appearance, and general style of self-presentation mark them as unwanted traffic.[10] In Anderson's view, "most residents ascribe criminality, incivility, toughness, and street smartness to the anonymous black male, who must work hard to make others trust his common decency."[11] This is the weight of race that anonymous black males must carry—it is the burden of proof that they are decent human beings. In anonymity, many black men are forced to share the negative traits of some not at all the same except in racial description. In light of the profound social marginalization that black males confront as unwanted traffic, some have persuasively characterized many young black males as obsolete.[12]

The portrayal of the black man as the criminal element dates back to slavery, and one has to wonder if today's image is a legacy of that institution.[13] However one chooses to answer that question, there is no doubt that the incarceration of black men is a devastating part of today's reality. According to a recent Justice Department report, an estimated 12 percent of black men between the ages of twenty and thirty-four are in jail or prison. By contrast, only 1.6 percent of similar-aged white men are incarcerated. According to the report, the Bureau of Justice Statistics calculates that a startling 28 percent of black men will be sent away to jail or prison during their lifetimes.[14]

In light of these developments, another wrinkle unfolds as Randall Kennedy raised the use of "color as a proxy for dangerousness."[15] When is this reasonable? Why is it reasonable? If reasonable, is it nonetheless at war with racial justice? Although I do not agree with many of Kennedy's policy recommendations, I think he framed the criminal justice issue well: "Whether the legal system ought to authorize people to take race into account in making calculations about the criminal propensity of others is a vexing question. Attuned to the reported demographics of crime, fearful people of all hues engage in race-dependent strategies either to apprehend criminals or to avoid them."[16] Thus stated, the basic issue is two pronged: one focusing on the operation of criminal law and the other on the responses by private persons and the community. At the end of the day, one must ask whether these responses represent self-protective racial discrimination that not only are reasonable but also legitimate.

Anderson argued that the racialized predicament of representing black men as unwanted traffic is worth examining for two reasons. First, the group situation of these men encapsulates the stigmatizing effect of "negative status-determining characteristics, in this case gender and race. Because public encounters between strangers on the streets of urban America are by nature brief, the participants must draw conclusions about each other quickly, and they generally rely on a small number of cues."[17] Second, in the neighborhood of Anderson's study, the presence and behavior of anonymous young black men is "the single dominating concern of many who use its public spaces. The central theme in maintaining safety on the streets is avoiding strange black males."[18]

The predicament of anonymous black men in public space extends, of course, from their own communities to broader society. Calls for heavier policing and disparate treatment in the administration of criminal justice are situated in both contexts. Do these calls represent legitimate expectations? How do legal analysis and the discourse on race and racism respond? How do we explain this and either challenge or legitimate this state of affairs?

Against this backdrop, I first rely on cultural studies in looking at the intersectional predicament—rather than at mere identity—of race, maleness, and space, building on Edward Soja's observation that there is no unspatialized reality. This circumstance has significant implications as blacks are constructed as unwanted traffic across time and space. I argue that if we are to generate effective resistance to this intersectional subordination, we must challenge the cultural construction of black males as unwanted traffic. In the next section, I situate myself as a privileged black male to demonstrate the way in which class mediates the phenomenon of black men as unwanted traffic. In doing so, I argue that there is a need for brother-to-brother connections and solidarity to struggle against the myriad effects of black men as unwanted traffic and as a feature of progressive black masculinity. The following section sets forth a form of praxis that employs intersectional identity as a tactic or strategy for privileged and unprivileged black men to connect. Lucie White's conception of *third-dimension lawyering*,[19] I suggest, provides a personal model for advocacy that brings collaboration among lawyers and others. Finally, I discuss felon disenfranchisement as another consequence of black men as unwanted traffic and as another site for activist intervention and solidarity.

The Unwanted Traffic of Black Males within Culture and Space

The Intersectional Challenge of Black Masculinity

As the introductory epigraphs suggest, there are many challenges to masculinity generally and to black masculinity particularly. Most of the discourse on intersectionality addresses the compounded identity of gender and race as it affects women of color.[20] Thus, for instance, in considering violence against women of color, Kimberlé Crenshaw argued that women of color are "erased by the strategic silences of feminism and antiracism."[21] Even though I agree with this, I think that a large segment of black men also suffer erasure by the strategic silence of antiracism and may find no place at all within any broad men's movement. These are the men who have been overinclusively lumped into the so-called underclass—the unfortunate term popularized in the 1980s to describe the violent, criminal, unemployed black men whose plight falls beyond antiracist concern and whose place within masculinity is at the demonized margin. Of course, many men who face intersectional challenges do not fit this description, and the social behavior attributed to the underclass suggested that black men were inherently violent and criminal. Many of the men constructed as unwanted traffic are neither violent nor criminal, unless it is considered a crime to be underemployed or unemployed. Though the characterization *underclass* is disfavored, the social marginalization it once described is accurate and continues.[22]

This chapter thus addresses the intersection of race and gender as it affects men. The intersectional identity and experience of black men present challenges including various practices that must be resisted, such as heterosexual black men engaging in violence toward women and gay men and in crime and violence toward others within their own neighborhoods. Additionally, many external constraints contribute to subordination whereby black men—because they are both black and men—live out their lives as those who are disproportionately despised, imprisoned, uneducated, and unemployed.

Culture's Designation of Black Males as Unwanted Traffic

To generate resistance to the construction of black males as unwanted traffic, the activist intervention must renegotiate culture. According to Stuart

Hall, the British scholar who has greatly influenced the development of cultural studies, *culture* refers to "the actual grounded terrain of practices, representations, languages and customs of any specific society … [and] the contradictory forms of common sense which have taken root in and helped to shape popular life."[23] Thus, the *cultural* is concerned with the issues that revolve around shared, perhaps hegemonic, social meanings that constitute the variety of ways people make sense of the world. Culture is malleable, not fixed. Society's cultural orientations should not be viewed as "incontestable givens, seamlessly transposed into social norms and institutions."[24] As society produces its cultural orientations, the process entails social contestation and social relations of domination. Thus, societal organization must be understood as "the changing, unstable, loosely coherent product of social relations, cultural innovation and political processes."[25] As Jean Cohen explained, this gives rise to agency: "Contemporary collective actors consciously struggle over the power to socially construct new identities, to create democratic spaces for autonomous social action, and to reinterpret norms and reshape institutions. It thus becomes incumbent on the theorist (a) to look into the processes by which collective actors create the identities and solidarities they defend, (b) to assess the relations between adversaries and the stakes of their conflicts, and (c) to analyze the structural and cultural developments that contribute to such heightened reflexivity."[26] Or, as Catherine MacKinnon asserted, "The first task of a movement for social change is to face one's situation and name it."[27] The situation I am recognizing is the cultural construction of black males as unwanted traffic. Initially, then, I enlist cultural studies for help in making sense of the world as it relates to the experience of the anonymous black man in public space. In relying on cultural studies, however, I do not want to sacrifice the sociological insight that emphasizes the social construction of reality—particularly, racial reality as socially constructed. Thus, cultural or symbolic construction of reality does not lie outside the social. Rather, the sociology of culture interacts symbiotically with cultural studies.[28]

It is impossible to mark the boundaries of cultural studies; there are no precedents or statutes. Cultural studies means different things to different people, but for purposes here the following definition can be adopted.

> (1) Cultural studies is an interdisciplinary field in which perspectives from different disciplines can be selectively drawn on to examine the relations of culture and power. (2) Cultural studies is concerned with all those practices, institutions and systems of classification through which there are inculcated in a population particular values, beliefs, competencies, routines of life and habitual forms of conduct. (3) The forms of power that cultural studies explores are diverse and include gender, race, class, colonialism, etc. Cultural studies seeks to explore the connections between these forms of power and to develop ways of

thinking about culture and power that can be utilized by agents in the pursuit of change. (4) The prime institutional sites for cultural studies are those of higher education and as such cultural studies is like other academic disciplines. Nevertheless, it tries to forge connections outside of the academy with social and political movements, workers in cultural institutions, and cultural management.[29]

Thus, cultural studies represents a potpourri, an eclectic tool kit of theory and practice. The discipline of cultural studies has developed, with all its complexities and self-contradictions, against the backdrop of major shifts in the social world that have changed many people's lives. In Elizabeth Long's view, "These same social changes, refracted through the academy, have made many scholars—perhaps especially those somewhat on the edges of traditional academic communities, disciplines, or careers—feel quite keenly the distance between their own disciplinary traditions and what seems in need of understanding."[30] As a legal scholar, I see the turn to cultural studies as both necessary and proper, because social injustice seems to have overwhelmed the ability of law to redress it. Additionally, legal scholarship, in the narrow sense, seems quite distant from the knowledge needed to open society and establish a more just order.

An additional feature of cultural studies that is helpful to my values and orientation is its identification with progressive and leftist politics. Its theoretical approaches and substantive concerns are conditioned by that identification. In particular, cultural studies has employed its theoretical aspects to engage in a critical commentary of social and cultural life. As Craig Calhoun said in a different context, at a minimum this means that cultural studies seeks "a constructive engagement with the social world that starts from the presumption that existing arrangements ... do not exhaust the range of possibilities. It seeks to explore the ways in which our categories of thought reduce our freedom by occluding recognition of what could be."[31] It thus fits within the critical tradition's imperative to examine and, often, to challenge the pregnant frameworks, categories, and assumptions about the world.

Again, from my view as a legal scholar, cultural studies represents a window of opportunity to construct a response to social change that makes more sense to me than the law's response to that change. The large shifts in society and culture over the fifty-some years since *Brown v. Board of Education* have outpaced the rights and remedies that are part of the Warren Court's legacy. Cultural studies is a tool to bridge this gap. Thus, as I draw on cultural studies, it reflects a realignment of disciplines. Particularly, what I want to suggest here is that the intersection of law and cultural studies provides an analytical framework that responds to the collapse of various explanatory paradigms associated with criminal procedure and civil rights law's ability to advance social justice. Here I use cultural studies as a tool kit with which we can assume a more enabled agency to renegotiate what David Theo Goldberg called our "racist culture."[32] I hope thereby to hint at ways to establish a re-presented image and experience that militate against the treatment of the anonymous black man in public space as unwanted traffic, inmates, and victims of justified homicide.

Resisting the Negative Intersection of Race, Maleness, and Space

According to the critical geographer Edward Soja, "All social relations become real and concrete, a part of our lived social existence, only when they are spatially 'inscribed.'"[33] In referring to the spatial inscription of social relations, Soja argued that social relations are concretely represented in the social production of social space. In his words, "social reality is not just coincidently spatial, existing 'in' space. Social reality is presuppositionally and ontologically spatial. There is no unspatialized reality. There are no aspatial social processes."[34] The factors of spatialized reality and spatial social processes often appear to be conspicuously absent when one can take his space for granted. Whites living in white neighborhoods generally live in unproblematic space; they are able, therefore, to ignore the facts and implications of spatialized reality and social processes. If, in contrast, someone lives in a neighborhood afflicted with toxic dumps and other manifestations of environmental racism, it becomes easy to see how reality and social processes are spatialized and racialized.[35] If someone lives in a hypersegregated neighborhood with all the constraints that suggests, this is seen as well.[36]

Thus, racialized space has a bearing on the treatment of black males as unwanted traffic. The "racialization of space" is "the process by which residential location is taken as an index of the attitudes, values, behavioral inclinations and social norms of the kinds of people who are assumed to live [there]."[37] This index of factors, rooted in racial presumption, gives space a racial identity. Within pockets of such space, race-neutral terms serve as racial code words, such as, for instance, those identified as residents of the inner city, those who occupy public housing projects, and even those housed in prisons or sitting on death row. Regardless of color or class, people are likely to see those within such space as black or Latino. Their images are associated with place, which is a result of space having been racialized.

Martha Mahoney offered a powerful summary of the effects of racialized space:

> Government-sponsored segregation helped inscribe in American culture the equation of "good neighborhoods" with White neighborhoods. The close correlation between employment opportunity and residential segregation meant that "Black" was increasingly linked with "inner-city" and with "unemployed or unemployable" in White consciousness; Whiteness was identified with "employed or employable," stability and self-sufficiency. In this way, residential segregation was both product and cause of racial constructions that ended to promote

further preferences for Whites and further exclusion for Black communities and individuals. White neighborhoods in this process of racial construction increasingly seem to be suitable sites for investment, while Black neighborhoods seem unsuitable.[38]

This process in the context of white supremacy has sanctified and edified white spaces against blackness. In such a context public space is also white space. Thus, those who represent threat are not welcome. No unwanted traffic is to enter.

So, I am talking here about the compoundedness—the synergistic features—of how race interacts with space to create identity. This process generates social relations, constructs cultural and social images of black males, extends or constricts social distance, and permits or prohibits justice in place and out of place. Black people are overly policed at home and are overly suspected away from home. As unwanted traffic within predominantly black space, say, Harlem or south central Los Angeles, a black man can be shot while reaching for his wallet. In predominantly white space, such as neighborhoods or in just about any public space, black men can be stopped while driving black, denied service at Denny's restaurant, passed by when the taxi is empty, or denied a housing opportunity. In each case, black men are unwanted traffic.[39]

There are many ways in which this spatial analysis bears on the institution of criminal justice. The isolation and marginalization of communities of color, as a result of residential segregation and neighborhood poverty, converge to provide an opportunity for strategically disparate treatment in law enforcement—that is, discrimination because of racialized space and racial identity; racial identity and racialized space compound the predicament of racism in law enforcement.[40]

As Elijah Anderson's work indicates, many black males are unwanted traffic even within their own space and even more so when they travel outside that space. The need for regulation of this traffic is never-ending, although the intensity of it may vary from place to place. Manifestations include the drug war within their space and the racial profiling when traveling beyond their space, and harsher penalties for using the drug at home (e.g., crack) than when away (e.g., powder). Neighbors experience victimization and fear of crime at their hands at home, whereas strangers experience mostly just fear while black men are away from home. Worst of all, perhaps, for many of these men home away from home is the state or federal prison, which too has become racialized space—a prototype of racialized space that now competes with the *ghetto*. Indeed, these two spaces represent the primary sites of containment—the space that sets the desirable bounds for regulating unwanted traffic in the hearts and minds of those who live outside of these spaces. Once the black male leaves either of these spaces—prison or the ghetto—there are societal, cultural, and institutional pressures, virtual conspiracies, to return him home, either to his prison home or to his ghetto home.

Douglas Massey argued that the unusually high degree of residential segregation of blacks from whites stems from the operation of three interrelated and mutually reinforcing forces in American society: (1) high levels of institutionalized discrimination in the real estate and banking industries, (2) discriminatory public policies implemented by whites at all levels of government, and (3) high levels of prejudice among whites against blacks as potential neighbors.[41] All three must be challenged, but it is prejudice against blacks that makes it very difficult to identify opportunities for intervention. That factor, moreover, is reinforced less by negative interaction between blacks and others and more by society's acceptance of negative cultural portrayals of the black male—stereotypic images in the mass media, from the eleven o'clock news to the crime reports in the local daily that distort white dreams of brotherhood into a multifaceted vision of black males as their worst nightmares.

This is why the renegotiation of culture is so important. If the cultural apparatus explains and justifies the treatment of black males, it often does so outside of the context of neighbors sharing residential space. Fear and loathing block even the potential for transformation of the opportunities for sustained interaction on a common ground. It makes it harder to question the common-sense understandings about the experience and the performance of black maleness. Charles Murray, the reactionary commentator, for instance, argued that liberals are mistaken in their reliance on the idea that whites discriminate against blacks based on "negative stereotypes about black neighbors [that] remain firmly entrenched in white psyches."[42] According to Murray, these stereotypes, which include the idea that blacks are more prone to violence and crime than whites, are more likely to live off welfare, and are lazier and less moral than whites, are "founded on empirically accurate understandings about contemporary black behaviour compared to contemporary white behaviour."[43] In other words, more bluntly, Murray appears to say that the negative stereotypes about blacks are true, consistent with accurate understandings about black behavior. In a similar vein, Nathan Glazer criticized liberal integrationists for not honestly addressing the negative effects of an increase in black population on property values. He argued that property values in neighborhoods decreased "not because blacks lived there, but because crime increased, schools declined, and the public sphere was neglected."[44] He concluded that black residential segregation will end when the black "behavior that induces the [white] motives of resistance or avoidance is reduced."[45]

Criminal and violent behavior lead the list of the negative behaviors that motivate white resistance and avoidance. The white fear of crime and violence is difficult to abate. Thus, the regulation of unwanted traffic remains paramount, and, worse, it extends not only to those far from home but also to those actually far from the image that generates the metaphor. The aversion of black males stems from conscious and unconscious racism that suggests to many—not just whites—that black males share a syndrome of negative traits.

Brother to Brother: Reaching across Class

Appreciating these observations, I address the challenge of black males of privilege, such as myself, standing in activist solidarity with black men who are primarily subordinated because they are black and male.[46] Moreover, as I am a Harvard-trained law professor, I am writing from the perspective of a privileged black male, although my privilege only approximates that of a similarly situated white male. Additionally, I am writing as a progressive, privileged black male. This is no simple task, writing from this complex, compounded perspective. Some might view me as necessarily an Oreo, because the cost of success within the mainstream opportunity structure not only distances me from most of my less privileged brothers but also de-races, or whitewashes, me to a large degree. But even from my privileged position, I still must negotiate race every day, and I still must clear racism's hurdles every day.[47] In my trek toward success in America, I have not given up my blackness, but all too often I have had to tailor it and to perform my black identity in a way that meets white societal expectations and approval. As I hold tightly to my blackness under these circumstances, however, I do not personify Horatio Alger in whiteface but, rather, in blackface. There is a caveat, though. As Mark Whitaker, the black editor of *Newsweek,* observed, "When Whites say they have an open mind about Blacks, they're talking about Blacks who are like them."[48] Though I reject integration as assimilation, I feel the pressures that Whitaker identifies. In short, as a relatively successful black male in America, I see what most whites seldom see, which is the pressure to stay black in predominantly white settings.

Another complicating feature of this experienced identity is the notion of success itself. Sociologist Raymond Mack argued that many whites "believe two things—that all people are created equal, and that Blacks are inferior to Whites."[49] Thus, I am often in the interesting predicament that as whites come to know, to accept, and to respect me, they simultaneously disassociate me from my racial group. Separated from the anonymous amalgam of black males and the negative stereotypes that freight their images, I am viewed as different. I am simply an individual, and these accepting whites do not alter their negative views of black males more generally. Indeed, Mack claimed, "[t]he truth is that if you succeed, Whites won't treat you as though you're Black. They treat you as though you're middle class."[50] Is it not ironic: I am black until I succeed.

Yet, of course, when I am out of the context of obvious success—not dressed in my suit or acting as the professor of law—I fall back into anonymity. Blackness then displaces the acceptance I get when I am not anonymous. Now, within this fluid context of success and anonymity, I must continually invent my black identity and connect it to other black males. If I am going to be progressive about my masculinity, moreover, I need to try and connect it to those black males who may not enjoy the trappings of my success—to blacks whom society sees as unacceptable because they are black. Of course, when I make this connection, heretofore accepting whites often rerecognize me as black, as an irritant within institutional and cultural frameworks who too often declares that race matters and who too often protests matters of race. Almost always, these accepting whites characterize me during these moments of manifested race consciousness as "playing the race card," "whining," or being "too sensitive." Nonetheless, I am unapologetically a critical race theorist.[51]

Although I am not sure that I can define *progressive masculinity,* I nonetheless claim to write from that perspective. To suggest that perspective's meaning, I briefly contrast two privileged black males who graduated from the prestigious Yale Law School: the late humanitarian and federal jurist A. Leon Higginbotham on one hand and Supreme Court Justice Clarence Thomas on the other hand. In speaking to graduating seniors at Wesleyan University in 1996, Judge Higginbotham told them, "I will make two requests of you. They are that you always attempt to see those human beings who become invisible to most people, and that you always try to hear the pleas of those persons who, despite their pain and suffering, have become voiceless and forgotten."[52] As Charles Ogeltree remarked on the passing of Judge Higginbotham, "[o]nce he succeeded, he was one who didn't hesitate to let the rope drop back down and help others who needed it."[53] The judge did not distance himself from his own blackness, and, moreover, he connected his work to broader humanity. Regardless of his individual success, he never removed himself from the struggles for social justice, open society, and inclusive democracy.

Justice Thomas represents a different view of black masculinity that is marked by a radical individualism, a formalized sense of race, and a thin sense of equality. In other words, he is colorblind. In 1998, Justice Thomas spoke to an eighteen-year-old black youth who was about to depart the housing projects of southeast Washington, D.C., to attend Brown University. He advised the young man, Cedric Jennings, "[n]o doubt one thing you'll find when you get to a school like Brown is a lot of classes and orientation on race relations. Try to avoid them."[54] Furthermore, he added, "[t]ry to say to yourself, 'I'm not a Black person. I'm just a person.' You'll find a lot of so-called multicultural combat, a lot of struggle between ethnic and racial groups wanting you to sign on, to narrow yourself into some group identity or other. You have to resist that, Cedric."[55] Finally, Justice Thomas told this student, "[w]hat I look for in hiring my clerks—the cream of the crop—I look for the math and sciences, real classes, none of that Afro-American study stuff. If they'd taken that stuff as an undergraduate, I don't want them."[56] As an expression of progressive black masculinity, I write not only within the tradition of Judge Higginbotham but also in resistance to the tradition of Justice Thomas.

Brother to Brother Again: Advancing Collective Identity and Solidarity in the Challenge to Felon Disenfranchisement

The discussion thus far has argued that racial residential segregation structures all anonymous black people as unwanted traffic in white and public space, marking their visibility and presence as out of place. Black men are paradigmatic representations of unwanted traffic, however, largely because their gendered images both historically and currently are so closely and dramatically associated with violence generally and violent crime particularly. This plays out in society as gendered racism, a phenomenon seldom acknowledged within a complex intersectional context of four features: race, space, maleness, and class.

Also, to this point, I have argued that the concept and practice of treating black men as unwanted traffic seems to augment, to justify, or to raise the stakes in assigning reasonable and unreasonable suspicion of black men just for being black men. These reactions lead to overpolicing black men within black communities and to practices of racial profiling, among others, when black men are outside of their communities. This overpolicing and racial profiling also seems, in part, to be responsible for high incarceration rates of black men and thus for their disenfranchisement in many states. As I shall elaborate, their disenfranchisement hurts me, other black men, and the larger black community because it dilutes what some might consider the black bloc vote and prohibits these men from voting and potentially changing laws and lawmakers that aid in their being profiled and incarcerated in the first place. The problem of voter disenfranchisement thus provides black people—all black people—with a concrete opportunity to engage politically and collectively.

The right to vote is cherished. Blacks have fought and died to secure this right and to make it a meaningful expression of democracy. Yet within a nation where there is virtually universal suffrage, over four million convicted felons cannot vote under varied circumstances.[57] They constitute the largest single group of citizens who are prohibited by state laws from voting in both state and federal elections. Among them, 1.5 million are African Americans. Although comprising 12 percent of the national population, blacks represent almost 38 percent of disenfranchised felons. Remarkably, nine states deny felons the right to vote for the rest of their lives. Disenfranchised black felons probably remain disenfranchised not only because of race but also because they stand pretty much alone and lack political support.[58] Progressive masculinity implores black people to engage this issue and to support their challenge to this predicament.

The problems in Florida during the 2000 presidential election indicate the common ground we share. As Lani Guinier pointed out, in Florida as a result of permanent disenfranchisement over 400,000 former felons—almost 50 percent of them black, mostly males—were ineligible to vote in the 2000 election.

She observed, moreover, that Florida has the largest number of people affected by the lifetime prohibition rule. A startling 30 percent of black men in some southern states are disenfranchised because of prior felonies.[59]

In 2000, during the presidential election, officials in Florida attempted to counter potential voter fraud by purging the rolls of felons. This effort had a racist impact, as 44 percent of the names on the felon list were black, and the felon purge eliminated 8,456 blacks from the voter rolls before the election.[60] It is said that justice delayed is often justice denied. Ultimately, of the 4,847 people who appealed after the election, 2,430 were determined not to have been convicted felons.[61] Given the profiles of the felons, disproportionately black and Latino, it is likely that if these voters had not been purged, the outcome of the presidential election may well have been different. In the blunt observation of Michael Tomasky, "A wildly inaccurate purge of voters, which the state of Florida knew to be inaccurate but did nothing to correct, cost Al Gore Florida, and the presidency."[62] This was part of the larger effort by state officials to play dirty tricks—"something purposeful and foul"—in a deliberate effort to disenfranchise blacks.[63]

Even though the events that unfolded in Florida were the most salient and perhaps the most egregious, the problem transcends its borders and demands that black people exercise activist solidarity and articulate a collective identity to redress the denial of democracy that occurred in 2000. According to Marc Mauer, "if current criminal justice trends continue, we can expect that 30–40 percent of black males born today will lose the right to vote for at least part of their adult lives."[64] Because the rate of incarceration has increased so dramatically in the last forty years, social scientists speculate that had the current level existed in 1960, "it is very likely that Richard Nixon would have defeated John Kennedy in the popular vote and possible that Nixon would have won the electoral college vote as well."[65]

Although litigation has been filed challenging the practices in Florida, it is uncertain how that will play out. Beyond the courtroom, black people must press the case to challenge the racial injustice of felon disenfranchisement. We must support efforts such as that of John Conyers, who has proposed legislation in Congress. Strategic use of the media must be engaged and scholarship produced to underscore that the United States has the most restrictive, unjust disenfranchisement laws of any democratic nation in the world, particularly laws that impose lifetime bans. The harsh consequences that can result represent not only an extreme construction of black men as unwanted traffic (in the voting booth), but also excessive racial injustice. Pursuant to Virginia law, for instance, an eighteen-year-old convicted of felony drug possession—not dealing—in that state who successfully completes his sentence to a drug treatment program is disenfranchised for life even though he may not have spent a single day in jail.[66]

As an attorney and legal scholar, therefore, I work within what Lucie White termed the *third dimension of advocacy*.[67] Therefore, I try to move beyond first-dimension test case litigation and law reform that seeks sweeping and innovative remedies. I even try to move beyond second-dimension work with marginalized, subordinated, and underrepresented communities to use litigation to "wide[n] the public imagination about right and wrong, mobilize political action behind new social arrangements, [and] pressure those in power to make concessions."[68] Here, law and litigation are viewed as public action with political significance. As with the legal challenge to felon disenfranchisement, the law and its practice in this dimension have cultural meaning, constituting a discourse about social justice. The advocacy seeks to influence public consciousness.[69] Believe me, this is exemplary progressive lawyering, but it is not enough. We must move to the next dimension.

Third-dimension lawyering entails collaborative work with the client community. This challenges subordination at the level of consciousness of the client community. The third dimension of lawyering involves "helping a group learn how to interpret moments of domination as opportunities for resistance."[70] Drawing on the work of Paulo Freire, third-dimension lawyering involves mutual consciousness rising between the lawyer and group, who learn together that "[i]t is an unconventional, non-hierarchal learning practice in which small groups reflect together upon the immediate conditions of their lives. The groups first search their shared reality for feelings about that reality that have previously gone unnamed. They then attempt to re-evaluate these common understandings as problems to be solved. They collectively design actions to respond to these problems and, insofar as possible, to carry them out. They then continue to reflect upon the changed reality, thereby deepening their analysis of domination and their concrete understandings of their own power."[71] This image, of course, is foreign to the traditional image of the lawyer. Indeed, one does not really need a law degree or an attorney's license to practice this dimension of advocacy. I think, however, that White is correct in observing that "fluency in the law—that is, a deep practical understanding of law as a discourse for articulating norms of justice and an array of rituals for resolving social conflict—will greatly improve a person's flexibility and effectiveness at 'third dimensional work.'"[72]

Brother-to-brother connection, activist solidarity, and collective identity implore black men to adopt the Judge Higginbotham sensibility and orientation I mentioned earlier as a demonstration of progressive black masculinity. We must recognize that felon disenfranchisement is a collateral consequence of mass incarceration—of a criminal justice system and prison industry gone wild. This outrageous state of affairs not only disproportionately affects black and brown brothers and their families and loved ones, but it also offends our legitimate expectations of racial justice and fundamental fairness. It embarrasses democracy.

Conclusion

The interaction and relations of black men must transcend particularized identity features associated with socioeconomic class, location and place of living, sexual orientation, and the like if we are to find the common ground to address injustice. One site of intervention is a racist culture that must be renegotiated so that our representation of black men as unwanted traffic can be destabilized, if not abolished. As I have emphasized, space constitutes a race-making situation, in that racialized space, in particular, associates black men with an index of attitudes, values, behavioral inclinations, and social norms imposed on them, more than they are chosen freely. In short, as Soja teaches, there is no aspatialized reality or social process. The cultural construction of black men as unwanted traffic illustrates the spatial inscription of social relations, both here and there. I have tried to show how the reasonable and unreasonable suspicion of black men has played out in devastating ways, particularly within the so-called criminal justice system. The ramifications are broad, including the denial of democracy through the felon disenfranchisement that brothers experience as a collateral consequence of mass incarceration.

As Kendall Thomas reminded, membership in a race, like membership in the national community, is "imagined."[73] Drawing on the work of Benedict Anderson, Thomas observed that most African Americans "will never know most of their fellow-members, meet them, or even hear of them, yet in the minds of each lives the image of their communion."[74] From this insight, Thomas declared, "the discourse of collective identity must, as a political matter, be understood and engaged as a technique or strategy."[75] Here, Thomas was focusing on the need to militate against "[t]he exclusion of Black gay men and lesbians from full, equal participation in African-American life … ."[76] In discussing the perils of black authenticity formation, Thomas argued, "We know that the obsessive preoccupation with proof of racial authenticity deflects attention and energy away from the need to come to grips with the real, material challenges in whose resolution black Americans of both genders and all sexual identifications have an immediate and urgent interest."[77] I see an analogous call for privileged black men to connect with marginalized black men. Though we sometimes share the status of unwanted traffic, I know full well that my being passed by when the taxi is empty is not the devastating experience that so many less privileged black men experience. Yet I also know that although I can vote, I have an immediate and urgent interest in securing that right for disenfranchised felons. Although I am subjected to reasonable and unreasonable suspicions, I know that I generally assume less risk of police misconduct than I would if I were poor and lived on a street with an inner-city zip code.

When the conference convened in Buffalo, New York, in April 2000 to explore the issues that revolve around progressive black masculinity, I had not thought very much about the subject matter. In some ways, I simply assumed that I represented progressive black masculinity. I know better now that this identity and its appurtenant values and practices cannot be simply assumed. After the conference and in writing this essay, I also know that brother-to-brother third-dimensional work is an urgent call. This essay is written in response to that call.

Notes

1. Michael S. Kimmel and Michael A. Messner, eds., *Men's Lives*, 5th ed. (Needham Heights, MA: Allyn & Bacon, 2001), intro., xv.
2. Manning Marable, "The Black Male: Searching beyond Stereotypes," in Kimmel and Messner, *Men's Lives*, 17.
3. *City of Memphis v. Greene*, 451 U.S. 100 (1981).
4. Ibid., 139.
5. See Edward J. Blakely and Mary Gail Snyder, *Fortress America: Gated and Walled Communities in the United States* (Washington, DC: Brookings Institution Press, 1997), 152, which describes gated areas as a concrete metaphor for exclusion of immigrants and nonwhites.
6. See, generally, Marc Mauer, *Race to Incarcerate*, (New York: New Press, 2001).
7. Leonard Steinhorn and Barbara Diggs-Brown, *By the Color of Our Skin: The Illusion of Integration and the Reality of Race* (New York: Dutton, 1999), 40.
8. John O. Calmore, "The Law and Culture-Shift: Race and the Warren Court Legacy," *Washington and Lee Law Review* 59, no. 4 (2002), 1095. Also, Latinos, Asians, and non-European immigrants are significant constructions of unwanted traffic. Kevin R. Johnson, "The Case for African American and Latina/o Cooperation in Challenging Racial Profiling in Law Enforcement," *Florida Law Review* 55, no. 1 (2003), 341.
9. Elijah Anderson, *Streetwise: Race, Class, and Change in an Urban Community* (Chicago: University of Chicago Press, 1990), 163.
10. Ibid.
11. Ibid.
12. Jewelle Taylor Gibbs, ed., *Young, Black, and Male in America: An Endangered Species* (Westport, CT: Auburn House, 1988).
13. Randall Kennedy stated, "Many jurisdictions that permitted slaveholding institutionalized the linkage of Blackness with suspiciousness by empowering all whites to demand proof of a black's status as a slave or free person. Since blacks were presumed to be slaves, any black person lacking obvious supervision by a white person was deemed to be suspect, a possible fugitive from bondage." Kennedy, *Race, Crime, and the Law* (New York: Pantheon, 1997), 138.
14. David A. Harris, "The Stories, the Statistics, and the Law: Why 'Driving While Black' Matters," *Minnesota Law Review* 84, no. 2 (1999), 301. "[O]ne in three black men between the ages of 20 and 29 were ... either in prison or jail, on probation, or on parole." Ibid.
15. Kennedy, *Race, Crime*, 136.
16. Ibid., 136–37.
17. Anderson, *Streetwise*, 163.
18. Ibid.
19. Lucie E. White, "To Learn and Teach: Lessons from Driefontein on Lawyering and Power," *Wisconsin Law Review* 1988 (1988), 699.
20. See Margaret L. Anderson and Patricia Hill Collins, eds., *Race, Class, and Gender: An Anthology*, 4th ed. (Belmont, CA: Wadsworth, 2001); and Adrien Katherine Wing, ed., *Critical Race Feminism: A Reader* (New York: New York University Press, 1997).
21. Kimberlé Crenshaw, "Mapping the Margins: Intersectionality, Identity Politics, and Violence against Women of Color," *Stanford Law Review* 43 (1991), 1253.
22. Michael B. Katz, ed., *The Underclass Debate: Views from History* (Princeton, NJ: Princeton University Press, 1993).
23. Chris Barker, *Cultural Studies: Theory and Practice* (London: Sage Publications, 2000), 8, quoting Stuart Hall, "Gramsci's Relevance for the Study of Race and Ethnicity," in *Stuart Hall: Critical Dialogues in Cultural Studies*, ed. David Morely and Kuan-Hsing Chen (New York: Routledge, 1996), 439.

24. Hall, "Gramsci's Relevance," 439.
25. Jean L. Cohen, "Strategy or Identity: New Theoretical Paradigms and Contemporary Social Movements," *Social Research* 52, no. 4 (Winter 1985), 699, quoting Alain Touraine, "Triumph or Downfall of Evil Society?" *Humanities in Review* 1(1982), 220.
26. Cohen, "Strategy or Identity," 690.
27. Catherine A. MacKinnon, *Toward a Feminist Theory of the State* (Cambridge, MA: Harvard University Press, 1989), 241.
28. See Victoria E. Bonnell and Lynn Hunt, eds., *Beyond the Cultural Turn: New Directions in the Study of Society and Culture* (Berkeley: University of California Press, 1999); and David Chaney, *The Cultural Turn: Scene-Setting Essays on Contemporary Cultural History* (New York: Routledge, 1994).
29. Barker, *Cultural Studies*, 7.
30. Elizabeth Long, "Introduction: Engaging Sociology and Cultural Studies: Disciplinarity and Social Change," in *From Sociology to Cultural Studies: New Perspectives*, ed. Elizabeth Long (Cambridge, MA: Blackwell Publishers, 1997), 17.
31. Craig Calhoun, *Critical Social Theory: Culture, History, and the Challenge of Difference* (Cambridge, MA: Blackwell Publishers, 1995), xviii.
32. David Theo Goldberg, *Racist Culture: Philosophy and the Politics of Meaning* (Cambridge, MA: Blackwell, 1993).
33. Edward W. Soja, *Thirdspace: Journeys to Los Angeles and Other Real-and-Imagined Places* (Cambridge, MA: Blackwell Publishers, 1996), 46.
34. Ibid.
35. Sheila Foster, "Justice from the Ground Up: Distributive Inequities, Grassroots Resistance, and the Transformative Politics of the Environmental Justice Movement," *California Law Review* 86, no. 4 (1998), 775.
36. Stephen Nathan Haymes, *Race, Culture, and the City: A Pedagogy for Black Urban Struggle* (Albany: State University of New York Press, 1995).
37. Calmore, "Racialized Space and the Culture of Segregation: 'Hewing a Stone of Hope from a Mountain of Despair,'" *University of Pennsylvania Law Review* 143 (1995), 1235–36.
38. Martha R. Mahoney, "Segregation, Whiteness, and Transformation," *University of Pennsylvania Law Review* 143 (1995), 1674.
39. Calmore, "Law and Culture Shift."
40. See Bela August Walker, "The Color of Crime: The Case against Race-Based Suspect Descriptions," *Columbia Law Review* 103, no. 4 (2003), 662; and Katheryn K. Russell, "The Racial Hoax as Crime: The Law as Affirmation," *Indiana Law Journal* 71, no. 3 (1996), 593.
41. Douglas S. Massey, "Getting Away with Murder: Segregation and Violent Crime in Urban America," *University of Pennsylvania Law Review* 143 (1995), 1203.
42. Charles Murray, "Class and Underclass," *New York Times*, May 21, 1993, sec. 7 (literary supplement), 9, which reviews Douglas S. Massey and Nancy A. Denton, *American Apartheid: Segregation and the Making of the Underclass* (Cambridge, MA: Harvard University Press, 1993).
43. Ibid.
44. Nathan Glazer, "American Apartheid: Segregation and the Making of the Underclass," *New Republic*, August 2, 1993, 40.
45. Ibid.
46. See Herb Boyd and Robert L. Allen, *Brotherman: The Odyssey of Black Men in America* (New York: Ballantine Books, 1995).
47. Ellis Cose, *The Rage of a Privileged Class* (New York: Harper Collins, 1993).
48. Mark Whitaker, "White and Black Lies," *Newsweek*, November 15, 1993, 52, 55.
49. Ibid.
50. Ibid.
51. As Cheryl Harris noted, "From this vantage point, the issue is not simply how societal bias is reflected in the legal system or how the law manages disputes that implicate race: The objective is to map the mutually constitutive relationship between race and the law. The law produces, constructs, and constitutes race, not only in domains where race is explicitly articulated, but also where race is unspoken and unacknowledged." Harris, "Critical Race Studies: An Introduction," *UCLA Law Review* 49, no. 5, (2002), 1216–17.

52. William Glaberson, "A. Leon Higginbotham, Jr., Federal Judge, Is Dead at 70," *New York Times*, December 15, 1998, B14.
53. Ibid.
54. Ron Suskin, "And Clarence Thomas Wept," *Esquire*, July 1998, 70–74.
55. Ibid.
56. Ibid.
57. Alexander Keysarr, *The Right to Vote: The Contested History of Democracy in the United States* (New York: Basic Books, 2000), 308.
58. Calmore, "Race Conscious Voting Rights and the New Demography in a Multiracing America," *University of North Carolina Law Review* 79, no. 5 (2001), 1274–75.
59. Lani Guinier, "What We Must Overcome," *American Prospect*, March 12, 2001, 28.
60. Melanie Eversley and Gary Kane, "Black Leaders Sense Sinister Motive in Purge," *Palm Beach Post*, May 27, 2001, 17A.
61. John Lantigua, "How the GOP Gamed the System in Florida," *Nation*, April 30, 2001, 11.
62. Michael Tomasky, "The Media and the Florida Fiasco," *TIKKUN*, May 1, 2001, 58.
63. Robert E. Pierre, "Botched Name Purge Denied Some the Right to Vote," *Washington Post*, May 31, 2001, A1.
64. Mauer, "Felon Voting Disenfranchisement: A Growing Collateral Consequence of Mass Incarceration," *Federal Sentencing Reporter* 12 (March–April 2000), 248.
65. Christopher Uggen and Jeff Manza, *The Political Consequences of Felon Disenfranchisement Laws in the United States* (draft presented to the American Sociological Association, August 11, 2000), discussed in Samuel Issacharoff, Pamela S. Karlan, and Richard H. Pildes, *Law of Democracy: Legal Structure of the Political Process* 10 (Supp. 2001), XX–XX. See also Uggen and Manza, "Democratic Contraction? Political Consequences of Felon Disenfranchisement Laws in the United States," *American Sociological Review* 67 (2002), 777–803.
66. Kendall Thomas, "'Ain't Nothin' Like the Real Thing': Black Masculinity, Gay Sexuality, and the Jargon of Authenticity," in Byrd and Guy-Sheftall, *Traps*, 338 39.
67. White, "Learn and Teach."
68. Ibid, 758–59.
69. White, "Learn and Teach."
70. Ibid.
71. Ibid.
72. Ibid, 765. See also Calmore, "Social Justice in the Third Dimension: Addressing the Problem of 'Preservation through Transformation,'" *University of Florida Journal of International Law* 16 (2004), 615.
73. Thomas, "'Ain't Nothin,'" 339.
74. Ibid., which quotes Benedict Anderson, *Imagined Communities: Reflections on the Origin and Spread of Nationalism* (New York: Verso, 1983), 15.
75. Ibid.
76. Ibid.
77. Ibid.

9
Incarcerated Masculinities

TERESA A. MILLER

The Re/construction of Masculinity in Prison

Much like military recruits, men entering the adult correctional system are presumed to bring identities that serviced them as criminal offenders but that are ill-suited to their new roles as correctional subjects. To reconstruct these men, the adult correctional system attempts to strip them of their previous identities and of all the symbols and insignia of status and social being.[1] In what Erving Goffman described as "mortification of the self," new prisoners are refashioned in state-issued clothing and are relegated to cramped living spaces shared by individuals of unknown history and status.[2] Within the institutional context of externally controlled relationships, close quarters, and near-total lack of privacy, new prisoners are quickly assessed for their potential for danger or threat, as collective safety depends on accurately assessing the type of man with which one is living or associating.[3] With resources for constructing manhood far more limited than those available to men "at liberty" or "on the street," prisoners employ physical space, their bodies, and language in distinctive ways to demonstrate masculinity.[4]

In the growing academic discipline of men's studies, researchers increasingly describe masculinity as a fluid and emergent construction rather than one based on physiology. Masculinity constructed in prison is neither static nor predetermined. It is based on social action tailored to particular circumstances and relationships and is renegotiated in each particular context.[5] Throughout the relatively brief history of prisons, many different masculinities have dominated—and coexisted—at correctional facilities at various times and places.

Whereas scholars have begun to analyze these masculinities through the lens of critical gender theory, these accounts have not adequately critiqued masculinity at the intersection of both race and gender. They leave unanswered the question of how prison masculinities are racialized and racializing and of how racialized prison masculinities more broadly produce and change masculinities in society. This chapter examines the racial and gender dimensions of the hyperaggressive prison masculinity that dominates many U.S. prisons and jails today. Specifically, I focus on the prominence of this masculinity among an expanding population of incarcerated black men. What emerges is a masculinity informed by a racialized system of sexual violence in which black men play a role. Whereas others have analyzed black men's embrace of this hyperaggressive masculinity in prison as an expression of black rage and rebellion against white authority, I demonstrate how this idea masks the structured vulnerability of black men as criminal subjects in the current era of mass incarceration wherein black and brown men are being imprisoned in record numbers. Furthermore, I explore the impact of incarceration on black ex-offenders and the urban, predominantly black communities to which they return, including the impact of this masculinity on those communities. Far from empowering black men, the hegemonic hyperaggressive masculinity and racialized sexual violence it generates work to further subordinate black men and their communities of origin.

Prison Masculinities within the "Total Institution" of the 1940s and 1950s

In the 1940s and '50s, a prisoner commonly established his masculinity within the prison context by observing the convict code. The convict code, or simply the code, is a set of social norms that establishes the moral order in a prison. It emerged in the context of prisons characterized as total institutions, where prison officials used force and unreviewable discretion to rule prisoners absolutely. It continues to influence the moral order among prisoners today.

Inmates strongly committed to living by the code are considered regular or stand-up guys and are accorded high status. Gresham Sykes and Sheldon Messinger summarized the norms or behavioral expectations comprising the code,[6] and Lee Bowker extracted from these norms the traits of an ideal prisoner who follows the code. Such an inmate is strongly pro-prisoner, hostile to the administration, tough, cool, and dependable. The system is the only common enemy; therefore, crimes committed in defiance of prison rules bolster an inmate's status, whereas snitching to prison officials relegates a prisoner to the lowest rung on the social ladder,[7] a position enforced by social rejection, and even sexual violence. In the context of the predominantly white prison population of that era, the dominant masculinity—the stand-up guy—was primarily performed by incarcerated white men. However, this dominant masculinity escaped the racialization that would attach to the masculinitis of the later, and considerably darker, prison population of the drug war era.

Muslim Masculinity of the Prisoners' Rights Era

Within the context of a politically militant civil rights movement, focused on racial uplift and equality, a new performance of masculinity became popular across the nation's prisons, coexisting with—and complementing—the code. Muslim masculinity emerged in the 1950s and '60s, reflecting the embrace of Islam as a religion of liberation by black convicts, a growing minority within the prison population. As more black prisoners renounced Christianity and joined the Nation of Islam, the values of that group permeated black prison masculinity: discipline, personal dignity, strict religious observance including prayer and dietary restrictions, and racial separatism. Since the 1930s, when Elijah Mohammed founded the Nation of Islam, these characteristics have been useful in helping black people on the outside concentrate economic resources and achieve a degree of economic self-sufficiency.

The well-known story of Malcolm X's prison transformation highlights the significance of Muslim masculinity to black prisoners of that period. In his autobiography, Malcolm Little described how by strictly disciplining himself to abstain from eating pork and smoking cigarettes, to pray, to study, and to completely distrust whites—who comprise the majority of prison guards—he reinvented himself as Malcolm X, a man whom other prisoners looked up to and emulated.[8] Malcolm described an encounter with a Harvard seminary student who was teaching a Bible class in Charlestown Prison. He challenged the tall, blonde, blue-eyed student on the racial identity of Jesus, forcing him to admit before a class of black inmates that Jesus, a Hebrew, was a black man. Malcolm wrote that "[e]xactly as I had known it would, almost overnight the Charlestown convicts, black and white, began buzzing with the story. Wherever I went, I could feel the nodding."[9]

Muslim masculinity furnished a form of resistance to an infantilizing, racially biased prison system. Muslim masculinity prioritized self-respect and personal dignity and was legitimated by religious doctrine. Owing largely to its rigid orthodoxy, the Nation of Islam became associated with the miraculous rehabilitation of hardened criminals for whom the prison disciplinary model was largely ineffectual.

The Hyperaggressive Prison Masculinity of the War on Drugs

The war on drugs and its burgeoning prison population intensified a particular expression of masculinity predicated on sexual violence, racial antagonism, predation, and misogyny. The construction of this hyperaggressive masculinity has been extensively studied across academic disciplines.[10] Early studies of male rape in prison suggested that the incidence of sexual assaults in prison was quite low. However, studies conducted since the late 1970s report much higher incidences of sexual victimization. In a 1994 study of a Nebraska prison, researchers found that 22 percent of the men they anonymously surveyed reported having been coerced into sexual acts against their will.[11] In a study of several prisons across the Midwest four years later, these same researchers found sexual coercion rates equally as high at 19 percent.[12]

Like mainstream masculinities on the outside, the hyperaggressive, drug-war-era prison masculinity is predicated on the domination of others, particularly women, complete with matching social and sexual roles. However, prison masculinities reflect a narrower, compressed range of masculinities due to the scarcity of resources over which prisoners can assert dominance. As such, sexual violence and domination become the key feature in this system, with men playing all the roles.

The dominant prisoner in the contemporary prison system is the *man* or the *jocker*. Although there are many linguistic variations on the term across the nation's prisons, as Stephen Donaldson explained, the term *man* is universal in prison slang.[13] *Men* occupy the dominant position in a social hierarchy of masculinities maintained through the subjugation of the feminine. *Men* have the greatest authority and power among male prisoners. In essence, *men* rule the joint. They establish values and norms for the entire prison population. They are political leaders, gang members, or organizers of the market economies within prisons, including the drug trade, sex trade, protection rackets, and contraband smuggling.

Manhood is established and maintained through the sexual penetration of less-dominant male prisoners. *Men, pitchers* or also called *jockers,* are sexually active men, usually black and Hispanic and under middle age. If a jocker is paired off with a mate, he is a *daddy*. If he maintains his status as a man through sexual coercion, he is a *booty bandit* or a *gorilla*.

A small class of *queens* exists below men. Generally comprising no more than 1 or 2 percent of the prison population, they seek and are assigned the passive sexual role traditionally associated with women. They are referred to with feminine pronouns and terms.[14] They have "pussies," not "assholes"; they wear "blouses," not "shirts"; and they are referred to as "her" or "she" rather than "him" or "he." Within a culture where manhood is established in opposition to the feminine, as in society in general, queens are highly desirable as sexual partners. Much like feminine "arm candy" on the outside, the queen is the foil who instantly defines her partner as a man and a jocker. In jails, many queens are street transvestites charged with prostitution.[15] However, consistent with the patriarchy that pervades the prison culture at all levels, queens are excluded from positions of power within the inmate economy. They are often scapegoated, prostituted, and viewed with contempt by both the men and prison staff.[16]

At the bottom of the social hierarchy are *punks* or *bitches*. Punks are male prisoners who have been forced into sexual submission through rape or the credible threat thereof, either by an individual or a group of prisoners (i.e., gang rape). Punks are treated as slaves. Sexual access to their bodies is sold through prostitution, is exchanged in satisfaction of debt, and is loaned to others for favors.[17] Punks tend to be younger prisoners, smaller in physical stature, inexperienced first timers, often incarcerated for nonviolent or victimless offenses, often middle class, and almost invariably white.[18]

Queens and punks, collectively referred to as *catchers,* are treated similarly in many respects. Both are denied the privileges of manhood, are enslaved by men, are excluded from positions of leadership, and are the subjects of sexual commerce. However, punks are lower in the prison social hierarchy because they bear the stigma of fallen men—incapable of resisting sexual penetration and thus of defending their manhood. Conversely, John Coggeshall suggested that queens maintain a higher status because they are able to maintain "control of their own lives and of their own self-concept."[19]

A catcher is required to act as a wife—keeping her man's cell tidy, doing laundry, making the bunk, and making and serving coffee.[20] Once coerced to assume the sexually receptive position, punks are considered fair game for any booty bandit. Hence, punks—and unpaired queens—quickly hook up with a jocker or a group of jockers for protection. Donaldson described the incentive for such pairings: "Usually a rape or two is sufficient to persuade an unattached Catcher to pair off as soon as possible."[21] Once claimed by a daddy, a punk gains protection. In return the daddy who owns him gains status.[22] The daddy has the reciprocal husbandly obligation to defend his *kid,* even at the cost of his own personal safety, although safety for the kid is relative. The daddy also has the privilege to use his kid as a source of revenue, prostituting her or loaning her to others. These relationships range from ruthless exploitation to romantic love.

Manhood is a tenuous status, constantly under siege. It can be lost irretrievably through a single incidence of sexual submission. *Men* must constantly demonstrate their manhood through sexual conquest or be challenged and risk being overpowered. Hence, the surest way to minimize the risk of demotion is to aggressively prey on other prisoners.[23]

The precariousness of manhood among prisoners creates an internal economy of prison sexual assault. Queens are vastly outnumbered by *men.* And according to Donaldson, the vast majority of punks are heterosexual by preference and history. Therefore, the conversion, or turning out, of heterosexual males to punks serves to maintain equilibrium within the prison subculture. In Donaldson's own words, "The total population of queens and punks is rarely high enough to meet the demand for sexually submissive prisoners ... and this imbalance of supply and demand is a key to understanding the social dynamics of relentless competition among the men, who in rough joints are in danger of 'losing their manhood' at any time."[24]

Prison masculinities diverge from constructions of masculinity outside of prison in several important respects. First, prison masculinities are largely unhinged from sexual orientation. On the street, a man's sexuality is a function of his sexual practices. With the exception of the deeply closeted, men who have sex with other men self-identify—and are identified by others—as homosexual or gay. In contrast, the vast majority of sexually active prisoners are having sex with other men.[25] With the exception of queens and some transgendered prisoners, these men self-identify as heterosexual or straight.

Second, within the prisoner subculture, sexual practice and social roles are fused. A male prisoner's sexual practices determine his social role. Male prisoners who sexually subordinate other male prisoners (i.e., pitchers) are exclusively privileged to be leaders, gang members, and control commerce (e.g., smuggling contraband, protection rackets, prostitution). Male prisoners unwilling or unable to resist sexual penetration (i.e. catchers) are uniformly excluded from leadership roles and are relegated to a feminine role, vastly subordinate to men.[26] Whereas the ideology of complementary social and sexual roles for men and women counsels a link between these roles, unlike life on the outside, for example, there is no social role for a macho homosexual male prisoner. As Donaldson reported, such a person who enters the prisoner subculture with "considerable fighting ability" may attempt to "pass" as a heterosexual jocker, displaying pornography in his cell to signal his heterosexuality. But as soon as his homosexual conduct "on the street" is discovered, he is relegated to the role of a queen; and if he resists that role, he may be coerced into the role of a punk [27].

Third, within the prisoner subculture there is little distinction between consent and coercion. Therefore rape, an offense premised on the crucial distinction between consent and coercion, has proven a difficult concept to employ in the prison setting.[28] Correctional officers have traditionally viewed any sexual contact among male prisoners as consensual. Their subculture equally stigmatizes the failure to fend off sexual overtures from other males. By refusing to police sexual conduct considered shameful and disreputatble they tacitly condone rape. Indeed they encourage the vulnerable inmate to act like a man and fight or fuck rather than to depend on their assistance. Consequently, sexual victimization of prisoners is vastly underreported.

The sexually predacious environment within some prison settings, and the unwillingness of prison officials to acknowledge it, jeopardizes the emotional and physical well-being of prisoners. The primary response of prison officials to sexual contact among prisoners is punitive. Prisons typically treat sexual contact among prisoners as a rule infraction and punish the inmates caught in *flagrante delicto*[29] with lockdown or solitary confinement.[30]

As James Messerschmidt noted, even in the contemporary prison system various performances of masculinity are present, some based on conveying information to prison officials (i.e., rats), others based on dealing in illegal economies inside prison (i.e., merchants), and still others based on using violence or the threat of violence to advance one's own interests (i.e., gorillas).[31] However, the dominant, or in R. W. Connell's words, the "hegemonic" masculinity that emerged in the era of "getting tough" on criminals was one based on sexual dominance.[32]

The concept of *hegemonic masculinity* helps us to put into perspective the social pecking order that dominates the culture of many prisons in this age of mass incarceration. According to Connell, hegemonic masculinity is the dominant performance of masculinity to which other variations of masculinity are subordinated.[33] In "The Cultural Constructions of Manhood in Prison," Jenny Phillips noted that the performance of masculinity is intensified by the isolated and harsh nature of prisons.[34] Indeed, Phillips's research supports the proposition that the construction of masculinity through sexual violence—or the threat of it—occurs most frequently in the most repressive prison environments, typically maximum-security settings.[35]

Racial Dimensions of the Construction of Masculinity in Prison

As the prison literature of the past twenty years documents, black men are disproportionately the aggressors in prison sexual violence. At the heart of the racial skew in prison sexual violence are the war on drugs and a criminal justice system that incapacitates vast segments of poor, urban neighborhoods—replete with the gang violence and drug addiction that plague them—in overcrowded, no-frills prisons. In this setting, the racialization of sexual violence in prison is the predictable result of confining unprecedented numbers of black and brown men in institutions with little security and no real objective beyond containment and incapacitation. Black men, as rational actors, use the few resources available to their advantage, hooking up for self-preservation, and sexually attacking to prevent their own sexual victimization. At the same time black men, by participating in this economy of sexual assault, are complicit in masculine violence and misogyny. However, black men are also victimized by theories that frame them as initiators of sexual violence in prison and ignores them as prison rape victims, while masking the fact that they were coerced into a predatory prison culture by a justice system that constructs urban black and brown men as criminal subjects. In the end, the problem is masculinity and how it is performed in prison rather than the black men who are disproportionately imprisoned.

One explanation of the tenacity of the hyperaggressive, sexually predacious masculinity in certain prisons and jails today is its utility as a demarcator of racial identity and power. Donaldson, Carroll, and others suggest that black male prisoners assert racial dominance over whites through the sexual subordination of white male prisoners. I refer to this notion as the *black rage theory* and argue that it constructs black men as inherently hyperaggressive, masking the manner in which get-tough policies used during mass incarceration structure black men as criminal subjects. In *Hacks, Blacks, and Cons*, Leo Carroll examined the role of race in many different aspects of prison life, including sexual violence, based on his study of race relations in a maximum-security prison in the earliest years of the 1970s. Carroll's interviews with inmate informants revealed that the vast majority of sexual assaults in the prison he studied were perpetrated by black aggressors on white victims. Although Carroll's data were collected in the earliest years of the war on drugs, he discerned a pattern of aggression and victimization that would intensify during the next two decades.

Carroll's interviews and observations revealed a complex choreography around the assertion of black and white masculinity. Four features of the racial landscape of sexual violence are significant. First, black male prisoners, particularly newly arrived prisoners, planned and initiated sexual attacks on vulnerable white inmates—and thus earned the reputation as *rippers*—as a means of gaining the support and acceptance of other black inmates.[36] Thus, he suggested that black on white sexual assaults were initiated as an expression of racial solidarity.

Second, within an institution in which race relations were tense, Carroll found that the vast majority of sexual assaults were by black male aggressors performing the hegemonic masculinity of pitchers on young, white, newly arrived male prisoners. These new arrivals were less likely to have formed bonds with other dominant males within the institution, and thus direct reprisal against the black ripper was unlikely. Carroll interpreted the motives of black rippers as expressing racial contempt for the racial oppression and psychological emasculation of black men in America.[37]

Third, though consensual relationships between black and white prisoners were universally condemned, black and white prisoners symbiotically cooperated to maintain a social system predicated on sexual violence. White prisoners were complicit in the racialized nature of black-on-white sexual violence. White pitchers directly benefited from the assaults of black rippers on young, white new arrivals, using the fear generated in the victim as a means of seducing him into the role of punk.[38] One white pitcher Carroll interviewed even admitted that he occasionally goaded black rippers into attacking white inmates to drive the victims to seek his protection and to become his punk.[39] Thus, as Carroll observed, "brutal racial conflict on one level creates a bond of tacit racial cooperation on another level."[40]

Much of the research on the racial dimensions of sexual victimization among prisoners mimics this theory, attributing the higher rate of black-on-white sexual assault to the emasculating racial marginalization of black men outside of prison, a phenomenon that goes beyond the symbolic emasculation they experience as prisoners. Several researchers explain black-on-white prisoner sexual assault as the product of an aggressive masculinity racially directed by black prisoners toward white prisoners who symbolize the source of the black prisoner's emasculation and racial oppression. From these various explanations, a picture emerges of black prisoners' racial anger expressed within the institutional setting of a well-established system of sexual subordination. Thus, manhood for black prisoners is reconstructed through the sexual subordination of those who symbolize their racial oppression—white men.[41]

This conceptualization of the racialized dynamics of prison sexual violence is intensely problematic and flawed. First, the black rage theory of prison sexual violence ignores the structural racism that positions the social networks of entire urban communities behind bars through racially biased criminal law enforcement, prosecution, and sentencing. Second, it normalizes the association of hyperaggressive masculinity with black males, for whom striking back at the white man is viewed as consistent with their inherently aggressive nature, and legitimates white racial panic rather than exposing it as a reflection of the vulnerability of black men as criminal subjects. Third, it constructs black men as emotional, hostile, and reactive rather than as rational actors operating within institutions characterized by arbitrary and extreme violence and employing violence as a means of constructing a social structure that rationally meets their need for security and protection. Finally, it misreads as black empowerment a racialized system of sexual violence that ultimately produces far more black victims when one considers the broader impact of prison sexual violence on the black victims within prisons, as well as black communities.

Although the black rage theory of black-on-white prisoner rape has gained a great deal of traction,[42] the social factors and policies producing mass incarceration clearly suggest an alternative hypothesis for the racialization of prison sexual violence. The policies surrounding the war on drugs and the get-tough political consensus have contributed to some of the significant factors playing a role in the racialization of prison violence, including the browning of the prison population, overcrowding, gang infiltration, declining security, and reduced prisoner protection.

The hallmark of the war on drugs was taking a get-tough approach to the problem of narcotics abuse, which had previously been treated as a medical problem and a public health issue. Conservative Republicans like Governor Nelson Rockefeller and the Ronald Reagan administration initiated a philosophical shift on this issue, rendering drug use, and the trafficking it supported, the subject of crime policy. The get-tough approach, however, was not limited to illegal drugs and crime policy but was extended to encompass welfare policies toward the poor. In this context, public support and government responsibility to the poor were drastically reduced, leaving them to mobilize new economic survival strategies in a period of unprecedented, postindustrial decline.[43] Those strategies often included participation in black-market drug sales. In addition, rehabilitation and crime-prevention strategies were abandoned in favor of stronger punishment of criminal offenders. Furthermore, a federal judiciary increasingly reflecting conservative appointments retrenched the rights prisoners had gained in the preceding decades during the prisoners' rights movement and broadly lowered the level of constitutional protection prisoners could expect while incarcerated.[44] Thus, prisoners of the war on drugs experienced reduced legal and political protection from violence and harassment initiated by guards as well as by other inmates. Within private prisons in particular, which flourished in response to the unprecedented expense of mass incarceration, the institutional goal of profit-making compromised prisoner safety through the use of nominally trained, minimally compensated guards and lower guard-to-inmate ratios. Mass incarceration also decreased prisoner security through overcrowding, another trademark of the war on drugs. Each of these factors contributed to the diminished security—and increased vulnerability—of prisoners that plays a crucial role in the increasingly racialized violence in prisons.

Second, the emergence of prison gangs increased racial polarization and the level of racial violence among prisoners. Prison gangs largely derived from street gangs that imported their organizational structure, leadership hierarchies, and activities into correctional facilities. However, the cycling of individuals into prison, back onto the street, and back into prison again has become so pronounced that it is hard to distinguish gang members recruited in prison from those recruited on the street. Gangs are established along racial lines. Gang alliances demand racial fealty, in return for which gang members are given protection. Under mass incarceration, the prominence of prison gangs has made it difficult for inmates to remain unaffiliated or neutral. Operating much as they do on the street, prison gangs take control of prison rackets (e.g., prostitution, gambling, trade in contraband) run by non-gang-affiliated prisoners. Further, lower-ranking gang members are frequently involved in the extortion and shakedown of unaffiliated inmates.[45] As a result, there is intense pressure to ally with black, Latino, Asian, or Aryan (i.e., white supremacist) gangs for protection. Prison gangs employ sexual violence as a means of challenging or asserting dominance. A gang seeking to assert its dominance over another gang may turn out one of the members of the rival gang and may exploit him as a punk.[46] These assaults almost always occur across racial lines.

Third, the influx of minorities with established racial bonds leaves white male prisoners more vulnerable to attack. Outside of prison, growing up in the "'hood" greatly disadvantages young men by narrowing their access to the networks and institutions that track many young people into the middle class. However, the disadvantage of growing up in racially stigmatized ghettos that are heavily policed and where incarceration is ever present in the machinery of the criminal justice system is an important asset for surviving in prison. Here, prior associations with fellow inmates based on neighborhood, family, street, or gang connections provide immediate allies and physical security in the uncertain and risky prison environment. Conversely, middle-class white men who are not from the 'hood and whose social networks and institutional affiliations track them for success on the outside are disadvantaged by the absence of prior associations on the inside. They are a racial minority in most prisons, prone to be tested and later assaulted because they lack networks that are highly functional for urban, minority prisoners.

The browning of the prison population that reconstructed prisons as majority minority institutions made white prisoners more vulnerable to attack. The war on drugs and its overincarceration of urban, poor racial minorities created a situation in which, as of 2000, blacks and Hispanics jointly comprised only

24.8 percent of the nation's population but represented 56.4 percent of all jail inmates[47] and 62 percent of all prison inmates.[48] As racial and ethnic minorities, whose inner-city communities are overpoliced and disproportionately imprisoned, blacks and Hispanics enter prison with a well-established sense of group affiliation and racial cohesion that distinguishes them from white prisoners who lack the consciousness of an oppressed minority on the street.[49] Within the context of overwhelmingly brown prison populations where racial antagonism is high, the threat of violent assault is ever present. Prisoners without close alliances to a tightly organized social network connected to family, friends, neighborhoods, gangs, or juvenile jails are vulnerable to attack because of the lesser likelihood of retaliation.[50]

Where Imprisoned Masculinities Meet the Street

Ninety-three percent of all prisoners are eventually released.[51] Each year, more than 600,000 adults—about 1,600 each day—leave state and federal prisons and return home to their communities of origin.[52] Joan Petersilia characterized the reintegration of these former prisoners, the vast majority of which return to inner-city metropolitan neighborhoods, as "one of the most profound challenges facing American society."[53] Until recently, little research has been undertaken to analyze the impact of mass incarceration on the individuals previously imprisoned or the families and communities to which they return. Recent studies by colleague Christopher Mele and me and Marc Mauer and Meda Chesney-Lind chronicled the disadvantages and struggles that a criminal record has on ex-prisoners.[54] Termed *collateral civil penalties,* these laws and policies effectively reduce the future life chances of ex-prisoners, making the payment of their debt to society interminable. However, with the notable exception of Petersilia's study of prisoner reentry,[55] little work has been done on the impact of mass incarceration on the communities that have to absorb people with such radically diminished prospects for the future. Nevertheless, there are four significant areas in which the impact of prison life plays out for these inner-city communities: economics, intimate social relationships, health, and culture/aesthetic. In each of these four areas, black masculinity is pivotal.

It is said that family members and friends "do time" right alongside their loved one. Indeed whole communities from which large numbers of incarcerated individuals are drawn feel the effects of the incarceration of their members long after they are paroled or released from prison. Families and communities—as well as individual ex-offenders—are burdened by the economic, cultural, social, and public health baggage of mass incarceration. Economically, incarceration frames the context in which black men reemerge from correctional facilities more of a burden to their families and their communities than a lost treasure. Prisons do not prepare black men to be prosperous breadwinners who can provide for their families and meet standards of successful masculinity on the outside. In addition, many black men emerge from incarceration profoundly affected—indeed traumatized—by the hyperaggessive masculinity they adopted (or submitted to) in order to survive in prison. As a result, the nature of incarceration itself, as well as prison masculinities, leave them ill-suited to be productive members of the society. Rather, they constitute obstacles to reintegration and, as such, negatively impact black communities. The cultural, social, and health impacts of incarceration—and incarcerated masculinities—on black communities are also toxic. Moreover, in the intimate social, cultural/aesthetic, and health spheres, incarceration and incarcerated masculinities have a direct negative impact upon black communities.

Economic Impoverishment

When a prisoner is released from the prison system, he is thrust back into a world in which masculinity is expressed through a variety of actions or performances including controlling others, acquiring material goods, providing for oneself and one's children, climbing hierarchies, and acquiring women. Although resources for demonstrating masculinity are less scarce on the street than in prison, ex-convicts nevertheless encounter formidable obstacles to establishing their masculinity outside the prison on these terms. The most obvious obstacle is that ex-convicts are overwhelmingly minority and unskilled. Ex-offenders released in the era of the war on drugs are likely to have been in custody before, to have a lengthy history of substance abuse, to have been involved in gang activity, and to have been unemployed and homeless for significant periods.[56] They are also likely, while incarcerated, to have spent significant periods in solitary confinement or supermax prisons and to have had little in the way of educational or vocational training during their incarceration.[57] Thus, the ex-offender's access to gainful employment and material possessions is limited. Additionally, most males coming out of prison have minor children with whom they have had limited contact while incarcerated.

For former prisoners, obstacles to the establishment of masculinity characterized by dominance, material wealth, and authority increase dramatically with the proliferation of collateral civil penalties that extend the punishment of criminal offenders far past their release from prison. Since the inception of the drug war, the notion that criminal offenders do their time in prison and pay their debt to society has become increasingly untenable as postincarceration penalties proliferated. The term *collateral civil penalties* characterizes a host of legal restrictions that hinder the ability of ex-offenders to successfully reenter society.[58] Enforced by civil law, these penalties include sanctions on certain types of employment, housing, education, civic participation, welfare eligibility, eligibility for federal loans, parental rights, and even the right of non-U.S. citizens to remain in the United States. Although the penalty of felon disenfranchisement was employed in some southern states as early as Reconstruction, the vast majority of collateral civil penalties were enacted on the heels of the contemporary war on drugs. In contrast to the high-profile criminal sentencing reforms of the 1980s and '90s, these penalties were enacted in civil, often omnibus, legislation of the same period. They are described as "invisible punishments"[59] because in criminal proceedings judges, prosecutors, and defense attorneys are rarely required to notify criminal defendants of the penalties and their harsh consequences; and the penalties tend to kick in automatically, without formal notice, typically after incarceration.[60]

Generally enacted in state law, collateral civil penalties mete out a range of harsh penalties for black male ex-offenders that limit their ability to acquire many of the mainstream indicia of manhood outside of prison. On release from prison, criminal offenders confront a range of ineligibilities and disqualifications that seriously hamper their ability to successfully parent, to find employment, and to provide for them and their families. Ex-offenders have an immediate need for housing. Without a permanent address, successful reentry—including finding and maintaining employment, reuniting with family and children, and tending to treatment needs—is thwarted.[61] Yet ex-offenders rarely rise to the level of a landlord's most desirable tenant. Landlords screen applicants based on criminal history, credit history, and work history, all of which present problems for the typical ex-offender.[62] Released prisoners have an immediate need for employment, yet they face significant formal barriers to obtaining certain forms of employment.[63] Moreover, ex-offenders face the loss of business or professional licenses, loss of parental rights for many whose children are in the foster care system, and ineligibility to vote or hold public office in many states.

Ex-offenders with drug convictions face a broader array of penalties. Individuals with drug convictions are banned from living in public or subsidized housing for three years unless they can demonstrate completion of an approved postrelease rehabilitation program.[64] Ex-drug offenders are banned from receiving cash subsidies from the government in the form of temporary assistance to needy families and food stamps.[65] They are ineligible for federal student loan assistance or the Hope Scholarship Credit and may face revocation of suspension of their driver's license.[66] They may even be ineligible to participate in federally funded health-care programs.[67]

The cumulative impact of these civil penalties on a newly released prisoner is nothing short of devastating. They frustrate his ability to find housing. They impede his ability to establish a legitimate income stream by posing obstacles to employment, occupational licensing, and public subsidy. Consequently, they weaken his ability to acquire food, shelter, or material goods for himself and to provide them for himself and his family. To the extent that vocational offerings for incarcerated men are limited to low-wage-earning vocations with little or no practical application on the streets, the prison system affirmatively shapes incarcerated masculinities that are detrimental to black communities.[68]

Quite aside from the impact of collateral civil penalties on individual ex-offenders, these sanctions operate on a community level to disadvantage poor, largely urban, and minority communities. Unprecedented numbers of prisoners are being released from prison as a "natural, predictable consequence of increased levels of imprisonment."[69] James Lynch and William Sabol found that the vast majority of released prisoners return to inner cities within the nation's metropolitan centers.[70] The disadvantaging effects of collateral civil penalties and their consequences are therefore clustered among poor, mostly minority, populations in core, inner-city communities, where the war on drugs has been most focused and concentrated. Thus collateral civil penalties pose barriers to reintegration and contribute to high recidivism rates at the community level, contributing further to the impoverishment of urban black communities.

Psychosocial and Physical Infirmity

The Psychosocial Impact of the Hyperaggressive Prison Masculinity on Black Communities   Very little research has been conducted on the impact of the hyperaggressive prison masculinity and the sexual violence it facilitates on the communities to which prisoners return on release. Nevertheless, the modest research that has been conducted suggests several harmful consequences for the mental and physical health of African Americans. Whereas the psychosocial impacts include severe psychological trauma and inappropriately aggressive conduct on the part of men who return home, the health consequences include HIV infection and AIDS.

Prison rape is so pervasive in U.S. prisons that it has been referred to as a collateral consequence of incarceration and even more poignantly an "unadjudicated death sentence."[71] Its impact on the black community from the standpoint of social functioning and public health has been significant. Many of the victims and perpetrators of prison rape carry psychosocial dysfunction and HIV back to the black communities they rejoin on release.

Survivors of sexual violence in prison commonly report nightmares, deep depression, shame, anxiety, suspicion, hypervigilance to danger, and suicidal thoughts. Some report increased anger and violent tendencies. These symptoms are associated with rape trauma syndrome, a variant of post-traumatic stress disorder. Most of the data on prison-rape trauma focus on the impact on prisoners in the prison setting and clearly establish that victims of sexual violence become predators to prevent their revictimization. Although little data exist on the psychosocial impact of prison-rape once prisoners are released, some researchers have suggested that prison-rape survivors perpetuate the cycle of sexual violence on the street or, at the very least, bring serious, untreated social and sexual dysfunction to intimate personal and familial relationships.

Although the impact of prison sexual violence on the communities to which prisoners return has yet to be widely studied by academics, at least one popular film has considered the subject. In *American Me*, director Edward James Olmos depicted the incarceration of a young Chicano prison gang leader from his time in a secure juvenile detention facility through his incarceration as an adult. Sexually assaulted by an older youth in the detention facility, he gains the respect of the other boys when he kills the victimizer with the very knife used to subdue him during the rape. The boy gets transferred to Folsom Prison and eventually rises to the head of the Mexican Mafia. Released after eighteen years behind bars, his romantic pursuit of a woman from his barrio ends in disaster. In bed with his new girlfriend, Santana, the gang leader played by Olmos, engages in rough sex during which he attempts to anally penetrate the woman, terrifying her and ending their relationship.[72]

Poor Prophylaxis and the Transmission of HIV to Black Communities Prison officials typically respond to sexual contact among prisoners punitively, as a disciplinary violation. In the face of widespread sexual contact among prisoners, treating it as rule breaking is inconsistent with providing condoms for prophylaxis. Indeed, all but a handful of prisons and jails prohibit the use of condoms. This has created a dire public health crisis within prisons as more and more prisoners report having contracted HIV in prison or jail[73] and puts black communities at risk. Prisoners who are released carry the infection back to their communities of origin. Therefore, it is hardly surprising that prisons and black communities report rates of HIV infection that exceed the national average. Nor is it surprising that public health researchers are starting to address HIV infection in prisons and black communities as intertwined epidemics requiring combined prevention and treatment strategies.[74]

On release, many male prisoners who were either victims or perpetrators of sexual violence in prison return to relationships that predate their incarceration or begin new relationships, typically with heterosexual women. Some, acting out the roles they adapted to in prison, carry on clandestine relationships with men "on the down low." Indeed, the down-low subculture of black men who lead double lives engaged in heterosexual relationships as boyfriends, husbands, or fathers by day and having clandestine sex with men by night reproduces the dual consciousness of the hyperaggressive prison masculinity within black communities on the outside.

Even more troubling for black communities from a public health standpoint is the apparent connection between men on the down low and high rates of HIV infection among heterosexual black women. A scant 13 percent of the U.S. population, African Americans accounted for more than half of new cases of HIV infection in 2002.[75] Whereas black men accounted for 44 percent of all new AIDS cases among all men, black women accounted for a staggering two-thirds of new AIDS cases among all women.[76] Since 2002, the leading cause of HIV infection among black women has been heterosexual contact. Some public health researchers and HIV educators hypothesize that down-low men are the bridge for HIV transmission to heterosexual black women, but no research data are available—and these are only suppositions. This apparent correlation should not be read to suggest that the harm to black communities emanates from gay black men or gay sex. The harm emanates from the failure to use condoms, as well as the repressive, homophobic climate in some black communities that deeply closets black men, discouraging them from openly discussing their sexuality with their wives, girlfriends, and families.

The Cultural/Aesthetic Impact of Prison Masculinities on Black Communities and Beyond

Subtle, yet most widespread, is the impact of prison masculinities and incarceration on black culture. The prison system leaves an enormous imprint on the young black men who are disproportionately confined in U.S. prisons and jails. For young black men, the experience of imprisonment has become a rite of passage, a transition to manhood. As Jerome Miller suggested, the experience of incarceration has become both a site of solidarity and a mark of subjugation for young black males whose peers, as well as uncles, fathers, grandfathers, and other adult male role models, have shared the same experience. Those who are not incarcerated themselves are indelibly marked by the surveillance, informing, profiling, harassment, and arrests that continually take place in inner-city neighborhoods.[77]

The influence of the prison system on black youth is clear in the music, fashion, and language of the generations of young men who have come of age since the imprisonment binge began. Life behind bars has become a major theme in street culture and hip-hop art.[78] The baggy-pants look that has become a fashion standard among inner-city youth originated in prison where prisoners—whose belts are confiscated at intake—lack a convenient and permissible means to keep their often ill-fitting, state-issue pants up. Likewise, the donning of elaborate tattoos under the scant coverage of muscle shirts, sneakers with fat, partially untied laces; cornrows tucked under do-rags or scarves; and cool, detached body postures and stares have become part of what one researcher refers to as "the aesthetics of criminalization."[79]

The cultural influence of prisons and jails is now felt far beyond the inner city, as the aesthetic of criminalization is consumed by black ghetto youth and white suburban youth alike and is exported through clothing styles, hairstyles, and music worldwide to such distant venues as Tokyo, London, Paris, and Bombay.

Like the black rage theory of race in prison rape, the aesthetic of criminalization can masquerade as empowerment absent a critical frame of reference for understanding the operation of race and gender within prisons and urban communities profoundly affected by them.

This chapter suggests that mass incarceration and the hegemonic hyperaggressive masculinity that dominates many U.S. prisons and jails is detrimental to urban black communities. It has further demonstrated the problematic nature of racial analyses of prison sexual violence that fail to critique structural racism at work within a violent and predacious prison culture. These analyses thereby privilege and legitimate white racial panic and the resulting calls for greater penal severity toward urban black men.

Notes

1. Jenny Phillips, "Cultural Construction of Manhood in Prison," *Men and Masculinity* 2, no. 1 (January 2001), 13–23.
2. Erving Goffman, *Asylums: Essays on the Social Situations of Mental Patients and Other Inmates* (Garden City, NY: Anchor Books, 1961), 14.
3. Phillips, "Cultural Construction," 13–23.
4. M. Nandi, "Re/constructing Black Masculinity in Prison," *Journal of Men's Studies* 11, no. 1 (Fall 2002), 91–108.
5. James W. Messerschmidt, "Masculinities, Crime, and Prison," in *Prison Masculinities*, ed. Donald F. Sabo, Terry Allen Kupers, and Willie James London (Philadelphia: Temple University Press, 2001), 71.
6. Gresham Sykes and Sheldon L. Messinger, "The Inmate Social System," in *Theoretical Studies in the Social Organization of the Prison*, ed. R. Cloward (New York: Social Research Council, 1960), 5–19.
7. Lee H. Bowker, *Prisoner Subcultures* (Lexington, KY Lexington Books, 1977), 26–27; Bernard T. Adeney, "Living on the Edge: Ethics Inside San Quentin," *Journal of Law & Religion* 6, no. 2 (1988), 440.
8. Malcolm X and Alex Haley, *The Autobiography of Malcolm X* (New York: Ballantine Books, 1964).
9. Ibid.
10. John M. Coggeshall, "'Ladies' behind Bars: A Liminal Gender as Cultural Mirror," *Anthropology Today* 4, no. 4 (August 1988), 6–8; Carl Bryan Holmberg, "The Culture of Transgression: Initiation into the Homosociality of a Midwestern State Prison," in Sabo and others, *Prison Masculinities*, 78–92; Phillips, "Cultural Construction," 13–23; Christopher D. Man and John P. Cronan, "Forecasting Sexual Abuse in Prison: The Prison Subculture of Masculinity as a Backdrop for 'Deliberate Indifference,'" *Journal of Criminal Law and Criminology* 92, no. 1/2 (Autumn 2001–Winter 2002), 127–186; James E. Robertson, "A Punk's Song about Prison Reform," *Pace Law Review* 24, no. 2 (Spring 2004), 527–562.
11. Cindy Struckman-Johnson and David Struckman-Johnson, "Sexual Coercion Rates in Seven Midwestern Prison Facilities for Men," *Prison Journal* 80, no. 4 (December 2000), 380.
12. Ibid., 384, 386.
13. Stephen Donaldson, "A Million Jockers, Punks, and Queens" in Sabo and others, *Prison Masculinities*, 118. Donaldson was a former prisoner, and this widely published essay is a first-hand account of sexual subordination in prison.
14. Ibid.
15. Ibid.
16. Ibid.
17. Ibid.
18. Ibid.
19. Coggeshall, "'Ladies' behind Bars," 7. However, this characterization overlooks the widespread and virulent homophobia that pervades prisons and impacts the construction of prison masculinities through the disgust and disdain with which all catchers are treated.
20. Donaldson, "Million Jockers," 120.
21. Ibid.
22. Ibid., 121.
23. Teresa A. Miller, "Sex & Surveillance: Gender, Privacy and the Sexualization of Power in Prison," *George Mason University Civil Rights Law Journal* 10, no. 2 (1999–2000), 303, citing Kevin Wright, "The Violent and the Victimized in the Male Prison" in *Prison Violence in America*, eds. Michael C. Braswell and Stephen Dillingham (Cincinnati, OH: Anderson Publishing Co., 1994), 104; and Robert W. Dumond, "The Sexual Assault of

Male Inmates in Incarcerated Settings," *International Journal of the Sociology of Law* 20, no. 1 (1992), 139.

24. Donaldson, "Million Jockers," 120.
25. Some sexually active prisoners have sex with women through conjugal visitation or custodial sexual misconduct. Conjugal visitation is infrequent and limited to married prisoners with clean disciplinary records. And sexual contact with guards and civilian staff may result in criminal prosecution of the nonincarcerated participant. As a result, sexual contact between women and incarcerated men is uncommon.
26. Donaldson, "Million Jockers," 120.
27. Ibid.
28. As Alan Davis concluded in his study of sexual aggressors and victims in the Philadelphia prison system and Sheriff's vans in the late 1960s, "[I]n our study of sexual assaults we excluded any that were cases of truly 'consensual' homosexuality. Nonetheless, it was hard to separate consensual homosexuality from rape, since many continuing and isolated homosexual liaisons originated from a gang rape, or from the ever-present threat of gang rape." Davis, "Sexual Assaults in the Philadelphia Prison System and Sheriff's Van," in *Male Rape: A Casebook of Sexual Aggressions*, ed. Anthony M. Scacco Jr. (New York: AMS Press, Inc., 1982), 112.
29. Meaning "in the very act of committing an offense; in the act of having sex." American Heritage Dictionary of the English Language, 4th ed., 2000.
30. Treating sexual contact as a disciplinary violation is inimical to disease-prevention strategies based on condom distribution to prisoners. As a result, AIDS is epidemic in prisons. In 2002, researchers estimated that nearly 3 percent of all state and federal prisoners are infected with HIV, four times the prevalence in the U.S. population. Robertson, "Rape among Incarcerated Men: Sex, Coercion and STDs," *AIDS Patient Care and STDs* 17 (2003), 423, available online at http://www.spr.org/en/academicarticles/robertson.html.
31. Messerschmidt, "Masculinities, Crime, and Prison," 67.
32. R. W. Connell, *Masculinities* (Cambridge: Polity Press, 1995).
33. Ibid.
34. "The rapid cutoff from the outside world is followed by a total indoctrination into a separate society behind the walls. A prison social system exerts a powerful shaping effect on the lives of inmates, thereby intensifying the enactment of masculinity." Phillips, "Cultural Constructions," 13.
35. Phillips reasoned that the harsher the environment, the more depleted the resources for augmenting manhood, thus the higher the stakes for accruing the honor and privileges that accompany high-status manhood. Ibid.
36. Leo Carroll, *Hacks, Blacks, and Cons: Race Relations in a Maximum Security Prison* (Lexington, KY: Lexington Books, 1974), 183–84.
37. Ibid., 184–87.
38. Ibid., 186.
39. "Sometimes if I really need a 'kid' and I see one that looks real good, th[e]n I might slip the word over to the spooks that he's really gay. Most of the time though I just sit back and watch the action. I wait till it looks like they're done with him then I come on like a knight in shining armor, see. I take him under my wing and start doing things for him and promise to keep the others away. After what he's been through it ain't nothing for him to take care of me and a coupla others. He's glad to do it." Ibid.
40. Ibid., 187.
41. The black rage theory tends to reduce a complex social and cultural phenomenon to racial politics. It encourages a monolithic construction of black men both in prison and on the street as deprived of masculine validation and unable to procure it without reference to white people. See Peter C. Buffum, "Racial Factors in Prison Homosexuality," in Scacco, *Male Rape*, 104–6, which characterizes the sexuality of "the Negro prisoner" as "more directed by dominance needs and sexual access than by strong needs for affective investment."
42. Carroll, *Hacks*, 184–85; Donaldson, "Million Jockers," 123, which describes black-on-white sexual assault in prison as "a symbolic attack on the manhood of all whites"; and Scacco, "The Scapegoat Is Almost Always White," in Scacco, *Male Rape*, 91–106. Scacco interviewed black sexual aggressors in a Connecticut training school for male

juvenile delinquents about their reasons for perpetrating sexual assaults on white male victims and concluded that "there are definite socio-racial overtones to the act of sexual victimization." Ibid., 91.

43. David Garland, *Culture of Control* (Chicago: University of Chicago Press, 2001); and Malcolm Feeley and Jonathan Simon, "The New Penology: Notes on the Emerging Strategy of Corrections and Its Implications," *Criminology* 30 (1992), 449–473.

44. See, generally, Marc Mauer, *Race to Incarcerate* (New York: New Press, 1999).

45. James B. Jacobs, "Stratification and Conflict among Prison Inmates," *Criminology*, 66, no. 4 (1976), 476–482.

46. Donaldson, "Million Jockers," 123.

47. Allen Beck and Jennifer Karberg, "Prison and Jail Inmates at Mid–Year 2000," *Bureau of Justice Statistics Bulletin*, March 2001, 7.

48. Beck and Paige Harrison, "Prisoners in 2000," *Bureau of Justice Statistics Bulletin*, August 2001, 11.

49. Well-known expert on prison gangs James B. Jacobs observed as early as 1976 that "Whites outside of prison rarely have the experience of having been treated on the basis of their race per se but on the inside they soon realize that their racial identity has the greatest implications for their inmate career." Jacobs, "Stratification and Conflict," 477.

50. As Carroll explained in *Hacks, Blacks, and Cons*, typically sexual assaults on prisoners who are subsequently "turned out" are typically preceded by a period of harassment and verbal threats designed to discover whether the victim has friends who will come to his defense. "If he has ties with any inmates who are able to mobilize any significant number in his defense, then the attack will be stopped." Carroll, *Hacks*, 183.

51. Joan Petersilia, *When Prisoners Come Home: Parole and Prisoner Reentry* (Oxford: Oxford University Press, 2003), 3.

52. Ibid.

53. Ibid., 3, 8.

54. Marc Mauer and Meda Chesney-Lind, eds., *Invisible Punishment: The Collateral Consequences of Mass Imprisonment* (New York: New Press, 2002); Christopher Mele and Teresa A. Miller, eds., *Civil Penalties, Social Consequences* (New York: Routledge, 2005).

55. Ibid.

56. Ibid., 21.

57. Ibid.

58. Christopher Mele and Miller, *Civil Penalties, Social Consequences*, 1.

59. Mauer and Meda Chesney-Lind, *Invisible Punishment*.

60. Mele and Miller, "Collateral Civil Penalties as Techniques of Social Policy," in Mele and Miller, *Civil Penalties*, 12.

61. Elizabeth Curtin, "Home Sweet Home for Ex-Offenders" in Mele and Miller, *Civil Penalties*, 113.

62. Ibid.

63. Ex-offenders commonly face legal prohibitions against employment in the fields of child care, education, security, nursing, and home health care. Since 1985, the number of barred occupations has increased dramatically. As the number of barred occupations has grown, the connection between ex-offenders' criminal history and the employment restrictions to which they are subject has become increasingly remote. Petersilia, *When Prisoners Come Home*, 113, 114. Ironically, while incarcerated, prisoners are frequently trained in trades for which they are legally barred from obtaining a license to practice. Petersilia cited the example of barbering, one of the most popular vocational training courses in the New York City Reformatory. The State of New York typically denies barber's license applications from individuals with a criminal record. Ibid., 114.

64. Curtin, "Home Sweet Home," 113.

65. Patricia Allard, *Denying Welfare Benefits to Women Convicted of Drug Offenses* (Washington, DC: The Sentencing Project, 2002).

66. Gabriel Chin, "Race, the War on Drugs, and the Collateral Consequences of Criminal Conviction," in Mele and Miller, *Civil Penalties*, 33.

67. Ibid.

68. For example, barbering and cosmetology courses are offered in New York state correctional facilities although collateral civil penalties disqualify ex-offenders from obtaining barbering and cosmetology licenses in the state of New York.
69. Petersilia, *When Prisoners Come Home*, 22.
70. James P. Lynch and William J. Sabol, *Prisoner Reentry in Perspective* (Washington, DC: Urban Institute, 2001).
71. Joanne Mariner, "No Escape: Male Rape in U.S. Prisons" (New York: Human Rights Watch, 2001). The report is available online at http://www.hrw.org/reports/2001/prison/report.html (accessed April 18, 2006).
72. *American Me* 119 min., 1992, distributed by Universal Pictures, New York.
73. The case of Michael Blucker is especially compelling. Blucker was able to prove with prison health records that he contracted the AIDS virus while incarcerated in the Illinois Department of Corrections Menard Prison. Blucker went to prison on a ten-year sentence for car theft at age twenty-eight and testified that he was gang raped, after which sexual access to his body was openly sold by gang members, leaving him with HIV.
74. Lynette Clemetson, "Links Between Prison and AIDS Affecting Blacks Inside and Out," The New York Times, August 6, 2004, A1; Linda Villarosa, "Patients With H.I.V. Seen as Separated By a Racial Divide," The New York Times, August 7, 2004, A1.
75. Jason B. Johnson, "Secret Gay Encounters of Black Men Could Be Raising Women's Infection Rate," *San Francisco Chronicle*, May 1, 2005, A1.
76. Ibid.
77. Jerome Miller suggested that the criminal justice system's massive reliance on confidential informants undermines and destroys social bonds within families and communities and on the street—bonds that in the past served to limit violence. J. Miller, *Search and Destroy: African-American Males in the Criminal Justice System* (Cambridge, MA: Cambridge University Press, 1996).
78. Ted Sampsell-Jones, "Culture and Contempt: The Limitations of Expressive Criminal Law," *Seattle University Law Review* 27, no. 1 (2003), 151.
79. Andrea Queeley, "Hip Hop and the Aesthetics of Criminalization," *Souls* 5, no. 1 (2003), 1–15.

Part 5
Black Men in (Re) View

10

Mirror's Fade to Black: Masculinity, Misogyny, and Class Ideation in *The Cosby Show* and *Martin*

NATHAN GRANT

Was my freedom not given to me then in order to build the world of the *You*?

Frantz Fanon[1]

Though I admired my father, I was more fascinated and charmed by black men who were not obsessed with being patriarchs ... . I remember them because they loved folks, especially women and children ... . They were black men who chose alternative lifestyles, who questioned the *status quo*, who shunned a ready made patriarchal identity and invented themselves ... . [T]here has never been a time in the history of the United States when black folks, particularly black men, have not been enraged by the dominant culture's stereotypical, fantastical representations of black masculinity. Unfortunately, black people have not systematically challenged these narrow visions, insisting on a more accurate "reading" of black male reality. Acting in complicity with the *status quo,* many black people have passively absorbed narrow representations of black masculinity, perpetuated stereotypes, myths, and offered one-dimensional accounts. Contemporary black men have been shaped by these representations.

bell hooks[2]

Salutary and viable notions of black masculinity appear to depend on expressions of action on the part of black men and of action in their own interest and in the interest of others. Racial representations that speak to issues of political and communitarian struggle best situate black men and women to answer the forces in society so reliably arrayed against people of color. Many everyday representations of blackness, however, do not suggest thoughtful, progressive action, succumbing as they do to those forces, some of which are subtle and insidious and sometimes generated by black people themselves. These representations have many conduits, but they are perhaps most regularly transmitted in various forms of leisurely activity, with the most common and far-reaching of these being television. Since its infancy in the mid–twentieth century, television has enjoyed near-totemic status in the American home. The images that television transmits are specular; they mirror the culture as they appear to cut across it, and viewers become as much the subjects of their discourses as they are the audience that consumes them. They come to us innocuously enough but are likely the more dangerous for our narrow or unconscious acceptance of them. Misrepresentations of blackness and maleness still abound in the mass market—that is, Hollywood cinema—although independent filmmaking most often offers the corrective. But television remains the medium with the greatest access to the American mind, as it generally and consistently severs blackness from social consciousness and political yearning. If black masculinity means acting consciously and politically, as much in this time as in any other, it is interesting to note that even with the current proliferation of black actors (i.e., thespians) on television screens, a serious prominence of the black male visage and voice and incisive treatment of the world in which he finds himself are sorely lacking.

There are more people of color in leading roles that tend to respect the ethnicities of audiences attracted to them; this perhaps invites us once again, however unconsciously, to court the notion that the country's racial problems are more or less solved. Before this era of inclusion, disenfranchised Americans readily understood that their absence from nightly television reflected their absence from daily society. Today, African American men now grace living rooms for an evening, as they have however infrequently since 1964, when Bill Cosby in NBC's *I Spy* was the first black man to star in a weekly prime-time broadcast. Cosby's starring role was all of a piece with a still-burgeoning civil rights movement whose next phase of consciousness raising included national on-screen black representation. But *I Spy* was a dramatic presentation with comic elements, a wry look at cold-war politics through a frame of light intrigue. Cosby and his white costar, Robert Culp, ordinarily treated the business of international espionage with humor, a feature of the show which was its own suggestion that television's black men, even with white costars of equal billing, were not quite to be taken seriously. Today's proliferation of black male actors has created the flawed presumption that this is no longer the case. Now many black men are cast in prominent and memorable roles on television, such as the hip, hard-boiled sex crimes detective Odafin Tutuola, played by rapper Ice T on NBC's *Law and Order: Special Victims Unit*, or the casino-savvy forensics investigator Warrick Brown, portrayed by Gary Dourdan on CBS's *CSI*, or Drs. Preston Burke and Richard Webber, played by Isaiah Washington and James Pickens Jr., respectively, on ABC's *Grey's Anatomy*. Yet all of these dramatic roles are performed by black actors who are parts of ensemble casts; they do not play the dramatic leads themselves. Although Steve Harris's character Eugene Young was a judge in ABC's legal drama *The Practice* and Dennis Haysbert played the president of the United States in Fox's espionage and terrorism thriller *24*, both roles were retired after one season: In Haysbert's case, it was the first season; in Harris's, the last. On CBS, Haysbert currently stars as the leader of a military covert special operations task force, but still, in *The Unit*, his boss is white.

In recalling black male television leads of the past, these were few and generally had the shortest television lives. Two classic cases are *Harris & Company* of the late 1970s, which starred Bernie Casey as a working-class, single father of five children; NBC yanked the series after only a few weeks. The other, CBS's *Under One Roof*, despite the caliber of its stars—James Earl Jones, Joe Morton, and Vanessa Bell Calloway—lasted exactly four episodes in 1995.[3] ABC's *Hawk*, a brief spin-off of the series *Spenser for Hire*, starred Avery Brooks as a flamboyant and unorthodox private detective. In *Spenser*, Brooks played "detective number two" to white actor Robert Urich's lead in the title role; he reappeared many years later as Captain Benjamin Sisko in *Star Trek: Deep Space Nine*. *Gideon's Crossing*, also on ABC, starred Andre Braugher as chief of surgery in a large metropolitan hospital, and CBS's *City of Angels* again featured a hospital setting, this time with a virtually all-black cast and with Blair Underwood and Vivica A. Fox in starring roles.

None of these shows appears today in prime time. Male leads in film or television control or direct a significant degree of the show's dramatic tension; it is this character's success or failure—and in the universe of weekly television drama, the success—that determines the audience's continuing appreciation of him. The appeal to fantasy that creates a show's following includes some of the most broadly referential considerations of the character's poise, consistency of response to particularly challenging or dangerous situations, and sexuality, among other things. This control of success by black men, particularly in areas of conflict with white men or sexual prowess, particularly with white women, would likely be discomfiting, especially on a weekly basis, to American audiences. The depiction of the black body, male and female, through nineteenth- and twentieth-century American visual culture provides ample evidence for this conclusion.[4]

The dearth of black male stars in dramatic roles may thus make one think of what the contemporary and instant meaning of comedy may be, for though black male actors are generally absent as dramatic leads, they still occupy the leads in many comedy series. If larger American audiences cannot adequately conceptualize the black male lead as a feature of dramatic realism, something about the comic black visage remains that is both deeply enduring and relentlessly specular. Comedic blackness becomes the cultural mirror in which white America sees and reaffirms itself; white audiences find reassurances of their social power within the contexts of contained black culture—a culture whose participants rarely act decisively for themselves or in communitarian struggles. Eric Lott, in discussing nineteenth-century blackface performance, writes that "the minstrel show was, on the one hand, a socially approved context of institutional control; and, on the other, it continually acknowledged and absorbed black culture even while defending white America against it."[5] Though Lott writes not about black comedians, but about white practitioners of blackface comedy, inherent in his remarks is the fact that such conditions are produced precisely because white minstrelsy represents blackness that ultimately surrenders the urge to resist. The same performance is all the more poignant in the actor whose mask cannot be wiped away.

Since comedy is the venue where now more than ever before black male leads are to be found, then comedy becomes very serious business indeed. One might fairly say that Bill Cosby's long career in stand-up comedy, even his early reputation for "blue" routines, actually did much to tailor the comic or semicomic roles he played later. But much of the success of *The Cosby Show*, the show that ultimately secured his fame, was shaped by a sense of controversy that helped frame the argument about what kind of contemporary black representation audiences wanted to see. *Cosby* had a pure comic flavor that became controversial because of the absence of a specific type of black representational focus: an existential center of black action. Shortly after *Cosby*'s success was acknowledged, Martin Lawrence's situation comedy *Martin* also stirred controversy as black audiences sometimes were dissatisfied with the show's blatantly racist and sexist humor. These shows represent opposing poles of the class divide, and their further interest lies in the fact that that divide is made wider through the fact of race: They reinvoke all of the old debates about white desire versus styles of black representation and fashion new ones about political acuity in foregrounding blackness, particularly in casting durable examples of black masculinity.

In the most common application of the term, a comedy is "a fictional work in which the materials are selected and managed primarily in order to interest and amuse us: the characters and their discomfitures engage our pleasurable attention rather than our profound concern, [and] we are made to feel that no great disaster will occur ... . "[6] Those discomfitures are important, since comedy in its classic definition derives its laughter, or its satire, from human weakness or failure. Comedy winds up being more serious than tragedy, for whereas tragedy makes us shrink from its horror comedy is the mirror held up by the comedian to his audience. I do not suggest that in looking either at *Cosby* or at *Martin* or at any other sitcom, black or white, audiences cannot or should not take advantage of comedy's warrant of release from the rituals of the actual world, its offer of renewal through laughter. But the world's everyday rituals do inexorably involve racial, class, and gender codes, and to the extent they achieve comic appraisal that appraisal relies on its efficacy to relieve the viewer from daily concerns by distorting visual and aural elements of racial representation. Comedy regularly invites the audience—whose season ticket is always already stamped—into the world of the uncomfortably familiar, the disquietingly recognizable. Where black progressivism is concerned, the uncomfortable familiarity is the ease with which black men and women appear to welcome its containment. *Cosby* and *Martin* are chosen here as examples because they are also often proposed as radical and diametrically opposed examples of black representation, poles between which more contemporary comedy featuring black men may be seen and evaluated.[7] Those poles are ordinarily defined through a valuation of class consciousness which inexorably creates the segments of black audience prepared to appreciate one position and denigrate the other, but I would like to suggest critiques of both that diminish the need for viewing either solely through the lens of class.

Cosby seems particularly complex because its Thursday night prime-time slot on NBC presented what was ostensibly a pleasant, wholesome view of an affluent, middle-class African American family whose male head of household is a pediatrician and whose female head is an attorney. Cliff and Claire Huxtable live a quiet existence, if harried by the antics of their children, friends, and in-laws, which, with Cliff as foil, provide much of the comedy. The domestic scene is one of humorous one-upmanship, with Claire appearing, for the most part, to hold the upper hand. The children are pleasant, energetic, and whimsical. The show presents a picture of a family's having achieved the vaunted American dream. The signal departure for this happy family tableau is that all of its members are black.

If in dramatic series black men are offered roles in society without on-screen leadership, comedy's *Cosby* offered leadership without roles. Though the Huxtables appeared to epitomize the kind of black bourgeois success that recalls W. E. B. Du Bois's notion of the talented tenth, and Cliff and son Theo, played by Malcolm-Jamal Warner, wore the logos and otherwise sported the symbolism of historically black colleges and universities (i.e., HBCUs), Cosby's character, Cliff, rarely practiced medicine on screen, and his wife, Claire, played by Phylicia Rashad, never practiced law. This observation may seem unfair, since the professional or occupational elements of characters are also not necessarily made central or functional in white sitcoms. But the use of the HBCU symbols and the family's apparent, though fleetingly portrayed, pro-black political stances seem to wish to make some capital of notions of black uplift through the exercise of a sense of communitarian responsibility that might include invoking the influence of one's profession. Although *Cosby* wanted to present wholesome family entertainment without making much of black political culture, these elements, as they occurred in the show from week to week, nevertheless make their own argument for examining the show in a larger political context.

Sut Jhally and Justin Lewis seek a balanced view of *The Cosby Show* in their study of the program. In reciting positions defending the show, they emphasize that *Cosby* was a significant departure from sitcoms with black casts that depended on racial stereotypes for their humor. But because of this fact, the show was originally not expected to make it to air. A black-oriented television series that either refused stereotypes, as *Cosby* did, or discussed politics and racism, would have a short life in prime time. "To attack the show because it panders to the needs of a mainstream white audience is to attack its lifeblood," Jhally and Lewis write. "In the TV culture of the United States, audience ratings determine whether a series lives or dies."[8] As such, *Cosby*, however well meaning its content, was ultimately designed to reassure white and black Americans that black life was realizable without the discomfiting problems of race and economics; indeed, this fate was inexorable, given the country's racial ideology and its ability to fashion the exceedingly narrow parameters within which a black sitcom could thrive.

For the late 1980s, *Cosby* did represent a signal departure from the common fare of black representation on television, especially regarding Cliff's feminist stances on behalf and at the behest of his wife and daughters. His challenges to an oppressive masculinity showed that black men could be nonsexist, and this positioning gave the show some political validity even if it was chary about issues of race. But so many of the show's moments seemed to desire racial discourses even as it felt itself to be prohibited from them, an urge Jhally and Lewis call the show's "quiet style."[9] The Huxtables' eldest daughter, Sondra, played by Sabrina LeBeauf, named her twins Nelson and Winnie, but no further reference was made as to the meaning of the choice. The reference to the Mandelas is thus placed just beyond the periphery of the spotlight for the viewer's briefest consideration; it is made "quietly and unobtrusively, relying on the audience's ability to catch the political ramifications of the statement."[10] In another instance during the show's second season, NBC wanted an anti-apartheid poster removed from Theo's bedroom door. Cosby fought to keep the sign and eventually won, but as Jhally and Lewis point out, "the network's desire to remove such a meek symbol of black resistance from the airwaves demonstrates what progressive voices on prime-time television are up against."[11] Even though *The Cosby Show* made statements against sexism, it ultimately muted even those statements, for it denied the impact of the masculine presence in matters of race; to the extent the show did not discuss race, it missed its opportunities to examine the ways in which race and gender are imbricated, a point to which I wish to return. Moreover, its refusal of class as a topic for exploration also muted discussions of alternate roles for the black professional, thus reerecting the stereotype of black bourgeois insouciance, the blithe lack of awareness of the real America of which these men and women are ordinarily accused.

In his incisive book *Black Skin, White Masks*, Frantz Fanon discusses the signal phenomenological feature of the black Antillean male. Having no discernible, inherent values of his own, this man depends on the presence and evaluation of the "other" to provide them. "The question is always whether he is less intelligent than I, blacker than I, less respectable than I," Fanon writes. "Every position of one's own, every effort at security, is based on relations of dependence, with the diminution of the other. It is the wreckage of what surrounds me that provides the foundation for my virility."[12] One way of preventing or reducing this human wreckage, for example, would be in the consciously human approach—thus leading to an increase in one's stature— with which one may attend the needs of the other. In the case of the black American physician, this would be a new feature of the relationship between a member of the so-called talented tenth and his patient. The very seeking of help by the other in crisis reaffirms the physician's consciousness of himself and, by extension, his value to his community. Fanon extends his critique through a return to Hegel's famous master–slave dialectic. Though "man is human only to the extent to which he tries to impose his existence on another man in order to be recognized by him,"[13] Fanon emphasizes the "absolute reciprocity" at the foundation of Hegelian dialectic, finding this necessity "in the degree to which I go beyond my own immediate being [and apprehend] the existence of the other as a natural and more than natural reality."[14] But this is a reciprocity, finally: The condescending subject must allow the other to perform this phenomenological function as well and to "restore to the other, through mediation and recognition, his human reality, which is different from his natural reality."[15] In this instance of transindividualism, class distinction, to a useful degree, is supplanted by a mutually recognized humanity.

This is not yet the case of Cliff. It is not immediately so because Fanon is discussing the Antillean black man—"the French Negro," as Fanon calls him, as opposed to "the American Negro, who is cast in a different play."[16] Because the Antillean man had never fought for his freedom, according to Fanon, becoming he "who can find in his memory no trace of the struggle for liberty or of that anguish of liberty of which Kierkegaard speaks," he is at variance with the black man in the United States, where "the Negro battles and is battled. There are laws that, little by little, are invalidated under the Constitution. There are other laws that forbid certain forms of discrimination. And we can be sure that nothing is going to be given free."[17] Now in this American instance, at least Claire is specifically implicated for her status as a member of the bar practicing in the United States, a status that appears to be limned only for an audience. It is thus not available to the other. Cliff could of course use his knowledge of medicine to help stem the crisis in health care for African Americans. But whether Cliff or Claire is expected to be the combatant, the fact is that there is no battle. If the notion of having a political battle of some sort seems a bit overwrought for a half-hour situation comedy, let us return for a moment to this chapter's working definition of comedy: a mirror of the human condition held up to an audience. This very idea of mirroring and recognition is also at the heart of these meditations of Fanon, and its angle of incidence is distorted by the omissions of *The Cosby Show*.

If part of the show's intent beyond the merely comic was to show that black professional success and laughter were possible—that one could show black possibility because one could show the irony of black struggle—then it is remarkable that on behalf of black communities Claire was never an advocate, remarkable that Cliff rarely healed. That message was consistently clouded by the mere wearing of certain HBCU colors. The mirror held up to the audience was one without backing, as if it were meant to see itself only as a transparency. Perhaps Cosby and his creative crew can finally be handed the last laugh in the class and representation wars surrounding the show after all, if we can deconstruct "Huxtables" into "Huck's Stables"—as if NBC, behaving as a corporate Huck Finn, were to command the trotting out of empty black shells for a forever faceless white viewing public. This is a public that is not only American but also international, as the show for much of its run was also rated number one in prime time in the Republic of South Africa during the years of apartheid. It is also ironic that whereas Cosby made television history with his appearance in *I Spy* at the height of the civil rights era, *The Cosby Show* flourished during the era of Reagan–Bush–Thatcher politics, which sought to undo civil rights—including education and means of economic advancement—for people of color and working classes on two continents. Indeed, the gains through political action that were realized in the 1960s by blacks and others, particularly in the United States, began to evaporate in this new era of downsized government and deregulation, and a new zeitgeist of conservatism, emboldened by colossal gains on Wall Street, arose. As Michael Dawson indicates, broad pessimism reemerged as a regular feature of life among African Americans and was well entrenched by the beginning of the Clinton era. In a 1993 poll taken by the National Black Politics Study, two-thirds of African American respondents believed that racial equality would either never be achieved or, at best, not be realized in their lifetimes.[18] "Very few African American political leaders," Dawson writes, "let alone White politicians, were willing to advocate broad-based economic redistribution after the Reagan ideological onslaught."[19] That *The Cosby Show* not only appeared during these years but became the cultural phenomenon that it was suggests popular acquiescence to this generalized unwillingness to ask searching questions about U.S. domestic policy and exemplifies the false comfort regarding race and economics in which Americans had managed to cloak themselves.

In returning to the idea of *Cosby*'s ultimate foreclosure of debate on sexism through its silence on racism, of particular interest for Claire, as both a woman and a practicing member of the bar, would have been the national attention during the same period given to Supreme Court confirmation hearings in which Clarence Thomas sought to fend off accusations of sexual impropriety from Anita Hill. But in that case, as in Claire's, and Cliff's, relative silence on the matter, specific issues of black masculinity loomed large. First there was the issue of the seat on the court itself, made vacant by the death of Thurgood

Marshall, a part of whose fame came from persuading the court of the invalidity of *Plessy v. Ferguson* in the landmark *Brown v. Board of Education* case, which charted the course for the same effort toward civil rights that saw Bill Cosby star in prime time a decade later. George H. W. Bush's nomination of Thomas to the bench was seen as cynical by many: The so-called black seat on the court was being given to an African American who appeared to be prepared to do the bidding of his conservative benefactors rather than, as did Marshall, to advance the progressive agenda on civil rights and social programs. More to the point in this, however, was Thomas's apparent lack of fitness to don the robes and the silence of black leadership regarding this lack. As Cornel West writes, "the very fact that no Black leader could utter publicly that a Black appointee for the Supreme Court was unqualified shows how captive they are to white-racist stereotypes about black intellectual talent."[20] With respect to Hill's accusations, Thomas could be seen to be shorn of an independent manhood by seeking refuge among his white male protectors in the Senate, while Hill, apparently fruitlessly, sacrificed what professional women like Claire Huxtable may take entirely for granted or may hold entirely sacred because of its fragility: the right to dignity and the respect of one's person. Toni Morrison uses the word *appropriate* to describe Thomas's secret swearing-in ceremony after his Senate confirmation, "for secrecy had operated from the beginning. Not only the dismissed and suppressed charges against the candidate, but also deeper, more ancient secrets of males bonding and the demonizing of females who contradict them."[21] The Hill–Thomas hearings drew in relief the forces of dominance and oppression that women face regularly and that black women have faced immemorially; the professional class status of this real-life drama's players proved only to be poor insulation from its effects.

Again, it may appear too much to ask of a weekly half-hour prime-time sitcom that it recognize these avenues of irony and ultimate deficiency and to develop material from them. But *The Cosby Show* took on that task when it conceived the cast. For virtually wherever blackness has appeared in literature or performance, it has been the sign of resistance; no other purpose of the black presence precedes this one. As Fanon remarked, "I am the slave not of the 'idea' others have of me but of my own appearance."[22] Embedded in his ironic statement is the fact that his appearance is the idea, as the insertion of the black body and voice into any discourse invests it with the sensibilities of difference and opposition; no valuation of social expression, once introduced to an awareness of the proximity of the black other, is ever again the same. *The Cosby Show* is more than liminally aware of this as it seeks to present innocuous and successful black life, for it revives the trappings of early black success and routes to empowerment with as much symbolism as, among other things, the donning of Morehouse and Spelman sweatshirts can convey. It tables its discussion of black progress exactly here, throwing a veil over the struggle that made this black success a possibility in the first place. But rather than that *Cosby* must show a responsibility to blackness because its cast is black, it must because the show's mimesis of black life is its irreducible responsibility.

In the comedy *Martin*, a very different emphasis is at work as the show's star Martin Lawrence crosses black masculinity with low humor. Here, Martin's collection of what he leads the audience to believe are his intellectually deficient male friends and neighbors, of his ordinary denigration of black women, and of his outlandish characterizations of some senior citizens probably leaves much to be desired in representations from black male comics. When Martin wears a "Free Mike Tyson" T-shirt in one episode, it is as abridged in its meaning as when the Huxtables model HBCU wear: Although Tyson is a much-maligned figure, having been manipulated by black as well as white handlers and boxing promoters, and is represented everywhere as a Bigger Thomas-like figure abused by American society, he has also lived the kind of black masculinity that women might do well to avoid. It is this specificity of Tyson's character that Martin's T-shirt cannot legitimate; its phrase mutes its efforts toward salutary black masculinity even as it announces them.

Kristal Brent Zook writes that although fans of *Martin* argue its precedence in showing a young, professional couple in love, "it was precisely this romantic vision of love which served to conceal and even mitigate the show's larger misogyny."[23] Many fans argue that such criticism betrays a fundamental class bias and that much of what is funny in the show depends on the audience's deletion of the reflexive nature of class consciousness, particularly that consciousness as it thrives in the black mind. Since class consciousness is muted in everyday discourse yet remains a lived reality, the show's display of black caricature is itself a defiant rejection of class judgment in its revelation of authentic black life before a larger, and thus potentially whiter, audience. This argument fails, however, before the blinding glare of the show's devaluation of black women. Its impetus toward a dominating black masculinity is the chief engine of the show's humor, an element that, on reflection, black progressive culturists may find difficult to absorb.

On the show, Martin Payne (Martin Lawrence) is a Philadelphia radio deejay who lives with his girlfriend, Gina Waters (Tisha Campbell), and consistently professes his devotion to her. But as Zook remarks, "Gina's physical comedy is often predicated on a certain fear of punishment. . . . In order to coax her man back to a less threatening self, Gina often resorts to trickery, home cooking, and especially sex."[24] Not only is this misogynist, but misogyny's byproducts for black maleness also become infantilization and primitivization. Lawrence's character neither knows nor understands the value for the relationship—and for the audience—that can ensue from recognizing black female struggle and autonomy; moreover, his insistence on domination diminishes the possibilities of a self-generating and independent masculinity that can otherwise accrue to him.

Other women and figurations of femaleness in the cast suffer as well. There is Gina's girlfriend Pam, played by Tichina Arnold, and two representations of women Lawrence plays in costume: Mrs. Payne, Martin's mother; and Sheneneh Jenkins, a next-door neighbor who, festooned with rings, bracelets, and hair decorations of various kinds, serves the function of the "'round-the-way" girl. Zook describes interactions among all four women as representing "dynamic struggles over how 'we' define black womanhood."[25] For example, Mrs. Payne, as the aggrieved mother hearing about injustices against her son, typically reacts with exaggerated indignation; "she has been known to fall out or faint with arms and legs spread-eagled and girdle exposed, to break into spontaneous somersaults, and even to eat furniture."[26] Martin ordinarily treats Pam as mannishly unattractive, and Sheneneh "is hopelessly mannish despite her devoted attention to hair and nails."[27] Sheneneh often resorts to a kind of masculine violence with others who cross her, or those who, even without malice, provoke her ire. "One of the key contradictions of gender representation in *Martin*," Zook explains, "is that while Pam, Sheneneh, and Mama Payne are constructed as strong, independent, 'authentic' black women, they are also represented as inherently unwomanly."[28] Zook also gives documentation of Lawrence sexually harassing his costar Campbell off screen, as well as being involved in incidents of partner and spousal violence against other women, all of which reveal genuine, real-life difficulties with women that Lawrence only reforegrounds in his stage and television work.[29] Zook calls Lawrence's use of drag in creating his female characters *gender-fuck*; here, she borrows from the black female impersonator Ru Paul, for whom the term describes the comic style of drag in which masculine body hair is part of the female mask. Along with the veneer of romance between young black professionals, it is the other means through which the show generates its misogyny. Sheneneh's mannishness and Mama Payne's exaggerated behavior have been noted already, but in these crossings of gender, blended with histrionics and violence, Lawrence's troubled and troubling urge toward masculine domination—hidden by make-up, jewelry, and accentuated body parts—is served entirely by locating the source of his humor in women's defeminization, as if making them monstrous by making them masculine consumes, and thus controls, their femininity. Lawrence's defeminized women become all of a piece with his off-screen efforts to control women with whom he has had relationships, for the masking—the putting-on the audience, the making of humor—is yet another form of sexual control. As Pierre Bourdieu writes, "To possess sexually, as in the French *baiser* or in the English 'to fuck,' is to dominate in the sense of subjecting to one's power, but also to deceive, mislead, or, as we say, 'to have' (whereas to resist seduction is not to be deceived, not 'to be had'). The manifestations of virility, whether legitimate or illegitimate, belong to the logic of prowess, the exploit, which confers honor."[30] Lawrence's assumption of the feminine visage and voice in creating Mama Payne and Sheneneh seems rather unlike that of the black comic Flip Wilson's creation of his feminine alter ego, Geraldine, whose tenderness craftily masked her dissatisfaction with sexism. Lawrence's women do not suggest the transgressive "eating of the other" about which bell hooks writes, the "longing for pleasure…projected as a force that can disrupt and subvert the will to dominate."[31] They rather replicate at the ground of gender the production of race that the black sitcom fashions for the comfort of white audiences, by assuming the feminine and discarding it in terms of laughter as commodity.

Martin's ultimate success, however, is based on Lawrence's deployment of his deception on black audiences. Viewers are indeed had when they accept a denigration of black femaleness that, despite the distorted sexualization framing it, is nevertheless carefully, cannily sanitized for family hour. Zook pertinently asks what black experience Lawrence is trying to represent and why so many African American viewers find such performances pleasurable and familiar. "The stakes here are about…who we allow to dance inside our imaginations and why. They're also about struggling with, and challenging the ways in which Martin Lawrence's memories and fantasies are our own as well."[32] It seems as well to have much to do with having failed to value black feminine presences on the one hand, and having begun, however haltingly, to articulate the importance of black masculine presences on the other. The mirror Lawrence holds up to audiences for their consumption forces them to witness men as devourers and women as their digested prey. To the extent the show may speak to black cultural specificities, it asks its audiences to continue to imbibe rituals of dominance and submission and to resist, for the remuneration from a larger commodity culture, any progressive alternative.

Audiences who abhor *Martin* and who consider *The Cosby Show* a more progressive, more wholesome alternative may find on deeper reflection that though *Martin*'s claims to black male virility lack legitimacy, *Cosby* renders black maleness politically impotent. Both shows mask the deferment of American dreaming either by distorting the black female visage and voice for the sake of masculine dominance, or by diminishing the exigencies of race and subordinating them to the fantasies of class. The idea of leisurely television watching is severely challenged if viewers can force the question of what kind of black representation, particularly black male representation, they should be prepared to watch. Since audiences have never adequately determined what black male possibilities exist in the public sphere, however, and since leisure and entertainment continuously involve the politics of their own time, a debate over the definition of *leisure* should be of immediate concern. Demands for an unusual vigilance by all progressive audiences against coded denigrations of blackness and calls for genuine representational balance over mere wholesomeness are also important, for when viewers are at their most relaxed, they are likely at their most vulnerable. The task is to discover how audiences can best give to their leisure some deeper structural understanding of the black male—to borrow from Ralph Ellison, how best to value his hidden name and complex fate.[33]

Notes

1. Frantz Fanon, *Black Skin, White Masks*, trans. Charles Lam Markmann (New York: Grove Weidenfeld, 1977), 232.
2. bell hooks, *Black Looks: Race and Representation* (Boston: South End Press, 1992), 89.
3. Robin R. Means Coleman, *African American Viewers and the Black Situation Comedy: Situating Racial Humor* (New York: Garland, 1998), 3–5.
4. See Patricia Hills, *The Painter's America: Rural and Urban Life, 1810–1910* (New York: Praeger, 1974); and Hugh Honour, *The Image of the Black in Western Art*, vol. 4 (Cambridge, MA: Harvard, 1989).
5. Eric Lott, *Love and Theft: Blackface Minstrelsy and the American Working Class* (New York: Oxford, 1993), 40.
6. M. H. Abrams, *A Glossary of Literary Terms*, 7th ed. (New York: Harcourt Brace, 1999), 38.
7. Coleman, *African American Viewers*, 10. *Martin* has often been seen, if anecdotally, as the "anti-Cosby"; inveighing against it have been Alvin Poussaint, Charles S. Dutton, and Bill Cosby himself, among others.
8. Sut Jhally and Justin Lewis, *Enlightened Racism: The Cosby Show, Audiences, and the Myth of the American Dream* (Boulder: Westview Press, 1992), 4.
9. Ibid.
10. Ibid.
11. Ibid.
12. Fanon, *Black Skin*, 211.
13. Ibid., 216.
14. Ibid.
15. Ibid., 217.
16. Ibid., 221.
17. Ibid.
18. Michael Dawson, "Black Discontent: The Preliminary Report of the 1993–1994 National Black Politics Study," National Black Politics Working Paper Series Report #1, University of Chicago, 1993–1994.
19. Dawson, "A Black Counterpublic?: Economic Earthquakes, Racial Agenda(s), and Black Politics," in *The Black Public Sphere*, ed. Black Public Sphere Collective (Chicago: University of Chicago Press, 1995), 219.
20. Cornel West, "Black Leadership and the Pitfalls of Racial Reasoning," in *Race-ing Justice, En-gendering Power: Essays on Anita Hill, Clarence Thomas, and the Construction of Social Reality*, ed. Toni Morrison (New York: Pantheon Books, 1992), 391.
21. Ibid., xx.
22. Fanon, *Black Skin*, 116.
23. Kristal Brent Zook, *Color by Fox: The Fox Network and the Revolution in Black Television* (New York: Oxford, 1999), 54. I am indebted to Zook's analysis of *Martin* for my insights here.
24. Ibid., 55.
25. Ibid., 57.
26. Ibid., 57–58.
27. Ibid., 58.
28. Ibid.
29. For a summary of these incidents, see ibid., 58–64.
30. Pierre Bourdieu, *Masculine Domination*, trans. Richard Nice (Stanford, CA: Stanford University Press, 2001), 19.
31. hooks, *Black Looks*, 27.
32. Zook, *Color*, 64.
33. Ralph Ellison, "Hidden Name and Complex Fate: A Writer's Experience in the United States," in *Shadow and Act* (New York: Random House, Inc., 1953), 144–66.

11

Welcome to the Terrordome: Exploring the Contradictions of a Hip-Hop Black Masculinity*

TIMOTHY J. BROWN

Bobbin' and weavin' and let the good get even
C'mon down
And welcome to the Terrordome.

Public Enemy
"Welcome to the Terrordome"
Fear of a Black Planet

The lyrics in the epigraph by legendary rap group Public Enemy continue to exemplify the struggle of being black in America. This struggle is defined by black men's contentious relationship with society, their culture, and each other in their attempt to construct their own identity. This is a relationship in which the dominant culture draws on historically developed stereotypes about black men to control and to minimize their potential. Over the centuries, black men have resisted this control over their persons by crafting new and different identities. The new generation too has resisted white appropriation and definition of them by crafting a new identity based on hip-hop culture. A hip-hop identity embodies both progressive elements of racial pride and masculinity as well as regressive elements drawn from American culture. The contentious relationship surrounding a hip-hop black masculinity was evident in an incident involving a hero of the hip-hop generation, Allen Iverson.

Iverson, the star shooting guard for the Philadelphia 76ers, is known not only for his quickness, crossover dribble, and rainbow jumpshot but also for embracing the cultural signifiers of the hip-hop generation such as cornrows, tattoos, and hip-hop music. As a product of the hip-hop generation, Iverson has been influenced by its music, fashion, and perspective. Rap music and

---

*Portions of this article were previously published in the *Journal of Intercultural Communication Research* 34, no. 1, 65–87.

hip-hop culture grew out of inner-city youth's discontent with a society that failed to hear their concerns or to address their problems. As an inner-city youth, Iverson identified with many of the themes articulated in rap music because his life experiences, such as growing up in a single-parent home in a poor neighborhood in Hampton, Virginia, paralleled those of many rappers. Not surprisingly, many of his generation listen to and have embraced rap music and hip-hop culture as part of expressing their cultural identity and class consciousness.[1]

During his National Basketball Association (NBA) career, Iverson was named rookie of the year, led the league in scoring four times, and was named the league's most valuable player in 2001. As one of the NBA's premier stars, Iverson enjoys a loyal following as his game jersey is consistently one of the top five NBA jerseys sold.[2] The stars of today, however, unlike past stars such as Michael Jordan or Magic Johnson, come from a different generation that has the league concerned about its crossover appeal.

This concern marks Iverson as one of the NBA's hip-hop icons and represents the volatile relationship between white society and hip-hop culture, the latter of which offers African Americans an alternative identity. Although Iverson is a successful multimillionaire who has economically surpassed the material desires of middle-class society, his persona and cultural identity are denounced and criticized by the same middle-class society.

The tensions between a hip-hop black masculinity and the dominant culture are best illustrated by the highly reported domestic incident involving Allen Iverson and his wife, Tawanna. During the summer of 2002 Iverson and his uncle, Greg Iverson, were accused of breaking into Iverson's cousin's apartment and threatening two occupants. The alleged incident occurred because Iverson was searching for his wife, who had left their home after a dispute. The media frenzy over the incident and the intense police investigation that took place were unprecedented for an incident that did not involve any physical abuse or injury.

An analysis of the Iverson incident reveals the media's reduction of Iverson to the familiar images that have been historically constructed about black men: that they are aggressive, angry, prone to violence, and sexually aggressive. Furthermore, Iverson's hip-hop black masculinity was a flash point for these media constructions because it embodies resistance though progressive elements of masculinity drawn from African American cultural traditions as well as regressive elements of patriarchy, competition, and individualism drawn from American culture but also present in African American communities.

Black Men and Popular Culture: Contemporary Constructions of Black Masculinity

Historically, black masculinity has been constructed and perpetuated in a negative way by popular culture texts. David Sibley explained how the positive meanings associated with the color white and the negative meanings associated with the color black gained greater currency during European colonialism where it was important to regulate and to dominate the colonized.[3] In time, popular culture took these negative associations and disseminated them through newspapers, film, radio, and television.[4] Furthermore, several studies have illustrated how African Americans have overwhelmingly played negative roles as Toms, coons, tragic mulattoes, mammies, and bucks,[5] as comedic characters,[6] and as characters that are inherently angry, potentially violent, and sexually aggressive.[7]

The negative constructions of African Americans through popular culture create, reproduce, and sustain racial ideologies.[8] These ideologies contain symbols, concepts, and images that act as a code through which individuals understand, interpret, and represent elements of our racial existence and African American culture.[9] Racial ideologies are often seen in sports, where the media often perpetuate racial stereotypes by highlighting white players' intellect with adjectives such as heady, good work habits, and cagey while instead emphasizing black players' athleticism as *a burner, a speedster,* and *talented.*[10]

The historical stereotypes associated with black men that have been perpetuated by popular culture have influenced the meanings and identities associated with black masculinity.[11] According to bell hooks, these stereotypes demonstrate how black men are living in a society that does not want them to succeed and offers narrow identities for them to enact.[12] Kobena Mercer further argued that black masculinity is a contradictory—and subordinated— form of identity, because historically African American males have been prevented from demonstrating aspects of patriarchal masculinity such as access to positions of power.[13]

The contemporary media and social images of black men can be categorized into three dominant types of black masculinity representative of contemporary culture: the *race man,* the *new black aesthetics,* and *the nigga.*[14] Todd Boyd argued that each identity is a representation of different expressions, meanings, and ideologies of black masculinity. The race man, signified by Bill Cosby, represents the ideology of cultural advancement by presenting images of the race that are acceptable to both the dominant white culture and African American culture: This identity is seen as a role model. Cultural advancement is based on the politics of integration and the establishment and normality of a black upper class. Meanwhile, the new black aesthetics, signified by Spike Lee, is based on the nationalist politics of Malcolm X. This representation of black masculinity infiltrated the dominant culture while still providing some sense of an African American aesthetic. Boyd argued that the new black aesthetics has led to individual black empowerment but has failed to create political and economic success for African Americans as a group. Finally, the nigga does not have an identifiable leader, nor does it have a traditional political agenda. Its primary concern is articulating the voice and lifestyle of the truly disadvantaged. The prominence of the nigga in contemporary society has moved the discussion of black masculinity from one solely of race to also include class. Furthermore, the nigga rejects the social acceptability of the race man and the traditional political nature of the new black aesthetics. Boyd further argued that the evolution of the race man to the new black aesthetics to the nigga demonstrates the contemporary articulations of black masculinity within class politics distinguishing one representation from another.

It is my contention that Allen Iverson is representative of the nigga identity, which I refer to here as a hip-hop black masculinity. This masculinity places Iverson in conflict with the dominant culture. Unlike the race man and the new black aesthetics, which ultimately are integrated into the dominant culture, a hip-hop black masculinity is countercultural and resists conforming to many of the dominant culture's precepts. As Boyd explained, "The modern-day 'nigga,' having come to prominence through several cultural arenas including rap music, African American cinema, and professional sports, equally defies aspects of mainstream white culture, as well as the [sometimes] restrictive dimensions of status quo black culture."[15] The icons of a hip-hop black masculinity such as Allen Iverson have acquired enough capital to uncompromisingly inhabit, construct, and express a black self-identity that connects them to the "hood." This wealth allows these icons to live in middle-class comfort while still presenting an image that retains lower-class signifiers and the mentality of the 'hood. This factor informs a hip-hop black masculinity and serves as a theoretical framework for understanding its contradictory nature of embodying the signs of both a progressive and regressive black masculinity.

Black Masculinities and the Court of Public Opinion

The stereotypical construction of black masculinity was illustrated by the nature of the media spectacle surrounding Allen Iverson's alleged domestic dispute. The media's[16] coverage of the incident reduced Iverson to the familiar images that have been historically constructed about black men and, as such, cater to the dominant culture's fears about black masculinity. Before articulating this point, a brief summary of the incident is provided.

During the summer of 2002, Iverson and his wife, Tawanna, allegedly had an argument, after which time Tawanna left their mansion in Gladwyne, Pennsylvania, an exclusive suburb that borders the city of Philadelphia. Allegedly, Iverson and his Uncle Greg, age thirty-nine, went to Iverson's cousin's (Shaun Bowman's) apartment in West Philadelphia looking for Tawanna. They entered the apartment, and Iverson confronted Shaun's roommate, Charles Jones, age twenty-one, and next-door neighbor Hakim Carey, age seventeen. According to Jones, Iverson, with a gun visible, forced his way into the apartment and threatened Jones with harm if he did not tell him where Tawanna and Bowman were. In the days following the incident, the Philadelphia media—talk radio, the major newspapers, and local and cable television news—along with national media began extensive coverage of the alleged incident, which was described as "All Allen All the Time."[17]

District Attorney Lynne M. Abraham announced that Iverson would be charged with fourteen offenses. A defense attorney, who has represented high-profile clients for thirty years, responded to the charges by saying, "They've thrown the book at him. From the information I have, this incident is domestic-related. This is an awful lot of charges for a guy who had an argument with his wife."[18] In the early hours of July 16, Iverson surrendered to police, where he was fingerprinted, photographed, and arraigned before being released eleven hours later on bail. By daybreak, an eclectic throng of media, supporters, opponents, street entertainers, and upstart entrepreneurs who sold items such as "Free Iverson" T-shirts, had gathered at police headquarters. ESPN's Sal Paolantonio referred to the media frenzy surrounding the case as "O.J. East."[19] Two weeks later at the six-hour preliminary hearing, the prosecution witnesses contradicted their earlier statements that Iverson had a gun and forced his way into the apartment. Judge James M. DeLeon dismissed all but two misdemeanor charges—making terrorist threats—against Iverson.[20]

Although Iverson's fans supported him, and though most defense attorneys overwhelmingly agreed that the district attorney's case was weak, some people strongly disagreed with the decision.[21] However, given the attorneys' perspective and the judge's dismissal of all but two of the charges, one can conclude that something larger was at work in the Iverson incident. An analysis of the media accounts that covered the Iverson incident reveal that Iverson's hip-hop masculinity was a source of the negative coverage he received and that individuals not identified as fans, and who tended to be nonblack, were more likely to believe all the allegations against Iverson. Columnist Johnette Howard picked up on this point: "Judging from TV interviews, plenty of people—whites in particular—seem focused on what punishment Iverson might receive, as if they suddenly find the wildly popular cornrowed and tattooed 76ers guard menacing, not just edgy or hip anymore. Plenty of people—African Americans in particular, at least those who were interviewed on TV outside Iverson's home and at the police station yesterday—seem focused on Iverson's treatment. They expressed a deep-rooted sense that Iverson is just another black guy who's getting a raw deal from the police."[22]

Ultimately, the media coverage of the Iverson incident constructed an image of Iverson as a menacing person whom people should fear. The most common way this image was invoked was by articulating the allegations of the incident over and over again until the alleged facts became normalized and reified as truth. This was a point *Philadelphia Daily News* sports reporter John Smallwood made on the cable television show *Daily News Live.*[23] It became accepted as fact that Iverson forced his way into his cousin's apartment. Over 150 documents generated primarily from the Philadelphia press, television news broadcasts, and three television news talk shows from July 12 to July 30 all emphasized that Iverson used force to gain entry into the apartment. When the reports also mentioned that Iverson had a heated argument with his wife, the media instantly constructed one of the most troubling stereotypes of black masculinity: the aggressive and angry black man.

The *Philadelphia Tribune,* the city's black-owned newspaper, was the only source that provided more insight into the alleged aggressive nature of this aspect of the incident. These reports quoted residents of the building saying that no one could enter the building unannounced because the front door was locked.[24] According to the residents, an individual either had to know the key code or be buzzed up by a tenant. This information, which was either ignored or downplayed, could have provided the public with a better understanding of the situation and could have challenged the validity of the information that was being reported by the media.

Besides portraying black men as aggressive, the image of black masculinity as prone to violence was also constructed for the public. When the incident was being discussed, most articles reviewed Iverson's past record, which included being arrested as a high school student and being convicted in 1993 for engaging in a bowling-alley brawl in Virginia. After the latter incident he spent four months in jail before governor Douglas Wilder granted him elemency; In 1997, he was arrested in Virginia after police found a gun and a small quantity of marijuana in a car in which he was the passenger.

This information, when mentioned, was often at the end of an article or report, which gave the impression that the current incident was simply a continuation of past misdeeds. This is illustrated by Karl Minor, who commented in the *Philadelphia Inquirer* on July 16, "The man [Iverson] has had more opportunities and breaks than anyone. He needs to pay for his actions now."[25] *Philadelphia Daily News* columnist John Baer wrote, "But, look, didn't he ask for this? And didn't we? Hasn't his pattern of behavior since high school reflected an outlaw, I'm a rebel style?"[26] The media constructions of Iverson's past actions were repeated to influence how the public interpreted the current incident. What was lost in these constructions was the roughly ten years between incidents, during which Iverson contributed positively to society as a father, husband, and as a community fundraiser. Instead, the media used only negative constructions to define black masculinity and in this case the negative images that present black men as prone to violence.

Further, the allegation that Iverson had a gun while at Shaun's apartment was also routinely repeated and used to construct him as prone to violence. This alleged fact was repeated so frequently that it too became normalized and reified as truth. Alan Taylor of the *Chattanooga Times/Free* Press presented the alleged fact as truth when he wrote, "As for her jumper-jacking hubby Allen Iverson, he certainly could use a shoulder holster. A superstar shouldn't have to tuck a handcannon in his waistband."[27] A *Philadelphia Daily News* editorial called for Iverson's immediate arrest and wrote, "NOTE TO ALL the gun-toting criminals in the greater Philadelphia metropolitan area: The next time Philadelphia police come knocking on your door with an arrest warrant in hand, tell them you'll turn yourself in just as soon as your attorney gets back into town. Maybe you'll get the same reaction Allen Iverson is getting."[28] Furthermore, the editorial stated, "The fact that Iverson is a free man, despite an arrest warrant that would make an al Qaeda operative blush, despite the fact that police know exactly where he is, shows the world that Iverson will be treated differently than everybody else."[29] These assumptions made by the media reinforce historical stereotypes about black men as violent.[30] As Paul Sniderman and Thomas Piazza contended, the dominant culture tends to believe the stereotype of black men as violent because the stereotype reinforces what has been disseminated throughout the mass media on a daily basis.[31]

Another construction of black men as being prone to violence was highlighted by the articles on domestic abuse written in connection to the case. Domestic abuse is a serious problem that should not be taken lightly, and clearly it is not an acceptable practice. In the Iverson incident, however, the shocking and horrifying violence associated with real domestic abuse were used to further vilify Iverson. A few articles discussed domestic violence as if it took place in the Iverson incident.[32] This speculation was made despite a lack of evidence of any emotional or physical abuse or any filing of a protective order. In fact, Tawanna was not even the one who filed the complaint against Iverson.

The true brutal nature of domestic violence was highlighted in a situation that occurred the same night as the Iverson incident but that was not as aggressively investigated. In this case, a woman's former boyfriend entered her apartment, verbally threatened her, and then beat her. The unidentified woman—who was black—filed a complaint with the police, but the police never pursued it, even after an inquiry from the reporter who wrote the story. Whereas this true case of domestic violence was ignored, in the Iverson case, where no abuse occurred, nine detectives worked on the case, supervisors oversaw the investigation, and the police commissioner was kept appraised of developments.[33] In response to the lack of attention to her case, the unidentified woman said, "They locked up this man, Allen Iverson, and he didn't even put his hands on the people. I get beat up and my face is all swollen and they won't call me back."[34] Consideration of how these two cases were handled exemplified how the police department and the media were fixated on the alleged crime due to Iverson's celebrity as a young black basketball star and not due to the nature of the assumed crime.

Besides being characterized as aggressive, angry, and prone to violence, one of the most prominent stereotypes about black masculinity involves the hypersexuality of black men. Historically, black men are seen as having large sexual appetites and as being sexually endowed but as psychologically too immature to have meaningful relationships.[35] Not surprisingly, sexuality was very prevalent in the Iverson case. One of the most reported alleged facts was that he kicked his wife out of the house "butt" naked. Similar to the other so-called facts, almost every article made reference to the "fact" that Tawanna was naked. This alleged fact supports Jones's argument that black sexuality is often represented by the dominant culture as animalistic and carnal with a lack of intimacy and true humanity.[36] These constructions help illustrate African American men as psychologically immature and less than human.[37]

In focusing on Tawanna's alleged nudity, the media also reinforced stereotypes of African Americans as being sexually driven people who do not have loving and mature relationships. As Leonard Fleming and Linda Harris wrote in their report, "Who could imagine that the king would be accused of tossing the queen from the mansion naked?"[38] Although no one was there to view the incident (this "fact" was noted by the accuser, Charles Jones), the mere repetition of this assumed fact became accepted as truth. This alleged fact was disputed by both parents, and later versions of the "facts" tended to report that Tawanna was half-naked.[39]

In addition to covering the suspected sexual nature of the case as scandalous, the media also made light of this alleged fact. In a very sarcastic and condescending column about the entire incident, Monica Kinney wrote hypothetical questions she would have liked to have asked during the police conference, such as "What are your personal feelings about fighting with your spouses while nude?"[40] Kinney also asked, "Would it be wise to advise the public to hide clean clothes, car keys, and a fully charged cell phone somewhere as a preventive measure for just this sort of situation?"[41] In another sarcastic remark, Alan Taylor asked, "Before we begin, can someone toss Tawanna Iverson a robe? And how about a Hide-a-Key?"[42]

The themes of domestic violence and sexuality the media constructed portray contradictory perspectives that underline two negative stereotypes of African Americans. On the one hand, reporting the case as domestic abuse signifies to the public a serious crime. Furthermore, as a black man who is constructed as aggressive and prone to violence, this portrayal of Iverson feeds into the dominant culture's fear of black masculinity. On the other hand, the sarcasm used to make light of and demean Iverson and his wife taps into the dominant culture's perception of African Americans as sex-crazed buffoons who are on public display.[43] Considering these two themes, the media can appeal to both those who are alarmed at domestic abuse and perceive black males in a suspicious and hostile way and those who view African Americans as comedians shucking and jiving their way in society.[44]

The media's intense coverage of the Iverson incident reflected a cultural divide between whites' belief about American society and blacks' experience within the American system. Within this cultural clash lies a hip-hop black masculinity that reflects both progressive and regressive elements in constructions of black masculinity.

Embracing Blackness as a Sign of Progressive Masculinity

The Iverson incident illustrates how identity continues to be a salient issue in contemporary society. Historically, African Americans have survived in an oppressive culture by inventing identities that either transcended or reinforced the stereotypes.[45] The hip-hop black masculinity does both. It resists certain stereotypes created by the dominant culture and black middle-class representations such as the race man or the new black aesthetics while simultaneously embracing patriarchal and individualist notions of masculinity that embody and reinstate aggression as a masculine practice.

The tension between the dominant culture and African American culture is in large part an example of the divided soul that W. E. B. Du Bois perceptively referred to as African Americans' double consciousness. A hip-hop black masculinity attempts to negotiate this contradiction by rearticulating African American cultural practices and values[46] from a hip-hop perspective. Although hip-hop culture is often labeled as perpetuating the worst aspects of African American culture, undermining traditional middle-class authority, a closer examination of the hip-hop black masculinity reveals, however, that it embraces valued cultural practices such as the oral tradition, call and response, and stylistic expression. In this sense, a hip-hop black masculinity is progressive because it defiantly values and elevates African American cultural practices in the construction of its identity.

A hip-hop black masculinity, however, also is influenced by patriarchal practices from the dominant and African American cultures. The tension between the progressive signs and patriarchal practices makes a hip-hop black masculinity problematic. As hooks argued, this tension is the result of black men living in a patriarchal culture that restricts and confines the black self. She further explained that "black men have had no dramatic say when it comes to the way they are represented. As a consequence they are victimized by stereotypes that were first articulated in the nineteenth century but hold sway over the minds and imaginations of citizens of this nation in the present day. Black males who refuse categorization are rare, for the price of visibility in the contemporary world of white supremacy is that black male identity be defined in relation to the stereotype whether by embodying it or seeking to be other than it."[47] Likewise, hip-hop has also addressed this problem as rappers such as Tupac Shakur have created a body of work that acknowledges the challenges of trying to remake oneself while living in an environment that makes change difficult.[48]

Therefore, how black men attempt to negotiate and to enact black masculinity in the face of negative stereotypes reflects the larger struggle between certain African American cultural values and patriarchal forms of domination perpetuated by the dominant culture. More specifically, the signs of a progressive hip-hop black masculinity can be found in the demonstration of

African American cultural practices and values in the construction of race, such as valuing blackness in defining one's cultural identity and enacting practices of the oral tradition such as boasting, and class, such as embracing the call-and-response communication pattern.

Race

The hip-hop black masculinity is the product of what Bakari Kitwana argued is the new black youth culture.[49] This cultural identity is defined by its defiant attitudes, through 'hood films, hip-hop magazines, and youth-oriented television programming such as MTV and through activism in opposition to both mainstream politics and older-generation African American activists. Those who enact a hip-hop black masculinity are viewed with suspicion from both the dominant culture and older African Americans.

Rarely is a hip-hop black masculinity perceived or considered to represent a progressive masculinity. Most conversations focus on the negative characteristics of the identity and the societal problems associated with an identity that glamorizes a hypermasculinity centered on materialism, sexism, and violence.[50] Iverson has been criticized for the hypermasculinity associated with a hip-hop black masculinity, most notably when he recorded a hard-core rap album. Because of its explicit lyrics, the album received so much negative publicity that the NBA prevented Iverson from releasing the album.

Nevertheless, a hip-hop masculinity is a progressive black masculinity in that it enables Iverson and others of the hip-hop generation to define their identity based on African American cultural values and practices that have shaped and been shaped by hip-hop culture. In essence, through hip-hop culture young black males are able to demonstrate a black identity or to elevate blackness. A hip-hop perspective on elevating blackness underscores how African Americans have always placed an emphasis on defining their cultural identity to counter oppression, social categorization, and stereotyping. Constructing a cultural identity provides individuals with a selected orientation toward their culture, and it serves as a means for demonstrating cultural kinship and pride.[51]

A hip-hop black masculinity enables individuals to elevate blackness by defining and retaining aspects of an authentic black self within a racially oppressive society. Elevating blackness is a way for African Americans to demonstrate identification with black culture, which includes adopting the various cultural practices, behaviors, and values of the group.[52] Throughout history, many individuals, such as Frederick Douglass, Sojourner Truth, and Malcolm X, have led movements to redefine the black self.

Likewise, a hip-hop black masculinity attempts to redefine the black self through the values of hip-hop culture. A hip-hop masculinity has simply taken African American cultural values such as the oral tradition, braggadocio, and stylistic expression and has repackaged them through hip-hop.[53] The reconstruction of these cultural values creates an alternative identity in relation to the dominant culture and the middle-class identities of the race man and the new black aesthetics. The bold attitude of a hip-hop black masculinity, which is based on the cultural value of boasting and stylistic expression, is best illustrated by Charles Barkley's famous comment when he referred to himself as a "'90s nigga." The reference, controversial at the time, articulated to the dominant culture a new liberated black identity that said, did, and represented itself regardless of acceptance by the dominant culture.[54]

The elevation of blackness and the claim to a new liberated black identity is facilitated and informed by the hip-hop icon's class position as well as his body politics. Icons of a hip-hop black masculinity have gained the financial freedom to express their blackness in an in-your-face and rebellious way. In fact, the often self-defined identity and mentality of the gangsta often articulated by rappers and embodied by the new youth culture represent the modern-day outlaw who lives his life outside the boundaries of the dominant culture.

Iverson is associated with hip-hop culture through its various signifiers such as cornrows, tattoos, baggy clothes, stocking caps, baseball caps, jewelry, music, and use of the vernacular. In fact, Iverson's cornrows, though making him a trendsetter, represent a sign of racial difference. Historically, African Americans' hair has been devalued as the most visible stigma associated with blackness, after skin color, because it represented qualities the dominant culture labeled as having less worth.[55] Iverson, by embracing the cultural signifier of cornrows, is ignoring the dominant culture's value system and is elevating the worth of black hair and thus blackness. It is a way of elevating his blackness by demonstrating the signifiers of a black self in a white society. More importantly, hip-hop artists who retain these signifiers are signaling their group membership even as their class status changes.

For black men who have not gained financial freedom, the hip-hop black masculinity enables them to demonstrate power in patriarchal culture—by posing and stylizing their bodies. In a patriarchal culture, black men's own bodies are the only aspect over which they have control. Since black men do not have power and status, they use their bodies to attain power and respect. As Cornel West proclaimed, "For most young black men, power is acquired by stylizing their bodies over space and time in such a way that their bodies reflect their uniqueness and provoke fear in others."[56] West further explained that the way young black men stylize their bodies is a form of self-identification and resistance to the dominant culture.[57] Therefore, the unique stylizing, posing, clothing, and dialect that signify a hip-hop black masculinity are a way for young people to exercise power. The stylin' and profilin' associated with a hip-hop black masculinity is perpetuated in videos, films, entertainment, and athletics as a way to demonstrate an oppositional identity that is reified as a sign of a strong black man.

Class

"Allen Iverson grew up in the inner city. He grew up in the projects. Iverson's role, I think, was to help society see that it is okay to dress differently and to talk differently and still to be a great athlete and still to be a good person. These latest incidents, though, I think, throw that into question." This statement by Stefan Fatsis of the *Wall Street Journal* not only illustrates the dominant culture's skepticism toward a hip-hop black masculinity, but also society's unwillingness to address class issues.[58]

The hip-hop black masculinity moves the discussion of black masculinity from one solely about race to include class, as this identity is based on a hard-core urban environment and mentality where being real is being wise and respected in the 'hood.[59] The hip-hop expression of class is facilitated by the hip-hop black masculinity's ability to elevate blackness and to do so freely because those who embody it have wealth. As Boyd explained, "Access to capital has made it possible for many hip-hop icons to defy the accepted codes of mainstream decorum in favor of displaying a defiant mode of aggression whenever desired."[60] Although individuals who enact a hip-hop black masculinity have reached elite status, they choose to retain their lower-class visual aesthetics and behaviors to defiantly reject the accepted norm of their acquired class position. This point is supported by Mark Neal, who argued, "In a league that commercializes black male urban expression, players are defined via their class interests or failure to accept the 'special' responsibilities and upper-middle-class sensibilities that being an elite athlete engenders."[61] A hip-hop black masculinity inhabits middle-class space while rejecting the attributes and requirements of middle-class values in two ways: (1) by inverting middle-class values; and (2) by rejecting the dominant culture's ideas about work.

Iverson's transcendence of middle-class values on his own terms highlights what Sibley called inversion.[62] According to Sibley, inversion occurs when individuals on the margin occupy the center and those on the center get displaced as spectators. With inversion, implicit boundaries and power relationships become more visible and explicit, and the transgressions are highlighted. Inversions represent a challenge to established power relations. Sibley's concept of inversion helps explain the tension between middle-class values and Iverson's values. Iverson's high-class status inverted the power structure of the dominant culture. Those displaced by Iverson perceive him as someone who has achieved a great deal, but having done so while circumventing the system and rejecting their values. The media and the police work in concert to help perpetuate the existing power relationships and control individuals—including Iverson—who attempt to invert the system. John Baer's comment clearly underscores Iverson's inversion: "We've ripped apart the private lives of Allen, his wife, his family, and his friends. Over what? Well, it's part of the deal. We make you an icon, we give you millions and then you are ours. We are, at all levels—media, law and justice, sports, entertainment—celebrity-driven, celebrity-obsessed."[63] By enacting a hip-hop black masculinity, Iverson inverts middle-class values by retaining his lower-class visual aesthetic and by boldly rejecting the accepted decorum of his recently acquired class.[64] Iverson represents a black masculinity influenced by hip-hop culture that has transformed the mainstream society but has refused to be compromised by that same society.

A second way a hip-hop black masculinity rejects the dominant culture's middle-class norms is by rejecting the limitations imposed by the American work ethic. Although the media tried to reduce Iverson's work ethic to the familiar stereotype of the lazy black man, his success shatters the stereotype and confounds a traditionalist view toward work. Hooks argued that one of the most oppressive places for black men is the workplace, which is a site of white male dominance.[65] She contended that "most black males suffer psychologically in the world of work whether they make loads of money or low wages from overt and covert racially based psychological terrorism. Integration has not intervened on the strategies of psychological terrorism that unenlightened white people use to maintain their dominance over black people."[66]

One explanation for why black men struggle in the workplace is due to the contrasting cultural values regarding work. As Thomas Kochman explained, in the workplace the dominant culture is governed by the norm of subordinating the self to the organization.[67] All individual efforts and decisions follow a highly structured plan that is implemented from the top down. The goal is to have predictability. By contrast, in African American culture the norm is not top down. Rather, it allows the individual to demonstrate improvisation and stylistic self-expression in accomplishing and possibly improving a task. In the work world, the dominant culture's values governing work conflict with the African American cultural values of improvisation and stylistic expression. Kochman best explained this African American cultural value as "Tell me what to do but not how to do it."[68] Whereas blacks place more emphasis on improvisation in completing the task, the dominant culture insists on consistently following a formal procedure to accomplish the job. In essence, the dominant culture's view of the American work ethic stifles black creativity.

The improvisation demonstrated by a hip-hop black masculinity reflects the African American cultural practice of the call and response, as a speaker's call, or message, is reinforced by audience feedback, or response. This interactive and participatory cultural practice relies on the improvisation skills of the individual and community to work together to construct a message. The call-and-response cultural practice is pervasive throughout the discourse of African American culture.[69] It is a progressive cultural value that relies on the harmony between the individual and community where the collective endeavor is greater than the individual or community effort. As West explained,

"As with a soloist in a jazz quartet or band, individuality is promoted in order to sustain and increase the creative tension with the group—a tension that yields higher levels of performance to achieve the aim of the collective project."[70] This cultural practice is characteristic of African American culture, with the most recognized cultural production being jazz.[71] A hip-hop black masculinity, often accused of being selfish and individualistic, is simply recreating the call-and-response cultural pattern. Hip-hop icons such as Iverson thrive in the call and response, as their individual skills are showcased by the team: Both individual and team performances are enhanced by working together. By enacting this cultural practice, a hip-hop black masculinity demonstrates a progressive masculinity.

Furthermore, Iverson represents in sports the cultural clash between the dominant culture's organizational values governing work that stress highly structured plans, captured in "play the right way," and African American norms that emphasize improvisation and spontaneity. Though Iverson is praised for his skill, he is often criticized for disregarding the strict organizational rules that govern meetings, routines, and practices.[72] As one letter to the editor said, "Just think how good he could be if he would practice."[73] Showing a lack of interest in practice is diametrically opposed to a fundamental middle-class value that Boyd argued is central to the dominant culture's idea of what makes a good citizen.[74] In questioning his practice habits, white society is clearly questioning Iverson's work ethic and dedication, which implicitly echoes the tired stereotype of black men as lazy and unproductive.

Contradicting the dominant culture's suspicion of Iverson's work ethic are his achievements that suggest he had to work hard to be the player he is today. The list includes being the first pick overall in the 1996 NBA draft, being the NBA rookie of the year for the 1996–97 season, leading the league in scoring four times, being an NBA all-star starter for five consecutive years, being the NBA all-star MVP, being the league MVP, leading his team to the NBA finals during the 2000–01 season, and being the cocaptain of Team USA's 2004 Olympic team. When Iverson's size is also considered—at barely six feet tall—it illustrates that he had to work extremely hard to excel at a game dominated by much larger and taller men. The dominant society's acceptance of racial folklore explains why Iverson's work is often overlooked. Racial folklore consists of stereotypes that associate African Americans with having natural physical ability.[75] Therefore, Iverson, despite his size, is not seen as having worked hard to achieve his athletic success; he is simply doing what comes natural to him. The belief in racial folklore not only undermines Iverson's hard work but also implies that intelligence is not needed to perform what comes naturally, evoking the stereotype of black men as physically talented but not very bright.

Despite his achievements, the media refused to construct Iverson as a modern-day Horatio Alger. Iverson, however rose from poverty to provide a better life for his family. It is a familiar story often celebrated in African American culture. Iverson has been a committed husband and father. He has also supported many of his extended family members, as well as the three children of his best friend, who was tragically killed during an altercation.[77] In addition, Iverson has created several charity events to give back to the community.[78] The charitable acts Iverson performs are not magnified by the media. Instead, the media constructed Iverson as yet another black male thug, who was roaming recklessly in society, assigning to him historical stereotypes of black masculinity. It portrayed him as a sensationalized black masculinity. John Hoberman argued that one consequence of this sensationalized black masculinity is that whites can develop an appreciation of black cultural styles via the media without developing a new understanding or liking of African Americans as their neighbors, friends, and colleagues.[76]

A Hip-Hop Black Masculinity as Regressive: The Perpetuation of Patriarchy

A consequence of living in a patriarchal society is that initiating individual, group, or societal change is difficult when the tools of domination are prevalent. The signs of a progressive masculinity found in a hip-hop black masculinity exist in a dialectical tension with forms of patriarchal domination, which understand masculinity in terms of physicality, aggression, and competitive individualism. The contradictory nature of a hip-hop black masculinity underscores that the choices available for black men to define their identities are limited and often unproductive.[79] Therefore, the signs of a progressive black masculinity, previously discussed, are contradicted by patriarchal forms of domination.

Race

Although elevating blackness, a hip-hop black masculinity also perpetuates the patriarchal practice of providing limited identities for black men. Although this identity is constructed in opposition to other identities assigned to black men such as the race man or the new black aesthetics, a hip-hop black masculinity is defined so narrowly—and often in countercultural ways—that the behaviors associated with the identities are sometimes counterproductive. African American cultural values such as the oral tradition, boasting, and stylistic expression are highly valued in the culture. However, a hip-hop black masculinity informed by definitions that men should be in control at all times tends to take the African American cultural values of boasting and stylistic expression to the extreme.

A hip-hop black masculinity intensifies the struggle of African Americans by enacting its defiance in most situations, even when it does not seem to be required. In other words, a hip-hop black masculinity can take the "ghetto" mentality to an extreme where masculinity is a continual process of demonstrating toughness and assertiveness and of not taking any shit from anyone for any reason. As Boyd stated, a hip-hop black masculinity "sees value only in being educated in the ways of the streets and the hard-core urban environment that [it] exists in."[80]

This rebellious attitude is best exemplified by Latrell Sprewell, who a few years ago choked his coach during an altercation at practice. The incident not only symbolized a new era in professional sports where star athletes could act on the power they had, but it also raised the bar for demonstrating the in-your-face defiant behaviors associated with a hip-hop black masculinity. Anything short of physically assaulting someone could be labeled "soft," which is definitely not a characteristic of a hip-hop black masculinity. As a result, black athletes who identify with a hip-hop black masculinity have to demonstrate their bravado in new and often aggressive ways. Another example of this type of hip-hop black masculinity is illustrated by the former Philadelphia Eagle, Terrell Owens. Owens, who was unhappy with his contract, demonstrated his bravado by getting into a fist-fight in the locker room and then challenging anyone who wanted to fight him. Owens' actions led to his suspension and eventual dismissal from the team. This example highlights how the tough-edged nature of a hip-hop masculinity in subverting dominant forms of oppression creates its own ideology and recreates power structures that subordinate other identities, namely those labeled as *soft* or *sellout*. Thus, a hip-hop black masculinity reproduces the capitalistic system and competitive individualism within a black space.

Class

The improvisational nature of the call-and-response cultural practice can also be a double-edged sword, particularly in the context of a dominant culture that prizes individualism to the exclusion of community. Excluding community and placing a higher value on individualism undermine African American cultural values such as community, cooperation, interconnectedness, and spirituality.[81] As Molefi Asante stated, "Within Afrocentric culture one sees a distaste for individual achievement that is not related to collective advancement."[82] It is only through cooperation between individual and community, as with a jazz concert, that results in the creation of harmonious tunes. As Kochman explained, individuals within the call-and-response communication pattern are "granted great license to improvise with regard to the text—in effect to generate new 'text' as they go along—and, through the simultaneous and direct demonstration of the individual performer's virtuoso ability and powers of evocation, to produce 'engendered feeling' in the audience."[83] However, as West argued, individuals living in a dominant culture that promotes competitive individualism too often do not see their interconnection to one another and thus act in inappropriate and unproductive ways for the common good.[84]

Competitive individualism is an American value that has also shaped the hip-hop black masculinity, and it is seen in the disharmony between a hip-hop black masculinity and the community. When there is discord between individual and community, which is often the result of an individual perceiving his or her role as being much more important than the collective effort, it undermines the African American cultural value of harmony. The lack of harmony results in reproducing patriarchal forms of domination by reestablishing hierarchies and power structures. Unfortunately, examples of competitive individualism and its destructive consequences abound as illustrated by individuals such as Terrell Owens, Randy Moss, and Rasheed Wallace.

A hip-hop black masculinity can reproduce hierarchies and power structures when the identity is so self-absorbed that it calls more attention to itself or downplays, or disses, the collective unit. This practice destroys unity to promote an individuality perceived to be more important or powerful than the group. Throughout his career, Iverson has been criticized for not being a team player, for taking too many shots, and for having his own set of rules. In other words, Iverson has been accused of being solely concerned about his game to the detriment of his teammates.

However, the most prominent discord to unity involves Shaquille O'Neal and Kobe Bryant. When both players were on the Los Angeles Lakers, their improvisation within the call-and-response pattern resulted in a collective effort of three championships. Both players were great due to their interconnectiveness and improvisation on the basketball court. Their collective success, however, was destroyed by the overly ambitious desire of both players to be the star of the team.

Conclusion

If nothing else, the Iverson incident and the construction of a hip-hop black masculinity demonstrates the compelling and complicated society in which African Americans continue to live. The incident reflects how a hip-hop black masculinity embodies a cultural site of struggle between those in power, who are only comfortable with narrowly defined identities for African Americans, and African Americans, who embrace many identities, one of which is associated with hip-hop culture. Neal explains the multitude of identities that comprise black masculinity: "While we embrace these identities as part of our being, we are also conscious of the fluidity of the communities to which we belong and the relative freedom to explore these identities, often playfully at the expense of white onlookers, in ways that our parents could never conceive."[85] At the same time, a hip-hop black masculinity is a site of struggle displaying both progressive and regressive constructions of masculinity. In referring to Iverson, Jere Longman and Richard Jones explained, "To some, he [Iverson] represents a threatening, gangster-rap lifestyle, yet he embodies the most traditional values of sports—loyal, courage, emotion, unbound determination. He has lived a roiling life that has left him both acutely fatalistic and poignantly hopeful."[86]

This modern-day double consciousness, of tension within and without, is what renders black men in general, and a hip-hop black masculinity more specifically, both the oppressed and oppressors. This is the real terrordome of black masculinity: In the process of creating the signs of a new progressive self, it relies on the old tools of domination. This cultural site of struggle merits attention, action, and strategies for transforming the center from the margins. One way to redefine black masculinity is to demythologized it. As Michael Dyson stated, "To demythologize black masculinity then is to understand its strengths and weaknesses, to understand not only its romantic elements but its powerfully progressive elements in the face of what we know about black masculinity."[87] The process Dyson speaks about starts with the ability to critique ourselves not in a hateful way but in a way that liberates black masculinity from racial folklore, cultural racism, historical stereotypes, and regressive constructions of masculinity that feature dominance and aggression.

Notes

1. Michael Eric Dyson, *Holler If You Hear Me: Searching for Tupac Shakur* (New York: Basic Civitas Books, 2001).
2. William Bunch and Rose DeWolf, "Wall Street Weighs in on A.I," *Philadelphia Daily News*, July 12, 2002, 10.
3. David Sibley, *Geographies of Exclusion* (New York: Routledge, 1995).
4. Manthia Diawara, "Black American Cinema: The New Realism," in *Black American Cinema*, ed. Manthia Diawara (New York: Routledge, 1993); John H. Franklin, *Race and History* (Baton Rouge: Louisiana State University Press, 1989); and Henry L. Gates, "TV's Black World Turns—But Stays Unreal," in *Race, Class, and Gender: An Anthology*, ed. M. L. Anderson and P. H. Collins (Belmont, CA: Wadsworth, 1992), 310–316.
5. Donald Bogle, *Toms, Coons, Mulattoes, Mammies, and Bucks—An Interpretive History of Blacks in American Films* (New York: Viking Press, 1973).
6. Richard J. Schafer, *Racial and Ethnic Groups* (New York: Harper Collins, 1993).
7. Mark P. Orbe, "Constructions of Reality on MTV's 'The Real World': An Analysis of the Restrictive Coding of Black Masculinity," *Southern Communication Journal* 64, no. 1 (1998), 32–47.
8. William Oliver, "Cultural Racism and Structural Violence: Implications for African Americans," in *Violence as Seen through a Prism of Color*, ed. Letha A. See (New York: Haworth Press, 2001), 1–25; and Michael Omi, "In Living Color: Race and American Culture," in *Cultural Politics in Contemporary America*, ed. Ian Angus and Sut Jhally (New York: Routledge, 1989), 111–122.
9. Dyson, *Between God and Gansta Rap: Bearing Witness to Black Culture* (New York: Oxford University Press, 1996); Dyson, *Race Rules: Navigating the Color Line* (New York: Vintage Books, 1996); and Mark Anthony Neal, *Soul Babies: Black Popular Culture and the Post-soul Aesthetic* (New York: Routledge, 2002).
10. Todd Boyd, *Am I Black Enough for You?: Popular Culture from the 'Hood and Beyond* (Bloomington: Indiana University Press, 1997); and Earl Ofari Hutchinson, *The Assassination of the Black Male Image* (New York: Simon & Schuster, 1996).
11. Lawson Bush, "Am I a Man?: A Literature Review Engaging the Sociohistorical Dynamics of Black Manhood in the United States," *The Western Journal of Black Studies* 23, no. 1 (1999), 49–57; Ronald Jackson and Celnisha Dangerfield, "Defining Black Masculinity

as Cultural Property: Toward an Identity Negotiation Paradigm," in *Intercultural Communication: A Reader*, 10th ed., ed. L. Samovar and R. Porter (Belmont, CA: Wadsworth, 2003), 120–130

12. bell hooks, *We Real Cool: Black Men and Masculinity* (New York: Routledge, 2004).
13. Kobena Mercer, *Welcome to the Jungle: New Positions in Black Cultural Studies* (New York: Routledge, 1994).
14. Boyd, *Am I Black Enough?*
15. Ibid., 31.
16. Jenice Armstrong, "'People Argue, That's What Happened' Just a Lover's Spat Tawanna's Mom: A.I. Loves My Daughter and She Loves Him," *Philadelphia Daily News*, July 16, 2002, 3. The Philadelphia newspapers—the *Inquirer*, the *Daily News*, and the *Tribune*—represent the primary media texts for analysis and were chosen for the following reasons. (1) The *Inquirer* and the *Daily News* are the largest circulated newspapers in the Philadelphia metropolitan area, which includes five suburban Pennsylvania counties, eight New Jersey counties, the cities of Atlantic City, Camden, and Trenton, and one county in Delaware and the city of Wilmington. Furthermore, during the time of the incident, the number of readers of the city's two largest papers increased. See Kathleen B. Shea, Matthew P. Blanchard, and Benjamin Lowe, "Too Much Iverson? Full Court Press Driven by 'High Interest,'" *Philadelphia Inquirer*, July 15, 2002, A1-2, A5, which makes what was written in the newspaper even more important to analyze. (2) As a Philadelphia 76er, Iverson's team is covered by these papers, the alleged crime took place in the city of Philadelphia, and it involved the Philadelphia police and Philadelphia's district attorney. Since the incident was a Philadelphia story involving most of the major players in the city of Philadelphia, it was important to analyze how the Philadelphia media covered the incident. (3) Philadelphia is known as one of the toughest—if not the toughest—sports media markets in the country with some of the most notorious sports fans in the nation. For example, the Philadelphia fans are known for pelting Santa Claus during the halftime of an Eagles football game and for cheering when Dallas Cowboy receiver Michael Irvin injured his neck and lay motionless on the artificial turf at since-demolished Veterans Stadium. (4) The Philadelphia newspapers represent different audiences. Although the *Inquirer* and the *Daily News* are owned by the same company, they appeal to two different demographics. The *Inquirer* is the hard-news paper, whereas the *Daily News* is more of a tabloid newspaper. The *Inquirer* is known for its international section, and the *Daily News* is known for its sports section, although individuals have raised the profile of the *Inquirer*'s sports section, like Steven A. Smith, who writes for the *Inquirer* and has crossed over into television as a basketball studio analyst for ESPN and TBS. The Iverson incident, however, propelled the story from the sports pages to the headlines in both newspapers. Therefore, analyzing how the incident was covered in both newspapers is important. The *Tribune* is the city's black-owned newspaper and provides an alternative perspective in its news coverage of the Iverson incident. Analyzing all three represents how the dominant culture and the African American culture constructed reports about the incident.
17. For sources used for the description of the Iverson incident, see "Affidavit against A.I.," *Philadelphia Daily News*, July 17, 2002, 5-6; Armstrong, "People Argue"; Will Bunch, "Arrest but No Rest," *Philadelphia Daily News*, July 17, 2002, 3-4; Mignon Brooks, "Who's Charles Jones?" *Philadelphia Tribune*, July 16, 2002, 3A; Kitty Caparella and Michael Hinkelman, "A.I.'s Accusers' Motives Questioned," *Philadelphia Daily News*, July 12, 2002, 8; Maryclaire Dale, "Iverson to Turn Himself In," *Philadelphia Tribune*, July 16, 2002, 5A; Ron Goldwyn and Joann McKoy, "Circus Surrounds Star's Surrender," *Philadelphia Daily News*, July 17, 2002, 6; Leonard Fleming and Linda Harris, "Tawanna, Allen: Love and Discord on Public Display," *Philadelphia Inquirer*, July 14, 2002, A1, A16; Thomas Gibbons Jr., "No Break for the Answer," *Philadelphia Tribune*, July 12, 2002, A1, A3; Scott Goss, "Until Police Book Him, Iverson Must Stay Home," *Philadelphia Inquirer*, July 12, 2002, A1, A10; Phil Jasner, "'He's Hurtin'" Concerned Brown Standing behind Iverson; Sixers' Brass Saddened but Supportive," *Philadelphia Daily News*, July 12, 2002, 141–12; Robert Moran, "Iverson to Surrender to Police Today," *Philadelphia Inquirer*, July 16, 2002, B1, B6; Moran, "Iverson Domestic Charges Unlikely," *Philadelphia Inquirer*, July 18, 2002, B1, B5; Moran, Benjamin Lowe, and Gibbons, "Until Police Book Him, Iverson Must Stay at Home," *Philadelphia Inquirer*, July 12, 2002, A1, A10; Moran, Lowe, and Gibbons, "Iverson Turns Himself In; D.A. Releases More Details," *Philadelphia Inquirer*,

July 17, 2002, A1, A16; Roscoe Nance and Donna Leinwand, "Iverson Faces Felony Charges," *USA Today*, July 12, 2002, 1C; Marc Narducci, "A Blend of Hurt and Concern," *Philadelphia Inquirer*, July 12, 2002, D1, D4; Ramona Smith, "For Iverson, the Buzzer Is About to Sound, and He's Off to a Holding Cell," *Philadelphia Daily News*, July 16, 2002, 4; and Skip Wood, "Iverson Will Need Some Answers," *USA Today*, July 12, 2002, 3C.

18. Quoted in Nance and Leinwand, "Iverson Faces Felony Charges," 1C.

19. Quoted in Bunch, "Iverson's Arrest," 4.

20. For sources used for the description of Iverson's preliminary hearing, see Theresa Conroy, "Court was a Magical Place," *Philadelphia Daily News*, July 30, 2002, 6; Monica Y. Kinney, "Sprague Notches a Blowout Victory," *Philadelphia Inquirer*, July 30, 2002, B1; James Nolan, "Rebound! Almost a Slam Dunk: Judge Tosses All but 2 Charges against A.I.," *Philadelphia Daily News*, July 30, 2002, 3–6; Jill Porter, "Normal Rules Didn't Apply," *Philadelphia Daily News*, July 30, 2002, 5; Michael Rubinkam, "Iverson Gets Favorable Call," *Delaware County Daily Times*, July 30, 2002, 3; and Jacqueline Soteropoulos, "Iverson Felony Charges Tossed: The Sixer and His Uncle Face 2 Misdemeanors," *Philadelphia Inquirer*, July 30, 2002, A1, A7.

21. Although the remainder of this chapter focuses on those who view Iverson negatively and thus felt he must be guilty, it is worth noting that Iverson had a groundswell of support within the black community and from his fans of all colors and ages. See "Even More 'as the Iverson Saga Turns,'" *Philadelphia Daily News*, July 17, 2002, letters to the editor, 16; Ira Porter, "Young Fans Continue to Support Iverson," *Philadelphia Inquirer*, July 12, 2002, A10; and John Smallwood, "Nothin' but Love for A.I. in Camden," *Philadelphia Daily News*, July 17, 2002, 9. On CN8, a Philadelphia Comcast cable news channel, a non-scientific Web poll conducted the night of Iverson's preliminary hearing reported that 95 percent of respondents agreed with Judge DeLeon's ruling. See *It's Your Call*, L. Doyle (host), Philadelphia, Comcast News Channel, July 29, 2002. Novella Williams, the spokes-person for Iverson's Celebrity Softball Classic, which took place in Camden, New Jersey, on July 20, and which Iverson participated in, stated, "I stand committed with my other young women to free him from the powers of evil. We will not allow anyone to throw another of our African-American heroes to the wolves. We cannot allow another young African-American millionaire to be taken down by a system." Smallwood, "Nothin' but Love," 9. Likewise, various attorneys were all in agreement that the case against Iverson was weak and that without Iverson's notoriety the case would not have gone to court. The lawyers explained that if the same incident had happened to the average person, it would have been quietly handled as a private domestic complaint and not as an intense criminal investigation. Nolan, "Being A.I. Might've Hurt Him," *Philadelphia Daily News*, July 29, 2002, 7. The Iverson case represented a minor case, considering the 1,550 cases handled by the Philadelphia courts each week. Brian McMonagle, a former homicide prosecutor, stated, "In 17 years, I've never seen a charge of the uniform firearms act in the absence of the gun or evidence of a shot fired," Nolan, "Rebound." Added attorney Leon Williams, "I think the district attorney's case is weak and I don't think you have to be a good lawyer to win that case." Dyana Williams, "DA's Case on Iverson Weak, Attorneys Say," *Philadelphia Tribune*, July 19, 2002, 5A.

22. Johnette Howard, "Police Arraign Iverson: With Black Star's Arrest Comes Racial Polarization," *Newsday*, New York: July 17, 2002, A70.

23. *Daily News Live*, M. Barkann (host), Philadelphia, Comcast Sportschannel, July 16, 2002.

24. Mignon Brooks, "Who's Charles Jones," 3A; and Scott Goss, "No Break for the Answer," *Philadelphia Tribune*, July 12, 2002, 1A, 3A.

25. Quoted in Fleming, "In Iverson's Hometown, Opinion Split," *Philadelphia Inquirer*, July 16, 2002, B1.

26. John Baer, "He's Still Thug-Prone; We're Still Icon-Crazy," *Philadelphia Daily News*, July 17, 2002, 5.

27. Quoted in "What They're Saying," *Philadelphia Daily News*, July 16, 2002, 7.

28. "Iverson Plays Defense While the Police & DA Stumble," *Philadelphia Daily News*, July 12, 2002, editorial, 15.

29. Ibid.

30. Trey Ellis, "How Does It Feel To Be a Problem?" in *Speak My Name: Black Men on Masculinity and the American Dream*, ed. Don Belton (Boston: Beacon Press, 1995), 9–11.

31. Paul Sniderman and Thomas Piazza, "Pictures in the Mind," in *Race and Ethnic Relations in the United States*, ed. C. G. Ellison and W. A. Martin (Los Angeles: Roxbury Publishing, 1999), 230–237.

32. Jane Eisner, "Iverson Saga Less about Sport than about Spousal Relations," *Philadelphia Inquirer*, July 18, 2002, A23; and Barbara Laker, "Abuse Victims Feel for Tawanna," *Philadelphia Daily News*, July 17, 2002, 8.

33. Christopher Hepp and Nancy Phillips, "Two Cases: Iverson's Got Full Focus, One Did Not," *Philadelphia Inquirer*, July 21, 2002, A1, A18.

34. Ibid.

35. Dyson, "Exploring, Constructing, and Sustaining Progressive Black Masculinities" (keynote address, Black Masculinities Conference, Buffalo State College and the University at Buffalo Law School, Buffalo, NY, April 12, 2002).

36. Jacquie Jones, "The Construction of Black Sexuality: Towards Normalizing the Black Cinematic Experience," in *Black American Cinema*, ed. M. Diawara (New York: Routledge, 1993), 247–256.

37. Ibid.

38. Fleming and Harris, "Tawanna, Allen," A1.

39. Armstrong, "Just a Lover's Spat"; Hepp, "For the Defense: Iverson's Mother," *Philadelphia Inquirer*, July 17, 2002, B1, B5.

40. Monica Y. Kinney, "So Few Answers on 'the Answer,'" *Philadelphia Inquirer*, July 12, 2002, B1.

41. Ibid.

42. "What They're Saying," 7.

43. Jones, "Construction of Black Sexuality."

44. Although not a historical stereotype, the media consistently justified its excessive coverage of Iverson by explaining that it was Iverson who brought the public attention on himself. As Tom Ferrick Jr. wrote, "Thanks to his antics in West Philly last week, Allen Iverson now goes from starring on the basketball court to starring in Municipal Court." Ferrick, "Possible Outcomes for the Answer," *Philadelphia Inquirer*, July 12, 2002, B1. Sam Donnellon, appearing on the Philadelphia Comcast cable television show *Daily News Live*, saw nothing wrong with the media coverage and said it was the media's duty to cover the story. According to Donnellon, the media did not create the circus, the defense attorneys being allowed to have their client wait created a time line for the media to gather and create the coverage. This point was repeated by Howard Eskin on the television talk show *It's Your Call*, which airs on Philadelphia Comcast:
    "If he hadn't stayed in his home and waited to turn himself in (the excessive coverage would not have happened). Once they got it out of the way (Iverson's arrest), we didn't do anything until the hearing. If he had gotten that out of the way, we wouldn't have had all the extra media coverage." *It's Your Call*, L. Doyle (host), Philadelphia: Comcast News Channel, July 29, 2002.

45. hooks, *We Real Cool*.

46. Through common experiences, groups of people share cultural values that comprise their social reality. In this essay, I draw on research from scholars who have analyzed various aspects of African American culture, have identified common experiences individuals used in response to their reality, and have identified many cultural values from the experiences of African Americans. These common experiences also form the basis of what the scholars label the African American community, or composite culture, or the African American experience. See Ronald L Jackson II, ed., *African American Communication & Identities: Essential Readings* (Thousand Oaks, CA: Sage, 2004); John Russell Rickford and Russell John Rickford, *Spoken Soul: The Story of Black English* (New York: John Wiley & Sons, 2000); and Geneva Smitherman, *Talkin' That Talk* (New York: Routledge, 2000).

47. hooks, *We Real Cool*, xii.

48. Timothy. J. Brown, "Reaffirming African American Cultural Values: Tupac Shakur's *Greatest Hits* as a Musical Autobiography." *The Western Journal of Black Studies* 29, no. 1 (2005), 558–573.

49. Bakari Kitwana, *The Hip-Hop Generation: Young Blacks and the Crisis in African American Culture* (New York: Basic Civitas Books, 2002).

50. Cornel West, *Race Matters*, 2d ed. (New York: Vintage Books, 2001).

51. Jackson, *African American Communication & Identities*.
52. Ibid.
53. For works that identify African American communication cultural values and practices, see Molefi K. Asante, *Afrocentricity* (Buffalo: Amulefi, 1980); Asante, *The Afrocentric Idea* (Philadelphia: Temple University Press, 1987); Brown, "Analyzing African-American Communication Patterns: Myrlie Evers-Williams Defines the NAACP's Image and Message," *New York State Communication Association's Proceedings* 11 (1997), 11–29; Melbourne S. Cummings and Jack L. Daniel, "The Study of African American Rhetoric," in *Rhetoric of Western Thought*, ed. J. L. Golden (Dubuque, IA: Kendell/Hunt, 1997), 360–385; Janice D. Hamlet, "The Reason Why We Sing: Understanding Traditional African American Worship," in *Our Voices: Essays in Culture, Ethnicity, and Communication*, 4th ed., ed. A. Gonzalez, M. Houston, and V. Chen (Los Angeles: Roxbury, 2004: 113–118); Jackson, *African American Communication & Identities*; Rickford and Rickford, *Spoken Soul*; and Smitherman, *Talkin' That Talk*.
54. Boyd, *Am I Black Enough?*
55. Mercer, *Welcome to the Jungle*.
56. West, *Race Matters*, 128.
57. Ibid.
58. Stefan Fatsis of the *Wall Street Journal*, quoted in "What They're Saying," 6.
59. Boyd, *Am I Black Enough?*
60. Ibid., 32.
61. Neal, *Soul Babies*, 145.
62. Sibley, *Geographies of Exclusion*.
63. Baer, "He's Still Thug-Prone," 5.
64. Boyd, *Am I Black Enough?*, 122.
65. hooks, *We Real Cool*.
66. Ibid., 24.
67. Thomas Kochman, "Black and White Cultural Styles in Pluralistic Perspective," in *Culture Communication and Conflict: Readings in Intercultural Relations,* 2d ed., ed. G. R. Weaver (Needham Heights, MA: Simon & Schuster, 1998), 293–308.
68. Ibid., 297.
69. Patricia H. Collins, *Black Feminist Thought*, 2d ed. (New York: Routledge, 2000); Kochman, "Black and White"; and Smitherman, *Talkin' That Talk*.
70. West, *Race Matters*, 150–51.
71. Boyd, *Am I Black Enough?*; and West, *Race Matters*.
72. Donnellon, "We're Talkin' Practice When It Comes to A.I. Plan," *Philadelphia Daily News*, July 29, 2002, 96; and Lowe, "Iverson Uses Decoy to Avoid Media," *Philadelphia Inquirer*, July 17, 2002, B5.
73. Quoted in "Community Voices," *Philadelphia Inquirer*, July 14, 2002, letters to the editor, C3.
74. Boyd, *Am I Black Enough?*
75. John Hoberman, "The Price of 'Black Dominance,'" *Society* 37 no. 3 (2000), 49–57; and Oliver, "Cultural Racism and Structural Violence."
76. Hoberman, "Price."
77. Ibid.
78. Armstrong, "The Host Couldn't Make It, but Va. Classic Goes On," *Philadelphia Daily News*, July 15, 2002, 5; Chris Gray, Gaiutra Bahadur, and Patrick Kerkstra, "Iverson Reaches Out to Avid Fans," *Philadelphia Inquirer*, July 21, 2002, A19; "Fans Support Iverson Charity," *Philadelphia Tribune*, July 23, 2002, 1A, 5A; and Smallwood, "Nothin' but Love," 9.
79. hooks, *We Real Cool*.
80. Boyd, *Am I Black Enough?*, 33.
81. Jackson, "Afrocentricity as Metatheory: A Dialogic Exploration of its Principles," in *Understanding African American Rhetoric: Classical Origins to Contemporary Innovations*, ed. Jackson and Elaine B. Richardson (New York: Routledge, 2003), 115–129.
82. Asante, "The Afrocentric idea," in Jackson, *African American Communication*, 26.
83. Kochman, "Black and White," 296.
84. West, *Race Matters*.

85. Neal, *Soul Babies*, 177.
86. Jere Longman and Richard Jones, "Iverson Is a Study in Contradictions," *New York Times*, July 21, 2002, 1, 8.
87. Dyson, "Exploring."

Part 6
Black Feminists Engaged

12

Beyond Competitive Victimhood: Abandoning Arguments that Black Women or Black Men Are Worse Off

STEPHANIE L. PHILLIPS

In 1991, Clarence Thomas was nominated to the Supreme Court of the United States. Because Thomas is a very conservative Republican who opposed affirmative action and was antipathetic to many commonly held views of African Americans, his nomination posed a dilemma for some. On the one hand, to have an African American on the court seemed a good thing. On the other hand, this particular African American was unlikely to represent the black community's point of view or to advance its interests. For many, the dilemma intensified when Anita Hill, also a very conservative Republican, testified at Thomas's confirmation hearings. She gave explicit examples of the highly sexualized commentary that regularly poured from Thomas's mouth when he headed the Equal Employment Opportunity Commission, where Hill had worked as his subordinate. According to Hill, Thomas's foul musings created such a hostile environment as to constitute sexual harassment.

Although a few applauded Hill's courage and certainly hoped her testimony would derail the Thomas nomination, most African Americans were appalled. The sexual explicitness on national television seemed akin to a pornographic display that reinforced white America's worst stereotypes about oversexed, degenerate black people, particularly black males. Moreover, the fact that a black woman was betraying a black man to whites—the Senate, white feminists, white America at large—meant that, once again, African Americans had to tangle with the hoary issue of whether black women owe unconditional support to any and all black men who stand before the white power structure. This supposed duty of loyalty comes from the idea that black Americans must present a united front against our enemy: white supremacy and its minions. Moreover, and more problematically, the obligation for black women to stand by our men is often assumed as a form of overcompensation: Black women are continually trying to disprove the allegation that we collude with white men to the detriment of black men. Colloquially, this charge is captured in the trope that "ain't nobody so free as a black woman and a white man." In the aftermath of the Thomas hearings, many scholars ruminated on the long history and seeming intractability of the trope, which implies, among other things, that black men are worse off than black women in the social order structured by American white supremacy. According to Nell Painter,

> The Black-woman-as-traitor-to-the-race is at least as old as *David Walker's Appeal* of 1829, and the figure has served as a convenient explanation for racial conflict since that time … [I]t should be remembered that in the tale of the subversion of the interests of the race, the Black female traitor—as mother to whites or lover of whites—connives with the white man against the Black man. Such themes reappear in *Black Skin, White Masks*, by Frantz Fanon; in *Black Rage*, by William Grier and Price Cobbs; and in *Madheart*, by LeRoi Jones, in which the figure of "the Black woman," as "Mammy" or as "Jezebel," is subject to loyalties to whites that conflict with her allegiance to the Black man. Unable to extricate herself from whites, the Black-woman-as-traitor misconstrues her racial interests and betrays Black men's aspirations to freedom.[1]

In Painter's view, Thomas deliberately cast Hill in the role of black-woman-as-traitor-to-the-race.[2] Indeed, one prominent black commentator explained to the *New York Times* how Hill evoked in black men an age-old fear that black women would betray them. Specifically, Alvin Poussaint, preeminent African American psychiatrist, had this to say about Hill's testimony that Thomas, now associate justice of the Supreme Court, had sexually harassed her: "There's a high level of anger among Black men, be they low-income or professional, that Black women will betray them; that Black women are given preference over them; that white men like to put Black women in between them to use them."[3]

The charge that black women collude with white men—again, colloquially, "ain't nobody so free as a black woman and a white man"—is sexual in origin, but has been generalized to the proposition that black men suffer more than black women as victims of white supremacy. The prime response of black feminists, including critical race theorists, has been to demonstrate that black women's sexuality has made us peculiarly vulnerable to white racist oppression rather than being a source of privilege.[4] Black feminists have also directed a great deal of attention to demonstrating that, in the aggregate, black women are economically more disadvantaged than black men.[5] Another prong of the response by black feminists has been to demonstrate that the false assumptions about black women's motivations and conditions that underlie the "ain't nobody so free" trope are used to excuse black male violence,[6] to privilege black male experience, and to validate black male sexism.[7] Furthermore, black feminists have frequently pointed out that the trope deflects attention from the social institutions and ideologies that are the principal sources of African

American oppression and that asking women to disempower themselves to bolster male ego is a formula that helps no one.[8]

Black feminists must continue to expose the myths, misinformation, and lies used to deny the oppression of black women. However, the defense of black women and explication of our suffering can be taken too far, yielding statements by some black feminists implying that black males consistently benefit from gender privilege, not only in relationships with black females but also in the comparative advantages of black males and females in American society at large. Correcting this distortion, which had been discernible in the work of some contemporary black feminists, was a probable precondition for furthering feminist ideas among black women, who live with and observe black men on a daily basis. If black feminism seemed to deny or to misapprehend the realities of black male oppression, then it was unsurprising that black women were reluctant to describe themselves as *feminist*.[9]

Some black feminists had done important work on the question of the gendered oppression of black males,[10] but there was no unanimity on the question whether black feminists should abandon the formulation that black women are more oppressed than black men or on the question whether it is beyond the scope of black feminism to pay particular attention to the forms of racist oppression specifically directed against black men. This lack of consensus caused theoretical and practical difficulties for black feminists, particularly in relation to the broad antiracist movement, tensions amply illustrated by Orlando Patterson's 1994 "Blacklash" article[11] and the black feminist responses to Patterson included in a 1995 symposium.[12]

Summarizing Patterson

According to Patterson, there is a crisis in relations between African American men and African American women, as evidenced by, among other things, a declining marriage rate.[13] The principal factor contributing to the African American gender crisis is that African Americans are racially subordinated and live in a hostile social, political, and economic environment. However, problems also are internally generated or perpetuated within the African American community.

With respect to the lower classes, Patterson traced the violent, misogynistic, and irresponsible behavior of many young African American males to the fact that they have been reared in single-parent households headed by women who are prone to brutal, abusive disciplinary methods.[14] Furthermore, Patterson ventured into Freudian theory: Because lower-class, black, male children have neither a father nor an effective father substitute present to model a healthy form of masculinity, they lapse into violence and predatory sexuality as the only means available for overcoming attachment to their mothers.[15] Moving on to examine the gender crisis in middle-class black America, Patterson pointed to a profound ideological misfit between African American women and men: "[R]esearchers have found serious mismatches and contradictions in the attitudes of middle-class black men and women. While middle-class black women have, with one notable exception, the most advanced set of gender attitudes in the nation, black men tend to remain highly traditionalist, believing in male dominance ideology in familial relations."[16] Having laid out his analysis of the gender crisis among lower- and middle-class African Americans, Patterson accused black feminists of having obscured these issues. Specifically, he blamed black feminists for distorting the inquiry into the actual state of African American gender relations by adopting the divisive and inaccurate formulation that African American women are more oppressed than African American men.[17]

As to the comparative situations of African American women and men, Patterson is himself both unclear and self-contradictory.[18] Given the impossibility of making coherent sense of his various propositions, it is not in the least surprising that two prominent black feminist theorists had starkly different responses to Patterson's article.

Feminist Responses

First, there is bell hooks, who responded to Patterson's essay with indignation.[19] Viewing Patterson's essay as "anti-feminist propaganda in Blackface,"[20] she pointed out that "[s]exist and misogynist thinking has always blamed mothers for the psychological dilemmas males face."[21] In response to Patterson's assertion that "contemporary African American feminist thought has badly obscured our understanding of gender relations,"[22] hooks objected to his "willingness to lump all black women who advocate feminist thinking together, even though our perspectives are not the same."[23] Hooks's anger at the fact that Patterson made sweeping generalizations about feminism was largely justified. Indeed, Patterson appeared totally unaware that the double-burden formulation he found problematic had been the subject of analysis, discussion, and critique by black feminists for at least fifteen years. Patterson wrote, "It has become almost a truism in discussions of black gender relations that African-American women are uniquely oppressed with a double burden. In today's usage, added to the burden of racism is the double jeopardy of mainstream gender discrimination. Following the Thomas hearings, in which an African-American woman was pitted against an African-American man, … many commentators and analysts emphasized yet a third burden experienced by African-American women: that of gender prejudice and exploitation by African-American men … ."[24]

Patterson, thinking that "the double burden argument, while not strictly incorrect, obscures more than it illuminates,"[25] wanted black feminists to abandon any formulation implying that black women are more oppressed than black men. Hooks's angry retort was, in effect, that many black feminists abandoned that formulation long ago, which Patterson would have known if he had taken feminism seriously.[26] The bottom line is that hooks was angry at Patterson for failing to realize that black feminists had been grappling for years with the issues that had just come to Patterson's attention. This is hooks's description of the strand of black feminism to which she adhered and of which Patterson was apparently ignorant:

> Truthfully, revolutionary visionary feminist thinking by Black females and males is one of the few places we can turn for an account of Black gender relations that does not seek to pit Black women and men against one another in an endless, meaningless debate about who has suffered more. This work courageously acknowledges that white supremacist capitalist patriarchy assaults the psyches of Black males and females alike. It is only by constructively articulating the nature of that assault and developing redemptive strategies for resistance and transformation that we can resolve the crisis of Black gender relations.[27]

In another symposium response to Patterson's "Blacklash" essay, prominent black feminist Michele Wallace recognized, like hooks, that Patterson was raising issues black feminists had been engaging for some time.[28] Unlike hooks, however, Wallace decided not to be angry with Patterson but rather welcomed him into the black feminist discussion.

Wallace began her article by writing that Patterson's "'Blacklash' is a wonderful and important piece."[29] Like hooks, but much more gently, Wallace chided Patterson for inaccurate overgeneralization of black feminist thought. She took issue with a passage written by Patterson, where he objects to "the tendency of black feminists, who dominate the discourse, to confine, and confound, the problems of gender—which concerns both males and females in their relations with each other—with those of women's issues, or, when relational problems are considered, to privilege the standpoint of women, on the assumption that they are always the victims of the interaction. Black men have as much at stake . . . ."[30] Wallace responded that she "no longer see[s] Black feminism as the discourse of victimization."[31] Rather, says Wallace, "In contemporary feminist discourse in the circles I frequent, . . . discussions of female gender and its construction rarely fail to take into account that constructions of female gender need to be thought in conjunction with constructions of masculinity."[32]

Pointing to the lack of unanimity among black feminists on basic issues, Wallace opined that "Black feminism today is . . . an odd and frail creature, not quite fish or fowl," wherein "[m]any black women who practice a brand of feminism can't even agree upon calling themselves feminists."[33] Although Wallace did not agree with everything Patterson wrote in his article, she was inclined to be generous, given the disarray of black feminist thought. Her bottom line with regard to Patterson is this: "The point is that he is proceeding in the right direction and that we need to be thinking along these lines."[34]

For purposes of the present inquiry, the important points in the hooks and Wallace articles are that neither one of them defended the formulation that black women are more oppressed than black men; both implicitly conceded that their early work reflected ideas on the relative position of black women and men to which they no longer adhered;[35] and both had come to include black masculinity within the purview of their work. It may nevertheless be the case, however, that the gendered oppression of black men is not a central black feminist concern, because black feminists prioritize exploration of the conditions in which African American women live and advocacy for African American women. Beyond these priorities, the full scope of black feminism becomes unclear. In fact, there has been such enormous contention surrounding the definition of *black feminism* that some thinkers have abandoned the phrase.

Pressing through the Boundaries: The Humanist Dimension of Black Feminism

Alice Walker coined the word *womanist* as, among other things, a synonym for the phrase *black feminist* and as a contrast to *feminism* in general. This is Walker's definition, quoted in full because it has been so influential:

> Womanist 1. From womanish. (Opp. of "girlish," i.e., frivolous, irresponsible, not serious.) A Black feminist or feminist of color. From the Black folk expression of mothers to female children, "You acting womanish," i.e., like a woman. Usually referring to outrageous, audacious, courageous or willful behavior. Wanting to know more and in greater depth than is considered "good" for one. Interested in grown-up doings. Acting grown up. Being grown up. Interchangeable with another Black folk expression: "You trying to be grown." Responsible. In charge. Serious.

> 2. Also: A woman who loves other women, sexually and/or nonsexually. Appreciates and prefers women's culture, women's emotional flexibility (values tears as natural counter-balance of laughter), and women's strength. Sometimes loves individual men, sexually and/or nonsexually. Committed to survival and wholeness of entire people, male and female. Not a separatist, except periodically, for health. Traditionally universalist, as in: "Mama, why are we brown, pink, and yellow, and our cousins are white, beige, and black?" Ans.: "Well, you know the colored race is just like a flower garden, with every color flower represented." Traditionally capable, as in: "Mama, I'm walking to Canada and I'm taking you and a bunch of other slaves with me." Reply: "It wouldn't be the first time."

> 3. Loves music. Loves dance. Loves the moon. Loves the Spirit. Loves love and food and roundness. Loves struggle. Loves the Folk. Loves herself. Regardless.

4. Womanist is to feminist as purple to lavender.[36]

Walker obviously is very woman oriented. At the same time, two of her phrases seem to press through the boundaries of a black feminism defined solely by reference to the interests of black women. According to Walker, a womanist is committed to survival and wholeness of entire people, male and female, and is traditionally universalist. The refusal to limit their scope to the interests of women and the emphasis on universalism have been prominent emphases in the work of other black feminists, beginning in the late nineteenth century[37] and continuing today.

Patricia Hill Collins is a contemporary black feminist who has drawn particular attention to the need for black feminism to be situated within broader humanist discourses and movements. In Collins's view, though black women experience many different forms of oppression that black feminism must address, black feminism has no special competence regarding all forms of oppression:

> Despite African-American women's potential power to reveal new insights about the matrix of domination, a Black women's standpoint is only one angle of vision. Thus Black feminist thought represents a partial perspective. The overarching matrix of domination houses multiple groups, each with varying experiences with penalty and privilege that produce corresponding partial perspectives, situated knowledges, and, for clearly identifiable subordinate groups, subjugated knowledges. No one group has a clear angle of vision. No one group possesses the theory or methodology that allows it to discover the absolute "truth" or, worse yet, proclaim its theories and methodologies as the universal norm evaluating other groups' experiences.[38]

Therefore, black feminism should be considered a subdivision of humanism, for "Black women's struggles are part of a wider struggle for human dignity and empowerment."[39] Even though the core agenda of black feminists may not encompass all forms of oppression, none fall outside the humanist commitments of black feminist thought.

The expansive description of black feminism, as committed to furthering the interests of black women; attentive to the race, class, and gender valences of black women's experiences; and part of a universalist quest for the principles and conditions of human flourishing has many and far-reaching implications. It means, among other things, that black feminists are concerned about issues that do not directly affect black women and that black feminists will not always insist that the interests of black women be given priority, when those interests conflict with other important projects. Nor should black feminists attempt to evade these complexities. The humanist stance is necessary to avoid parochialism,[40] to work effectively for social change, and to develop principled bases for coalition.[41]

Notes

1. Nell I. Painter, "Hill, Thomas, and the Use of Racial Stereotype," in *Race-ing Justice, En-Gendering Power: Essays on Anita Hill, Clarence Thomas, and the Construction of Social Reality*, ed. Toni Morrison (New York: Pantheon Books, 1992), 204. Additional historical references to accusations by black men that black women corruptly and willingly had sex with white men can be found in Paula Giddings, *When and Where I Enter* (New York: William Morrow, 1984), 61–62, notes 16–19.
2. Painter, "Hill," 204. Nellie McKay and Margaret Burnham made the same observation. McKay, "Remembering Anita Hill and Clarence Thomas: What Really Happened When One Black Woman Spoke Out," in Morrison, *Race-ing*, 284; and Burnham, "The Supreme Court Appointment Process and the Politics of Race and Sex," in Morrison, *Race-ing*, 312.
3. Lena Williams, "Blacks View Dispute as Very Embarrassing and Deeply Divisive," *New York Times*, October 15, 1991, A19.
4. See, e.g., bell hooks, *Yearning: Race, Gender, and Cultural Politics* (Cambridge, MA: South End Press, 1990), 57–60.
5. See, e.g., Giddings, *When and Where*, 344–45; Judy Scales-Trent, "Black Women and the Constitution: Finding Our Place; Asserting Our Rights," *Harvard Civil Rights–Civil Liberties Law Review* 24, no. 1 (1989), 29. Barbara Smith said that one of the effects of black feminist inquiry into the situation of black women was "to deflate some of the cherished myths about Black Womanhood, for example, ... that we are more economically privileged than Black men." Smith, ed., *Home Girls: A Black Feminist Anthology* (New York: Kitchen Table/Women of Color Press, 1983), xxxii.
6. See Patricia Hill Collins, *Black Feminist Thought: Knowledge, Consciousness and the Politics of Empowerment* (Boston: Unwin and Hyman, 1990), 186–89.
7. See Painter, "Hill"; McKay, "Remembering Anita Hill"; and Burnham, "Supreme Court." See also Michele Wallace, *Black Macho and the Myth of the Superwoman* (New York: Verso Classics, 1979), 17–19.
8. See Collins, *Black Feminist Thought*, 184, and sources cited therein.
9. For a partial analysis of black women's worry that embracing feminism would be tantamount to betrayal of black men, see hooks, *Yearning*, 59–60.
10. See, e.g., hooks, *Black Looks: Race and Representation* (New York: Routledge, 1992), 87–113.
11. Orlando Patterson, "Blacklash: The Crisis of Gender Relations among African Americans," *Transition: An International Review* 62 (1994), 4–26.
12. bell hooks, "Feminist Transformation," in *Transition: An International Review* 66 (1995), 93–98; Michele Wallace, "Neither Fish nor Fowl," in *Transition* 66, 98–101.
13. Patterson, "Blacklash," 19.
14. Ibid., 13–14.
15. Ibid., 16–17.
16. Ibid., 20. The exception to black women's otherwise advanced gender attitudes is "their unusually high valorization of mothering," which Patterson viewed as an "oddly traditionalist element in the otherwise radical structure of Black middle-class women's beliefs on gender." Ibid. Although Patterson did not clearly state what should be done to correct the clash of gender ideologies, the adjectives he used to describe middle-class women's stance, e.g., *liberated* and *autonomous*, are complimentary. Ibid., 25. By contrast, his characterization of middle-class males' gender ideology is pejorative; he referred to them as "the most sexist and self-excusing of men." Ibid. I therefore infer that Patterson thought black middle-class males should change their thinking.
17. Ibid., 7–8.
18. Having lambasted black feminists for saying that black women are worse off than black men, he conceded that "it is not a myth that African-American women have been more burdened than African-American men," suggested that careful analysis yields the conclusion that it is impossible to determine whether black women or black men are worse off, admonished that the attempt to rank oppressions is, at any rate, wrong-headed and divisive, and, despite all the aforementioned, opined that black men are in fact worse off than black women. Ibid., 8–10.
19. hooks, "Feminist Transformation," *Transition: An International Review* 66 (1995), 93–98.

Beyond Competitive Victimhood • 225

20. Ibid., 94.
21. Ibid., 96.
22. Ibid., 98, quoting Patterson, "Blacklash," 7.
23. hooks, "Feminist Transformation," 98.
24. Patterson, "Blacklash," 8.
25. Ibid.
26. The evolution of hooks's thinking regarding the relative positioning of African American women and men is clear in her published work. For instance, in her first book, *Ain't I a Woman: Black Women and Feminism*, written when hooks was a nineteen-year-old college student, many passages reflect hooks's broad, humanist commitment to end domination in all its forms. hooks, *Ain't I a Woman: Black Women and Feminism* (Cambridge, MA: South End Press, 1981). However, passages also can be found stating that black women are more oppressed than black men. See, e.g., ibid., 52–53: "As far back as slavery, white people established a social hierarchy based on race and sex that ranked white men first, white women second, though sometimes equal to Black men, who are ranked third, and Black women last." This strand of hooks's thinking, positioning black men as better off than black women in the overall social hierarchy, did not, however—even in 1981—represent the views of all black feminists. Smith, for one, launched a scathing critique of *Ain't I a Woman* for, among other things, minimizing African American male oppression. Smith, "Black Feminism Divorced from Black Feminist Organizing," *Black Scholar* 14 (1983), 38. Furthermore, several years before Patterson wrote his "Blacklash" article, hooks had drawn attention to the changes in her thinking regarding the comparative situations of black women and men, pointing to the contrast between *Ain't I a Woman* and her later work. See hooks and Cornel West, *Breaking Bread* (Cambridge, MA: South End Press, 1991), 106.
27. hooks, "Feminist Transformation," 98.
28. Michele Wallace, "Neither Fish nor Fowl," *Transition: An International Review* 66 (1995), 98.
29. Ibid., 98.
30. Ibid., 99, quoting Patterson, "Blacklash," 7.
31. Wallace, "Neither Fish," 99.
32. Ibid.
33. Ibid.
34. Ibid., 101.
35. Legal academics who write black feminist theory have followed a similar trajectory in coming to a nuanced theoretical treatment of the positioning of black men. See, e.g., Kimberlé Crenshaw, "Demarginalizing the Intersection of Race and Sex: A Black Feminist Critique of Antidiscrimination Doctrine, Feminist Theory, and Antiracist Politics," *University of Chicago Legal Forum* 1989 (1989), 139, 140, 157, note 46; and Crenshaw, "Mapping the Margins: Intersectionality, Identity Politics, and Violence against Women of Color," *Stanford Law Review* 43 (1991), 1252, 1287.
36. Alice Walker, *In Search of Our Mothers' Gardens* (Orlando: Harcourt, 1983), xi–xii. Black feminists who have adopted Walker's womanist concept include Sherley Anne Williams. See Williams, "Some Implications of Womanist Theory," in *Reading Black, Reading Feminist*, ed. Henry L. Gates (New York: Plume Books, 1990), 68. However, it is important to note that black women who, like Walker, (1) are feminists; (2) see race, gender, and class as interlocking systems of domination; and (3) reject the proposition that her gender is necessarily the most significant determinant in a black woman's life, do not all embrace Walker's womanist terminology. Hooks, for one, described herself as "feminist" or "a person who supports feminist movement," in part because "Black women must continue to insist on our right to participate in shaping feminist theory and practice that addresses our racial concerns as well as our feminist issues." hooks, *Talking Back* (Cambridge, MA: South End Press, 1989), 182. Furthermore, hooks declined to use the womanist terminology because she was bothered by the tendency of some black women to use the word *womanist* in opposition to the term *feminist*. Ibid., 181–82.
37. See, e.g., Collins, *Black Feminist Thought*, 37, which discusses a speech made by Anna Julia Cooper in 1893.
38. Ibid., 234–35.
39. Ibid., 37. See also ibid., 37–39, which discusses the humanist vision of black feminism.

40. The humanist discourse that, in the present day, seems actually or potentially to be a universal touchstone is the international human rights discourse, especially as embodied in the International Covenant on Civil and Political Rights, 999 U.N.T.S. 171 (1966), and the International Covenant on Economic, Social, and Cultural Rights, 993 U.N.T.S. 3 (1966). These covenants are not unproblematic. For instance, there is an African critique of these documents and current international human rights discourse for embodying a distinctively Western notion of individualism, to the disrespect of more communal traditions. See, e.g., *Human Rights in Africa: Cross-Cultural Perspectives*, ed. Abdullahi Ahmed An-Na'im and Francis M. Deng (New York: Brookings Institution Press, 1990); Josiah A. M. Cobbah, "African Values and the Human Rights Debate: An African Perspective," *Human Rights Quarterly* 9, no. 3 (1987), 309–331; Timothy Fernyhough, "Human Rights and Pre-Colonial Africa," in *Human Rights and Governance in Africa*, ed. Ronald Cohen, Goran Hyden, and Wiston Nagan (Gainesville: University Press of Florida, 1993), 39–73; Chris Mojekwu, "International Human Rights: An African Perspective," in *International Human Rights: Contemporary Issues*, ed. Jack L. Nelson and Vera M. Greene (New York: Earl M Coleman Enterprises, 1980), 85–95; Makau Mutua, "The Banjul Charter and the African Cultural Fingerprint: An Evaluation of the Language of Duties," *Virginia Journal of International Law* 35, no. 2 (1995), 339–380; and Dunstan M. Wai, "Human Rights in Sub-Saharan Africa," in *Human Rights: Cultural and Ideological Perspectives*, ed. Adamantia Pollis and Peter Schwab (Westport, CT: Praeger Publishers, 1979), 115–144. Furthermore, some countries, including the United States, refuse to endorse the aspirations included in the International Covenant on Economic, Social, and Cultural Rights, including the right of every individual to meaningful work and health care. Despite these and many other problems, international human rights discourse has the most credibility and the broadest endorsement of the currently extant humanist discourses. Collins confirmed that black feminists should pay attention to international human rights discourse, noting that black feminism's humanist vision is "reflected in the growing prominence of international issues and global concerns in the works of contemporary African-American women intellectuals." Collins, *Black Feminist Thought*, 39 (citations omitted).

41. It is possible, for instance, that, despite affirming foundational principles of humanism and equality, see Jerome H. Schiele, *Human Services and the Afrocentric Paradigm* (New York: Haworth, 2000), Afrocentrists will not readily enter into coalition with black feminists because of differences on the questions of gender roles and homosexuality.

13

Gender Justice: Linking Women's Human Rights and Progressive Black Masculinities

M. BAHATI KUUMBA

Black Masculinities, Black Feminists, and Gender Justice

The construction and promotion of progressive black masculinities is as necessary for achieving gender justice as is women's empowerment and the development of black feminist consciousness and praxis. Of course, a radical shift in gendered power relations within African diasporan communities is not, in itself, sufficient for all women's or men's liberation. Achieving gender justice will ultimately mean confronting and transforming the interconnected hierarchies and inequalities of race, ethnicity, nation, class, sexuality, and culture. Patriarchy operates on the level of the nation-state, community, and household and intricately connects and supports other systems of oppression on multiple levels. As such, masculinities, and black masculinities in particular, comprise a distinct site for women's human rights struggle.

The project of confronting and dismantling male dominance in all of its forms is embedded in the black feminist mission. As most activists for social justice would concede, the complexities of global inequality and multiple terrains of interacting oppressions require multiple strategies for effective transformation. Women's liberation has often been a lower-level concern relative to other areas of struggle including the struggles for racial justice and national liberation throughout Africa and the African Diaspora. As a result, the detrimental impact of patriarchy and male dominance within the black community is often muffled and eclipsed by the efforts to overcome other systems of domination, particularly of race, nation, and class. However, not only is patriarchy essential to current socioeconomic and political systems of dominance, but the manifestation of dominant and dominating forms of masculinity also supports it and often thwarts truly collective efforts for social and personal change.

As a result, black women, feminist or not, have a stake in the transformation of oppressive black masculinities and the development of progressive black masculinities. Not only are expressions of hypermasculinity expressed in the personal lives of African American women, but oppressive masculinities are also manifest in the organized movements for social change. Black feminists and activists from a wide range of struggles would agree that the move toward more humanistic and holistic expressions of gender in African diasporan communities is imperative for the human liberation struggle. However, black feminists differ on how progressive black masculinities are best aided and achieved and what the appropriate expenditure of black women's energy should be in this gender transformation. Specifically, black feminist perspectives diverge on the strategies for, and even the possibilities of, transforming systems of male dominance within African and African diasporan communities.

In the present discussion, I explore a range of black masculinities and their relationship to social justice movements in general and to the struggle for women's liberation specifically. I then turn to a discussion of black feminist interventionist approaches to aid in the development of progressive black masculinities. I focus on two groups' efforts: the All-African Women's Revolutionary Union (AAWRU) and the National Center for Human Rights Education (NCHRE). The latter's efforts are particularly interesting because of the way men were engaged in consciousness-raising methods often employed by black feminist collectives.

Spanning the Spectrum: The Range of Black Masculinities

In the United States, historically men of African descent have been dually in the positions of victim–victimizer in relation to the dominant construction of manhood.[1] The conception of the African–black[2] man as the strong, hypersexualized primitive was perpetuated as justification for colonization, enslavement, and European dominance. Sociologist Anthony Lemelle characterizes masculinity in the black male experience as a "structural trope, the figurative use of representation to covertly portray and reproduce power relations of a social formation."[3] The manipulation of patriarchy and maleness was a central ingredient in the development of racial oppression and capitalist accumulation in the United States. Enslavement was justified by the perpetration of pseudoscientific and religious myths centered on the pathological nature of African people's gendered natures. The myth of the primitive and aggressive black man was exploited on both productive and reproductive levels. This dominant notion of African–black manhood was established, and at the same time exploited, as part of the process of colonial–capitalist accumulation in the new world.

These same gendered and racialized constructions of black masculine gender served as justification for lynching, sexual assaults, and other forms of gender violence against both black men and women. Angela Davis articulated this relationship clearly in her essay titled "Rape, Racism, and the Myth of the Black Male Rapist." In her analysis, the construction and "political invention" of a feared and violent black masculinity was useful in maintaining racist economic and political oppression.[4] So, from an early point, the development of black masculinities as situated within the United States has been intimately linked to the dominant Western construction of manhood. These problematic masculinities occupy a hegemonic position in relation to other black masculinities and black female identities in the contemporary moment.[5]

The range of black masculinities and patriarchies expressed throughout the African Diaspora have been constructed and structured through the particularities of the specific social, cultural, and political contexts in which they arise. Black male identities can be placed along a continuum from compliance with, to resistance against, the systemic oppressions of patriarchy and its handmaidens—racism, classism, sexism, homophobia, and imperialism.[6] On one end of the spectrum are expressions of manhood within African and African diasporan communities, black masculinities that embody and emulate the Western model of male dominance, violence, aggression, hierarchy, and privilege. These dominant and dominating constructions of black masculinity in the United States are both reflective of and intertwined with the historical development of systemic inequalities.

There are, on the other end of the spectrum, submerged and less visible black masculinities. In *Feminism Is for Everyone*, bell hooks wrote a brief chapter on *feminist masculinity*, which discussed antisexist men, along with some feminists, who came to recognize "that patriarchy stripped men of certain rights, imposing on them a sexist masculine identity."[7] In addition, the expressions of progressive and humane masculinities such as mothering fathers, protective older brothers, community workers, healers, and other life teachers are woven throughout African descendent communities. Unfortunately, these more humane versions of black masculinity rarely serve as models against which or as measures by which black men gauge their maleness.

Contested and Contesting Masculinities in Movements

At different points in the black liberation and social justice struggle, constructions of black masculinities and gender hierarchies of power have taken distinct forms and have posed particular problems or opportunities.[8] On the one hand, *movement masculinities* that reinscribe power disparities and hierarchies create structural and ideological constraints to prioritizing women's human rights. Contests over gender roles have, at times, negatively impacted or devalued the contributions made by black women to liberatory efforts. Where African diasporan women's contributions to liberation struggles have not been stymied, their activist labor has been exploited and appropriated in service of these male-dominated models of liberation. In these cases, as is common in racial justice and national liberation movements, "national independence [and racial equality are] posed as a necessary precondition for women's liberation. At the same time, women's contributions are sought after and needed in the struggle for nation/race independence and equality."[9] In some cases, male dominance has been fused with and seen as synonymous with equality.

There are, though, instances in which black men in the United States have committed gender suicide and have attempted to dislodge their identities and behaviors from male dominance and hierarchy. A collective of such men calling themselves "Black Men for the Eradication of Sexism" at Morehouse College in the early 1990s wrote the following in their mission statement: "We believe that although we are oppressed because of our color, we are privileged because of our sex and must therefore take responsibility for ending that privilege… . We're here to redefine ourselves so one day we can all realize what it really means to be a man and to be human."[10] In cases like these, black men have struggled against the dominant paradigm by linking the transformation of gender hierarchies to other liberatory projects.

So for instance, in 1998 close to 2,000 activists of African descent attended the Black Radical Congress (BRC) held in Chicago, Illinois, under the thematic banner "Setting a Black Radical Agenda for the Twenty-First Century." The BRC is a contemporary attempt to "reinvigorate and redirect the movement toward liberation."[11] A caucus was established to correct the tendencies and practices associated with oppressive black masculinities that served to split the movement around questions of gender. At the end, an attending African American male activist reported, for example, that "gender, especially the concerns of women, [is] central to the BRC's theory, strategy, and tactics. The Black Radical Congress is being structured on gender equality. Most roles or functional positions in the BRC consist of women and men co-chairs."[12] The BRC is the first national-level, gender-integrated coalition of African American activists and organizations to put antisexism and the eradication of women's oppression in the forefront of its mission. On the structural level, women's representation at leadership levels was made a priority in the organization and, in addition, a black feminist caucus was formed to spearhead and to refine the theoretical and practical applications of black revolutionary feminism. These efforts have the potential of transforming the ideas and behaviors of African American men and women in the future of social justice struggles on structural, ideological and praxis levels.

However, not all black masculinities that claim allegiance to human liberation and social justice on some level are working in the interests of women's human rights. As Manning Marable observed, "From the very beginning of Black political activism in the United States, Afro-American men had real difficulty in considering the 'triple oppression' of Black women with any degree of seriousness. Part of the problem stemmed from the evolution of patriarchal institutions within Black civil society."[13] He went on to identify the male-dominated and male-defined black church, schools, economic enterprises, media and officially political organizations as cases in point. In this sense, these patriarchal masculinities were in conflict with the interests of the African American community as a whole.

Thus, there have also been movement phases in which black masculinities recreated patriarchal dominance and thereby thwarted African American women's contributions and narrowed the range and form of their movement participation. The latter part of the 1960s, for example, which ushered in the more militant and nationalist black power phase of the movement, tended to equate liberation with reasserting black manhood as opposed to establishing peoplehood. Black masculinities were used not only as weapons against "The Man" but also, most problematically, as dominance over African American women. During this era, the racially separatist and masculinized politics of cultural nationalism reasserted patriarchy as the movement's objective. The wide participation enjoyed by African American women in the earlier period of the struggle narrowed in the face of the quasimilitary and masculinized strategies adopted by groups like the Black Panther Party for Self Defense and the Black Liberation Army.

This is not to say that African American women did not participate in these emergent forms of social struggle and reconstruction. Women made significant contributions through the main organizational structures of the period. The women in the Black Panther Party often adopted the masculinized symbolism associated with militancy and armed defense. The image of Black Panther leader Kathleen Cleaver in black leather, holding a rifle to her breast, was in some ways even more oppositional to the capitalist–racist patriarchy because it challenged both the normative ideology of femininity and the enforced norm of African American passivity. However, this masculinized shift in the ideology and symbolism of the movement widened the gender gap within the African American community in particular ways. Specifically, there was a devaluation and deemphasis on gender justice and fewer opportunities for women to engage equally in movement activities in gender-integrated organizations of this period.

The development of a critical black feminist discourse was incubated during this period of gender polarization in the black liberation struggle. Autonomous African American women's collectives emerged as a result of gender splits, tensions, and the expanded consciousness within the racial and social justice movement. At this point, responses of black masculinities within the movement became synonymous with antiblack feminism. The Combahee River Collective observed in the 1970s that "the reaction of Black men to feminism has been notoriously negative ... . They realize that they might not only lose valuable and hardworking allies in their struggles but might also be forced to change their habitually sexist ways of interacting with and oppressing Black women."[14] These antifeminist black masculinities can still be seen in efforts such as the Million Man March sponsored by the Nation of Islam, which took place in Washington, D.C., in 1995, as a "Holy Day of Atonement and Reconciliation." Although the march served as a strong symbol of continued dissatisfaction with U.S. race relations and included select African American women as participants and organizers, it flowed from the conservative and patriarchal traditions in the movement. The stated objective was to have African American men atone for their transgressions and to resume leadership over family and community responsibilities. This idea was based on an underlying assumption of male-dominance and individual-level causation, ignoring structural causes, for the plight of African Americans. Though the gender segregationist tone was softened as the time of the march approached, the original call, which excluded African American women, was hotly contested in the black community. Clarence Lusane observed that:

> Although women did much of the work of organizing the march—as has been the case historically in black politics—the march explicitly privileged the plight of the most serious issue facing African Americans, and women were asked to stay at home that day and educate the children … . The problem, in a larger sense, was the political exclusion of black women's issues and concerns … . The politics of the march's leaders essentially said that only issues facing black men were issues for the whole black community, while the issues facing black women were not.[15]

This position is reminiscent of an earlier phase in the movement, which essentially premised the liberation of African American people on the rejuvenation of the black patriarchy and male dominance.

Nevertheless, there have been phases in the struggle for racial equality within the United States in which black masculinities were deployed in ways that empowered the community. For example, a long history of African and African diasporan men have championed the need to prioritize women's rights and, according to Johnnetta Cole and Beverly Guy-Sheftall, have been actively "disloyal to patriarchy."[16] In *Traps: African American Men on Gender and Sexuality*, Rudolph Byrd and Guy-Sheftall compiled an impressive list of antisexist black male writing from profeminist forefathers including Frederick Douglass, Alexander Crummell, and W. E. B. Du Bois. Even these progressive expressions of masculinity were not completely aligned with black women's interests and rights. As Cole and Guy-Sheftall further observed, "Douglass argued for the greater urgency of race over gender" in advocating for the vote.[17] Thus, even black masculinities that are counterhegemonic on some level are not necessarily concerned with human liberation, including the liberation of black women and their human rights.

A Black Feminist Role in Transforming Black Masculinities?

Today, black feminists and gender activists in African and African diasporan communities continue to differ on their perspectives relative to the most effective strategies for undermining patriarchy and transforming gender relations. Although most agree that gender transformation is a necessary part of the struggle for liberation in other areas of oppression, black feminist perspectives on how to achieve this objective vary as widely as the spectrum of black masculinities. Further, even though most agree that men must play a substantial role in changing gender relations, these women also differ about what role women should play in engaging black men about black men's own gendered roles and expectations as well as about educating them about sexism and the achievement of women's human rights. The same gendered tensions that stimulated the emergence of black feminism underlie the complex range of positions held by black feminists on the strategies they employ to eradicate patriarchy and to engage black men in these efforts.

At a seminar on global black feminisms held at Spelman College in June 2002, for example, two distinct philosophical positions emerged among the participants on the degree to which black women should expend efforts to engage, to educate, or to organize men about gender oppression generally and women's human rights in particular. For some participants, black women's work was best directed toward strengthening collective power with other women. There was, in their mind, enough work to do in the process of consciousness raising and organizing women against multiple oppressions. They argued that their contributions through diverse women-only and semiautonomous women's spaces offer the greatest opportunity to challenge multilevel oppression.

In fact, women in the "antiapartheid, civil rights, and Black Power movements developed alternative women-only spaces that provided other strategic opportunities for resistance."[18] Within these autonomous spaces, women could engage in social change efforts as deeply as they wanted without having to confront or to be marginalized by the debilitating impact of sexism internal to their organizations. Indeed, African woman-only spaces and semiautonomous organizations have been catalysts for movements with a range of objectives including environmental justice, racial equality, and gay liberation.

From this perspective, efforts on the part of black women in politicizing black men about gender oppression is seen, at best, as another expression of women's stereotypical and disproportionate caring and servicing responsibilities. This work can also lead to overburdening and to exploiting women's movement efforts much like the workings of patriarchy in the larger society. For instance, although the Combahee River Collective proposed that black feminists join with black men in the struggle against patriarchy and other forms of oppression, it simultaneously acknowledged the deep divides and problematic cleavages that exist in the black community as a result of patriarchy and gender oppression.[19]

Others black feminists take a more interventionist approach in countering patriarchy and oppressive black masculinities. In their view, black feminists have to take a more engaged role in undermining patriarchal identities, expressions, and structures. The efforts put forth by black feminists in this endeavor are seen, from this perspective, as worth the sacrifice. As a result, shifting away from the gender polarization of the 1970s and 1980s, there are increasing tendencies toward more interventionist and gender-integrated efforts to aid in the radical transformation of oppressive black masculinities and patriarchy within black institutions.

In the following discussion, I draw from examples of these interventionist approaches that were either black feminist led or informed. Each of these cases presents a distinct type of effort in which women have been active in raising consciousness about and organizing men against patriarchy and around women's human rights. These strategies provide useful lessons and salient issues related to the struggle to forge progressive and profeminist black masculinities.

From the Inside Out: The Impact
of the All-African Women's Revolutionary Union

The All-African Women's Revolutionary Union (AAWRU), the women's wing of the All-African People's Revolutionary Party (AAPRP), was formed in 1980 with the purpose of facilitating a semiautonomous space within the organization for the development of women's radical Pan-African consciousness. The union was also a vehicle for educating the wider organization and constituency, both men and women, about patriarchy and the woman question as they relate particularly to African people worldwide. All women in the AAPRP were considered members of the union. Though most union members would not have considered themselves feminist, the party and its women's wing promoted an African-centered race–gender–class analysis very similar to black feminist social philosophy.[20]

The AAWRU was charged with the task of developing antipatriarchal political education and action within the AAPRP. A central mission of the wing was to educate the brothers about sexism and to reconstitute the organization away from male dominance. The AAWRU held regular meetings discussing readings on various aspects of women's oppression, liberation, and antipatriarchal struggle internationally. These meetings were considered a requirement for sisters of the party but were only optional for male members, who could attend but not vote. In addition to AAWRU meetings, the women's wing sought to raise gender consciousness within and outside of the party by organizing internal forums on the system of patriarchy from an African perspective, by sponsoring external events and speakers that addressed topics related to African women, and by developing an approved AAWRU reading list to supplement the main reading list. In addition to this ideological offensive, structural processes also were established to alter the typical masculine paradigm and to bring more women into leadership positions.

The results of this strategy of engaging black men around issues of sexism were both ideologically and structurally uneven. Needless to say, the task of attempting to change structures, belief systems, attitudes, and behaviors within the organization created extra work for the women. This work only slightly challenged the male-informed model of social resistance and individual practices of male dominance that prevailed in the AAPRP overall.

Wing members and leadership experienced high levels of burnout and over-burdening as a result of their added responsibility of trying to address the male dominance in the organization. Further, in addition to their political education and programmatic work, the AAWRU was responsible for organizing the Young Pioneers Institute and child care. The implementation of the child-care work was supposed to equally draw from men and women's labor. It rarely did.

The fact that the AAPRP brothers were often able to do their party work unhampered by the constraints of family labor in some ways mirrors the exploitative processes characteristic of patriarchal capitalist accumulation.[21] The limited impact on reconstructing oppressive masculinities and patriarchy within the organization was due in part to the self-selective nature of the consciousness-raising process. This meant that only the most interested, and potentially only the already gender-conscious male militants, availed themselves of AAWRU-sponsored meetings and events. The degree to which male members engaged, or did not, with the women-centered readings, speakers, and issues varied and was highly dependent on their own assessment of its importance.

In this case, the interventionist approach reinforced patriarchal gender splits and patriarchal norms in two ways. First, structurally linking the union to youth and child-care responsibilities not only replicated normative gender roles but also structurally supported the exploitation of women's labor. Another rigid boundary was enforced between the political and the personal. Further, the issues of male dominance and patriarchy leveled by the union had extremely limited impact outside of official party politics. No mechanisms existed for challenging men in the organization on their expressions of male dominance on interpersonal levels, an area deemed inappropriate and off-limits to the real political work. The degree to which the party was committed to the development and activities of the union also varied widely by chapter and region. The idea of antipatriarchal struggle, of course, resulted in a wide range of responses from men within the party, from rabid antifeminist to truly humane, egalitarian, and pro-feminist and -womanist.

From the Outside In: Bringing Human Rights Home

Black feminist and international activist Loretta Ross founded the National Center for Human Rights Education (NCHRE) in 1996 as the "first human rights education organization in the United States that focuses primarily on domestic human rights violations."[22] Unlike most U.S. and Europe-based human rights organizations that focus on atrocities elsewhere in the world, the NCHRE brings human rights home, so to speak. The organization is also committed to gender justice based on the principles of the Universal Declaration of Human Rights and other international treaties that safeguard women's rights and challenge sexist discrimination. As part of a larger strategy of incorporating women's concerns into the broader human rights framework, the NCHRE organized a Gender Justice Retreat to "train men on women's human rights" in May 2002, under the leadership of Ross and NCHRE's women's human rights project manager Dazon Dixon Diallo.[23] Though not all of the participants in this retreat were male, or of African descent, the issues that arose during the four-day session are helpful to understanding the range and possibilities of black feminist interventionist approaches to transforming oppressive black masculinities.

The Gender Justice Retreat was conceptualized as "an opportunity for a group of progressive social justice workers and educators to reflect on ways to develop popular education models and training techniques to advance men's understandings of gender related social injustices and women's human rights."[24] The themes and questions that emerged from this black feminist-led effort to teach men about gender relations and women's human rights are instructive and have implications for the actual work needed to dislodge patriarchy.

The central question posed during this retreat was, "What do men need in order to become proactive, positive agents for change regarding women's oppression?" For my purposes, I pose several other questions: "What are the issues and questions that emerge from this type of black feminist interventionist approach to antipatriarchy work? How is black feminism implicated and what impact can it and its proponents have in the struggle to create and sustain progressive black masculinities?" During the retreat, several issues emerged related to both the possibilities and problems using black feminist praxis to aid in transforming black masculinities. A key concern was the tightrope that feminist interventionists were walking between helping to reinvent masculinities toward a progressive politic without recentering men and, as a result, remarginalizing women.

In contrast to the AAWRU, the Gender Justice Retreat was consciously grounded in, emerged from, and utilized a black feminist framework. The organizers drew from their experience in the black women's health movement in creating a strategy to teach men about women's human rights. This black feminist praxis was especially evident in the use of the self-help model, a method of engaging the participants and connecting them to human rights through their personal, lived experience.

As a way of introduction, each participant engaged in confidential, personal experiences, especially as they answered the following three crucial questions: (1) name an experience when your human rights were violated; (2) name an experience when you may have violated someone else's human rights; and (3) name an experience when your human rights were protected.[25]

In the retreat, personal disclosures were shared through their relationship to human rights, either as victim, violator, or protector. This process is a direct reflection of one of the main tenets associated with black feminism: concrete experience as a criterion for meaning.[26] The centering of lived experience is based on the belief that concrete knowledge comes from living life as oneself:

in the black feminist context as a black woman; at the retreat as a black man. Concrete experience offers a particular position from which to view and to theorize about the social world. In this case, the purposive selection of participants played a role.

The self-help process also embodies the "ethic of caring": the idea that personal expressiveness, emotions, and empathy are central to the knowledge-validation process.[27] This emphasis builds a dialogue between reason and emotion, a form of connected knowing, as opposed to these being diametrical opposites, as in reason versus emotion. The self-help process draws from the value placed on individual expressiveness, on the appropriateness of emotions, and on the capacity for empathy.

How effective is black feminist praxis and the self-help model with men? According to the organizers of the retreat, "this was the first time that many of the men had ever spoken of experiences in their lives that were personally relevant to understanding the concept of human rights."[28] The novelty of this type of disclosure for men led one participant to remark, "The processing of the 'stuff' [self-help and personal experiences] became pivotal to the process of developing best human rights practices."[29] Expressing emotions and exposing vulnerabilities are diametrically opposed to the dominant construction of masculinity. The participants determined that it would be necessary to "stretch the boundaries of masculinity" to even engage in antipatriarchal human rights discourse.

Throughout the course of the retreat, the other discussions and sessions focused on the human rights framework, men and feminist theory, homophobia, and male feminist identity.[30] The retreat participants noted the fact that the constraining impact of categorical, binary, and oppositional thinking had a negative impact in all of these areas. This binary thinking, characteristic of Western thought, is fundamentally related to the emergence and justification of oppressive and unequal power relationships, including gender oppression and oppressive expressions of black masculinity. Oppositional categories that emerged at different points in the retreat process included self, or individual, versus system, center versus margin, woman versus man, gay versus straight, victim versus victimizer, scholar versus activist, nationalism versus feminism, and black versus white. It became clear that reinforcing these dichotomous splits on any level in the context of multiple identities and oppressions undermines efforts to dislodge patriarchy and to do women's human rights work.

Some of the tensions that emerged during the retreat led participants to the conclusion that men would have to transform and to work on themselves to do effective gender and women's rights work. During the retreat, the "participants, especially the majority group of black men, requested a shift in the agenda to allow space and time for them to meet in separate groups, so that the black men and the white men would have the opportunity to address some of the issues discussed in an even safer space."[31] Clearly, the multilayered and reflexive process of human rights work means that internal issues men have within and among themselves have to be included in the transformational process. As one participant observed, "In social work theory we've looked at fixing individuals and ignoring systems. As activists we do the opposite [focus on systems and ignore the individuals]. We need to address both and recognize the relationship between the two."[32]

During the retreat, these divisions and tensions among men along lines of race–ethnicity, class, status, and sexuality came to the surface and were addressed and momentarily resolved. While men broke away to work on and to discuss intragender issues, organizers became concerned about the possibilities of centering men once again, a key characteristic of a patriarchal society. How can men's issues be negotiated, even in same-sex spaces, without marginalizing women and minimizing their agency? "What is the risk of re-centering men into the frame and moving women back to the margins?"[33] How do we create same male-only space without recentering men as the ultimate decision maker, ultimate player, or ultimate victim?

One answer that emerged during the retreat was the suggestion that part of raising political consciousness means recognizing and discussing the relationship between dominating masculinities and other lines of oppressions. That is, male power and hegemonic men, or masculinities, in black and other communities are only possible through the subjugation and oppression of other identities. As one retreat participant commented, "Women's human rights are deprived so that someone else can have a dominant identity."[34]

Toward Wo/Men's Liberation: Which Way?

Should African and African diasporan men work autonomously and among themselves to forge more progressive and antipatriarchal black masculinities, or should they be aided in some way by their sisters in struggle? How helpful is black feminist theory and praxis in this process? How appropriate or effective with men, particularly black men, are the strategies black feminists have developed to confront and to transform themselves? How is this work done without either re-erasing or overburdening black women? These crucial questions emerged in an examination of these divergent strategies engaged by black feminists as they sought strategies to aid in the development of progressive black masculinities.

In these cases, the projects of the AAWRU and the NCHRE are evidence of the impact that black feminist and woman-led interventions can have on black masculinities. It is evident, based on the black feminist analysis of interlocking and multiple oppressions,[35] that black women have a vested interest in transforming oppressive black expressions of manhood. As a result, black feminist interventionist approaches to aiding in transforming black masculinity models are emerging internationally. Part of the overall objective is to create environments in which the work that black women are doing to transform and to empower themselves is supported. Both examples involved a small cadre of men, whether through their own self-selection or by design. The strategy was to create a vanguard of profeminist, antipatriarchal men to take the struggle more deeply into the ranks of their brothers. The nature of patriarchal thought, which devalues women's contributions in general, makes it impossible for black feminists to do this transformational work on a grand scale.

The expressions of black maleness that are defined by their power or hierarchical positioning over others, whether in the form of gender violence or extreme cultural nationalism, have had limited utility in the struggle for racial equality or social justice. Audre Lorde's prophetic statement that "the master's tools will never dismantle the master's house" is just as relevant for black masculinities and the black freedom struggle as they were for women and the women's liberation movement.[36] As the struggle for social equality and justice is increasingly globalized and international, activists have stressed the importance of being aware of the interrelation among multiple forms of oppression, dominance, and resistance. Further, transformation on the individual level in forging new black masculinities would have to be accompanied by broader activities to be supported or sustained. For example, since most of the male participants were engaged in antisexism work of some form already, they were able to identify the "significant stigma attached to men who are able to envision a society without patriarchy."[37]

To rebuild and to revitalize the movements for progressive social change, it is imperative that the vision include mechanisms to create and fortify humanist, feminist, and liberatory black masculinities and female identities. Within African and African diasporan communities, particularly those in the United States, these visions could take the form of:

- black masculinities defined to include active engagement with social change movements that undermine the range of systemic oppressions affecting people of African descent (e.g., feminist and reproductive rights; socialist, gay and lesbian, and antiglobalization movements);
- black masculinities approaching black liberation and racial equity as more than merely a reassertion and reinvention of patriarchy within African descendent communities;
- black masculinities not dichotomously constructed against either a submissive or castrating black female persona or placed in hierarchies;
- black masculinities conscious and ever vigilant of the multiple expressions of male privilege and consistently seeking to deconstruct and to dismantle this privilege;
- black masculinities devoid of narcissism and definitions of reality through a masculinist gaze and male-centered interests;

- black masculinities proceeding from the premise that the personal is political but also acknowledging that the political is not limited to the personal, (i.e., the interpersonal expression of progressive maleness).

A crucial aspect of the development of progressive black masculinities is the recognition of, and struggle for, women's human rights. In a special issue of the South African feminist journal *Agenda*, Thulani Nkosi, the coordinator of a young men's group, defined the *new man* as "gender sensitive, not afraid to express his emotions, shares in the daily household chores, views women as equals and as partners, is not abusive and respects women's rights as human rights."[38] Progressive black masculinities are essential for the development of an inclusive and transformative resistance and reconstructive movement in the United States. At the same time, social activism that consciously opposes racial, gender, and class oppression, as well as heterosexism, is necessary for, and has to become an essential part of, the construction of black manhood and womanhood.

Notes

1. National Center for Human Rights Education (NCHRE), *Minutes from the Gender Justice Retreat: Training Men on Women's Human Rights, October 2002* (Atlanta: NCHRE.
2. Throughout this chapter, I use *African* and *African diasporan* as synonymous with *black*. I use *African American* as shorthand for people of African descent in the United States. *African diasporan* includes African Americans as well as people of African descent located in and throughout the Americas, the Caribbean, the United Kingdom, Asia, and the Middle East.
3. Anthony J. Lemelle, "The Political Sociology of Black Masculinity and Tropes of Domination," *Journal of African American Men* 1, no. 2 (1995), 88.
4. Angela Davis, *Women, Race, and Class* (New York: Vintage Books, 1983).
5. R. W. Connell, *Gender and Power: Society, the Person and Sexual Politics* (Stanford, CA: Stanford University Press, 1987); bell hooks, *Feminism Is for Everybody* (Boston: South End Press, 2000); and Lemelle, "Political Sociology."
6. Connell, *Gender and Power*; and Lemelle, "Political Sociology."
7. hooks, *Feminism*, 68.
8. M. Bahati Kuumba, *Gender and Social Movements* (Walnut Creek, CA: AltaMira Press, 2001).
9. Kuumba, "Engendering the Pan-African Movement: Field Notes from the All-African Women's Revolutionary Union," in *Still Lifting, Still Climbing: African American Women's Contemporary Activism*, ed. Kimberly Springer (New York: New York University Press, 1999), 169.
10. Black Men for the Eradication of Sexism at Morehouse College, 1994, "Mission Statement" in *Traps: African American Men on Gender and Sexuality*, ed. Rudolph P. Byrd and Beverly Guy-Sheftall (Bloomington: Indiana University Press, 2001), 200, 202.
11. Sundiata Keita Cha-Jua, "The Black Radical Congress and the Reconstruction of the Black Freedom Movement," *Black Scholar* 28, nos. 3–4 (1998), 9.
12. Ibid., 10.
13. Manning Marable, "Groundings with My Sisters: Patriarchy and the Exploitation of Black Women," in Byrd and Guy-Sheftall, *Traps*, 124.
14. Combahee River Collective, "The Combahee River Collective Statement," in *Home Girls: A Black Feminist Anthology*, ed. Barbara Smith (New Brunswick, NJ: Kitchen Table Press 2000), 264, 274.
15. Clarence Lusane, *Race in the Global Era: African Americans at the Millennium* (Boston: South End Press, 1997), 205.

16. Johnnetta Betsch Cole and Guy-Sheftall, *Gender Talk: The Struggle for Women's Equality in African American Communities* (New York: Ballantine Books, 2003), 43.
17. Ibid., 75.
18. Kuumba, *Gender and Social,* 14.
19. Combahee River Collective, "Statement."
20. Kuumba, "Engendering."
21. Ibid., 184.
22. National Center for Human Rights Education (NCHRE), *Final Report on the Gender Justice Retreat, October 2002.* (Atlanta: National Center for Human Rights Education and the Shaler Adams Foundation, 2002).
23. Ibid.
24. The Gender Justice Retreat was sponsored by the Shayler Adams Foundation. Ibid.
25. Ibid., 3.
26. Patricia Hill Collins, *Black Feminist Thought: Knowledge, Consciousness, and the Politics of Empowerment* (New York: Routledge, 1991), 208–12.
27. Ibid., 217.
28. Diallo, "Gender Justice," 3.
29. Ibid., 6.
30. Ibid., 4.
31. Ibid., 5.
32. NCHRE Retreat.
33. Diallo, "Gender Justice," 18.
34. Ibid., 6.
35. Collins, *Black Feminist Thought,* 225–30.
36. Audre Lorde, "The Master's Tools Will Never Dismantle the Master's House," in *Feminist Postcolonial Theory: A Reader,* ed. Reina Lewis and Sara Mills (New York: Routledge, 2003), 27.
37. Diallo, "Gender Justice," 4.
38. Thulani Nkosi, "Young Men Taking a Stand," *Agenda* 37 (1998), 37.

Part 7
Walking the Talk

14

Breaking the Silence: The Role of Progressive Black Men in the Fight against Sexual Assault

THEMA BRYANT-DAVIS, Ph.D.

I am an African American psychologist. I am a rape survivor. I am a woman who is blessed to have a brother, father, and husband who have spoken out against the violation of women, including me. Though it is good to see and experience some progressive African American men speaking out actively against sexual violence, the unfortunate reality is that many men in the African American community, as in other communitites, often respond to reports of rape with silence, denial, and victim blaming. This chapter is both a celebration of brothers who have stood firm and loud in the fight against sexual violence and a call for brothers who are in denial. This is a call for all brothers to adopt progressive activist masculinities.

A number of social, political, and psychological factors contribute to the silence surrounding rape in the African American community. We cannot, however, continue to allow these barriers to block the possibility of dialogue, healing, and justice. Taking into account our shared history of oppression, we have to actively promote a masculinity that resists both rape and the passive acceptance of sexual objectification. This chapter first reviews some of the contributing factors to African American male silence in the fight against rape. Later, I explore the need for progressive African American men's participation in the fight against sexual violence. Finally, the chapter outlines some of the numerous ways brothers have stood and can stand against sexual violence. This chapter includes reflections by various African American men between the ages of twenty and sixty-five. These are men of varying educational and vocational backgrounds whom I asked to share their reflections concerning sexual violence in the African American community. The quotations offered by these men open each section of the chapter. As an African American woman scholar writing a chapter on progressive black masculinity, it was important for me to create a forum in which the voices of African American men are heard so we can shatter the silence together.

Why the Silence?

There is a tacit agreement amongst our folk that we should not "air our dirty laundry" in public. Many think that to do so indicates that we are "out of control" or "weak." These perceptions inhibit African Americans (particularly men) from seeking help in other areas as well. In addition, we tend to protect each other (for good or ill) from the rest of society because historically, the sins of one Black person become the sins of us all—thus, if one man engages in sexual violence, in the media we all become sexual predators. Unfortunately, some men have a stereotypic view of what "maleness" is. According to this view, a man must be in "control" at all times—anything else is perceived as "weakness." This view dictates that all other people (i.e., women, children, and other men) must be subordinate. This perspective does not promote partnerships with women—indeed, it suggests that women are and should be fairly child-like and acquiescent instead of fully functioning adults. Such a power differential in relationships can only be maintained by violence or the threat of violence.

Dr. Ralph Piper, psychologist

When African Americans are asked what comes to mind at the thought of the words *rape* and *black men,* the answer often includes the false reports of rape by white women and the consequent lynching of African American men. This has been a reality in American history that has left a permanent mark in African American consciousness. It is a fact that due to the false accusations of white women numerous African American men were tortured and lynched. During and long after slavery, there has been both a fascination with and a fear of African American men's sexuality. There is the stigma and stereotype that most African American men are rapists. This myth, as with all racist myths, is not true. African American men are not genetically or culturally predisposed to rape. In addition, the fear of African American men by white women ignores the reality that intraracial rape is more prevalent than interracial rape, meaning a white woman is more likely to be raped by a white man than by a black man.

As a result of the widespread jailing, torture, and lynching of African American men due to rape reports of white women, the African American community has adopted a protective stance around African American men who are accused of rape. Though this was a reasonable response to the killing of innocent African American men, it has set up a community system that ignores and even destroys African American survivors of intraracial rape—that is, the rape of African American women by African American men. There is, it seems, a mandate in our community requiring individuals to sacrifice the self for the sake of the group. This is most often translated to mean that African American women who are raped by African American men should remain silent for fear that their stories will contribute to society's negative view of African American men. This problem is compounded by a racist judicial system, so that when an African American woman presses charges against an African American man for rape, she is often seen as betraying him to a racist system. The judgment and burdens of these acts are placed on the woman's shoulders. It is, however, rare that members of the community see the act of rape by an African American man as a violation and betrayal of the woman and the community. It is rarely recognized that the African American male who rapes is complicit in and perpetuating a society that says African American women are whores unworthy of respect and protection. The rapist is not categorized as the betrayer of the race; instead, the survivor who comes forward is judged a tool of the racist enemy in the destruction of African American manhood.

Progressive African American men, however, practice and promote the kind of respect for community based on consent and equality of all members, including African American women. Progressive African American men acknowledge that there are African American women who have been raped by African American men and that these rapes must be brought to light for the community to heal and to grow. In thinking about this issue, I penned the following poem.

Protecting Judas
 Sister said she didn't want to tell on her rapist
 Didn't want to betray the race
 Didn't want to turn over another brother into the hands of the system
 But I wonder if the brother was thinking of the race
 When he punched her in the jaw
 Wonder if he was saluting Mother Africa
 When he pinned her arms down
 Wonder if he was contemplating the NAACP
 When he ignored her cries to…stop
 Wonder if he was thinking about kente cloth
 When he tore open her shirt and ripped off her panties
 Wonder if he was performing community service
 When he stabbed her with the sword of his redemption again and again
 Was it once for Malcolm?
 Once for Martin?
 Once for Marcus Garvey?
 Once for Nelson Mandela? Once for Kunta Kente?
 Once for Rosa? Once for Sojourner? Once for Harriet?
 Again and Again
 Did he shed her blood for the people?
 It is impossible to betray Judas.
 It is impossible to betray Judas.

But she grew up in silent sanctuaries
Although that was no silent night
It was the unholiest of nights

Maps of Africa keep her busy but not healed
She keeps so busy praising her Jesus
Keeps busy serving her people
Keeps busy trying to stay busy
But her heart and hymen are broken

She thinks her silence redeems
But only Judas is redeemed
What about the woman on the fourth cross
Who will redeem the life of this lamb?
Her shed blood
Broken for what?
Where is the community?
When will we stop shouting
Crucify her
Crucify her/Crucify her

She lays awake at night
Hanger in hand
Waiting
She's waiting for fathers that will stand in the gap
For brothers who will believe her
For sisters who will sit with her until the storm learns to peace be still
She's not calling for lynch mobs
But an oasis of truth telling where healing can begin
She doesn't want any more certificates for her silence
She doesn't want another plaque for her nervous grin
She's not calling for a mere nation of women whistle blowers
But of sons that are raised to keep their brothers in check

She keeps so busy trying to stay busy
She ain't got time to die
But her joy bells are broken
She ain't got time to die
But she can't sleep at night
She ain't got time to die
But sex makes her cry
She ain't got time to die
But her appetite is gone

She ain't got time to die
But one hundred showers later she's still dirty
She ain't got time to die
But silent blood is still blood all the same
She ain't got time to die
But the silence is killing her softly

Holy Mary
Mother of God
Who will redeem the life of this lamb?
Is there one
Some man—some woman—some boy—some girl
Is there one who is not afraid to shatter the silence?
Are you the one—?
Who will help her
Lay down her burdens
Down by the riverside
So she can study war no more

Were you there when he pinned her to that bed
Were you there when we all sat on our hands
Were you there when we all set Judas free
Oh—oh sometimes it causes me to tremble, tremble, tremble
Enough is Enough
We will accept not one more silenced lamb

Silenced Lambs: Myths about Rape

The black man's attitude toward rape requests correction less than his definition of it. Not only must he know that "one who rapes" is wrong, but he must also comprehend completely what constitutes "rape."
Kwesi Davis, Production Engineer, DreamWorks Animation SKG

There is a myth that the silenced lambs among us are only African American female survivors. However, the number of African American boys and men who have been molested and raped is staggering. These assaults occur in apartments, schools, houses, alleys, gyms, religious sites, and penitentiaries. Whether or not they have disclosed their experience, everyone knows a boy or man who has been violated, yet these violations are met with community silence. Most men who are sexually assaulted are violated by men who identify themselves as heterosexual. A large part of the silence in the African American community, however, is rooted in the fear of a homophobic response. There is the fear on the part of the male survivor that others will perceive him to be less manly or will categorize him as having been a consenting participant and, therefore, gay. The magnitude of this fear is based on the wrongful and unacceptable emotional rejection, verbal harassment, and physical assaults to which many gay men in the community are subjected. But many men believe that there are already too many barriers to African American men's sense of manhood, including racism and poverty, to acknowledge yet another obstacle such as rape.

Another myth and barrier to African American men's participation in the movement against rape is misconceptions about the definition of rape. Many within the community—men and women alike—still only consider physically violent rape, perpetrated by a stranger, to be real rape. If a strange man with a gun breaks in and sexually violates a woman, or if an unknown man with a knife sexually assaults a preadolescent boy, most people understand that rape has indeed occurred. However, the truth is that most people are raped by acquaintances, not by strangers. Further, most rapists do not carry a weapon. Sexual assault is legally defined as unwanted physical sexual contact as a result of violence, threat of violence, intimidation or with a person unable to give consent as a result of being under the age of legal consent or under the influence of alcohol and drugs, including date-rape drugs. Community education is needed on the reality of acquaintance rape and rape that occurs as a result of coercion, threat, and intimidation.

Progressive African American men adopt a consensual model for sexual intimacy. They do not assume that consent to sex is based on such factors as a person's dress or level of intoxication or having had consensual sex with the person in the past. Further, progressive African American men know that going to a person's home does not equal consent to sex and that even consensual kissing does not amount to consent to intercourse. Progressive African American men acknowledge that acquaintance and stranger rape are both violations of the human person and cannot be condoned or ignored.

Still another myth, held within and outside of the African American community, is that women who report rape are liars. The Department of Justice has found that the number of false reports of rape is extremely low, which is consistent with the low rates of false reports of other crimes. And we instinctively know this. When people say they have been robbed or physically assaulted, we do not question their motives or their report. Yet many people assume that women routinely lie about rape because they believe that reporting rape leads to some sort of benefit and positive attention. The opposite is actually the case. As a matter of fact, the majority of victims never come forward because they know they will not be believed or supported. Reporting sexual crimes is a very difficult, not enticing, experience. We should be as—and even more—concerned with the many people who continue to suffer in silence as we are about the relatively few false reports of rape.

Unfortunately, in contemporary times the judicial system is seen as being primarily controlled by whites. As a result, when survivors of sexual violence report the crime, they are seen as reporting a black person to a white system. If we created institutions and systems within our community that would handle cases of intraracial violence in a just fashion, I would encourage my sisters and brothers to use that system. But we do not currently have those systems in place. So if the choice is between silent injustices and suffering, or reporting injustice and seeking emotional and physical support from institutions that are predominantly white, I think the African American community needs to choose healing and justice.

Finally, another myth that exists both within and outside our community is the belief that rapists are unattractive, unpopular men who are socially awkward or visibly recognizable. This is based on the premise that rape is committed by men who either are unable to obtain sex due to lack of social skills or sex appeal or who are clearly mentally ill and visibly identifiable maniacs who rape because they are insane. Since many people believe this myth, when someone reports sexual violence that has been perpetrated by someone we consider charismatic, attractive, sexy, and mentally stable, people believe that the person making the report must be lying. As with domestic violence, many perpetrators of sexual violence are clean-cut, intelligent, sociable people. Rape is a choice. It is a crime based on power and intimidation. It is a crime committed by persons turned on by power and control. Whether a person is attractive or not, popular or not, intelligent or not, talented or not, he may be a rapist. Progressive men are not fooled into believing they can pick out a rapist based on physical attractiveness, social status, money, or charisma. Progressive men understand that rapists come from all walks of life. Progressive men understand that rape is about power, not about lack of sexual options. A rapist may be married, successful, and handsome. A rapist may be an important community leader, a popular minister, a famous rhythm and blues singer, a gifted politician, or the person standing on the corner. Progressive men do not let the status of the rapist silence their stance against sexual violence.

Why Should Black Men Care about Rape?

In America, where the unspeakable becomes commonplace, where forced breeding and rape sustained African slave populations for centuries, the black man has but one option: Dismantle sexual violence, to quench the wrath of his ancestors.
Kwesi Davis, Production Engineer, DreamWorks Animation SKG

If there were a physical marker for all the rape survivors among us, there would be more awareness that a crisis is occurring—just imagine if one in four women were walking around with amputated right arms and one in seven men were walking around with amputated left arms. We would have a million rap songs, hymns, panels, community rallies, marches, e-mails, and books on the topic. Most often, however, the scars of rape are invisible to the physical eye. The invisibility of our scars does not negate the reality of our experience. Rape negatively affects individuals, families, and the community as a whole. Rape can lead to depression, drug and alcohol addiction, anxiety, distrust of others, difficulties with sexual intercourse, and even suicide. Community-level effects include loss of safety and trust among community members, anger, hopelessness, powerlessness, and isolation. With the societal barriers impeding the self-esteem and self-efficacy of African Americans, we cannot afford to continue the destruction of ourselves through rape and the silent acceptance of rape.

Progressive African American men who want to save and to transform their community understand the necessity of standing against rape. When the marginalization and oppression of some of us is accepted then the entire community remains stuck. Growth based in silent genocide is death, and the continued raping of our sisters and brothers is genocide. It kills spirits, hearts, minds, families, and sometimes bodies. Progressive black men want us all to live, including those of us who have been molested, raped, assaulted, harassed, and silenced. Progressive black men do not allow fear of the fallout to keep them silent. They want to create space for the truth, no matter how painful the story or the voice. Progressive black men love truth and justice more than silence and cover-ups.

What Can Progressive Black Men Do?

It is the black male's responsibility to be on task with his male peers regarding their views on sexual violence. It is not OK to allow your brothers to brag about participating in domestic violence or sexual violence, not even in jest. If they do, it is your responsibility to check them about their behavior and to speak up on behalf of our sisters. If you do not do this, you are a participant in your brothers' violent behavior. One of the biggest barriers that keeps black men from working against sexual violence is fear. We sometimes feel that if we speak out against it to our peers that we will be seen as weaker or not living up to some people's definition of what a man really is. A true man does not allow his sisters to be violated and denigrated because he knows that the negative impact on his community will be grave.

Shawn Peterson, actor and pianist

Progressive black men have already been active in the fight against sexual violence in a number of ways: in personal commitments to resist participation or support for sexual violence, in personal responses to friends and family members who have been assaulted, and in publicly providing their support in books, rap songs, sermons, and film. We need the activity of a few to become contagious to change the mindset of many. That every revolution has been sparked by the energy of a few makes me hopeful that an army of progressive black men will stand and make it unacceptable and unthinkable for the community to stand by and condone the rape of any of us.

Individual Commitment

As an African American male who was raised in an environment where manhood, male/female relationships, and sexuality in general were clouded by negative images of pimps, hustlers, and "free-spirited" sexaholics, my views on the subject of "sexual violence" are intense. I believe the bulk of the issues stem from ignorance around what really happened to our sense of "family" and "love of self" during the slave trade. Silence with this issue, for the black man, is clearly the result of fear around how to communicate [effectively] on getting help. Most black men in the 'hood, regardless of spiritual, mental, or emotional maturity, have issues with "opening up" to a specialist if they are struggling with an issue. As a progressive Black man, one way that I'm combating this issue is through education and healthy dialogue with my wife. I wanted to know why our women are treated the way they are by society in general. I read the book *Stolen Women* by Dr. Gail Wyatt. That book opened my understanding to the issues from a historical context. Of course, that's just the beginning—staying in a prayerful posture around "holistic knowledge" is the other piece. However, I recommend that book to anybody who loves our people, and particularly our sisters.

Wyatt Jackson, dancer and choreographer

Progressive black men work to ensure that they never sexually violate anyone. Progressive men think about the verbal and nonverbal ways people communicate consent. They model their relationships with others on principles of respect, communication, and equality. They never use physical force or verbal intimidation to obtain sex. Progressive men are not aroused by the words "*no*" or "*please stop.*" Progressive men do not believe it is their job to convince women to have sex with them. Tears, pain, fear, or abuse of power is not a turn-on for progressive men. They find equality and mutual consent sexy.

In terms of promoting an antirape society, progressive black men do not make or laugh at rape jokes. If one of their friends describes a situation that sounds like rape, progressive men do not remain silent. They confront and speak up. Progressive men do not respond to gang rape charges by saying, "I was in the room, but I didn't touch her." Passively accepting the rape of another when one has the power to intervene is against the values of progressive men. Progressive men do not teach younger men that no means yes. They do not put pressure on young men to obtain sex at all costs. They do not model sexual violence against wives, girlfriends, relatives, friends, or strangers. Progressive men understand that when it comes to the war against rape, there are no sidelines. Silence is acceptance of the status quo, and the status quo is that rape is not taken seriously. When it comes to rape, every man is either a supporter of rape or a resister of rape; there is no middle ground.

Community Organization

> A growing minority of men of color are increasingly engaged in dialogue about sexual violence. This has been spawned in part by critiques of heterosexism's tendency to effectively silence conversations about antigay violence of any kind, and the steady growth of sexual violence in prisons amidst an incarceration crisis that has devastated communities of color increasingly since the 1970s. Small numbers of progressive Black men, usually all male, are coming together in safe spaces and beginning to address issues of sexual violence they might feel uncomfortable discussing openly in the presence of women. These spaces need to be encouraged, expanded, and informed by the experience of elders sympathetic to an antisexist politic. But we must also encourage the proliferation of critical coeducational spaces where survivors and supporters who have overcome the aversion to speak freely in the presence of the opposite sex can learn from each other's experiences as well. Broadening our understanding and analysis of the historical and contemporary relationship between the sexual violence facilitated by patriarchy and White supremacy is an essential step towards effectively liberating Black communities.
>
> **Bryonn Bain, law student and poet**

Black men who are progressive have worked together to form organizations that fight against rape. These organizations are all over the country. Some are focused on African American men and some are interracial organizations of men who stand against rape, such as Men Against Rape in Washington, D.C. These groups provide education in the community at schools, religious sites, and recreation centers. They have media and poster campaigns that promote antirape messages. Progressive black men think of ways to organize other black men against rape.

Religious Leaders

> Historically, the black church has not been a supportive place when it comes to addressing sexual violence. The basic response of clergy members was to fix the conflict through prayer, getting an apology, and asking that people who were violated move on. Two factors have helped

the church become more progressive in addressing sexual violence. The first is the inclusion of more women in leadership as officers and in the ministry. The second is that secular society has begun to hold the church accountable for sexual assault, abuse, and harassment. Due in part to this new reality, the church has become more responsive and proactive in addressing sexual violence.

Bishop John Bryant, African Methodist Episcopal Church

Progressive black male religious leaders work actively in the fight against rape. They preach about it, pray about it, and organize about it. They do not stand before their members and silence rape survivors by calling them liars or betrayers of the race or immoral women. They do not hold up rapists as community leaders. They do not remain silent on the subject of rape. If a religious leader has been a minister for over a year and has never spoken against rape or molestation, he is not progressive. He is helping to sustain a rape society. If the leader has spoken about rape, and the central theme of the message was for survivors is to simply forgive and get over it, he is still helping to sustain a rape society. Progressive black male religious leaders assist in the provision of counseling of survivors and perpetrators, sponsor support groups for survivors, and provide special prayer services for survivors, education for church members on sexual violence, and protocols to deal with violations. Progressive black male religious leaders work to ensure that their organizations have policies on sexual harassment and assault. Progressive black male religious leaders do not promote rapists to leadership positions. Progressive black male religious leaders do not rape, molest, or harass anyone. More religious leaders need to uphold these guidelines and to organize to combat silence in religious institutions.

Unfortunately, regressive traditions and mentalities also exist within black religious institutions that promote sexual violence. One of these is the use of scripture to demean women and girls. Religious leaders who teach that women are less valuable, less intelligent, and less important than men contribute to violence against women. Some religious leaders teach men and women that within marriage physical, sexual, and verbal violence against women is acceptable when the women is disrespectful in some way. Religious leaders must teach that violence is never acceptable within marriage or outside of marriage.

Another way religious institutions may promote sexual violence is by banning the appointment of females to leadership positions. When women are not a part of the development of an institution's policies and procedures, the institution often ends up ignoring or minimizing the experiences and needs of women. Finally, it is also noteworthy that the response of religious leaders within the community when there has been a charge of sexual violence by black men against black women has been one of silence or victim blaming. Consistently religious leaders support the male and require that members support, pray for, and encourage the perpetrator and discount the survivor. This teaches members that black women are liars, whores, or simply are irrelevant and that black men are the true victims. This regressive theology is based on a God who despises or devalues women and that kind of faith will not enable the African American community to heal or to grow.

Scholars

> It was in the seventeenth century that American property law first began supporting the sexual dominance of enslaved Africans by plantation owners—as a means of expanding the value of their investment. In economic terms, blacks were dehumanized to mere objects, and the dollar value obtainable for us was enhanced by our ability to readily reproduce. The offspring from the rape of enslaved African women made slave owners wealthier, and so sexual violence was permitted and promoted early on in our American experience. As a matter of law, both black women and men were customarily violated sexually as a result of this legislation. Furthermore, blacks had no legal recourse for rape until long after slavery was abolished.
>
> **Bryonn Bain, law student and poet**

All too often, scholarship concerning sexual assault is written by women. Progressive black male sociologists, psychologists, and political scientists examine the realities of rape in their work. They conduct research, create theories, and evaluate programs around antirape constructs, attitudes, and behaviors. Some progressive black male scholars are already doing this work, but many more are needed. Just as racism is not a problem for blacks to solve alone, rape is not a problem for women to solve alone. Collaboration is a requirement for the cure. There has been enough gender division, distrust, and antagonism within the black community. To tackle major issues such as racism and rape, sisters and brothers must work together. It is through sustained dialogue and relationship that we will find our voices and our healing. Those who by profession study issues of mediation, justice, violence, and community must play an active role in this process.

Hip-Hop Artists

> Dr. King spoke over thirty years ago about the deafening silence of the moral majority. His argument posits that those who advocate evil are vocal while those on the side of justice are mute. Black men who sit silently by while our women are defamed in videos, disrespected in movies, and degraded in barber shops have a responsibility to speak up on behalf of their daughters, mothers, wives, and sisters. There are rules of the street in the arena of the illegal; black men must cultivate rules of the street in the dimension of the immoral. The old

adage is true: if you're not a part of the solution, you are a part of the problem.

Reverend Jamal H. Bryant, founder and pastor,
Empowerment Temple

Progressive black male artists have lyrics and videos that articulate the realities of sexual violence. Some artists have addressed such issues as incest and rape, but only a few. Hip hop is a powerful communication device that is able to spread messages both nationally and internationally. Artists have a divine mandate to speak truth to power. Artists are not politicians searching for votes, although some artists are focused solely on selling CDs and making their way up the music charts. The authentic gift of artists, however, is their ability to get people to see reality and to see the possibility of transforming reality. In various hip-hop songs, the artists share their dreams and realities, from gangsta rap dreams for material wealth to socially conscious rap dreams of racial justice. This is a call, however, for more hip-hop artists to name the realities of rape as well as the possibility of creating an antirape society.

Some dynamics within certain rap lyrics and videos currently promote sexual violence. These include threats to sodomize and to rape women and men. A number of lyrics and videos also objectify women and girls. In addition a few rap artists have talked specifically about the desire to be with underage girls and have written lyrics that promote using coercion and physical force to obtain sexual pleasure. Members of the African American community need to take into account the appropriate response to such music and to the rap artists charged and convicted of sexual violence. Often the community has defended the perpetrator or has ignored the charges at the expense of the survivor, who is most often also a member of the African American community. Some may argue that all music forms include perpetrators of sexual violence. This is true, but since hip hop is the most popular contemporary form of African American music it can and should play an integral role in the healing of our community.

I dream of the day when antirape lyrics come across the radio waves, and little girls and boys dance freely in living rooms, school houses, and block parties, knowing that rape is not tolerated. I want to snap my fingers and bop my head to the sound of my brothers speaking about safety, respect, and consent. I know that this is not an impossible dream. I know that we can and will make videos and songs that are not just about diamonds, cars, and women in bikinis. Considering this call for my brothers who are hip-hop artists, I wrote the following poem.

A Note to My Brothers

Too many kings are posing as pimps
Laying juicy Judas kisses on the community
Taking pride in tricking Queens into selling themselves

For Tim shackles and gold chains
Not realizing that making teenage Queens into hoes
Ties the lynch ropes around their own necks
So where my real kings at?
Cause true soldiers got heart &
True gangsters don't walk in fear
While pimps feel so small they wear their sisters' backs
Like high heel shoes
So where my true kings at?
Walking with the Wisdom of Solomon
Immune to the ignorance of the big Willy shiny apple syndrome
So where my true kings at?
Confident enough to bask in the glory of Nefertiti
Without needing to knock her to her knees
Not needing the booster chair of pride based in platinum
Talkin' bout pimpin' ain't easy
Knowing full well pimpin' is easier than manhood
So where my true kings at?
Feeding their minds with self-knowledge
Feeding their souls with melodies from heaven
Feeding their hearts with the blood of truth
Feeding their people with hope
Standing not as sell-out pimps and hustlers
But making the world marvel at their beautiful manhood
I said where my true kings at?
Not playin' women
But playing the whole notes of a people determined to live
Not focused on blowin' up
But focused on breathing the divine breath of supernatural reality
Not settling for the lazy work of convincing undeveloped minds to undress
Unprotected bodies
But stepping up to the royal plate of nourishing emancipated spirits
Showing their sisters that their dreams are just reality waiting for
Wings
Where my true kings at
Rhymin' about revolution
Freestylin' about true solutions
Investing in our people's evolution
Where you at?
Put your hands up cause
We don't need any more court jesters
Making us the laughingstock of the nation
The pitied generation of the universe

The forgotten peoples of the millennium
We don't need any more clowns
Creating chaos by promoting materialism
To a people hungry for knowledge
So where my true kings at?
Under the clown costumes and lazy lyrics
Your souls stand draped in true royalty
So uncover your minds and free your spirits
My kings arise
We've been holding our breath waiting for you
Staying awake looking for you
Standing on tip toe hoping for you
Praying and crying for you
Through this prolonged midnight
Believing this day would arrive
When you remembered yourself
Stood in your true glory
And sent out the proclamation
Ring the alarm
Our kings have returned
And they're taking no prisoners
Flashback
"I'm not Toby—I'm Kunta Kente"
Flash forward
"I'm not a hot boy or a nigger—a pimp or a hustler
I am King Solomon
Here to bring down Babylon
Restore my people's crown
Bring them up from the ground
I embody the vastness of the night
The depth of the oceans
The might of the earth's core
The mind of the Creator
I have come to myself and
Yesterday was the last day of our kingdom's demise
We are rising up
Past pimp villages to the kingdom of manhood
We are rising up
and all the women exhaled
We are rising up
and all the children laughed
We are rising up
and all the elders whispered "a-sha"

Conclusion

One of the things that is most important in the fight against sexual violence, and I would say this applies especially to the Black community, is to talk about it. Everyone feels uncomfortable talking about sexual violence, as men tense up feeling that they are being attacked. But this is usually only the response in the presence of women. When men are in groups alone, allusion to sexual violence is suddenly somehow acceptable. Often, the achievement of sexual fulfillment becomes the most important thing, and the woman's treatment often comes second. This attitude is proliferated by men who disagree but do not speak out about their disagreement. When there is a group ringleader who is supporting a certain behavior, people often go along with that behavior without giving a second thought. This practice leads men to eventually convince themselves that sexual violence is not so bad, that it is actually a rather popular thing to do. But if there is just one man in the group who will stand against the viewpoint, who speaks what he knows is right, who will stand and say that sexual violence is wrong and it is not at all acceptable, most of the men present will give the issue some thought, and come to the same conclusion. It is all a matter of stopping men from following the wrong leadership and getting them to reach within themselves for the right answers, which most of them already know.

Michael Jenkins, college student and sexual health peer educator

Sexual violence is prevalent in the African American community, as it is in other communities. The fight against sexual violence needs to be adopted by black men and women. Progressive black men examine their own conceptions of power, sex, relationships, respect, and justice. Progressive black men make mutuality and reciprocity a necessary part of their relationships. They support consensual and respectful sexual expression between adults. They reject and speak out against forced sexual contact, whether the force is by violence, threat, or manipulation. Progressive black men also stand against the sexual violation of children, including adolescents. My hope is for the eradication of sexual violence, which depends on the community of black men and women who are committed to restoring the wholeness of our people. Certainly we have been bruised by slavery, lynching, rape, and contemporary racial stereotypes, but we cannot allow those scars to permit us to wound each other. Enough is enough. Progressive black men will not allow fear or shame to silence them about the truth of sexual violence. They are courageous enough to shatter the silence—they are strong enough to demand healing and justice. The reality of sexual violence makes me cringe, but the landscape of brothers and sisters speaking, rapping, singing, preaching, and organizing gives me hope.

Recommended Reading

Akbar, Na'im. *Chains and Images of Psychological Slavery*. Jersey City, NJ: Mind Productions and Associates, 1984.

———. *The Community of Self*, rev. ed. Tallahassee, FL: Productions and Associates, Inc., 1985.

Bryant-Davis, Thema. *Thriving in the Wake of Trauma: A Multicultural Guide*. Westport, CT: Praeger Press, 2005.

Collins, Patricia Hill. *Black Feminist Thought*. New York: Routledge, 2000.

Gunning, Sandra. *Race, Rape, and Lynching*. New York: Oxford University Press, 1996.

hooks, bell. *Ain't I a Woman: Black Women and Feminism*. Boston: South End Press, 1981.

Franklin, Anderson. *From Brotherhood to Manhood: How Black Men Rescue Their Relationships and Dreams from the Invisibility Syndrome*. New York: Wiley & Sons, 2004.

Majors, Richard, and Janet Billson. *Cool Pose: The Dilemmas of Black Manhood in America*. New York: Lexington Books, 1992.

Pierce-Baker, Charlotte. *Surviving the Silence: Black Women and Rape*. New York: W.W. Norton and Company, 1990.

West, Carolyn. *Violence in the Lives of Black Women: Battered, Black, and Blue*. Binghamton, NY: Haworth Press, 2002.

Wyatt, Gail. *Stolen Women: Reclaiming Our Sexuality, Taking Back Our Lives*. New York: Wiley & Sons, 1997.

15

Bringing Up Daddy: A Progressive Black Masculine Fatherhood?

MARK ANTHONY NEAL

My wife, Gloria, and I were heartbroken. I was at a conference in Houston, Texas, when she finally got through to me by cell phone to tell me the news that all potential adoptive parents dread. Folk privy to the adoption process are all too familiar with the possibility that at the last hour, a woman, who months earlier agreed to give her unborn child up for adoption, will take one look at her newborn baby and change her mind. My wife and I kept our impending adoption a secret from just about everyone including parents, close friends, and even our then-four-year-old daughter for that very reason. So there I was alone, on the brink of tears, walking through an FAO Schwarz toy store in Houston, looking at the toys and stuffed animals I was not going to buy for our newborn daughter. I was also relieved. Camille Monet, as we had planned to name the newborn girl, was to be our second adopted child. My wife and I had talked for some time about adopting a second child, but the reality was that I was not looking forward to having another baby in the house. The often-prohibitive cost of adoption conspired to keep Misha Gabrielle our only child, and I looked forward to giving her all of the love and support that comes with being an only child—as I am. My ambivalence about adopting a second child caused me to revisit my hesitancy to adopt four years earlier.

My wife and I were among the millions of couples whose difficulties with conception meant hours of testing, manufactured copulation, and the prospect of costly in vitro fertilization, none of which guaranteed that we would become pregnant. Though I had resisted—ignored, really—my wife's suggestion that we consider adoption, I finally relented and agreed to take a look-see at the process. Adoption was always a last resort and one that I was prepared to let be just that, as we waited for the research around in vitro fertilization to improve to the point that it was more of a viable option for us. In our early thirties then, my wife was unwilling to wait and in one tear-filled episode finally convinced me that adoption was our only option. At the time I guess I was like so many black men, who view the process of getting a woman pregnant as an affirmation of our masculinity—think of how many black men describe their kids as their seeds—particularly in a society that has historically denied us the fullest expression of our masculinity. Thus, the idea that I could not produce a seed somehow meant that something was wrong with me, that I was less than a man. As Thaddeus Goodavage rhetorically asked about the impact of adoption on black men, "How does a Black man, already disaffirmed and demasculated by the wider society, affirm his own manhood when he cannot create, produce, or sustain anything, even children?"[1] As long as we did not adopt, I could always say that our childlessness was a lifestyle choice.

My visions of fatherhood, and manhood for that matter, were naturally influenced by the black man I called *Daddy*. Old-school in every sense of the word, from his Georgia-bred slowness and assortment of Old Spice bottles, to the way he counted his money (in the dark while my mother and I slept), I cannot say that my father taught me anything about fatherhood other than the fact that a good father—a good man—put in a day's work and provided for his family. Legal scholar Nancy E. Dowd observed that "the most critical way of proving one's masculinity is by being an economic provider, and it is precisely in that respect that Black men are denied the means to be men in traditional terms."[2] And that was indeed a mantra for my father, who through most of my childhood trekked three hours back and forth to work every day from the Bronx to Brooklyn, where he worked twelve-hour days, six days a week as a short-order cook and dishwasher at a combination drugstore and grill in Crown Heights. On most days, Daddy was out of the house before I woke and did not get home until I was fast asleep. Save Friday and Saturday nights in the summer, when he allowed me to walk with him to the bodega to get beer, cigarettes, pork rinds, and the Hostess cupcakes I craved and the Sunday mornings when he shared the sounds of the Mighty Clouds of Joy, The Dixie Hummingbirds, B. B. King, and Bobby "Blue" Bland with me and allowed me to help him with Sunday morning breakfast, I cannot say that I remember my father as a parenting presence. Certainly he was of a generation of men who accepted that things like changing diapers, boiling bottles, and making formula were considered women's work. And my mother held out no other expectations of him, save the occasional request to mop the kitchen floor or to wash the dishes.

Because adoption caused me to reassess my ideas of what black manhood meant—as if our only value in the world was to get women pregnant, to make money, and to provide patriarchal leadership in our families and communities—I was also forced to reconsider what roles fathers play in the parenting process.

Sociologist Sandra Walker acknowledged, "When children see their father wash dishes, clothes, and become involved in school activities, it presents a broader and more positive picture of what a black man can be."[3] Though I had considered myself a feminist long before I became a father, it was the birth and adoption of my daughter that forced me to understand that a shared parenting process was as important as notions that women should get equal pay for equal work. We give children very little credit for being able to discern that the division of labor between Mommy and Daddy in the household is often reflective of the value accorded Mommy and Daddy in the real world. Thus, a woman's work is that of the professional nurturer, whether at home, at child-care facilities, at primary schooling, or in the workforce.

Examining the impact child-care activities can have on men, sociologist Scott Coltrane argued that "given women's biological capacity to bear and nurse children, men's participation in early childcare necessarily entails a minimum level of male–female cooperation. Sharing child-rearing tasks probably creates expectations for male–female cooperation in other, more public, activities and may enhance women's opportunities to exercise public authority."[4] Not only does the sharing of child-care activities help provide a more egalitarian view of how can gender function in the real world, but it also has the potential to help young children embrace those views. My daughter, for example, has never expressed the idea that there are things Daddy does or Mommy does, because she sees us sharing or rotating everyday child-care activities—though that has not kept her from expressing a preference for my wife's cooking ("Daddy, you always make chicken!").

It certainly was not easy. I have never been dutiful about picking up after myself, and my wife has always had to prod me—sometimes under threats of violence—to do things like mop the kitchen floor or even take out the trash. And I guess that somewhere in my upbringing I accepted that housework, including child care, was the kind of domestic work naturally assigned to the women in the house. Virtually every family-oriented television show I have watched over the last forty years, from *I Love Lucy* to *Roseanne*, confirms the perception that women were naturally endowed domestics, giving some support to my mother's quips during my childhood that she was more than a glorified maid. Sociologists Coltrane and Masako Ishii-Kuntz suggested that there are specific contexts when men begin to wrap their heads around the concept of shared domestic work, notably when husbands and wives delay having children and "in response to the husband's ideology and time availability." According to the researchers, "husbands' less traditional gender/family ideology and fewer employment hours were strong predictors of their performing more mundane and routine family work."[5] In the context of my own life my views as a feminist and my career as a writer and academic provided the circumstances in which I was at least open to the idea of sharing mundane housework when my wife and I first decided to adopt.

Saving Daddy

In steps our brown-skinned shortie, and spending only a few short months with her after which it became clear that we had a diva on our hands, was affectionately referred to as the "baby-girl diva." No one ever believes our story, but less than one month—twenty-five days officially—from the time we walked into the adoption agency, got a few brochures, and took home an application, we brought seventeen-day-old Misha Gabrielle into our home. The quickness of the adoption process is in part due to that tragic state of black adoption: Potential white parents often wait as long as three years—hence the sudden focus on interracial adoption, particularly of Asian newborns—whereas newborn black babies often languish for months in foster care until adoptive parents are found. Needless to say, we were—especially me—absolutely unprepared for parenthood. To be honest, I had come to enjoy the freedom our childless existence allowed, and as an up-and-coming black scholar I relished the time I could spend in Starbucks getting my "read and write" on. My wife sensed very early after we were made aware of Misha's birth and the possibility that we could adopt her that I was hesitant and issued to me an ultimatum that shall remain unrepeated—my wife has a gift for witty venom.

Misha Gabrielle was born a preemie and came into the world three weeks before she was supposed to be here. I was in the car one day listening to N'dea Davenport's "Placement for the Baby," a song about adoption whose lyrics I really had not listened closely to, and I literally broke down thinking about what kind of spirit this baby girl possessed that she willed herself into the world three weeks early. It was like she knew we were the adoptive parents she was supposed to be with and forced herself into the world before schedule, just so we would be the ones to adopt her. It was the first glimpse I would have of the baby-girl diva's independent spirit and the first of many life lessons she would teach me during her now seven-year-old life. In the classic narratives associated with adoption, it is always about what the adoptive parents bring to the table, as they are often seen as rescuing a child, particularly black children, from a life of poverty and neglect. But with Misha Gabrielle it has always been about what she brings to the table. I can honestly say that she has fundamentally changed my life. The very spirit that brought her into the world early she brought to her role as my daughter as if it were her ordained duty to make me an engaged father and a better man.

But Misha's impact on me was so much deeper. Yes, she has made me a better man, but she also saved my life. For more than a decade I had suffered with what could only be described as an earth-shattering snore. Soon that snoring was accompanied by sudden waking episodes during my nighttime sleep followed by morning headaches. It was only when I began inexplicably falling asleep during the course of the day that I gave any thought that perhaps something was awry. By the time Misha was in the mix I was deep in the throes of a ginseng addiction, somehow believing that my sleeping and waking problems were the product of undernourishing my over-250-pound frame. Unbeknownst to me at the time, I had all the classic signs of sleep apnea (apnea is Greek for "without breath"), a condition in which folks awake suddenly from their sleep several times a night after they have stopped breathing for small periods of time, often as long as a minute. The disease causes a restless sleep, which the body attempts to compensate for during the course of the day through unplanned naps while those who suffer from the disease sit quietly behind a desk, watch television on the couch, and perhaps most tragically are behind the wheels of moving vehicles. According to the American Sleep Apnea Association an estimated ten million Americans have unrecognized sleep apnea.[6] What this all meant for me was that when my sleep apnea was combined with the general sleeplessness that comes with having a newborn in the house, I was for all intents a walking zombie.

I have vivid memories of two early morning feedings with my daughter, then still very much an infant, where I fell asleep only to awaken a half-hour later with her fast asleep on the floor where I had apparently dropped her. (I just got around to sharing that story with my wife about a year ago.) At four or five months old my rather precocious daughter was apparently already hip to the deal and would often smack me across the face when I fell asleep while we played on the couch. The stories of Mark falling asleep mid-conversation or snoring loud enough to be heard across the street were humorous at the time but were no longer funny when my still-undiagnosed sleep apnea often caused me to doze off while behind the wheel of the car. Since my daughter's child care was five minutes from the campus where I taught at the time, it meant that most often she was in the car with me as I struggled to stay awake. After a small fender bender, I finally got serious about the sleep problem and went to the local sleep center to be tested. Shortly thereafter, I was hooked up to an array of apparatuses, and my sleep was monitored overnight. The morning after my sleep patterns were monitored, the attending technician informed me that I had seven hundred apneic events. I stopped breathing seven hundred times during the course of a six-hour sleep. In other words, I had a severe case of sleep apnea, one that if left untreated would likely end up with me having a heart attack or stroke while still in my early thirties. Sleep apnea is caused when air passages are closed shut during sleep, causing those afflicted with the condition to gasp for air during their sleep, hence the loud snoring sounds and sudden waking. Sleep apnea is generally caused by obesity. Men, people with large necks, and young African Americans are part of the likely at-risk group. Besides daytime drowsiness, there is a noticeable drop-off in motor skills, short-term memory, and the development of a less-than-engaging personal disposition.

Having been together for more than ten years at the time, my wife often commented that I had changed. It is a comment, along with complaints of snoring, often made by the partners of those who suffer from severe cases of sleep apnea. A few months after my sleep test I began receiving treatment for my sleep apnea. Treatment meant wearing a mask to bed, even during quick naps. The mask is connected to a machine known as a continuous positive airway pressure (CPAP), which pushes air into my nose, keeping my air passages open and allowing me to have a restful sleep. The machine is small enough to fit in a shoulder bag, thus making it easy to travel with. When on business trips, very often the first thing I do when I get to a hotel is to identify an outlet close to the bed to plug in my CPAP. The morning after I was first hooked up the CPAP I remember telling my wife that it was like I had been born again. My doctor at the sleep center cautioned that a significant number of folks do not recover sufficiently because they do not consistently use the machine because of discomfort and other factors including forgetfulness. I can honestly say that after that first night of sleep, I cannot imagine ever being without my CPAP. In the months after I began treatment it was like Misha and I were both newborns trying to make sense of the world. In my mind, I should have died while Misha was still a baby, but my life was saved by a little brown girl who willed herself into the world and then willed herself into her daddy's heart. What did my wife and I bring to the table? Yeah, we brought a stable home and a loving environment, but it was my daughter who brought me life.

Father Bias

In the context of all of these events, I really began to take the idea of father-hood, even in a traditional sense, very seriously. The demands of my wife's own professional career often meant that I could not simply see myself as a part-time babysitter—as one brother once described spending time with his kids—or the one who just picked up our daughter from school—the kinds of things that most fathers do regularly at one time or another—but rather as a conurturer. I remember the very first day my wife left me alone with Misha. Gloria had returned to work after taking a month-long maternity leave, and we decided that on the days I did not teach I would stay home with Misha instead of sending her to day care. I remember meticulously picking out the music that I wanted her to listen to as we sat at home that day, beginning with Marvin Gaye and Tammi Terrell's "Ain't No Mountain High Enough" and "You're All I Need to Get By," which I quietly sang in her tiny ear. Truth be told, once the romance died off, it was something that I could not sustain—the sleep apnea was kicking my ass—and months later Misha was in day care full time. Nevertheless, for most of my daughter's life I have prepared the family dinner, have done the grocery shopping, have given her nightly baths, and have put her down to sleep at night, things I can rarely remember my own father doing. Granted, my dad's work schedule made such things impossi-ble, but as I noted, there was never an expectation that he would be a more engaged parent. Both my parents were the products of a generation of people who really believed that black men were incapable of playing such a role, so even when those women felt imposed upon at times, there was little drama. I am not saying that all black families functioned this way thirty years ago, but it was clearly an accepted trend.

The fact that so many black fathers were not expected to be involved fathers speaks to an underlying father bias that exists in the larger society and often discourages men from playing such roles. In their book *Throwaway Dads,* child psychologists Ross D. Parke and Armin A. Brott observed that stereotypes that "dads are lazy, dangerous, biologically unfit or deadbeats powerfully shapes our impressions about fathers."[7] The authors also noted that within children's literature, "fathers, if they're shown at all, are generally portrayed as indifferent, uncaring, buffoonish characters who do little more than come home late after work and bounce baby around for five minutes before putting her to bed."[8] For example, the very reason we all found a film like Eddie Murphy's *Daddy Day Care* so damn funny was because the idea that a group of men would run a child-care facility is utterly preposterous to our sensibilities. Yes, the men in the film were challenged to run a day-care facility, as any novice child-care worker would be regardless of gender, but the subtext of the film was that we found these men incapable of being engaged fathers. Because of my flexible work hours as a college professor and writer, I was often the one charged with day-care duty and sick days, and it was during those many, many hours riding around in my old Honda Accord listening to *Veggie Tales* tapes and the music of Lenny Kravitz or sitting in Starbucks reading Faith Ringgold picture books—*Tar Beach* in particular—or any of the books in David Kirk's *Miss Spider* series—Miss Spider was adopted—or playing tackle in the living room that we formed the ultimate father–daughter bond. I began to refer to her as my "soul sister." But also in this context I began to deal firsthand with issues of father bias.

I have found myself offended, for example, on occasions when folks assume that the time I put in with and for my daughter is somehow an aberration. There are times when I go into children's clothing stores—*Children's Place* is a favorite of mine—to buy a cute pair of shoes or a sweater for my daughter, and the salesperson doggedly asks me if I need help (the assumption being that I could not possibly know anything about children's sizes, let alone the clothing size of my own child and no doubt complicated by the fact that I am black) or if I want a gift box, as if the only reason a man would be in a store like that was because he was buying a gift. Then there are the day-care providers who never feel the need the share the intricacies of my daughter's day but offer them gratuitously to my wife whenever she picks Misha up. In his book *The Nurturing Father*, Kyle D. Pruett observed the ways fathers are sometimes treated when they accompany their children to doctor's appointments. As one pediatrician told Pruett, "I just thought the father was doing the 'well-baby visit' as an interested escort."[9] And then there are the subtleties, like the general lack of baby-changing stations in men's public restrooms or the great drama of being the only man—and more often than not the only black—in a room full of mothers at my daughter's various extracurricular activities. Political scientist and feminist dad Isaac Balbus recalled his feelings while accompanying his daughter once to her weekly playgroup: "I feared that a male would not be entirely welcome at an otherwise entirely female affair. This was 'women's space' into which I was not inclined to intrude. I was received cordially, but it seemed to me that there was little, if anything, to talk about."[10] And like Balbus, I am cordially received, but there is also a discomfort, likely informed by the fact that most of the white women in the room have rarely had a conversation with a black man who was not serving them in some capacity.

Even worse are folk who want to bestow the Nobel Peace Prize of parenting on me simply because they have never seen a black man as a good parent. When the wife of one of my colleagues once remarked to me that she had never seen a man so attentive to his child, I was not quite sure whether she was talking about men in general or black men in particular, especially because I saw her husband as a man who was particularly attentive to his son. Throughout their book Parke and Brott often compared the stereotypical treatment that fathers face in American society to that of African Americans, arguing that "it's humiliating, degrading, and ultimately psychologically damaging."[11] Although I would challenge the full weight of such a comparison, what does their analysis say about the ways society views black fathers? And I have to admit that at times I have to resist patting myself on the back for doing the kinds of things society would have us believe black men were genetically challenged to do. What I do is not exceptional; it comes with the territory of being a parent in the twenty-first century. When I talk with so many of my friends and colleagues who are fathers—half of my conversations with fellow hip-hop scholar S. Craig Watkins are about our daughters—or see the number of public figures who alter their lifestyles so their children can be part of their professional lives, I realize that many black men are dramatically altering the larger society's views of black men as parents.

Black Men as Nurturing Fathers

One good example of this trend of public figures altering their lifestyles to nurture their children is baseball manager Dusty Baker and his relationship with his young son, Darren. When managing the San Francisco Giants a few years ago, Baker allowed the children of his players—most often boys—to have a visible presence in the clubhouse and in the dugout. The sons of a few of his players at the time, including Barry Bonds's son, Nikolai, and Darren Baker, rotated as team batboys. In the eyes of many, the normally surly Bonds became human—even endearing—as he kissed his son, Nikolai, at home plate after hitting home runs. But Darren Baker, only three years old when he served as the Giants' batboy in the last two months of 2002, was the most endearing. Dusty Baker's parenting skills, however, were called into question during the 2002 World Series, when Darren ran out on the field during a game. The young boy was saved from being in the middle of a possible collision at home plate when the Giants' J. T. Snow grabbed him by the back of his collar and pulled him out of danger.

At the time of the incident Baker was fifty-three years old and less than a year removed from a bout with prostate cancer. Given his career he understood he was not always going to be around to be a regular presence in his young son's life, so he instead chose to have his son come to work with him, particularly in the years before Darren was of school age.[12] The first thing Baker did, after the Giants lost the final game of the 2002 World Series, was to reach down and console his crying son. It is the kind of image of black fathers we rarely see in American society.

Unknown to many folks though, Baker's decision to have Darren around may have also been in response to his own estranged relationship with his father earlier in his baseball career. Johnny Baker, Sr., had been an influence on Dusty Baker as a youth, often coaching him in Little League, but the two fell out when the younger Baker was drafted by the Atlanta Braves in 1967 and signed a contract with the team against his father's wishes. When his father attempted to challenge the signing in court, Dusty Baker cut his ties with him. As a seventeen-year-old playing professional sports and being away from his family for the first time, Baker sought out another father figure, finding him in the figure of Henry Aaron. When Aaron went through a divorce and lamented about missing his children, Baker reevaluated his relationship with his father. According to sportswriter Tom Stanton, "For years, Baker had little or nothing to do with his father. He didn't call him, and he didn't include him in his life … . But seeing how much Aaron missed his children helped open his eyes, and it was one of the factors among several that led him to reconnect with his own father."[13] The weekend after the San Francisco Giants lost the 2002 World Series, Dusty Baker accompanied his then-seventy-seven-year-old father to a Notre Dame football game, telling reporters, "It's something he always wanted to do."[14] Dusty Baker's relationship with his father and son highlight the significance American society, and black communities specifically, have placed on the relationship between fathers and their sons and on fatherhood and masculinity. As Goodavage asserted, "Fathering a biological son provides a certain space to celebrate intergenerationally and genetically. In the elite context of biological father–son relationships, maleness—that sacrosanct quality grounded on falsely constructed notions of power—moves along uncriticized, as father essentially remakes himself in another who closely resembles him."[15] Journalist Jonetta Rose Barras, who examined fatherlessness in the lives of black women in her book *Whatever Happened to Daddy's Little Girl?*, adds that "most of the data on fatherlessness in America captures the effect on boys and men, little of it references girls and women."[16] I have no qualms with celebrating the impact engaged black fathers have on their sons, but the patriarchal focus of those relationships often obscures the impact black fathers can and do have on their daughters. In this case I am not just talking about little black girls seeing their fathers as strong, protective, and responsive to their needs and to the needs of their family and community, which are absolutely laudable attributes for any daughter to have access to. Instead, I mean a black fatherhood that attempts to embody, to the extent that a man can, the realities of being a young black girl and woman in American society. In other words, I am calling for a black feminist fatherhood that not only has an impact on the lives of black girls and women but also is tied to a reconsideration of what black masculinity can be.

In her book *Redefining Fatherhood,* Dowd argued that "men's identities as fathers do not exist in isolation from their identities as men. Indeed, that broader masculine identity arguably poses the most difficult challenge to a redefined and differently lived fatherhood. As long as masculinity identifies nurture and care as feminine and unmanly, men's socialization will work against them rather than for them."[17] Other scholars and psychologists also support the notion that fathers must embrace the idea of being a nurturer. According to Pruett, "The only way for many men to find nurturing quality in themselves is to stop restricting and strangling it—to allow it to come forward," adding that "a father may embrace his children, but until he embraces his own unique, irreplaceable value to them as a parent, he does not have as much in his arms as he thinks."[18] Psychologist Louise Silverstein took it a step further, arguing that the "experience of nurturing and caring for young children has the power to change the cultural construction of masculinity into something less coercive and oppressive for both women and men."[19]

Many black women have discussed the importance of their relationships with their fathers, particularly in the context of their father's absences, because of work or other more dramatic issues. Qubilah Shabazz, who witnessed the assassination of her father, Malcolm X (El-Hajj Malik El-Shabazz) in 1965, sweetly recalled her father's presence: "He almost had me convinced that I was made up of brown sugar …. Every morning, he'd take my finger and stir his coffee with my finger. He said it was to sweeten it up."[20] In her book *When Chickenheads Come Home to Roost: My Life as a Hip-Hop Feminist,* journalist and critic Joan Morgan wrote, "From the ages of four to seven I cried inconsolably each time my father left the house. No one knew quite what to make of this. I was too young to understand the dangers that lurked outside our South Bronx apartment, and because my father didn't keep odd, inexplicable hours, my tantrums were dismissed as the unbridled passion of first love."[21] Reflecting on her own childhood of fatherlessness, Jonetta Rose Barras wrote that a "girl abandoned by the first man in her life forever entertains powerful feelings of being unworthy or incapable of receiving any man's love. Even when she receives love from another, she is constantly and intensely fearful of losing it. This is the anxiety, the pain, of losing one father. I had three fathers toss me aside."[22]

In many ways, Barras's admission helps highlight the common thinking that young black girls and women are in need of strong patriarchal figures in their life, but there are other examples of black women who discuss the absence of black fathers in their lives in ways that speak more broadly to the impact of nurturance. For example, even though the parents of literary scholar and activist Sharon Patricia Holland divorced when she was seven years old and her father, who was a doctor, was not always a presence in her life, she recalled a time when "this woman came in because her daughter was bleeding uncontrollably. My Dad treated her, called the ambulance and when the woman tried to pay him, he put his hand around hers and held her. I'll never forget that moment—although I knew he wasn't always there for me—I also knew that he was caring about black women often left behind by their families, communities and the District of Columbia. I carry that image of him with me and conjure it often—especially in those moments when I want to walk away, or when I want to be angry at him for something."[23] Morgan recalled a father who was "a serious womanizer" and "pretty chauvinistic in some senses when it came to mom, he totally didn't support her dreams and visions of higher education, travel...and expected total support for his. And I can honestly say he is the source of all of my abandonment and commitment issues of which I have many." But she admitted, "On the other hand, he adored me and there is something to be said for being a daddy's girl ... . And he really believed, or at least made me believe I could be prime minister of Jamaica one day if I wanted and I think he would have really been thrilled if I'd gone to law school and went into politics. I NEVER got the message that I couldn't do anything because 1 was a girl."[24]

Parke and Brott argued that girls have "a lot to gain emotionally, socially, intellectually, and psychologically from greater contact with their fathers."[25] This point is reinforced by Nicole Johnson, who said, "I can't imagine who I would be without my father...my father was my primary caretaker from about 2–4 [years of age] because he worked nights ... . I consider my father one of my best friends," adding that "he has always been accessible to me .... He always told me the truth even when I didn't want to hear it [and] he had faith in the way he raised me to go out in the world and not mess up too much."[26] Literary scholar Daphne Brooks was even more specific about the role her father, a public school administrator and activist, had on her intellectual development. According to Brooks, "[My father] was my first and most brilliant professor, and he taught me the meaning of words, of intellectual power, African-American history, literature, and culture. He recognized the critical importance of how black people in particular might use language as a tool for transformation ... . He and my mom gave me the courage to write, to dream, to imagine." She added, "I know that my voice as a scholar and as a writer is that of my father's. Daddy always encouraged me to make my voice heard, to use my voice and my love of writing as an instrument for change."[27] One reason why nurturing fathers tend to have the kinds of impact on their daughters that both Johnson and Brooks's fathers did on them is because they often offer their daughters more open space to develop beyond traditional gender roles. For example, Coltrane noted that traditional fathers "tend to sex-type their children, overstimulate infants, and engage in rough and tumble play," and "caretaking fathers tend to interact verbally with their children, allow for self-direction, and treat sons and daughters similarly."[28] Indeed, my wife often blames Misha's verbosity on me: too many lectures attended, too many interviews overheard, and too many complex ruminations on the most simplistic of things. And I would be lying if I did not admit that I do want to recreate myself in my daughter, encouraging in her love of words, art, music, and creativity.

Black men seeing themselves as nurturing fathers is only the beginning of a process in which a progressive black masculine fatherhood can be realized. Using Pruett's logic here, it is about black fathers seeing themselves as having something unique and important to offer to their sons and daughters that will productively influence their lives as boys and later men and girls who later become women.

Part of my role as a so-called feminist father, as a progressive father, is to encourage Misha to do the kinds of things she wants—within reason—regardless of whether the larger society finds such things strange for a little girl. Nowhere has this been more explicit than with Misha's verbal skills. In this case I am not simply talking about her ability to express herself verbally but about her comfort in saying anything that reflects her desires and feelings at any given time; admittedly, it is something about which my wife and I sometimes disagree. My wife and I were both raised in families in which children just did not get involved in grown folk conversations. But in the spirit of a feminism that speaks back, I have thought it important for Misha to indeed speak back to whatever, with the caveat that she remain respectful. I would be lying if I said there were times when her ability to speak back has not been absolutely maddening and exasperating, but I also realize how well this will serve her as a young woman. Parke and Brott noted the importance of such a strategy, stating that "girls whose fathers play with them a lot, for example, tend to be more popular with their peers and more assertive in their interpersonal relationships throughout their lives."[29] The researchers also cite further evidence that "extremely competent and successful women frequently recall their fathers as active and encouraging, playful and exciting."[30] Ironically, both my wife and my mother-in-law possess sarcastic wits that suggest they, too, understand the importance of women being able to speak back to the world.

But even as I pursue the idea of a progressive black fatherhood, I admittedly am driven by the very issues that drive most responsible fathers, like the examples of my father and late father-in-law. Thus, there are so many moments where I am literally frozen by the fear of not being able to provide economically for my family. Though I make a fairly comfortable living as a writer and academic—most comfortable because of my flexible schedule—my fear of not providing, in collaboration with the overachiever in me, often means I struggle mightily with the tensions of being on my grind and being a progressive daddy. According to Silverstein, this tension "addresses one of the paradoxes of patriarchal society in that although fathers have had enormous economic power over their children, they have remained emotionally isolated from the intimate relationships of family life."[31] I still struggle with this notion of intimacy with my daughter and wife, though my ability to come to terms with its importance has manifested itself in my hyperawareness of my mortality. That same fear of not being able to provide for my family is often expressed in the fear of dying suddenly and not being around for my family, particularly my daughter. As for so many Americans, the tragedy of September 11, 2001, was a reminder of just how fleeting life can be. Some of my most cherished memories of being a father are of trying to protect Misha from any knowledge of the attacks and any knowledge that the world in which she would grow up had changed in serious and fundamental ways. In this way, my fears underlie an urgency I now feel as a father, fears that often manifest themselves in a commitment to creating moments where I can truly be that engaged, nurturing, and, yes, progressive father.

Yet there is still that small part of me that cannot help but think about Misha as simply daddy's little girl, something I am reminded of when I break down in tears, virtually every time I hear Johnny Hartman's vocal rendition of Bill Evans's 'Waltz for Debby": "In her own sweet world/populated by dolls and clowns and a prince and a big purple bear/lives my favorite girl, unaware of worried frowns that we weary grownups all wear." Ironically, Misha came to a sense of feminism on her own, courtesy of a Disney Channel production of all things. *Cheetah Girls* was based on a series of 'tween novels written by journalist Deborah Gregory that focus on five teenage girls of color living in New York City. The film featured Raven (Symone) and singing group 3LW members Adrienne Bailon and Kiely Williams. "Girl Power" and "Cinderella" were two of the songs featured on the film's soundtrack. The former celebrated the potential of little brown girls ("Throw your hands Up/if you know that you're a star"), but it was the explicitly feminist "Cinderella" that captivated Misha. Taking aim at *Cinderella,* one of the defining myths of childhood femininity, the Cheetah Girls defiantly state that they do not want to be like Cinderella, coyly singing, "I can slay my own dragons...my knight in shining armor is me," and I thought it was such a wonderful sentiment to pass on to little girls in a world that encourages them from the time of their birth to seek out a male protector and provider, whether Prince Charming or the baby-daddy around the way. As I rummaged through Misha's CD collection one day trying to find her *Cheetah Girls* CD, she asked why I was looking for it, and before I could answer she said, "I know you want to listen to it, Daddy, because it's cool." I could not help thinking to myself, "Yes, baby-girl, brown girl feminism is cool."

In her essay "Fathering Is a Feminist Issue" Silverstein made explicit connections between fatherhood and feminism, suggesting that "redefining fathering to reflect a primary emphasis on nurturing and caretaking, as well as providing, is the next necessary phase in the continuing feminist transformation of patriarchal culture for the benefit of women as well as men."[32]

Nurturing in a Patriarchal World: The R. Kelly Case

Silverstein's assertion became most clear to me when my role as a nurturing father—a feminist or progressive father—ran into conflict with my career as a music journalist. For some time I had been a strong supporter of R&B vocalist R. Kelly, arguing in my book *Soul Babies: Black Popular Culture and the Post-soul Aesthetic* that the artist often functioned in the role of a social critic who "provides meaningful critiques of contemporary black life."[33] But I had to reevaluate my relationship to Kelly and his music when he was indicted on twenty-one counts of child pornography in June 2002.[34] Six months later an additional twelve counts were added. A month after the last set of indictments, Kelly released his sixth CD, *The Chocolate Factory*. Thinking about reviewing the CD for one of the publications for which I wrote, I could not help but think that such a review would make me a criminal, or rather a critical, accomplice.

The indictments against Kelly stem from a series of widely distributed videotapes in which he is purported to have sex with young girls as young as thirteen years of age. Throughout his career, R. Kelly has been haunted by rumors of his rapturous relations with underage girls. His brief marriage to the late Aaliyah in 1994, in which she was fifteen at the time, was just the most visible proof of those rumors. In late 2000, allegations against Kelly became public as two different women alleged that the adult Kelly had sex with them when they were minors. Both women were students at Kenwood Academy in Hyde Park (Chicago), which Kelly also attended as a teen. Kelly settled a suit with another accuser in 1998.[35] By the time the videotape emerged in February 2002—on the eve of Kelly's performance at the opening ceremonies of the Salt Lake City Olympics—a clear pattern had emerged: R. Kelly was likely a pedophile and a child pornographer. In response to the indictments, folks went into celebrity surveillance mode, as Kelly's music, movements, and mediated messages were subject to intense scrutiny. Many urban radio outlets were at the center of the frenetic coverage as program directors were faced with decisions over whether to continue to play Kelly's music. When stories about Kelly's problems surfaced in 2000, Todd Cavanah, the program director at Chicago's WBBM-FM, admitted, "We play hit songs from hit artists that our audience likes, and R. Kelly is one of them."[36] Cavanah's tone was very different when Kelly was indicted two years later and he decided to pull Kelly's music from his station's playlist: "Now that it's a real case, with a grand jury indictment, it's a serious issue … . We have community standards to live up to, and this is the right thing to do." In contrast, Mary Dyson, the general manager at WGCI-FM, also in Chicago, offered, "He's innocent until proven guilty … . At this moment our plan is to continue playing his music."[37]

When bootlegged videos of *R. Kelly Exposed* began to appear on the streets of major cities, and when various links to the so-called R. Kelly sex video began to circulate throughout the Internet, it was clear that folks were more interested in the R. Kelly angle than the well-being of the young girls in the video. Seemingly lost in the exchange of dollars and Internet links was the fact that those folks who sold and bought *R. Kelly Exposed* or who forwarded and opened Internet links, were also trafficking in child pornography. Such oversights are likely to occur within a culture that valued Kelly's celebrity over the lives of the young black girls who accused him of having sexual contact with them. The issue of race was easily glossed over in much of the coverage of Kelly's sexcapades. Mary Mitchell was one of the few commentators who addressed the significance of the racial identity of the girls, writing, "As long as [Kelly] is being accused of having sex with underage black girls, the allegations will draw a collective yawn." In contrast, she wrote, "What would have happened had Kelly gone to an affluent area like Naperville or Winnetka to recruit choir girls…had Kelly been accused of touching a golden hair on just one girl's head, he would have been put under the jail."[38]

And this was part of the irony I considered as I began to write about R. Kelly's *The Chocolate Factory*. What if Kelly had been Justin Timberlake or Eminem? Would the conversation fall back so easily into one where a white man mistreated and exploited—raped?—a young black girl because of his racist views of black women? And of course it did when Benzino (Ray Scott), a marginal hip-hop artist and part owner of the now-defunct magazine *The Source*, tried to incite black audiences against Eminem when a tape that the white rapper made when he was a teenager was unearthed. On the tape he dissed black girls by referring to them as "Adumb."[39] Pearl Cleage addressed such a reality in *Mad at Miles* as she wondered "what if Kenny [G] was revealed to be kicking men's asses all over the country…what if Kenny [G] wrote a book saying that sometimes he had to slap black men around a little just to make them cool out and leave him the fuck alone."[40] For Cleage, the idea that black folks would close ranks around folks who harmed other black folks is unconscionable, be those folks black or white. Not surprisingly, R. Kelly's *Chocolate Factory* sold over 550,000 copies in its first week, making it the number-one recording on the Soundscan chart for the week.

As a long-time fan of Kelly's music I was one of those who purchased the recording. Three of the songs on *Chocolate Factory* were originally slated for *Loveland*. The latter recording was scrapped because of bootlegging. I was forwarded a bootlegged copy of *Loveland* in early 2002 and listened to it regularly, as it was the most mature and sophisticated music of Kelly's career. A favorite of mine was the original version of the song "Step in the Name of Love," a tribute to the stepper-set culture of Kelly's native Chicago. As innocuous as Kelly's "I Believe I Can Fly" or the "Electric Slide," the song quickly became one of Misha's favorites, and very often the two of us could be heard chanting

"Step, step, side to side, round and round, now, dip it now, separate, bring it back, let me see you do the love slide" while bumping down the highway in the car. But one day when Misha asked to hear the song again, it finally struck me that if she was ten years older I would not even want her in same room with R. Kelly. Suddenly it became clear to me that a figure like Kelly posed a threat not only to my daughter but to a host of other daughters. In the aftermath of the disturbing commercial success of Kelly's *Chocolate Factory*—in which I am admittedly implicated—there were even more disturbing moments like when Kelly stood in front of the audience at the Black Entertainment Television Awards in June 2003 to acknowledge the importance of "black folk standing up for each other," as if trying to protect young black girls from pedophiles and other sexual predators is not about standing up for black folk.

No doubt R. Kelly's incredible level of productivity in the aftermath of his indictments has been motivated by escalating legal expenses and calculated payoffs to the families of women who could be called to testify against him in a court of law. There is something terribly insidious about listening to R. Kelly floss about being the "Pied Piper of R&B." For whatever reasons, audiences seem to gravitate toward the man's worst—and least artistic—impulses. So tracks like "The Snake" and "Thoia Thoinga," from his greatest hits package *The R in R&B,* which folks treated as if it was the new jump-off, represent so little of the genius that Kelly is capable of, genius that was powerfully evident on the bootlegged *Loveland.* But paying close attention to the fable to which Kelly attaches himself, folks seem to forget that the piper took off with the town's kids when they did not pay up for his getting rid of the rats. And let us be straight: R. Kelly is making off with our kids, but not necessarily as the thirty-something man-child eyeballing our fourteen-year-old in the plaid skirt but rather as the songwriter and producer of the little shorties that our kids swear are the second coming.

What has made R. Kelly peerless over the last several years is his abilities as a recording artist, songwriter, arranger, and producer. Years ago it was the late Aaliyah and Changing Faces; most recently it has been the Isley Brothers and Ginuwine, but today Kelly is reproducing himself right at the center of black kiddie pop, working with acts like the now-defunct B2K, Marques Houston, Cassidy, Nick Cannon, JS (The Johnson Sisters), and Nivea. Kelly got into the mix with B2K on the group's second disc, *Pandemonium,* producing the track "Bump, Bump, Bump." He also produced the song "Girlfriend," one of the additional tracks on the deluxe upgrade of *Pandemonium* that was released in March 2003. Kelly wisely chose not to appear in many of these videos, including for Nivea's "Laundromat," though he does in fact sing opposite her on that song. A man accused of inappropriate sexual behavior with minors obviously cannot show up in a music video cooing in the ear of a teenager. Kelly's stand-in for the "Laundromat" video was Nick Cannon, of the films *Drumline* and *Love Don't Cost a Thing* and long-time veteran of the Nickelodeon channel.

Like Britney Spears before him and Hillary Duff currently, Cannon is trying to translate kiddie fame into a sustainable career. As a label-mate—both Cannon and Kelly record for Jive—Kelly was more than willing to lend a hand and in fact cast Cannon as the DJ in the video for his song "Ignition (remix)." Perhaps feeling his oats and no doubt feeling all the love pouring from the folks up in the balcony (a metaphor for folks who do not care who you molested but still want to get down), Kelly is very present in Cannon's video "Feeling Freaky," which also featured B2K.

I was in the living room one evening watching the Nickelodeon channel with Misha, when Nick Cannon's image came across the screen. As my daughter yelped, "Look, Daddy, it's Nick Cannon!" I thought about the fact that if she were ten or eleven years old, I probably would have had to take her to the *Scream III* tour Cannon, B2K, and Marques Houston were headlining during summer 2003. But there is indeed something to consider when the music performed at a major kiddie pop tour featured music written and produced by a man accused of sexual relations with underage women. The Pied Piper indeed.

Conclusion

Four-year-old Misha Gabrielle was with my wife and me the day after Thanksgiving 2002 as we sat in a local restaurant. It was our first time out since we heard that we would not be adopting a second child. Symbolically, the day out was an acknowledgment on the part of my wife and me that we were finally moving on from a very painful and disappointing situation. While sitting there, as we thought about using the money we set aside for the adoption to plan a trip to Disney World, we got the call on my cell phone from our lawyer letting us know that the birth mother had again changed her mind and had decided to go ahead with the adoption. Camille Monet has been with us since December 2002, a day before my birthday. These days my notions about my masculinity are firmly tied to how good a parent I am to my two daughters. Despite my hang-ups initially about having a new baby in the house, fatherhood has been a breeze the second time around, and I am more confident than ever in my skills as a father and conurturer. It is me who now asks my wife, "When are we going to adopt the next one?" I am in a house full of women, and I am thinking that it is time to bring a little boy into the mix, if only so that there will be another black boy in the world who will grow up to become an engaged, nurturing, feminist, and, yes, perhaps a progressive black father.

Notes

1. Thaddeus Goodavage, "Are You My Father?" in *Father Songs: Testimonies by African-American Sons and Daughters*, ed. Gloria Wade-Gayles (Boston: Beacon, 1997), 23.
2. Nancy E. Dowd, *Redefining Fatherhood* (New York: New York University Press, 2000), 73.
3. Quoted in Lynn Norment, "They Call Them Mr. Mom: A Growing Number of Black Fathers Raise Daughters and Sons by Themselves," *Ebony*, June 1991, 52.
4. Scott Coltrane, "Father–Child Relationships and the Status of Women: A Cross-Cultural Study," *American Journal of Sociology* 93, no. 5 (March 1988), 1089.

5. Coltrane and Masako Ishii-Kuntz, "Men's Housework: A Life Course Perspective," *Journal of Marriage and the Family* 54, no. 1 (February 1992), 54.
6. See American Sleep Apnea Association, http://www.sleepapnea.org.
7. Ross D. Parke and Armin A. Brott, *Throwaway Dads: The Myths and Barriers that Keep Men from Being the Fathers They Want to Be* (New York: Houghton Mifflin, 1999), 77.
8. Ibid., 78.
9. Quoted in Kyle D. Pruett, *The Nurturing Father* (New York: Warner, 1987), 59.
10. Isaac D. Balbus, *Emotional Rescue: The Theory and Practice of a Feminist Father* (New York: Routledge, 1998), 104.
11. Parke and Brott, *Throwaway Dads*, 101.
12. George Vecsey, "More Bench for Darren This Time," *New York Times*, October 26, 2002, D1.
13. Tom Stanton, *Hank Aaron and the Home Run that Changed America* (New York: Morrow, 2004), 141.
14. Hal Bodley, "Baker Is the Man among Giants," *USA Today*, October 29, 2002, 4C.
15. Goodavage, "Are You My Father?" 22.
16. Jonetta Rose Barras, *Whatever Happened to Daddy's Little Girl?: The Impact of Fatherlessness on Black Women* (New York: Ballantine, 2000), 39.
17. Dowd, *Redefining*, 181.
18. Pruett, *Nurturing*, 281.
19. Louise B. Silverstein, "Fathering Is a Feminist Issue," *Psychology of Women Quarterly* 20 (1996), 31.
20. Quoted in Barras, *Whatever Happened*, 137.
21. Joan Morgan, *When Chickenheads Come Home to Roost: My Life as a Hip-Hop Feminist* (New York: Simon & Schuster, 1999), 126.
22. Barras, *Whatever Happened*, 1.
23. Sharon Patricia Holland, interview with the author, May 10, 2004.
24. Morgan, interview with the author, May 16, 2004.
25. Parke and Brott, *Throwaway Dads*, 10.
26. Nicole Johnson, interview with the author, May 14, 2004.
27. Daphne Brooks, interview with the author, May 21, 2004.
28. Coltrane, "Father–Child Relationships," 1089.
29. Parke and Brott, *Throwaway Dads*, 10.
30. Ibid.
31. Silverstein, "Fathering Is a Feminist Issue," 30.
32. Ibid., 4.
33. Mark Anthony Neal, *Soul Babies: Black Popular Culture and the Post-soul Aesthetic* (New York: Routledge, 2002), 13.
34. Abdon M. Pallasch and Jim DeRogatis, "R&B Superstar Hit with 21 Counts of Child Porn," *Chicago Sun-Times*, June 6, 2002, 6.
35. Jim DeRogatis and Pallasch, "City Police Investigate R&B Singer R. Kelly in Sex Tape," *Chicago Sun-Times*, February 8, 2002, 1.
36. DeRogatis and Pallasch, "R. Kelly Report Sparks Anger," *Chicago Sun-Times*, December 22, 2000, 3.
37. Mary Houlihan, "Kelly Tunes Get Boot at One Station," *Chicago Sun-Times*, June 6, 2002, 8.
38. Mary Mitchell, "Latest Allegation Unlikely to Get Kelly in Big Trouble," *Chicago Sun-Times*, February 14, 2002, 14.
39. Glenn Gaboa, "A War of Words," *Newsday*, New York: December 21, 2003, 22.
40. Pearl Cleage, *Mad at Miles: A Blackwoman's Guide to Truth* (Southfield, MI: Cleage Group, 1990), 20.

Selected Bibliography

Abrams, M. H. *A Glossary of Literary Terms*. 7th ed. New York: Harcourt Brace, 1999.

Akbar, Na'im. *Chains and Images of Psychological Slavery*. Jersey City, NJ: Mind Productions and Associates, 1984.

———. *The Community of Self.*, rev. ed. Tallahassee, FL: Productions and Associates, Inc., 1985.

Akbar, Na'im. *Visions of Black Men*. Nashville: Winston-Derek Publishers, Inc., 1991.

Anderson, Elijah. *Code of the Street: Decency, Violence and the Moral Life of the Inner City*. New York: W. W. Norton, 1999.

———. *Streetwise: Race, Class, and Change in an Urban Community*. Chicago: University of Chicago Press, 1990.

Anderson, Margaret L., and Patricia Hill Collins, eds. *Race, Class, and Gender: An Anthology*. 4th ed. Belmont, CA: Wadsworth, 2001.

Asante, Molefi K. *Afrocentricity*. Buffalo: Amulefi, 1980.

———. "The Afrocentric Idea." In *African American Communication and Identities*, edited by R. Jackson, 16–28. Thousand Oaks, CA: Sage, 2004.

———. *The Afrocentric Idea*. Philadelphia: Temple University Press, 1987.

———. *Erasing Racism*. Amherst, NY: Prometheus Books, 2003.

Baker-Fletcher, Garth Kasimu. *Xodus: An African American Male Journey*. Minneapolis, MN: Fortress Press, 1996.

Baldwin, James. *Nobody Knows My Name*. New York: Vintage, 1993.

bandele, asha. *The Prisoner's Wife: A Memoir*. New York: Scribner, 1999.

Barker, Chris. *Cultural Studies: Theory and Practice*. London: Sage Publications, 2000.

Battle, Juan, Cathy J. Cohen, Dorian Warren, Gerard Fergerson, and Suzette Audam. *Say It Loud, I'm Black and I'm Proud: Black Pride Survey 2000*. New York: Policy Institute of the National Gay and Lesbian Task Force, 2002.

Belton, Don, ed. *Speak My Name: Black Men on Masculinity and the American Dream*. Boston: Beacon Press, 1995.

Bender, Leslie, and Daan Braverman, eds. *Power, Privilege and the Law: A Civil Rights Reader*. St. Paul, MN: West Publishing, 1995.

Blount, Marcellus, and George P. Cunningham, eds. *Representing Black Men*. New York: Routledge, 1996.

Bogle, Donald. *Toms, Coons, Mulattoes, Mammies, and Bucks—An Interpretive History of Blacks in American Films*. New York: Viking Press, 1973.

Bonhoeffer, Dietrich. *The Cost of Discipleship*. New York: Macmillan, 1959.

Bonnell, Victoria E., and Lynn Hunt, eds. *Beyond the Cultural Turn: New Directions in the Study of Society and Culture*. Berkeley: University of California Press, 1999.

Bourdieu, Pierre. *Masculine Domination*. Translated by Richard Nice. Stanford, CA: Stanford University Press, 2001.

Boyd, Herb, and Robert L. Allen. *Brotherman: The Odyssey of Black Men in America*. New York: Ballantine Books, 1995.

Boyd, Stephen B., W. Merle Longwood, and Mark W. Muesse, eds. *Redeeming Men: Religion and Masculinities*. Louisville, KY: Westminster John Knox Press, 1996.

Boyd, Todd. *Am I Black Enough for You?: Popular Culture from the 'Hood and Beyond*. Bloomington: Indiana University Press, 1997.

Brakke, David. "Ethiopian Demons: Male Sexuality, the Black-Skinned Other, and the Monastic Self." *Journal of the History of Sexuality* 10, nos. 3–4 (2001): 501–35.

Brandt, Eric, ed. *Dangerous Liaisons: Blacks, Gays, and the Struggle for Equality*. New York: New Press, 1999.

Brod, Harry, and Michael Kaufman, eds. *Theorizing Masculinities*. Thousand Oaks, CA: Sage Publications, 1994.

Brooten, Bernadette J. *Love between Women: Early Christian Responses to Female Homoeroticism*. Chicago: University of Chicago Press, 1996.

Bryant-Davis, Thema. *Thriving in the Wake of Trauma: A Multicultural Guide*. Westport, CT: Praeger Press, 2005.

Bush, Lawson. "Am I a Man?: A Literature Review Engaging the Sociohistorical Dynamics of Black Manhood in the United States." *Western Journal of Black Studies* 23, no. 1 (1999): 49–57.

Byrd, Rudolph P., and Beverly Guy-Sheftall, eds. *Traps: African American Men on Gender and Sexuality*. Bloomington: Indiana University Press, 2001.

Byron, Gay L. *Symbolic Blackness and Ethnic Difference in Early Christian Literature*. New York: Routledge, 2002.

Cade, Toni, ed. *The Black Woman: An Anthology*. New York: Mentor, 1970.

Calhoun, Craig. *Critical Social Theory: Culture, History, and the Challenge of Difference*. Cambridge, MA: Blackwell Publishers, 1995.

Calmore, John O. "The Law and Culture-Shift: Race and the Warren Court Legacy." *Washington and Lee Law Review* 59, no. 4 (2002): 1095–139.

———. "Race-Conscious Voting Rights and the New Demography in a Multiracing America." *University of North Carolina Law Review* 79, no. 5 (2001): 1253–1281.

———. "Racialized Space and the Culture of Segregation: 'Hewing a Stone of Hope from a Mountain of Despair.'" *University of Pennsylvania Law Review* 143 (1995): 1233–73.

Carbado Devon W., ed. *Black Men on Race, Gender, and Sexuality*. New York: New York University Press, 1999.

Carroll, Leo. *Hacks, Blacks, and Cons: Race Relations in a Maximum Security Prison*. New York: Lexington Books, 1974.

Castelli, Elizabeth A. "Paul on Women & Gender." In *Women & Christian Origins*, edited by Ross S. Kraemer and Mary Rose D'Angelo 221–35. New York: Oxford University Press, 1999.

Cazenave, Noel. "Race, Socioeconomic Status, and Age: The Social Context of American Masculinity." *Sex Roles* 11 (1984): 639–56.

Chaney, David. *The Cultural Turn: Scene-Setting Essays on Contemporary Cultural History*. New York: Routledge, 1994.

Cho, Sumi K., "Converging Stereotypes in Racialized Sexual Harrassment: Where the Model Minority Meets Suzie Wong." In *Critical Race Theory: The Cutting Edge*, ed. Delgadö and J. Stefancic. Philadelphia: Temple University Press, 2000, 532–542.

Cohen, Jean L. "Strategy or Identity: New Theoretical Paradigms and Contemporary Social Movements." *Social Research* 52, no. 4 (Winter 1985): 663–716.

Cole, Johnnetta B., and Beverly Guy-Sheftall. *Gender Talk: The Struggle for Women's Equality in African American Communities*. New York: Ballantine, 2003.

Coleman, Robin R. Means. *African American Viewers and the Black Situation Comedy: Situating Racial Humor*. New York: Garland, 1998.

Collins, Patricia Hill. *Black Feminist Thought: Knowledge, Consciousness, and the Politics of Empowerment*. New York: Routledge, 2000.

———. *Black Sexual Politics: African Americans, Gender, and the New Racism*. New York: Routledge, 2004.

———. *Fighting Words: Black Women and the Search for Justice*. Minneapolis: University of Minnesota Press, 1998.

Cones, James H. *God of the Oppressed*. New York: Seabury Press, 1997.

———. *Risks of Faith: The Emergence of a Black Theology of Liberation, 1968–1998*. Boston: Beacon Press, 1999.

Connell, R. W. *Masculinities*. Cambridge, MA: Polity Press, 1995.

———. "Very Straight Gay: Masculinity, Homosexual Experience, and the Dynamics of Gender," *American Sociological Review* 57, no. 6 (1992): 735–51.

Constantine-Simms, Delroy, ed. *The Greatest Taboo: Homosexuality in Black Communities*. New York: Alyson Books, 2000.

Cose, Ellis. *The Envy of the World: On Being a Black Man in America*. New York: Washington Square Press, 2002.

———. *The Rage of a Privileged Class*. New York: Harper Collins, 1993.

Crenshaw, Kimberlé, and others, eds. *Critical Race Theory: The Key Writings that Formed the Movement*. New York: New Press, 1997.

———. "Demarginalizing the Intersection of Race and Sex: A Black Feminist Critique of Antidiscrimination Doctrine, Feminist Theory, and Antiracist Politics." *University of Chicago Legal Forum* 1989 (1989): 139–67.

———. "Mapping the Margins: Intersectionality, Identity Politics, and Violence against Women of Color." *Stanford Law Review* 43 (1991): 1241–99.

Cruse, Harold. *The Crisis of the Negro Intellectual.* New York: William Morrow & Co., Inc., 1967.

Cummings, Melbourne, and Jack L. Daniel, "The Study of African American Rhetoric." In *Rhetoric of Western Thought.*, edited by J. L. Golden, 360–85. Dubuque, IA: Kendell/Hunt, 1997.

Curtin, Elizabeth. "Home Sweet Home for Ex-Offenders." In *Civil Penalties, Social Consequences,* edited by Christopher Mele and Teresa Miller, 111–120. New York: Routledge, 2005.

Davis, Angela. *Women, Race, and Class.* New York: Vintage Books, 1983.

Dawson, Michael. "A Black Counterpublic?: Economic Earthquakes, Racial Agenda(s), and Black Politics." In *The Black Public Sphere.* Chicago: University of Chicago Press, 1995: 199–227.

Dawson, Michael. "Black Discontent: The Preliminary Report of the 1993–1994 National Black Politics Study." National Black Politics Working Paper Series, Report #1, University of Chicago, 1993–94.

Diawara, Manthia, ed. *Black American Cinema.* New York: Routledge, 1993.

Dines, Gail. "King Kong and the White Woman: *Hustler Magazine* and the Demonization of Black Masculinity." *Violence against Women* 4, no. 3 (June 1998): 291–307.

Douglas, Kelly Brown. *Sexuality and the Black Church: A Womanist Perspective.* Maryknoll, NY: Orbis Books, 1999, 68–83.

Du Bois, William E. B. *Darkwater: Voices from within the Veil.* New York: Harcourt, Brace, 1921.

Dyson, Michael E. *Between God and Gansta Rap: Bearing Witness to Black Culture.* New York: Oxford University Press, 1997.

———. "Exploring, Constructing, and Sustaining Progressive Black Masculinities." Keynote address, Black Masculinities Conference, Buffalo State College and the University at Buffalo Law School, Buffalo, NY, April 12, 2002.

———. *Holler if You Hear Me: Searching for Tupac Shakur.* New York: Basic Civitas Books, 2001.

———. *Is Bill Cosby Right? Or Has the Black Middle Class Lost Its Mind?* New York: Basic Civitas Books, 2005.

———. *Race Rules: Navigating the Color Line.* New York: Vintage Books, 1996.

Ehrenreich, Nancy. "Subordination and Symbiosis: Mechanisms of Mutual Support between Subordinating Systems." *University of Missouri Kansas City Law Review* 71, no. 2 (2002): 251–308.

Eversley, Melanie, and Gary Kane. "Black Leaders Sense Sinister Motive in Purge." *Palm Beach Post,* May 27, 2001, 17A.

Fanon, Frantz. *Black Skin, White Masks.* Translated by Charles Lam Markmann. New York: Grove Press, 1967.

Foster, Sheila. "Justice from the Ground Up: Distributive Inequities, Grassroots Resistance, and the Transformative Politics of the Environmental Justice Movement." *California Law Review* 86, no. 4 (1998): 775–841.

Franklin, Anderson. *From Brotherhood to Manhood: How Black Men Rescue Their Relationships and Dreams from the Invisibility Syndrome.* New York: Wiley & Sons, 2004.

Franklin, Clyde W. II. "Surviving the Institutional Decimation of Black Males: Causes, Consequences, and Intervention." In *The Making of Masculinities: The New Men's Studies,* edited by Harry Brod. Boston: Allen & Unwin, 1987.

Franklin, John H. *Race and History.* Baton Rouge: Louisiana State University Press, 1989.

Gates, Jr., Henry Louis, ed. *Reading Black, Reading Feminist: A Critical Anthology.* New York: Meridian, 1990.

Giddings, Paula. *When and Where I Enter.* New York: William Morrow, 1984.

Glancy, Jennifer A. "Protocols of Masculinity in the Pastoral Epistles." In *New Testament Masculinities,* edited by Stephen D. Moore and Janice Capel Anderson, 235–64. Atlanta: Society of Biblical Literature, 2003.

Goldberg, David Theo. *Racist Culture: Philosophy and the Politics of Meaning.* Cambridge, MA: Blackwell, 1993.

Golden, Marita. *Saving Our Sons: Raising Black Children in a Turbulent World.* New York: Doubleday, 1995.

Gomes, Peter J. "Black Christians and Homosexuality: The Pathology of a Permitted Prejudice." *African American Pulpit* (Summer 2001): 30–33.

———. *The Good Book: Reading the Bible with Mind and Heart.* San Francisco: Harper, 2002.

Goss, Robert E., and Mona West, eds. *Take Back the Word: A Queer Reading of the Bible.* Cleveland: Pilgrim Press, 2000.

Guinier, Lani. "What We Must Overcome." *American Prospect,* March 12, 2001, 28.

Gunning, Sandra. *Race, Rape, and Lynching.* New York: Oxford University Press, 1996.

Hamlet, Janice D. "The Reason Why We Sing: Understanding Traditional African American Worship." In *Our Voices: Essays in Culture, Ethnicity, and Communication,* 4th. ed., edited by A. Gonzalez, M. Houston, and V. Chen. Los Angeles: Roxbury, 2004.

Harris, Cheryl I. "Critical Race Studies: An Introduction." *UCLA Law Review* 49, no. 5 (2002): 1215–36.

———. "Whiteness as Property." *Harvard Law Review* 106, no. 8 (1993): 1709–91.

Harris, David A. "The Stories, the Statistics, and the Law: Why 'Driving while Black' Matters." *Minnesota Law Review* 84, no. 2 (1999): 265–326.

Harris, Ian. *Messages Men Hear: Constructing Masculinities.* Bristol, PA: Taylor & Francis, 1995.

Hills, Patricia. *The Painter's America.* New York: Praeger, 1974.

Hine, Darlene Clark, and Earnestine Jenkins, eds. *A Question of Manhood: A Reader in U.S. Black Men's History and Masculinity.* Vols. 1 and 2. Bloomington: Indiana University Press, 1999.

Hoberman, John. "The Price of 'Black Dominance'." *Society* 37, no. 3 (2000): 49–57.

Honour, Hugh. *The Image of the Black in Western Art.* Vol. 4. Cambridge, MA: Harvard University Press, 1989.

hooks, bell. *Ain't I a Woman: Black Women and Feminism.* Cambridge, MA: South End Press, 1981.

———. *Black Looks: Race and Representation.* Boston: South End Press, 1992.

———. *Feminism Is for Everybody.* Boston: South End Press, 2000.

———. *From Margin to Center.* Boston: South End Press, 1984.

———. *Killing Rage: Ending Racism.* New York: H. Holt & Co., 1995.

———. *We Real Cool: Black Men and Masculinity.* New York: Routledge, 2004.

hooks, bell, and Cornel West. *Breaking Bread.* Cambridge, MA: South End Press, 1991.

Hope, Cain, ed. *Stony the Road We Trod: African American Biblical Interpretation.* Minneapolis, MN: Fortress, 1991.

Hunter, Andrea G., and James E. Davis. "An Exploration of Afro-American Men's Conceptualization of Manhood." *Gender & Society* 6 (1992): 464–79.

———. "Hidden Voices of Black Men: The Meaning, Structure, and Complexity of Manhood." *Journal of Black Studies* 25 (1994): 20–40.

Hutchinson, Earl Ofari. *The Assassination of the Black Male Image.* New York: Simon & Schuster, 1996.

Iglesias, Elizabeth M. "Identity, Democracy, Communicative Power, International Labor Rights and the Evolution of LatCrit Theory and Community." *University of Miami Law Review* 53, no. 4 (1999): 575–682.

———. "Rape, Race, and Representation: The Power of Discourse, Discourses of Power, and the Reconstruction of Heterosexuality." *Vanderbilt Law Review* 49, no. 4 (1996): 869–960.

Iglesias, Elizabeth M., and Francisco Valdes. "Religion, Gender, Sexuality, Race and Class in Coalitional Theory: A Critical and Self-Critical Analysis of LatCrit Social Justice Agendas." *Chicano-Latino Law Review* 19 (1998): 503–88.

Jackson, Ronald, and Celnisha Dangerfield. "Defining Black Masculinity as Cultural Property: Toward an Identity Negotiation Paradigm." In *Intercultural Communication: A Reader,* 10th ed., edited by L. Samovar and R. Porter. Belmont, CA: Wadsworth, 2003.

Jackson, Ronald, and Elaine B. Richardson. eds. *Understanding African-American Rhetoric: Classical Origins to Contemporary Innovations.* New York: Routledge, 2003.

James, David. C. *What Are They Saying about Masculine Spirituality?* New York: Paulist Press, 1996.

Jhally, Sut, and Justin Lewis. *Enlightened Racism: The Cosby Show, Audiences, and the Myth of the American Dream.* Boulder: Westview Press, 1992.

Johnson, Kevin R. "The Case for African American and Latina/o Cooperation in Challenging Racial Profiling in Law Enforcement." *Florida Law Review* 55, no. 1 (2003): 341–63.

Katz, Michael B., ed. *The Underclass Debate: Views from History.* Princeton, NJ: Princeton University Press, 1993.

Kelley, Robin D. G. *Freedom Dreams: The Black Radical Imagination.* Boston: Beacon, 2002.

Kennedy, Randall. *Race, Crime, and the Law.* New York: Pantheon, 1997.

Keysarr, Alexander. *The Right to Vote: The Contested History of Democracy in the United States.* New York: Basic Books, 2000.

Kimmel, Michael S. *The Gendered Society.* New York: Oxford University Press, 2000.

———. "Masculinity as Homophobia: Fear, Shame, and Silence in the Construction of Gender Identity." In *Men and Masculinity: A Text Reader,* edited by Theodore F. Cohen, 29–41. Belmont, CA: Wadsworth Thomson Learning, 2001.

Kimmel, Michael S., and Michael A. Messner, eds. *Men's Lives.* 5th ed. Needham Heights, MA.: Allyn & Bacon, 2001.

Kitwana, Bakari. *The Hip-Hop Generation: Young Blacks and the Crisis in African American Culture.* New York: Basic Civitas Books, 2002.

Kochman, Thomas. "Black and White Cultural Styles in Pluralistic Perspective." In *Culture Communication and Conflict: Readings in Intercultural Relations,* 2d ed., edited by G. R. Weaver, 293–308. Needham Heights, MA: Simon & Schuster, 1998.

Kuumba, M. Bahati. "Engendering the Pan-African Movement: Field Notes from the All-African Women's Revolutionary Union." In *Still Lifting, Still Climbing: African American Women's Contemporary Activism,* edited by Kimberly Springer, 167–88. New York: New York University Press, 1999.

———. *Gender and Social Movements.* Walnut Creek, CA: AltaMira Press, 2001.

Lance, H. Darrell. "The Bible and Homosexuality." *American Baptist Quarterly* 8 (1989): 140–51.

Lemelle, Anthony J. "The Political Sociology of Black Masculinity and Tropes of Domination." *Journal of African American Men* 1, no. 2 (1995): 88.

Lemons, Gary L. "To Be Black, Male and 'Feminist'—Making Womanist Space for Black Men." *International Journal of Sociology and Social Policy* 1, no.2 (1997): 35–61.

Long, Elizabeth. "Introduction: Engaging Sociology and Cultural Studies: Disciplinarity and Social Change." In *From Sociology to Cultural Studies: New Perspectives,* edited by Elizabeth Long, 17. Cambridge, MA: Blackwell Publishers, 1997: 1–35.

Lorde, Audre. *Sister Outsider: Essays and Speeches.* Freedom, CA: Crossing Press, 1984.

Lott, Eric. *Love and Theft: Blackface Minstrelsy and the American Working Class.* New York: Oxford, 1993.

Loughlin, Gerard. "Refiguring of Masculinity in Christ." In *Religion and Sexuality,* edited by Michael A. Hayes, Wendy Porter, and David Tombs. Sheffield, UK: Sheffield Academic Press, 1998.

Lusane, Clarence. *Race in the Global Era: African Americans at the Millennium.* Boston: South End Press, 1997.

MacKinnon, Catherine A. *Toward a Feminist Theory of the State.* Cambridge, MA: Harvard University Press, 1989.

Madhubuti, Haki. *Black Men: Obsolete, Single, Dangerous? Afrikan American Families in Transition: Essays in Discovery, Solution, and Hope.* Chicago: Third World Press, 1990.

Mahoney, Martha R. "Segregation, Whiteness, and Transformation." *University of Pennsylvania Law Review* 143 (1995): 1659–84.

Majors, Richard, and Janet Mancini Bilson. *Cool Pose: The Dilemmas of Black Manhood in America.* New York: Lexington Books, 1992.

Majors, Richard G. and Jacob U. Gordon, eds. *The American Black Male: His Present Status and His Future.* Chicago: Nelson-Hall Publishers, 1994.

Malcolm X and Alex Haley. *The Autobiography of Malcolm X.* New York: Ballantine Books, 1964.

Marable, Manning, ed. *Dispatches from the Ebony Tower: Intellectuals Confront the African American Experience.* New York: Columbia University Press, 2000.

———. "Groundings with My Sisters: Patriarchy and the Exploitation of Black Women," In *How Capitalism Underdeveloped Black America: Problems in Race, Political Economy and Society,* edited by Manning Marable, 69–104. Boston: South End Press, 1983.

Massey, Douglas S. "Getting Away with Murder: Segregation and Violent Crime in Urban America." *University of Pennsylvania Law Review* 143 (1995): 1203–32.

Mauer, Marc. *Race to Incarcerate.* New York: New Press, 1999.

McKenzie, John. "The Gospel According to Matthew." In *The Jerome Biblical Commentary,* vol. 2, edited by Raymond E. Brown, Joseph A. Fitzmyer, and Roland E. Murphy. Englewood Cliffs, NJ: Prentice-Hall, 1968.

Mele, Christopher, and Teresa A. Miller, eds. *Civil Penalties, Social Consequences.* New York: Routledge, 2005.

Mercer, Kobena. *Welcome to the Jungle: New Positions in Black Cultural Studies.* New York: Routledge, 1994.

Miller, Teresa A. "Sex and Surveillance: Gender, Privacy and the Sexualization of Prison." *George Mason University Civil Rights Law Journal* 10, no. 2 (2000): 291–356.

Moore, Stephen D. *God's Gym: Divine Male Bodies of the Bible.* New York: Routledge. 1996.

Morrison, Toni ed. *Race-ing Justice, En-Gendering Power: Essays on Anita Hill, Clarence Thomas, and the Construction of Social Reality.* New York: Pantheon Books, 1992.

Murray, Pauli. "The Liberation of Black Women." *Voices of the New Feminism* 10, no. 2 (1970): 87–102.

Mutua, Athena. "The Rise of Critical Race Theory in Law." In *Handbook Series of Race and Ethnic Studies,* edited by Patricia Hill Collins and John Solomos. Thousand Oaks, CA: Sage Publications, forthcoming 2006.

National Center for Human Rights Education (NCHRE). http://www.nchre.org.

Neal, Mark Anthony. *Soul Babies: Black Popular Culture and the Post-soul Aesthetic.* New York: Routledge, 2002.

Newsom, Carol A., and Sharon H. Ringe, eds. *The Women's Bible Commentary,* expanded ed. Louisville, KY: Westminster John Knox Press, 1998.

Nissinen, Martti. *Homoeroticism in the Biblical World: A Historical Perspective.* Minneapolis: Fortress Press, 1998.

Nkosi, Thulani. "Young Men Taking a Stand." *Agenda* 37 (1998): 30–31.

Oliver, William. "Cultural Racism and Structural Violence: Implications for African Americans." In *Violence as Seen through a Prism of Color,* edited by Letha A. New York: Haworth Press, 2001: 1–26.

Omi, Michael, "In Living Color: Race and American Culture." In *Cultural Politics in Contemporary America,* edited by Ian Angus and Sut Jhally, 111–122. New York: Routledge, 1989.

Omi, Michael, and Howard Winant. *Racial Formation in the United States from the 1960s to the 1990s.* New York: Routledge, 1994.

Omolade, Barbara. *The Rising Song of African American Women.* New York: Routledge, 1994.

Orbe, Mark P. "Constructions of Reality on MTV's 'The Real World': An Analysis of the Restrictive Coding of Black Masculinity." *Southern Communication Journal* 64, no. 1 (1998): 32–47.

Paris, Peter J. "The Bible and the Black Churches." In *The Bible and Social Reform,* edited by Ernest R. Sandeen, 134–35, Philadelphia: Fortress Press, 1982.

Petersilia, Joan. *When Prisoners Come Home: Parole and Prisoner Reentry.* Oxford: Oxford University Press, 2003.

Pierce-Baker, Charlotte. *Surviving the Silence: Black Women and Rape.* New York: W. W. Norton and Company, 1990.

Pinar, William F. *The Gender of Racial Politics and Violence in America: Lynching, Prison Rape, and the Crisis of Masculinity.* New York: P. Lang, 2001.

Rickford, John Russell, and Russell John Rickford. *Spoken Soul: The Story of Black English.* New York: John Wiley & Sons, 2000.

Russell, Katheryn K. "The Racial Hoax as Crime: The Law as Affirmation." *Indiana Law Journal* 71, no. 3 (1996): 593–621.

Sabo, Donald F., Terry Allen Kupers, and Willie James London, eds. *Prison Masculinities.* Philadelphia: Temple University Press, 2001.

Scacco, Anthony M. Jr., ed. *Male Rape: A Casebook of Sexual Aggressions.* New York: AMS Press, Inc., 1982.

Schiele, Jerome H. *Human Services and the Afrocentric Paradigm.* New York: Haworth, 2000.

Scroggs, Robin. "Paul the Prisoner: Political Asceticism in the Letter to the Philippians." In *Asceticism and the New Testament,* edited by Leif Vaage and Vincent L. Wimbush, 187–207. New York: Routledge, 1999.

Seidman, Steven. *Beyond the Closet: The Transformation of Gay and Lesbian Life.* New York: Routledge, 2002.

———. ed. *Queer Theory/Sociology.* Cambridge, MA: Blackwell, 1996.

Sibley, David. *Geographies of Exclusion.* New York: Routledge, 1995.

Simmons, Ron. "Some Thoughts on the Challenges Facing Black Gay Intellectuals." In *Brother to Brother: New Writings by Black Gay Men,* edited by Essex Hemphill, 211–28. Boston: Alyson Publications, 1991.

Smitherman, Geneva. *Talkin' That Talk.* New York: Routledge, 2000.

Sniderman, Paul, and Thomas Piazza. "Pictures in the Mind." In *Race and Ethnic Relations in the United States,* edited by C.G. Ellison and W.A. Martin, 230–37. Los Angeles: Roxbury Publishing, 1999.

Soja, Edward W. *Thirdspace: Journeys to Los Angeles and Other Real-and-Imagined Places.* Cambridge, MA: Blackwell Publishers, 1996.

Staples, Robert. *Black Masculinity: The Black Male's Role in American Society.* San Francisco: Black Scholars Press, 1982.

——. "The Myth of Black Macho: A Response to Angry Black Feminists." *Black Scholar* 10, no. 6 (1979): 24–33.

Steinhorn, Leonard, and Barbara Diggs-Brown. *By the Color of Our Skin: The Illusion of Integration and the Reality of Race.* New York: Dutton, 1999.

Takaki, Ronald T. *A Different Mirror: A History of Multicultural America.* Boston: Little Brown and Co., 1993.

Thurman, Howard. *Jesus and the Disinherited.* Boston: Beacon Press, 1996.

Valdes, Francisco. "Identity Maneuvers in Law and Society." *University of Missouri Kansas City Law Review* 71, no. 2 (2002): 377–98.

Vawter, Bruce. "The Gospel According to John." In *The Jerome Biblical Commentary,* vol. 2, edited by Raymond E. Brown, Joseph A. Fitzmyer, and Roland E. Murphy. Englewood Cliffs, NJ: Prentice-Hall, 1968.

Wade, Jay C. "African American Men's Gender Role Conflict: The Significance of Racial Identity," *Sex Roles: A Journal of Research* 34, nos. 1–2 (1996): 17.

Walker, Alice. *In Search of our Mothers' Gardens.* Orlando: Harcourt, 1983.

Walker, Bela August. "The Color of Crime: The Case against Race-Based Suspect Descriptions." *Columbia Law Review* 103, no. 4 (2003): 662–88.

Wallace, Michele. "Neither Fish nor Fowl." *Transition: An International Review* 66 (1995): 98–100.

West, Carolyn. *Violence in the Lives of Black Women: Battered, Black, and Blue.* Binghamton, NY: Haworth Press, 2002.

West, Cornel. *Race Matters.* 2d ed. New York: Vintage Books, 2001.

Wetherell, Margaret, and Nigel Edley. "Negotiating Hegemonic Masculinity: Imaginary Positions and Psycho-Discursive Practices." *Feminism & Psychology* 9, no. 3 (1999): 335–56.

White, Joseph L., and James H. Cones III. *Black Men Emerging.* New York: W.H. Freeman, 1999.

White, Lucie E. "To Learn and Teach: Lessons from Driefontein on Lawyering and Power." *Wisconsin Law Review* 1988 (1988): 699–726.

Wicker, Kathleen O. "Ethiopian Moses (Collected Sources)." In *Ascetic Behavior in Greco-Roman Antiquity: A Source Book,* edited by Vincent L. Wimbush, 329–48. Minneapolis: Fortress Press, 1990.

Wideman, John Edgar. *Brothers and Keepers.* New York: Penguin, 1984.

Williams, Craig A. *Roman Homosexuality: Ideologies of Masculinity in Classical Antiquity.* New York: Oxford University Press, 1999.

Wilson, William Julius. *The Truly Disadvantaged: The Inner City, the Underclass, and Public Policy.* Chicago: University of Chicago Press, 1987.

——. *When Work Disappears: The World of the New Urban Poor.* New York: Knopf, 1996.

Wimbush, Vincent L., ed. *African Americans and the Bible.* New York: Continuum, 2000.

Wing, Adrien Katherine., ed. *Critical Race Feminism: A Reader.* New York: New York University Press, 1997.

Wyatt, Gail. *Stolen Women: Reclaiming Our Sexuality, Taking Back Our Lives.* New York: Wiley & Sons, 1997.

Zook, Kristal Brent. *Color by Fox: The Fox Network and the Revolution in Black Television.* New York: Oxford, 1999.

Contributors

Timothy J. Brown

Born and raised in Coatesville, Pennsylvania, Timothy J. Brown received his Ph.D. in rhetoric and public address from Ohio University in 1997. He received his B.A. and M.A. degrees in communication studies from West Chester University. He is currently associate professor of communication studies at West Chester University. Prior to his appointment there, Brown was assistant professor of communication at Buffalo State College from 1997 to 2002. He also served as associate chair of the department from 2001 to 2002. Brown is a rhetorical scholar whose research interests include culture and communication, African American rhetoric, ideology and race, and popular culture. He is also a motivational speaker and has been a successful speech and debate coach. Brown's most recent publications include coauthoring the public speaking textbook *Public Speaking for Success: Strategies for Diverse Audiences and Occasions* (Plymouth, MI: Hayden-McNeil, 2005); "Allen Iverson as America's Most Wanted: Black Masculinity as a Cultural Site of Struggle" (*Journal of Intercultural Communication Research* 34, no. 1, 2005); and "Deconstructing the Dialectical Tensions in *The Horse Whisperer*: How Myths Represent Competing Cultural Values" (*Journal of Popular Culture* 38, no. 2, 2004).

Thema Bryant-Davis

Thema Bryant-Davis, a rape crisis counselor for over ten years, is assistant professor at California State University, Long Beach. She earned her doctorate in clinical psychology from Duke University and completed her postdoctoral training at Harvard Medical Center. For three years she coordinated the Princeton University Sexual Harassment/Assault/Advising, Resources, and Education (SHARE) program, which addresses sexual assault and harassment. Bryant-Davis served for three years as an American Psychological Association representative to the United Nations, where she advocated for mental health at the World Conference Against Racism. Bryant-Davis is author of the book *Thriving in the Wake of Trauma: A Multicultural Guide* (Praeger, 2005). She was honored among "Women Who Are Shaping the World" in 2005 by *ESSENCE* magazine. Bryant-Davis is also a poet and motivational speaker who uses the arts to bring healing to the lives of trauma survivors.

Gay L. Byron

Gay L. Byron is Baptist Missionary Training School associate professor of New Testament and Black Church Studies at Colgate Rochester Crozer Divinity School in Rochester, NY. She received her Ph.D. in New Testament and Christian origins at Union Theological Seminary in New York. Her research interests include Pauline literature and theology, New Testament ethics, womanist and feminist biblical hermeneutics, literary and cultural approaches to the Bible, and early Christian asceticism. She is the author of *Symbolic Blackness and Ethnic Difference in Early Christian Literature* (Routledge, 2002) and the recipient of a Luce fellowship through the Association of Theological Schools (2005–06). Her current research identifies and examines ancient Ethiopic (Ge'ez) sources for the study of the New Testament and other early Christian writings. Byron is an ordained minister of the Word and Sacrament in the Presbyterian Church USA. For over two years she served as pastor of the Laconia Community Presbyterian Church in the Bronx, New York. She is married to the Rev. Philip B. Davis Sr., pastor of the First Presbyterian Church of East Rochester. Together they are the parents of two young sons.

John O. Calmore

John O. Calmore joined the faculty at the University of North Carolina in fall 1997. After graduation from law school, Calmore was named a Reginald Heber Smith Fellow and was assigned to the Western Center on Law and Poverty in Los Angeles and to the Boston Legal Assistance Project in Roxbury, Massachusetts. He has been staff attorney for the Legal Aid Foundation of Los Angeles, the Western Center on Law and Poverty and the National Housing Law Project. Calmore became director of litigation at the Legal Aid Foundation of Los Angeles in 1982. He began teaching law in 1985 first at North Carolina Central University, then at Loyola Law School in Los Angeles, and finally at University of North Carolina. He has served as a program officer in the Rights and Social Justice Program at the Ford Foundation in New York City, executive committee member of the Association of American Law Schools Section on Minority Groups, and chair of the Section on Property Law. Calmore has also served on the boards of directors of the National Asian Pacific American Legal Consortium, the New World Foundation, the National Advisory Board for the Institute on Race and Poverty, the American Bar Associations Commission on Homelessness and Poverty, the Bank of America Social Policy Advisory Committee, and currently on the board of Oxfam America. Calmore teaches antidiscrimination law, social justice lawyering, torts, and a seminar on critical race theory.

Patricia Hill Collins

Patricia Hill Collins received her B.A. and Ph.D. degrees from Brandeis University and an M.A.T. degree from Harvard University. Although her specialties in sociology include such diverse areas as sociology of knowledge, organizational theory, social stratification, and work and occupations, her research and scholarship have dealt primarily with issues of gender, race, and social class, specifically relating to African American women. She has published many articles in professional journals and edited volumes. Her first book, *Black Feminist Thought: Knowledge, Consciousness, and the Politics of Empowerment* (Unwin Hyman, 1990), has won many awards. Her second book, *Race, Class and Gender: An Anthology* (coedited with Margaret Andersen, Wadsworth Publishing, 1992), with a sixth edition in preparation for 2006, is widely used in undergraduate classrooms throughout the United States. Her other books include *Fighting Words: Black Women and the Search for Justice* (University of Minnesota Press, 1998), *Black Sexual Politics: African Americans, Gender, and the New Racism* (Routledge, 2004), and *From Black Power to Hip Hop: Racism, Nationalism, and Feminism* (Temple University Press, 2005). Collins has taught at several institutions, has held editorial positions with professional journals, has lectured widely in the United States and abroad, has served in many capacities in professional organizations, and has acted as consultant for a number of businesses and community organizations.

Nathan Grant

Nathan Grant, who received his Ph.D. in 1994 from New York University, is an Associate Professor of English at the University at Buffalo and has worked extensively with issues of literary masculinity. He has edited previously unpublished poetry of Owen Dodson and written essays on such figures as James Baldwin, Ed Bullins, Charles Burnett, Jacob Lawrence, and August Wilson for *Callaloo, African American Review,* and *American Drama*; he has also written on Jean Toomer, Frantz Fanon, Lacan, and Foucault for the French journal *Q/W/E/R/T/Y*. In addition to also having appeared in several anthologies in black popular culture, art, and film, Grant is also author of *Masculinist Impulses: Toomer, Hurston, Black Writing and Modernity* (University of Missouri Press, 2004).

Beverly Guy-Sheftall

Beverly Guy-Sheftall is the Anna Julia Cooper Professor of Women's Studies and founding director of the Women's Research and Resource Center at Spelman College. She is coeditor of *Sturdy Black Bridges: Visions of Black Women in Literature,* eds. Roseann P. Bell, Bettye J. Parker and Beverly Guy-Sheftall, Garden City, NJ: Anchor Books, 1979; and *Double Stitch: Black Women Write about Mothers and Daughters* (Patricia Bell-Scott and Beverly-Guy-Sheftall, eds., Beacon Press, 1991) She is the author of *Daughters of Sorrow: Attitudes toward Black Women, 1880–1920,* volume eleven (Carlson Publishing, 1990) and is founding coeditor of *SAGE: A Scholarly Journal on Black Women.* She consults and speaks widely on issues relating to race, gender, and multiculturalism. Her latest books are: coeditor with Rudolph P. Byrd, of *Traps: African American Men on Gender and Sexuality* (Indiana University Press, 2001) and coauthor with Johnnetta Betsch Cole, of *Gender Talk: The Struggle for Women's Equality in African American Communities* (Ballantine, 2003).

Whitney G. Harris

Whitney G. Harris currently serves as executive director of diversity and multiculturalism in the Office of the Chancellor of the Minnesota State Colleges and Universities System. His affiliations include membership in the American Association for Affirmative Action, Phi Kappa Pi Honor Society, National Association for the Advancement of Colored People, American Civil Liberties Union, Phi Delta Kappa, the National Human Rights Campaign, and the Southern Poverty Law Center. He is past president of the African-Americans in Louisiana Higher Education and current board member of the American Men's Studies Association, Michigan Equality, and the Ruth Ellis Center. He holds a doctorate in educational foundations and administration from The Union Institute and University in Cincinnati, a master's degree in special education and psychology from Louisiana State University, degrees in theology from the University of Ottawa and St. Paul University in Ottawa, and a bachelor's degree with honors in special education and elementary education from McNeese State University. In 1996, he earned a certificate in higher education from the Harvard Management Development Program.

Elizabeth M. Iglesias

Professor Elizabeth M. Iglesias holds a B.A. (magna cum laude) from the University of Michigan and a J.D. (with honors) from Yale Law School. She is the cofounder of Latina and Latino Critical Theory, Inc. (LatCrit, Inc.), which she incorporated in 1998 and codirected until 2003. She has received numerous honors and awards as a scholar, activist, citizen, and poet. Some of these include being honored with the "Most Outstanding Faculty Award" by the University of Miami Public Interest Law Group; named the 1999–2000 Dean Thomas Lecturer at Yale Law School; being named among "Women Who Make a Difference," an award presented by Miami Law Women; having June 14, 2000 proclaimed "Elizabeth M. Iglesias Day" by Alex Penelas, Mayor of Miami–Dade County, Florida, and being awarded the Tompkins Poetry Prize. In 2003, Professor Iglesias cofounded LisaLeine Productions, a multimedia woman-owned production company devoted to the advancement of human rights through the creation, exhibition, and distribution of independent film and art. Her first documentary, entitled *Scaring Miami: Anarchists, RoboCops, and Corporate Globalization*, explores the mass convergence of labor, environmental, peace, and justice activists in Miami in November 2003 to protest the Free Trade Area of the Americas.

Michael Kimmel

Sociologist and author Michael Kimmel has received international recognition for his work on men and masculinity. His books on masculinity include *Changing Men: New Directions in Research on Men and Masculinity* (Sage, 1987) and *Men Confront Pornography* (Crown, 1990), which was called "revelatory" (*Kirkus*) and "timely and valuable" (*Village Voice*). His book *Against the Tide: Pro-feminist Men in the United States, 1776–1990* (Beacon, 1992), is a documentary history of men who supported women's equality since the founding of the country. His book *Manhood in America: A Cultural History* (Free Press, 1996) was published to significant acclaim. One of Kimmel's latest books is titled *The Gendered Society* (Oxford University Press, 2000). Kimmel is also a well-known educator concerning gender issues. His innovative course, "Sociology of Masculinity," is one of the few courses in the nation that examines men's lives from a profeminist perspective and has been featured in newspaper and magazine articles and on television shows. His college textbook, coedited with Michael Messner, is entitled *Men's Lives* (6th edition, 2004) and has been adopted in virtually every course on men and masculinity in the country. Kimmel is editor of the international, interdisciplinary journal *Men and Masculinities*. He is also the national spokesperson for the National Organization for Men Against Sexism. On the basis of his expertise, Kimmel served as an expert witness for the U.S. Department of Justice in the Virginia Military Institute and Citadel cases.

M. Bahati Kuumba

M. Bahati Kuumba earned her Ph.D. in sociology at Howard University in 1993 and is currently associate professor of women's studies and associate director of the Women's Research and Resource Center at Spelman College. Her scholarship, activism, and teaching focus on African and African diasporan women in the areas of social movements and activism, the political economy of reproductive and population policies, and comparative feminisms. She has been widely published in scholarly journals such as *Gender and Society, Sociological Forum, Mobilization,* and *Africa Today* and recently guest edited a special issue of *Agenda,* a South Africa–based journal. Her publications also include numerous anthologized essays; the book *Gender and Social Movements* (AltaMira Press, 2001), a comparative analysis of black women and their organizations in the civil rights, black power, and anti-apartheid movements; and a collection of essays on African women's activism, titled *Transnational Transgressions: African Women and Struggle in Global Perspective* (Africa World Press, 2004), coedited with Monica White. Currently, Kuumba is researching and writing on the topic of African women's transnational and comparative activism. In addition to her scholarship, she remains active in a range of women's and human rights organizations and was the 2005 recipient of Spelman College's Fannie Lou Hamer Achievement Award.

Teresa A. Miller

Teresa (Teri) A. Miller is professor of law at the State University of New York at Buffalo. She was an Angier B. Duke Scholar at Duke University, where she earned her B.A. in psychology in 1982. She received her J.D. from Harvard Law School in 1986. She was a Hastie Fellow at the University of Wisconsin–Madison, earning her LL.M. in 1988, and clerked for the Honorable William M. Hoeveler in the Southern District of Florida from 1990 to 1991. Miller has taught Prisoner Law and theories of criminal punishment for a decade. More recently, Miller began teaching immigration law, and focusing on the growing convergence of traditional civil deportation law and criminal punishment policy, and the extent to which it reflects neoliberal, postwelfare penal practices of the war on drugs. In "Blurring the Boundaries between Immigration and Crime Control after September 11" (*Boston College Third World Law Journal* 81, 2005), Miller extended this analysis to immigration reforms enacted to support the war on terror. She is married and raising three young children: a daughter and two sons.

Athena D. Mutua

Athena D. Mutua is associate professor at the University at Buffalo Law School. She received a B.A. from Earlham College, a J.D. and M.A. from The American University in Washington, D.C., and an LL.M. from Harvard Law School. She teaches banking law, corporations, critical race theory, and civil rights and writes in the areas of critical race theory and feminist legal theory. Some of her recent works include: Introduction and Afterword, "Who Gets In? The Quest for Diversity After Grutter," 2004 Mitchell Lecture, 52 *Buff. L. Rev.* 531, 587 (2004); and "The Rise of Critical Race Theory," *Handbook on Race and Ethnic Studies*, Sage, forthcoming 2006. She also recently published a series of essays and training materials on women rights in Kenya. This was in connection with a year-long stay there where she was a consultant to several human rights organizations involved in the ongoing Kenya Constitutional Review process. An examination of this work is captured in "*Gender Equality and Women's Solidarity across Religious, Ethnic, and Class Difference in the Kenya Constitutional Review Process*," 13 Wm. & Mary J. of Women's L. 1 (2006). She organized the project on progressive black masculinities and lives with her spouse, Makau Mutua and their three young sons.

Mark Anthony Neal

Mark Anthony Neal is associate professor of black popular culture in the Program in African and African-American Studies at Duke University. He holds a doctorate in American Studies from the State University of New York at Buffalo. Neal's scholarly interests are in black popular culture, black feminist and queer theory, and black intellectual production. He is the author of three books: *What the Music Said: Black Popular Music and Black Public Culture* (Routledge, 1998), *Soul Babies: Black Popular Culture and the Post-soul Aesthetic* (Routledge, 2002), and *Songs in the Key of Black Life: A Rhythm and Blues Nation* (Routledge, 2003).

Stephanie L. Phillips

Stephanie L. Phillips is professor of law at the State University of New York at Buffalo School of Law and is presently pursuing a Master of Arts in Theology from Colgate Rochester Crozer Divinity School. She received her J.D. in 1981 from Harvard University. She teaches in the areas of conflict of laws, securities regulation, law and religion, and race and American law. Her work in black feminist theory and narrative analysis has been published in the *Hastings Women's Law Journal* ("Claiming our Foremothers: The Legend of Sally Hemings and the Tasks of Black Feminist Theory," 8, no. 2, Fall 1997).

Index